A Commentary on the New Code of Canon Law

A COMMENTARY ON
THE NEW
CODE OF CANON LAW

By THE REV. P. CHAS. AUGUSTINE, O.S.B., D.D.
Professor of Canon Law

VOLUME VI
Administrative Law
(Can. 1154-1551)

B. HERDER BOOK CO.

17 SOUTH BROADWAY, ST. LOUIS, MO.
AND
68, GREAT RUSSELL ST., LONDON, W. C.
1921

CUM PERMISSU SUPERIORUM

NIHIL OBSTAT

Sti. Ludovici, die 18. Nov. 1920

F. G. Holweck,
Censor Librorum.

IMPRIMATUR

Sti. Ludovici, die 22. Nov. 1920

✝Joannes J. Glennon,
Archiepiscopus
Sti. Ludovici.

Copyright, 1921
by
Joseph Gummersbach

VAIL-BALLOU COMPANY
BINGHAMTON AND NEW YORK

CONTENTS

CONTENTS

THE NEW CODE OF CANON LAW

BOOK III—PART II
SACRED PLACES AND TIMES

INTRODUCTION

After the treatise on the Sacraments and Sacramentals, we come to sacred *places* as the next subject of consideration. Sacred places partake, as it were, of the sacramental nature and may, therefore, be truly called vehicles of sanctification. Besides, being consecrated or blessed, they may be claimed by the ecclesiastical authorities as their own, and are not subject to civil power.

Means of sanctification are also sacred *times,* namely holydays and days of fasting and abstinence. These form the subject-matter of Part II of the Third Book of the Code.

SECTION I

SACRED PLACES IN GENERAL

CAN. 1154

Loca sacra ea sunt quae divino cultui fideliumve sepulturae deputantur consecratione vel benedictione quam probati liturgici libri ad hoc praescribunt.

Sacred places are places set aside for divine worship, or for the burial of the faithful, by a consecration or blessing prescribed for this purpose by the approved liturgical books.

The custom of withdrawing certain buildings from profane uses and dedicating them to the divinity, is as old as divine worship itself. The act by which a place is made sacred, is called *consecration* or *blessing*. The *canonical effects* of both are the same. These effects consist partly in the destination of an otherwise profane thing for sacred functions and worship, partly in the prohibition of profane acts being performed in sacred places. Hence Can. 1172 mentions the violation or defilement of a church if certain acts are committed therein. Besides, the sacred character is apparent from the *ius asyli* referred to in Can. 1179. Finally, though this is not specially mentioned in the text, certain profane acts must not be performed in sacred places. Such acts are civil trials, theatrical and purely secular entertainments,

2

political or merely worldly meetings, and every species of buying and selling.[1]

As we said, the canonical effects of consecration and blessing are identical. But there is a difference in the sacramental effects. *Consecration* is an act performed by the bishop with certain prayers and anointing with oil and chrism, whereas a *blessing* consists of prayers and aspersions with holy water, which, even though reserved to the bishop, may also be performed by priests.[2] Consecration, therefore, is also called solemn dedication, whereas a blessing is a less solemn initiation.[3]

The liturgical books which contain the formularies for consecrations and blessings are the Roman Pontifical and the Roman Ritual.

THE MINISTER OF CONSECRATION

Can. 1155

§ 1. Consecratio alicuius loci, quanquam ad regulares pertinentis, spectat ad Ordinarium territorii in quo locus ipse reperitur, dummodo Ordinarius charactere episcopali sit insignitus, non tamen ad Vicarium Generalem sine speciali mandato, firmo iure S. R. E. Cardinalium consecrandi ecclesiam et altaria sui tituli.

§ 2. Ordinarius territorii, licet charactere episcopali careat, potest cuilibet eiusdem ritus Episcopo licentiam dare consecrationes peragendi in suo territorio.

Our canon substantially repeats the old law, which made it very plain that no strange bishop, even though he

1 Cfr. Aichner, *Compendium Iuris Eccl.*, § 203, 3.

2 Cfr. *Pontificale Rom., De ecclesiae dedicatione sive consecratione; Rituale Rom*, tit VIII, c 27.

3 Wernz, *Ius Decretal*, III, n. 436, p. 437, ed. 1.

has built a church at his expense in another diocese, may consecrate a temple outside his own territory.[4] Abbots were forbidden to consecrate churches and altars.[5] This provision is here reenacted, for even *regulars* have to call in the bishop in whose territory a church is to be consecrated. Only in case the local Ordinary, after repeated requests on the part of the regulars, should refuse to perform the consecration, are they permitted to call in another bishop, as Leo X had enacted at the Vth Lateran Council.[6]

A *Vicar General* who is endowed with the episcopal dignity, may consecrate sacred places only by special commission from the Ordinary, which should be repeated every time a consecration is to take place.

Cardinals who are not bishops may by law validly consecrate the churches and altars of their own title. Cardinals who are endowed with the episcopal character may, in virtue of a special privilege, consecrate churches and altars everywhere with the consent of the local Ordinary.[7]

An Ordinary who is not endowed with the episcopal character may grant the faculty of consecrating places to any bishop of the same rite. Thus a *Prelate or Abbot Nullius,* if he is not a bishop, may call any bishop of the same rite into his diocese for that purpose. The same applies to *vicars-capitular* or administrators. *Sede vacante* the regulars also must apply to the latter, who shall call in a bishop for the purpose.[8]

From all the ancient texts, which in this case have not been abolished, it follows that the *episcopal character* is

4 Cc. 1, 3, C. 16, q. 5

5 C 10, C. 16, q 1.

6 " *Dum intra,*" Dec. 19, 1516, § 12.

7 See can 239, § 1, n. 20. The Cardinal-Vicar of Rome is not en-titled to consecrate titular churches and altars of other cardinals; S Rit C., Jan 30, 1879 (*Dec Auth.,* n. 3478).

8 Many, *De Locis Sacris,* 1904, p. 32.

required for valid consecration, although this requisite is of merely ecclesiastical (but universal) law. The consequence is that the Pope, and he alone, can dispense from this law and grant the faculty to consecrate places to such as are not bishops. Benedict XIV granted to Abbot Engelbert of Kempten in Bavaria the privilege of consecrating his abbey-church. A personally granted privilege seems to be required, as Benedict XIV insinuates in his letter.[9] If an abbot claims the right to consecrate a church, he must possess a special privilege of the Apostolic See and exhibit it to the bishop who would otherwise be entitled to perform the function.[10]

A consequence of this requirement is that any validly consecrated bishop, even though he be a heretic, or a schismatic, or under censure, may validly, though not licitly, consecrate churches and altars.

Notice the term *"eiusdem ritus,"* which excludes a mixture of rites. Hence a Latin Ordinary may not licitly grant permission, say to the Ruthenian bishop of our country or Canada, to consecrate a Latin church.[11]

Observe, finally, the expression, *"Ordinarius territorii,"* which includes all Ordinaries, whether their territories are large or small, and also the abbots and prelates mentioned in can. 319, § 2.

It may be added that a metropolitan has no right to interfere with consecrations in the territories of his suffragan bishops.

---

[9] *"Ex tuis precibus,"* Nov. 16, 1748

[10] *S. Rit. C*, April 14, 1674 (*Dec. Auth.*, n. 1505).

[11] S O, June 16, 1831 (*Coll P F*, n 822): *"non expedire,"* which means that the consecration would be valid, but illicit.

THE MINISTER OF A BLESSING

Can. 1156

Ius benedicendi locum sacrum, si hic pertineat ad clerum saecularem vel ad religionem non exemptam, vel ad laicalem, spectat ad Ordinarium territorii in quo locus reperitur; si ad religionem clericalem exemptam, ad Superiorem maiorem; uterque vero potest alium sacerdotem ad hoc delegare.

The right of blessing a sacred place belongs (1) to the Ordinary in whose territory the place is situated, concerning all places which belong to the secular clergy, or to non-exempt religious, or to lay persons, even though these be an ecclesiastical corporation which constructed the church; [12] (2) to the *major superior*, if the place belongs to exempt religious, *i. e.*, who are such either in virtue of their regular character or by reason of a special privilege.

The Ordinary as well as the religious superior may delegate another priest, whether secular or religious, whether pastor or not,[13] to bless a place, but not to consecrate it.[14] Hence provincials, abbots, guardians, conventual priors and all who enjoy the power of quasi-provincials, may bless churches and altars either themselves or through others.[15]

Can. 1157

Non obstante quolibet privilegio, nemo potest locum sacrum consecrare vel benedicere sine Ordinarii consensu.

---

12 S Rit C., Oct. 7, 1645 (*Dec. Auth*, n. 889).

13 *Ibid.* and Aug. 7 1875 (*ibid*, n. 3364, ad 1)

14 S. Rit. C, Oct 7, 1645

15 Reg. Iuris, 68, 72 in 6°.

No one may bless or consecrate a sacred place without the consent of the Ordinary, notwithstanding any privilege.

The Ordinary whose consent is required for consecration, is the one in whose territory the church or altar is located. This rule, we repeat, binds all, regulars and seculars, individuals and corporations, no matter whether or not they have built, or helped to build, the church or altar.[16] To *bless* a church or altar the consent of the Ordinary is required, as explained under can 1156.

The name of Ordinary, in this latter case, also comprises the higher religious superiors.

The required consent may be given either in writing or orally, but should, in ordinary cases, be express. In urgent cases we believe consent may be lawfully presumed for a blessing, but hardly for a consecration, because a consecration is a pontifical right, which may not be exercised in alien territory.[17]

REGISTRATION AND PROOF

CAN 1158

De peracta consecratione vel benedictione redigatur documentum, cuius alterum exemplar in Curia episcopali, alterum in ecclesiae archivo servetur.

CAN. 1159

§ 1. Consecratio vel benedictio alicuius loci, modo nemini damnum fiat, satis probatur etiam per unum testem omni exceptione maiorem.

§ 2. Si de ea legitime constet, nec consecratio nec

---

16 Cc. 1, 3, C. 16, q. 5; S. Rit C., Oct. 7, 1645 (*Dec. Auth*, n 889). 17 *Trid*, Sess. 6, c. 5, *de ref.*; c. 28, C. 7, q. 1, inflicts one year's suspension *a divinis,* but our Code contains no penalty.

benedictio iterari potest; in dubio autem, peragatur ad cautelam.

After the consecration or blessing a report should be drawn up, of which one copy is to be kept in the episcopal court, and another in the archives of the church.

Consecration or blessing can be proved by one trustworthy witness, provided no damage is done to a third person.

Neither consecration nor blessing is to be repeated after legal proof has been furnished that it has taken place; but if there is doubt, the act may be performed provisionally (*ad cautelam*).

A sufficient proof would be the testimony of an authentic document or the deposition of an eye-witness.[18] Damage would be caused if a consecrated or blessed church were given over to profane uses. Formerly one who consecrated a church or an altar was entitled to the tithes offered there. Hence the requirement of an unprejudiced witness.

Reconsecration is forbidden for an analogous reason as rebaptism, *viz.:* because the ceremony imprints an indelible character.[19] For this reason canonists have taught that if a positive doubt exists as to whether a church or an altar has been consecrated, the consecration should take place, and Benedict XIV sanctioned this teaching, now embodied in the Code.[20] The mere age of a church would not create a positive doubt as to its not being consecrated or dedicated. The constantly observed anniversary of the dedication, especially if for the consecration of the main altar some kind of document were preserved, would make reconsecration unnecessary, even though there were no

18 C 16, Dist 1, *de cons* , S. Rit C , Aug. 19, 1634 ad 1 (*Dec. Auth.,* n. 611).

19 C 3, Dist 68; C 10, Dist L, *de cons* , c. 111, Dist. 4, *de cons* 20 "*Iam inde,*" Nov. 17, 1706.

authentic document and no traces of the crosses appeared on the walls.[21] If neither crosses nor documents are available, and the church was entirely remodelled or rebuilt, consecration must take place.[22] If the doubt cannot be dispersed, consecration should be performed provisionally. This does not mean conditional consecration, but, as the text says, *ad cautelam,* according to the formula contained in the Roman Pontifical.

IMMUNITY OF SACRED PLACES

CAN. 1160

Loca sacra exempta sunt a iurisdictione auctoritatis civilis et in eis legitima Ecclesiae auctoritas iurisdictionem suam libere exercet.

Sacred places are exempt from the jurisdiction of the civil authority, and the lawful ecclesiastical authority freely exercises jurisdiction in them.

This is what is called *localis immunitas,* or exemption from civil power in the use and administration of these places. Even the pagans felt awe and reverence for sacred places. The very terms ἱερόν and *sanctum* instilled respect for the spot or district set apart for the gods. No criminal or unclean person was allowed to enter these *temene* or sacred precincts, and no animal was admitted into them. The fact that such places were either erected or protected by public authority shielded them from vexation and profanation.[23] All this goes to show that there is in man what we might call a natural instinct of

---

21 S. Rit. C., Nov. 27, 1706 (*Dec. Auth.,* n. 2174).

22 S. Rit. C., Dec. 17, 1875; Aug. 19, 1878 (*Dec. Auth.,* nn. 3385, 3462).

23 Cfr. Stengel, *Die Griech. Kultusaltertümer,* 1898, p. 18 ff.; Ramsay-Lanciani, *Manual of Roman Antiquities,* p. 372 ff.

reverence for things that belong to God. It was not priestly arrogance, then, on the part of the Christian Church that she claimed these natural prerogatives and that the Christian emperors accorded them, as it were, spontaneously. A specific exemption was the *ius metatus* or right of quartering soldiers in churches. The Church would not permit secular trials, civil or criminal, to be held in sacred places, nor purely worldly meetings, markets, and political assemblies.[24] This immunity still exists. *Our States* have enacted laws which protect at least the safety and decorum of church meetings. While no church is "established" here in the European sense of the word, all are "established for the purpose of the security of the worshippers from penalties or from molestation in the act of worship "[25] Church purposes in the United States are strictly private purposes, it is true, but they are of more than passing interest to the general public.[26] This, of course, naturally implies that the administration and government of a sacred place belonging to the Catholic Church must be acknowledged and carried out according to its own constitution and laws. For without such authority the important provisions in the constitutions which guarantee the free enjoyment of religious beliefs and worship to every person would become nugatory.[27] The Catholic Church cannot permit her temples to become — as was customary before 1776 [28]— places for town meetings, lectures, concerts, temperance or political meetings and for other profane purposes.

24 Cfr. cc 1, 5, X, iii, 49, c. 2, 6°, III, 23

25 Cfr Zollmann, *American Civil Church Law,* 1917, p. 286

26 *Ibid.,* p. 407: "Says the *Missouri* court in a dedication case: it is presumed that in the nineteenth century, in a Christian land, no argument is necessary to show that church purposes are public purposes."

27 *Ibid ,* p. 286.

28 *Ibid.,* p. 407.

Here we may add some practical observations occasioned by the recent influenza epidemic. The Church is not opposed to sanitary and hygienic regulations intended to safeguard the public health and welfare. But she cannot recognize the authority of a local board of health to close a church or to command the clergy to do so. Such measures, when necessary, have to be taken through the hierarchy, *i. e.*, the bishop of the diocese, who should not shirk his duty. This is an act of jurisdiction proper to the diocesan court.

A last remark: The text does not state on what ground the Church claims immunity for sacred places, whether by divine or ecclesiastical law. The majority of canonists attribute it either to divine law or (at least) to the natural dictates of reason. The latter view may be safely defended on the basis of universal consent.

TITLE IX

CHURCHES

CAN. 1161

Ecclesiae nomine intelligitur aedes sacra divino cultui dedicata eum potissimum in finem ut omnibus Christifidelibus usui sit ad divinum cultum publice exercendum.

By the term *church* is understood a sacred building dedicated to divine worship, chiefly for the purpose that it may be made use of by all the faithful for public services.

The Latin term *ecclesia* (from ἐκκαλέω) was the first in vogue among Christians for their meeting places.[1] "Temple" was rarely used up to the fourth century, probably to avoid confounding Christian places of worship with Jewish and pagan temples.

The definition of "church" in the Code contains three characteristics: (a) *sacred building*, to distinguish it from altars and furniture and common buildings; (b) *dedicated to divine worship*, by consecration or solemn blessing; and (c) chiefly for the purpose that it be *open* to *all the faithful*. The last-named characteristic distin-

---

[1] Cfr I Cor. 11, 12, Tertull, *De Velandis Virg.*, 13, *De Pudicitia*, 4. The term *dominicum*, from the Greek κυριακόν, was also used early; from this latter expression the Scotch *kirk*, English *church*, and German *Kirche* arose. Other terms, like *basilica* and *martyrium*, have a specific meaning as to form or kind.

guishes a church from an oratory, either domestic or semi-public, for oratories may vie with, or even surpass churches in size and be consecrated like them, but, unlike churches, are intended only for certain classes of people or certain families.[2]

BUILDING OF CHURCHES

CAN. 1162

§ 1. Nulla ecclesia aedificetur sine expresso Ordinarii loci consensu scriptis dato, quem tamen Vicarius Generalis praestare nequit sine mandato speciali.

§ 2. Ordinarius consensum ne praebeat, nisi prudenter praeviderit necessaria non defutura ad novae ecclesiae aedificationem et conservationem ad ministrorum sustentationem aliasque cultus impensas.

§ 3. Ne nova ecclesia ceteris iam exsistentibus detrimentum afferat, maiore fidelium spirituali utilitate non compensatum, Ordinarius, antequam consensum praebeat, audire debet vicinarum ecclesiarum rectores quorum intersit, firmo praescripto can. 1676.

§ 4. Etiam sodales religiosi, licet consensum constituendae novae domus in dioecesi vel civitate ab Ordinario loci retulerint, antequam tamen ecclesiam vel oratorium publicum in certo ac determinato loco aedificent, Ordinarii loci licentiam obtinere debent.

CAN. 1163

Benedicere et imponere primarium ecclesiae lapidem, ad eos spectat, de quibus in can. 1156.

2 S. Rit C , May 18, 1883, ad IV, 5; June 5, 1899 (*Dec. Auth*, nn. 3574, 4025).

CAN. 1164

§ 1. Curent Ordinarii, audito etiam, si opus fuerit, peritorum consilio, ut in ecclesiarum aedificatione vel refectione serventur formae a traditione christiana receptae et artis sacrae leges.

§ 2. In ecclesia nullus aperiatur aditus vel fenestra ad laicorum domus; locaque, si adsint, subter ecclesiae pavimentum aut supra ecclesiam, ad usum mere profanum ne adhibeantur.

Can. 1162 provides that the *consent of the Ordinary* must be obtained for building a church. No church, says § 1, may be built without the express consent, in writing, of the diocesan Ordinary. The Vicar General cannot give this consent without a special mandate from the Ordinary.

This is partly old and partly new law, as far as the written consent is concerned. The Council of Chalcedon forbade religious to construct oratories without the consent of the diocesan.[3] Other synods also insist upon this formality.[4]

§ 2 rules that the Ordinary shall withhold his consent until he is convinced that the necessary means for building and maintaining a new church, and for supporting the ministers and defraying other expenditures of religious worship, will not be wanting. This, too, is ancient practice. Ancient councils insisted on the necessary dowry (*dos*) for every new church.[5] This requirement is also stated in the Roman Pontifical.[6] The Ordinary is

---

3 C. 10, C. 18, q. 2.
4 Cfr. c. 44, C. 16, q. 1 (Worms); c. 9, Dist. 1, *de cons.* (Orleans).

5 C. 26, C. 16, q. 7; c. 8, x, III, 40.
6 P. II, tit., *de benedictione et impositione primarii lapidis.*

therefore most solemnly charged to examine the financial prospects of a new church.

§ 3 of can. 1162 adds another condition for the consent: In order that the new church may not become a detriment to churches already existing, if the loss would not be compensated by the spiritual advantage of the faithful, the Ordinary shall, before giving his consent, hear the interested rectors of the neighboring churches, with due regard, however, to can. 1676. This canon is a repetition of an old Roman Law which passed into the Decretals,[7] and rules that everyone,— in our case every rector of a church already in existence,— who believes himself to be injured by the erection of a new church, may sue for an injunction before the judge. The effect is somewhat similar to legal estoppel, but is only temporary, until the judge has decided the case. But although the new building should not be continued while the case is pending, the builder may go on with the work, provided he gives security to restore everything to the condition before the work commenced in case the sentence should be against him. Our Code grants two months to the plaintiff or objector to prove his contention. This term may be prolonged or shortened by the competent judge. Hence the bishop has to listen to the objections of the interested rectors, summon the parties and witnesses, in fact, conduct an ecclesiastical trial, at least in summary form.

§ 4 mentions *religious* who wish to build a church or public oratory. These, although they have already obtained the consent of the local Ordinary for establishing a house in the diocese or city, must obtain the permission of the local Ordinary before they can build a church or

---

7 Cfr. Dig. 39, 1; Cod. VIII, 10, 14; X, V, 32, *de novi operis nun-* *tiatione;* Gasparri, *De SSma Euch.,* 1897, I, n. 125, p. 81.

public oratory in a certain and specified place) Concerning this we have said enough elsewhere,[8] and nothing we have said needs modification. We will only add a case: A religious community had received permission to build a house in a certain city. They did so, and opened a public oratory within the boundaries of a parish church as yet in the "catacomb" or basement stage. This drew some substantial and perhaps niggardly parishioners to the new chapel, who contributed neither to the oratory of the religious nor to the parish church. The solution is evident. The bishop had to stop the new chapel or else cut off part of the parish and give it to the religious.

Note that after the promulgation of the Code no religious, however exempt, can escape the law; and if the bishop granted permission before the promulgation, he may now withdraw it, provided the building was not commenced or the site changed. For the Code says: in a certain and specified place. Besides, under § 1 of can. 1162 written consent is required.

Can. 1163 rules that the *blessing and laying of the cornerstone* belongs to those who are entitled to bless the church. Hence the Ordinary or his delegate, or the superior of exempt religious or his delegate, may bless and lay the corner-stone.

Can. 1164 admonishes Ordinaries to see to it that new churches are built and old ones repaired in accordance with the time-honored laws of Christian architecture and the rules of sacred art.

This can best be explained in the school-room, where lectures on Christian art should be given. The earliest form of church building was the *basilica,* which was

8 Cfr. Vol. III, p. 89, can. 497. Formerly they only needed the permission of the Holy See for building a monastery; c. 4, 6°, V, 7.

evolved from the ancient Roman dwelling-house.[9] About the eighth century the Romanesque style absorbed the basilica, and later the Gothic style added its distinct and pointed features. Out of these arose two mixtures, *viz.*, Barocco and Rococo, of which the former may have some claim to the name of traditional architecture, whereas the extreme Rococo can hardly be called anything else but a mental and architectural aberration. Then there is the Byzantine style, which has found favor here and there, even in our country, and certainly comes up to the requirements of Christian art.

Our text adds that, if necessary, experts should be consulted. This is a dictate of common sense. The rules of art demand that the style should fit into the landscape and its surroundings. The financial resources also must be considered. But a well-trained taste will be able to erect a monument even of cheaper material. Finally the practical and acoustic side should receive attention. Too many and heavy pillars are hardly practicable for a parish church; too great a distance between people and altar is not compatible with the all-absorbing idea of the sacrifice. These are merely suggestions based on experience.

§ 2 of can. 1164 says that no opening or window may lead from the church into the house of lay people and that the space underneath or above the church should not be used for profane purposes.

As to the first clause it may be noted that an episcopal palace [10] or priest's residence may be built in such a way that a gate or window leads into the church. Religious, with the permission of the bishop, may have a choir built in their house leading into the church, from which they may assist at Mass or pay their visits to the Bl. Sacrament.

9 Cfr. Lowrie, *Monuments of the Early Church,* 1901, p. 83 ff.

10 This was formerly refused; cfr. Gasparri, *l. c.,* n. 127, p. 83.

The next clause may cause surprise to more than one pastor, for it would seem to affect the so-called combination-buildings (church and school combined) so often found here. If there is nothing else attached to such a building, we believe it is not forbidden, for the text says, *" ad usum mere profanum,"* which cannot be applied to a parish school. The case is different if the basement or the hall above the church would be used for merely profane meetings or entertainments. The decisions are decidedly against such use, even if the basement were only used as a theatre for the school-children.[11] The reason is that the church together with the basement is, *as a whole, consecrated (per modum unius).* The decisions have consecration in view. Do they apply to churches which are blessed? There is no doubt that, as stated above, the canonical effect of consecration and blessing, as far as the church is concerned, is the same. However, there *is* a difference between consecration and blessing, and we hardly believe that a combination building could be consecrated. Besides, as shall be seen under can. 1172, the defilement of a church must affect the church itself. Hence it is commonly taught that the sacristy or tower of a church, or a crypt which has neither chapels nor a burial place, is not polluted by acts performed therein.[12] From this it would seem to follow that the basement or hall of a church is not, strictly speaking, included in the church proper. The consequence would be that the hall or basement of the church (if this were merely blessed) might be used for purposes which would otherwise be excluded.

We would also draw attention to the fact of necessity which exists in many places. However, we must add

[11] S Rit C, May 4, 1882 (*Dec. Auth*, n. 3546).   [12] Many, *l. c*, p 78 ff.

that the intention of the lawgiver certainly is to prohibit merely worldly uses which have no connection with the church. Dances, balls, and noisy banquets should not be held in these places.

We add some decisions. A dormitory, even for clerical students, is not permitted immediately above the ceiling of the chapel or church; only if it is separated by an intervening space or room provided with solid walls, may it be placed above the church.[13] There should be no cellar under the church.[14]

DEDICATION OF A CHURCH

CAN. 1165

§ 1. Divina officia celebrari in·nova ecclesia nequeunt, antequam eadem vel sollemni consecratione vel saltem benedictione divino cultui fuerit dedicata.

§ 2. Si prudenter praevideatur ecclesiam conversum iri ad usus profanos, Ordinarius consensum eius aedificationi ne praebeat, aut saltem, si forte aedificata fuerit, eam ne consecret neve benedicat.

§ 3. Sollemni consecratione dedicentur ecclesiae cathedrales et, quantum fieri potest, ecclesiae collegiatae, conventuales, paroeciales.

§ 4. Ecclesia ex ligno vel ferro aliove metallo benedici potest, non autem consecrari.

§ 5. Altare consecrari potest etiam sine ecclesiae consecratione; sed una simul cum ecclesia debet saltem altare maius consecrari aut altare secundarium, si maius sit iam consecratum.

§ 1. Divine service may not be held in a new church

---

13 S. Rit. C, May 11, 1641, July 27, 1878 (*Dec Auth*, nn 756, 3460). 14 S Rit C, Aug 31, 1867 (*ibid*, n 3156)

before it has been solemnly *consecrated* or at least dedicated to the worship of God by a *blessing*.

This law dates back to remote antiquity. Eusebius, the "Father of Church History," tells us that, soon after the persecutions had ceased, churches were dedicated in the presence of gatherings of bishops, priests, and a great multitude of lay-people, who counted distance nothing, being united in love and joy on the occasion. He inserts his own discourse delivered at the dedication of a church at Tyre.[15]

No special ritual for church dedications can be traced before the eighth or ninth century. According to the two most ancient *Ordines Romani,* the chief ceremony appears to have been the translation of relics. A description of the liturgical act of dedication in use in France at the beginning of the eighth century shows that it closely resembled the present rite, as found in the Roman Pontifical.[16] Thus we may say that, although at first churches were perhaps dedicated by celebrating the divine mysteries, yet from the eighth century onward a special ritual was followed, which finally developed into the present rite.

Dedication then is performed by either consecration or blessing.

Consecration essentially consists in anointing with chrism the twelve crosses which are placed on the walls or pillars of the church, with the formula: "*Sanctificetur et consecretur hoc templum in nomine Patris et Filii et Spiritus Sancti, etc*"[17] The bishop should go around the whole church three times. If this cannot be done, he

---

[15] *Hist Eccl*, X, 3, 1 ff. (cfr. *Die Griech. Christl. Schriftsteller*, by Schwarz-Mommsen, Vol. II, 860 ff.)

[16] Cfr Duchesne-McClure, *Divine Worship*, 1903, p 407 ff.

[17] S Rit C., April 12, 1614 (*Dec. Auth*, n. 319).

should at least go about those parts which are accessible.[18] If (*e. g.*, on account of bad weather) the prayers and sprinkling of the outside walls cannot take place, what is to be done? The S. Congregation answered as follows: If possible, recourse should be had to the Holy See; but if the consecration cannot be delayed, the solemn function may begin in the sacristy, or in the vestibule, or in some other convenient place, and the outside walls should be sprinkled as well as it can possibly be done; but the people are not to be admitted into the church from the beginning of the ceremony.[19] One and the same bishop must consecrate the church and the main, or at least one, altar.[20]

Blessing a church consists essentially in sprinkling the upper and lower part of the walls, either inside or outside, with holy water. All churches and public oratories must be at least blessed according to the formula in the Roman Ritual.[21] Unless they are blessed no titular feast may be celebrated.[22] Nor does the fact that the cemetery is blessed create a presumption in favor of the church.[23] Before the blessing is imparted, *divine service* may not be celebrated in a church. This means that Mass may not be said, the sacraments may not be administered, and there is to be no preaching; for these offices especially constitute *divine worship* (cfr. can. 2256).

§ 2. If it can be reasonably foreseen that a church will be turned to profane uses, the Ordinary shall not consent to its being built, nor consecrate or bless it after it is built. There would be room for prudent fear if a church

---

18 S. Rit. C., Sept. 19, 1665, ad 1 (*ibid.*, n. 1321).

19 S. Rit. C., Feb. 22, 1888 (*ibid.*, n. 16).

20 S. Rit. C., March 3, 1866 (*ibid.*, n. 3142).

21 S. Rit. C., June 5, 1899 (*ibid.*, n. 4025).

22 S. Rit. C., Sept. 2, 1871, ad II, 3 (*ibid.*, n. 3255).

23 S. Rit. C., Feb. 21, 1896, ad IV, (*ibid.*, n. 3888).

or public oratory belonged to a private family and thus be liable to transfer and subsequent profanation by way of sale or alienation.[24]

§ 3. *Cathedral churches* and also, as far as possible, *collegiate, conventual, and parish churches,* should be solemnly *consecrated.*

§ 4. Churches built of wood or iron, or some other metal, may be blessed, but not consecrated.

As to rural chapels and oratories of confraternities or pious associations, they may be consecrated if built of stone or brick, but if the bishop does not wish to consecrate them he may delegate a priest to bless them.[25]

Churches built of reinforced concrete (*caementum armatum*) may be solemnly consecrated, provided that the places for the twelve crosses and the door posts of the main entrance be of stone [26]

§ 5. An altar may be consecrated even if the church is not consecrated; but together with the church the main altar (or, if the main altar is already consecrated), a side altar must be consecrated This section embodies the substance of former decisions of the S. Congregation, as summarized in a decree of the S. Rit. C., June 8, 1896. This decree states that the consecration of a church without the simultaneous consecration of at least one altar is valid but illicit if performed without Apostolic dispensation [27] The reason is to be sought in the integrity of the whole ceremony.

24 S. Rit C , May 4, 1882, ad I (*ibid* , n 3546)

25 S Rit C , Aug. 7, 1875, ad 1 (*ibid.,* n. 3364).

26 S. Rit C , Nov. 12, 1909 (n. 4240)

27 *Dec Auth.,* n 3907 (also nn. 1321, 2177).

THE CONSECRATION OF CHURCHES AND ALTARS

CAN. 1166

§ 1. Ecclesiarum consecratio, quamvis quolibet die fieri possit, decentius tamen diebus dominicis aliisve festis de praecepto peragitur.

§ 2. Episcopus consecrans et qui petunt ecclesiam sibi consecrari, per eum diem qui consecrationem praecedit, ieiunent.

§ 3. Cum consecratur ecclesia vel altare, Episcopus consecrator, licet iurisdictione in territorio careat, indulgentiam concedit unius anni ecclesiam vel altare visitantibus in ipsa consecrationis die; in die vero anniversaria quinquaginta dierum, si sit Episcopus; centum, si Archiepiscopus; biscentum, si S. R. E. Cardinalis.

§ 1. Although churches may be consecrated on any day, it is meet that *Sundays* or *holydays of obligation* be chosen for that purpose

§ 2. The consecrating bishop as well as those who have petitioned for consecration, shall *fast* on the day preceding the consecration.

This fast is of *strict obligation*. It is personal as well as local.[28] Thus if a founder asks the bishop to consecrate a church or public oratory, he is bound to fast the day before; if a chapter or corporation (*v. g.*, parish) or religious community ask for consecration, the whole chapter, etc., are bound to fast, including those who voted against the consecration.[29] But the chaplain of religious communities of sisters who asked for the favor would not have to fast, even though he submitted the petition to the

28 S. Rit. C., July 29, 1780; Sept. 12, 1840 (*Dec. Auth*, nn. 2519).

29 Many, *l. c*, p. 33.

bishop. Of course, if he had asked for it personally, he too would be bound to fast.

§ 3. At the consecration of a church or altar the consecrating bishop, though he may not have jurisdiction over the territory, grants an indulgence of one year to all who visit the church or altar on the day of the consecration; of fifty days for the anniversary of the consecration; of 100 days if he be an archbishop, 200 if he be a cardinal.

ANNIVERSARY OF CONSECRATION

CAN. 1167

Festum consecrationis ecclesiae quotannis celebretur ad normam legum liturgicarum.

The feast of the consecration of a church is to be celebrated annually according to the rubrics.

The latest decrees [30] concerning this subject are: Provided the cathedral church has been consecrated and not merely blessed:

(a) The feast of the dedication is a primary feast and *festum Domini;*

(b) The anniversary must be celebrated as a first-class feast with octave throughout the diocese by the secular clergy and also by the religious clergy if the latter follow the diocesan calendar; if they have their own calendar, they must celebrate the anniversary of the dedication of the cathedral as a feast of the first class without octave;

(c) The anniversary must be celebrated on the day proper and not transferred to a Sunday; [31]

(d) The anniversary of the dedication of the cathe-

---

30 S Rit C., Nov 1, 1911 (*A Ap S*, III, 646 f)

31 If the day is not recorded or remembered, the Ordinary, with the advice of the chapter, may *semel pro semper* assign a day.

dral must be celebrated separately from the dedication of
all the churches of the diocese; for the latter feast (*dedi-
catio omnium ecclesiarum dioeceseos*) a day may be designated by the Ordinary;

(e) The same rule must be observed by religious orders or congregations with regard to the celebration of the
dedication of all the churches of their institute;[32]

(f) The feast of the dedication of all the churches of
a diocese (or institute) must be understood in the sense
that each church celebrates its own dedication.[33]

TITLES AND TITULAR FEASTS

CAN. 1168

§ 1. Unaquaeque ecclesia consecrata vel benedicta
suum habeat titulum; qui, peracta ecclesiae dedicatione, mutari nequit.

§ 2. Etiam festum tituli quotannis celebretur ad
normas legum liturgicarum.

§ 3. Ecclesiae dedicari Beatis nequeunt sine Sedis
Apostolicae indulto.

§ 1. Each consecrated or blessed church must have its
own title, which cannot be changed after the dedication.

§ 2. The titular feast is to be celebrated annually according to the rubrical laws.

§ 3. Churches cannot be dedicated to a *Beatus* without
an Apostolic indult.

Titulus[34] is the name by which a church is known and
distinguished from other churches. It is not unlike the
name given in Baptism. If the name is that of a person,

32 S Rit C, Oct 28, 1913, I, 3,
c f (A Ap. S, V, 458)
33 S Rit C, Feb. 12, 1914 (A
Ap S., VI, 76)

34 Cfr Gasparri, *De SSma Euch.*,
1907, I, n. 137 ff., Many, *l. c*, p.
52 ff.

this person is called the *patron* of the church, provided he or she be a Saint (*persona creata, non increata*), for patron signifies *advocate,* which does not apply to a Divine Person.

Titles of churches may be: the Blessed Trinity or one of the three Divine Persons,[35] Jesus Christ or one of the biblical mysteries, the Blessed Virgin or any one of her special attributes, the angels and saints or some conspicuous events in their lives, as, for instance, the conversion of St. Paul.

When two saints are chosen as patrons for one church, they are generally taken *per modum unius, e. g.,* SS. Philip and James. But if at the dedication two different saints are chosen *divisim,* they are celebrated on their respective days. Sometimes it happens that a secondary title or patron is added because it has been transferred from a church forsaken or destroyed.

The text says that the *title cannot be changed.* For the title being chosen at the laying of the corner-stone and made stable or perpetual at the dedication, is the distinctive and permanent attribute of a church. Hence it has been decided more than once that the bishop cannot of his own accord change the original title, but an Apostolic indult is required for the purpose.[36] If the Holy See adds the title of an abandoned church to another, the title thus added is a secondary one.[37]

§ 3 says that no church shall be dedicated to a *Beatus, i. e.,* one who is beatified, but not yet canonized by a formal decree of the Holy See. In the case of such as have been venerated as saints by a constant tradition before the

35 God the Father is, as far as we know, not chosen, because of the fact that He is not represented as sent (*defectu missionis divinae*)

36 S. Rit. C., Sept. 6, 1834, ad 2; Sept. 12, 1857, ad 17 (*l. c.,* nn. 2719, 3059)

37 S. Rit. C., April 20, 1822, n. 1 (*ibid.,* n 2619, t IV, p 221).

time of Alexander III (1159–1181), the public veneration takes the place of the formal decree of the Apostolic
See,[38] and they may therefore be chosen as patrons for
churches.

§ 2 concerns the *titular feast*. The chief rules as to
that are the following:

1. The titular feast of the cathedral church must be
celebrated with octave by the whole clergy of the diocese,
including those religious who follow the diocesan calendar. Regulars (not religious who have no calendar of
their own) must observe the feast as one of the first class,
but without octave, if they have their own calendar.[39]
This celebration includes office and Mass

2. The *church* whose clergy is obliged to observe the
feast is any *consecrated* or *blessed* church. Oratories,
either public or semi-public, are included, provided they
are either consecrated or solemnly blessed; likewise episcopal chapels, oratories of seminaries, hospital chapels,
chapels of religious houses, etc.[40]

3. The *clergy* obliged to say the office and Mass of the
titular feast are: (a) the pastor and his assistants [41] (b)
Missionaries assigned to several missions, but residing at
one, are bound only to the feast of the residential
church [42] (c) Rectors, seminary professors, and students
who live in the seminary, must recite the office of the
seminary church.[43]

4. *Regulars* must celebrate the feast of their own
church; [44] but if they merely live in a house adjoining a

---

38 Many, *l c*, p 54 f
39 S Rit C, Nov. 11, 1911 (*A.
Ap S.*, III, 647 f.).
40 S Rit C, June 5, 1899 (n.
4025).
41 S. Rit C, Sept. 2, 1871, Aug.
11, 1877 (*ibid*, nn 3255, 3431)

42 S. Rit C, Aug. 25, 1882, Feb.
27, 1883 (*ibid*, nn 3554, 3571).
43 S Rit C, Feb. 27, 1847 (*ibid*,
n 2939)
44 S. Rit C, Sept. 18, 1877, ad 1
(n 3437)

church which they do not own, they are not allowed to recite the office of that church.[45]   A religious community in charge of a public church must recite the office of the titular feast of that church with octave [46]

5. *Chaplains of sisters* are not bound to say the office of the titular feast of the chapel which they serve.

6. The bishop must recite the office of the titular feast of the cathedral church, and if he has two bishoprics *aeque principaliter* united, he has to recite the office of both cathedral churches, if they have different titles.

If a church is simply called " St. Mary's," the proper title is the Assumption ; " Our Saviour's " is celebrated on the feast of the Transfiguration.[47]

CHURCH BELLS

CAN. 1169

§ 1. Cuilibet ecclesiae campanas esse convenit, quibus fideles ad divina officia aliosque religionis actus invitentur.

§ 2.   Etiam ecclesiarum campanae debent consecrari vel benedici secundum ritus in probatis liturgicis libris traditos.

§ 3.   Earum usus unice subest ecclesiasticae auctoritati.

§ 4.   Salvis conditionibus, probante Ordinario, appositis ab illis qui campanam ecclesiae forte dederint, campana benedicta ad usus mere profanos adhiberi nequit, nisi ex causa necessitatis aut ex licentia Ordinarii aut denique ex legitima consuetudine.

§ 5.   Quod ad campanarum consecrationem vel ben-

---

45 Gasparri, *l. c.*, p 96.
46 S Rit. C , April 7, 1876, ad IV (n. 3397).
47 Gasparri, *l. c* , p 95, 97.

edictionem attinet, servetur praescriptum can. 1155, 1156.

§ 1. It is becoming that every church have bells, by which the faithful may be called to the divine service and other religious acts.

§ 2. Church bells must be either consecrated or blessed according to the rites prescribed in approved liturgical books.

§ 3. Their use is regulated exclusively by the church authorities.

§ 4. Aside from the stipulations made by the donor with the approval of the Ordinary, a blessed bell cannot be used for merely profane purposes, except in case of necessity, or by permission of the Ordinary, or by lawful custom.

§ 5. The consecration or blessing of bells is governed by can. 1155 and 1156.

We need not dwell on the origin of bells. Suffice it to say that from the word " *signum,*" used in ancient monkish rules,[48] to *campana,* or bell proper, which appears in the *Liber Pontificalis* under Stephen II (752–757), there lie about 250 years [49] The eighth century witnessed the development which gave rise to the use of bells for churches as we know it. Complaint was made by the regulars against prelates who forbade religious to have church bells, and Pope Gregory IX put an end to these molestations.[50]

§ 1 simply affirms the convenience and propriety of having bells in every church, whether in charge of secular or religious clergy. Nothing is said about their number or size.

---

48 *Reg. S Bened* , c. 43.
49 Cfr *Cath Encyc* , II, 418 ff
Bells are often called *nolae*, which is a reminder of the legend that St. Paulinus of Nola invented them
50 C 16, x, V, 31.

§ 2 mentions the *consecration and blessing of bells,* which, as § 5 enacts, must be regulated according to can. 1155 and 1156.

The formula of *consecration* is found in the *Pontificale Romanum.* It should be used for the bells of consecrated churches.[51]

According to can. 1155, the consecration of bells is reserved to the local Ordinary, and delegation to a simple priest can only be given by the Holy See.[52]

There is also a formulary for *blessing* bells in the Roman Ritual [53] It is intended for bells to be used for church or chapel purposes.[54] For this function the Ordinary or an exempt religious superior may delegate any priest without recourse to the Holy See.[55] If the *consecration* is performed on several bells, the washings and anointings are made *per modum unius* during the recitation of the Psalms. The water must be blessed for each function, but not for each bell, if several are consecrated at the same time.

If a delegate performs the consecration and has received delegation for one bell only, whilst there are several, delegation for the others may be presumed.

If, for some reason, there is no water blessed by the bishop available, the delegate may, in case of necessity, bless water himself.[56]

One delegated to consecrate bells must strictly follow the *Pontificale;* he must not omit the anointings or muti-

---

[51] S Rit. C, Jan. 22, 1908 (*Dec. Auth.,* n 4211).

[52] S Rit. C, April 19, 1687 (*ibid.,* n. 1781). The anointing may not be omitted.

[53] See ed. Pustet, 1913, p. 77* ff.

[54] There is also a blessing of bells not intended for church uses; see *ed cit.,* p 84.*

[55] It is not becoming that the bishop *in pontificalibus* should climb a ladder to bless bells which cannot be taken down; S Rit. C, July 16, 1594 (*l. c.,* n. 52).

[56] S. Rit. C, April 14, 1885 (n. 3630).

late or change the formula, and he must employ a deacon.[57]

Nothing forbids the consecration of bells made of pure iron or steel.[58]

Bells consecrated or blessed for the service of churches or chapels, are strictly sacred things and, as such, subject to the exclusive jurisdiction of the Church. They must not be rung for merely secular purposes, worldly festivities, political meetings, executions, etc. Their guardian is the pastor or the sacristan canon of the cathedral chapter, who, in case of doubt, especially when serious consequences are to be apprehended, is bound to report to the Ordinary.

§ 4 leaves a wide margin in regard to the use of church bells. (a) The will of the founder must be respected, if any stipulations have been made with the approval of the bishop. (b) Necessity justifies the ringing of church bells in time of flood, fire, war, etc.[59] (c) The permission of the Ordinary may be given for any laudable purpose, e. g., to celebrate a victory or the restoration of peace, the return of soldiers, civic festivals, etc. (d) Lawful custom sanctions the use of church bells for any of the aforesaid or similar purposes.

But it must be emphasized that the ringing of bells consecrated or blessed for church purposes cannot lawfully be dictated by the civil authorities, since, as said above, by consecration or blessing these objects have a sacred character imprinted upon them.

The question whether bells used by a church are its property or belong to some one else can sometimes be

57 S. Rit C, June 23, 1853 (n. 3015)

58 S. Rit. C, Feb. 6, 1858 (n 3067).

59 In that case the sexton or any parishioner may ring the bell without asking the pastor or bishop, especially if there are no other means of communication.

determined only by the intention of the founder, but unless the stipulated and proved intention of the founder [60] makes an exception, the control of church bells lies solely with the ecclesiastical authority, *i. e.,* the Ordinary of the diocese.

LOSS OF CONSECRATION OR BLESSING

CAN. 1170

Consecrationem vel benedictionem ecclesia non amittit, nisi tota destructa fuerit, vel maior parietum pars corruerit, vel in usus profanos ab Ordinario loci redacta sit, ad norman can. 1187.

A church does not lose its consecration or blessing unless it is totally destroyed, or the larger part of the walls has collapsed, or the Ordinary has turned the building over to profane uses, according to can. 1187.

It would be equal to entire destruction if the whole wall, apse and roof had been removed.[61] But a partial repair of, say, two-fifths of the walls would not require re-consecration. Thus, *e. g.,* if the framework or joists of a church were consumed by fire, or the framework of the tower had fallen upon the arch of the middle aisle and damaged the walls, no reconsecration would be required [62] Even if the whole church is successively repaired, re-consecration is not required, provided each part repaired is smaller than the parts not repaired.[63] Furthermore, although the whole plastering (*intonaco*) were removed

---

60 Zollmann, *American Civil Church Law,* 1917, p. 374 f If the civil authorities should ask the church authorities to moderate the ringing of bells, no one would object to such a petition, provided it were reasonable.

61 S Rit C., Sept 4, 1875 (n 3372)

62 S Rit C., July 13, 1883 (n. 3504)

63 S. Rit. C., Aug 31, 1872 (n. 3269).

together with the crosses, and new plastering, stucco, or marble substituted, no re-consecration or re-blessing would be necessary; but the crosses should be painted anew or replaced by new ones.[64] Even if the church is considerably enlarged and interiorly embellished with marble or stucco, as long as the old walls remain in the proportion of 3 to 2 or 5 to 3, no re-consecration or re-blessing is required, though the crosses, as stated above, must be renewed.[65]

As to the reduction of a consecrated or blessed church to profane uses we refer to can. 1187. The Ordinary alone can do this, and hence, if a church was turned over to profane uses by human malice or violence, it may be called defiled, provided Can. 1172 is verified, but it is not execrated, and execration is here to be understood.[66]

EFFECT OF CONSECRATION OR BLESSING

Can. 1171

In sacra aede legitime dedicata omnes ecclesiastici ritus perfici possunt, salvis iuribus paroecialibus, privilegiis et legitimis consuetudinibus; Ordinarius autem, praesertim horas sacrorum rituum, potest, iusta de causa, praefinire, dummodo ne agatur de ecclesia quae ad religionem exemptam pertineat, firmo praescripto can. 609, § 3.

One of the effects of consecration or blessing is that, in every sacred edifice properly dedicated, all ecclesiastical rites may be performed, with due regard to parochial

---

[64] S. Rit C, May 4, 1882; June 8, 1896, ad II; Aug 9, 1897 (*l. c*, an 3345, 3907, 3962).
[65] S. Rit. C, Jan 16, 1886 (n.

3651); this holds good even if the primary intention was to repair or enlarge the whole church
[66] Many, *l c*, p 66

rights, privileges, and lawful customs.   But the Ordinary may, for a just cause, determine the hours of service, provided the church does not belong to exempt religious.

This law comprises every church or public oratory duly consecrated or blessed.   The ecclesiastical rites which may be performed in such sacred edifices are the divine offices mentioned in can. 1165, § 1.

The Code adds: *salvis iuribus paroecialibus, privilegiis et legitimis consuetudinibus.*   This means that a church or public oratory may be solemnly consecrated or blessed, yet, as long as it is no parish church, no parochial rights can be exercised therein, unless the parish priest should choose it for parochial functions.   Besides it may happen that, for instance, a confraternity enjoys certain privileges for its members, *e. g.,* the burial right may be attached to a church, even though it is not a parish church.

Lawful custom may introduce rights which might otherwise be claimed by the parish church, for instance, that of having a *baptismal font.*[67]

As to the *hours of service,* it has been more than once decided that the bishop may, either at a synod or outside, determine the hour of the parochial Mass, as well as forbid that Mass be said in secular chapels before the parochial Mass.   However, the S. Congregation has repeatedly urged pastors to say Mass at hours convenient for the faithful   The pastor is not entitled to forbid that Mass be said before the parochial Mass.[68]   It was declared that an archpriest has no right to forbid chaplains of a public oratory to say Mass before the parochial Mass, unless this oratory was subject to the parish church, whose archpriest attempted to enforce the prohibition in question.[69]

---

[67] Cfr. S C. C , May 17, 1749 (Richter, *Trid,* p. 131, n. 8); can. 775

[68] Bened. XIV, *Inst.,* 44, nn 9 ff.

[69] S. Rit C., July 11, 1643 (n. 842).

Exempt religious, even though warned by the bishop, are not obliged to abstain from celebrating Mass or performing other functions even while the bells are ringing for the parochial Mass   Thus the S. C. Concilii has decided several times.[70]

Our canon refers to can. 609, § 3, which has been sufficiently explained in Vol. III of this Commentary.

DESECRATION OF A CHURCH

CAN. 1172

§ 1. Ecclesia violatur infra recensitis tantum actibus, dummodo certi sint, notorii, et in ipsa ecclesia positi:

1°. Delicto homicidii;

2°. Iniuriosa et gravi sanguinis effusione;

3°. Impiis vel sordidis usibus, quibus ecclesia addicta fuerit;

4°. Sepultura infidelis vel excommunicati post sententiam declaratoriam vel condemnatoriam.

§ 2. Violata ecclesia, non ideo coemeterium, etsi contiguum, violatum censetur, et viceversa.

By desecration (*pollutio ecclesiae,* as it was formerly called) is here understood a moral violation of a church by diverting it from a sacred to a profane use.   It is induced only by acts described in the law and differs from *execration* in as much as the latter entails the loss of consecration or blessing, whilst desecration only requires reconciliation or rehabilitation.

Up to the time of the Decree of Gratian no clear distinction can be established between desecration and execration, as may be seen from the canons the Master

---

70 Cfr. Richter, *Trid.,* p 136, n. 45.

alleges.[71] The term "*pollutio*" does not occur in the classical texts of Gratian, but was probably brought in by the glossators. *Violatio* is used by Pseudo-Hyginus.[72] *Pollutio* and *reconciliatio* are the terms employed in the Decretals.[73]

The Code has apparently omitted from the list of acts which induce violation the *seminis effusio*,[74] but instead of it has inserted a new mode of desecration, which can only be determined by subsequent practical legislation.[75]

§ 1. A church is violated (or desecrated) by the following acts, provided they are certain, notorious, and committed in the church itself, to wit:

1. The crime of homicide;

2. Injurious and serious shedding of blood;

3. Impious or sordid use to which the church was diverted;

4. The burial of an infidel or one excommunicated by a declaratory or condemnatory sentence.

§ 2. The desecration of a church does not entail the desecration of the cemetery, even though the latter adjoins the church, and *vice versa*, desecration of the cemetery does not involve desecration of the church.

Homicide must here be strictly understood, as the killing of any human being, whether young or old; hence it also covers abortion and suicide. It does not matter whether the crime is committed by poison, or hanging, or the use of a weapon.

The text further says *delicto*. A crime supposes a

---

71 C 3, Dist 68; cc 19, 20, 27, 28, Dist. 1, *de cons*

72 C 19, Dist 1, *de cons.*

73 Cc. 7, 10, x, III, 40.

74 C 10, x, III, 40

75 Whether the *effusio seminis humani* is included in § 1, n. 3° (as the *Irish Eccl. Record*, 1919, 460, maintains) seems doubtful, because *usus* is hardly ever employed in such connection, unless a church were used for a brothel, which is a repulsive thought.

grievous fault, and therefore homicide committed by a child, or by an insane or frenzied person, would not desecrate a church. If a drunkard perpetrates such an act, it depends on whether the action was in any way foreseen or not. If it was not foreseen, it does not desecrate the church.[76] Lynching, however, and even the judiciary execution of a sentence of capital punishment would induce desecration. No crime is involved if one kills an aggressor in self-defence.

Iniuriosa et gravis sanguinis effusio means the shedding of human blood in such quantity that it may be called a pouring out. Hence a few drops, or the oozing from a light wound would not desecrate a church, and the authors[77] speak of a *copious* shedding of blood. The word *gravis* may have another meaning, *viz. graviter culpabilis*, grievously sinful. Hence if boys would beat one another, or if a teacher would punish boys in church, it would scarcely amount to a grievous fault.[78] If by a serious blow from another the nose would bleed copiously, some assert desecration, while others deny it.[79] The correct answer depends partly on the interpretation of *iniuriosa*, because the injury may be referred either to the sacred edifice[80] or to the person[81] injured. The text does not decide which is meant. But most probably the act must be injurious to both edifice and person, so that the person injured is really damaged, and the people who witnessed the act look upon it as a serious irreverence done to the church.

The third act which induces desecration is giving the church over *to impious or sordid uses*. Here the terms

76 Cfr Gasparri, *De SSma Eucharistia*, n 250, Vol. I, p. 177.

77 Gasparri, *l c.*, n. 251; Many, *De Locis Sacris*, p 72.

78 Reiffenstuel, III, 40, n. 16.

79 Gasparri, *l. c*

80 *Idem, l. c.*

81 Many, *l. c*, p 71

require attention, because, as stated, this cause is new.

Impious has many meanings: ungodly, irreligious, irreverent, unnatural, detestable, etc. Hence using a church for orgies, as happened in the French Revolution, or for Masonic rites, would, in our opinion, desecrate it. Sacrilegious robbery would also have this effect.

Sordidus may be compared with the sordid or mean offices forbidden to the clergy. Thus a church may be called desecrated if it was used for a barracks, especially if it has also served to quarter horses or mules;[82] although the S. Congregation[83] in one instance of a two days' occupation by soldiers decided only for provisional reconciliation. Sordid would also be the use of a church for merely political meetings, if this should happen frequently and under great agitation.

Lastly, *the burial of an infidel* or an excommunicated person also desecrates a church. By infidels are here understood persons who have never been baptized. Catechumens must not be classed with infidels[84] Besides, a more benign interpretation would, in our case, exclude from the class of infidels all children of Catholic parents, whether buried with the mother or not[85] But if this be admitted, why not extend it to the husband or wife of a Catholic partner, since the unbelieving party, according to I Cor. VII, 14, is sanctified by the believing party? We make this suggestion with due reserve and because some canonists[86] interpret the term *pagans* and *infidels* as including grown persons only, or such as are wilful infidels. Our Code, which does *not* receive its juridical value from the spurious texts of Gratian's Decree, simply mentions

82 S Rit C , March 3, 1821 (*Dec. Auth*, n 2612)

83 S Rit C , Feb 27, 1847 (*ibid.,* n. 2938).

84 Cfr can. 1239, § 2

85 Gasparri, *l c.,* n. 253; Many, *l. c*, p 75 f.

86 Gasparri, *l. c* , see, however, can. 1239

infidels, without distinction, thereby including all who are destitute of baptismal grace through their own fault.

Excommunicati must also be interpreted strictly. It includes only those who have been declared excommunicated or condemned to the penalty. It does *not* include those under suspension or interdict, and therefore the burial of a suspended or interdicted person would not desecrate a church

Excommunicati are either *vitandi* or *tolerati.* Both kinds are here included, provided a declaratory or condemnatory sentence has been given.[87]

Concerning heretics or schismatics it may be asked whether their burial in a church would defile it. A decision of the S. Congregation[88] would seem to include all non-Catholics. However, since the Code[89] requires a declaratory sentence even for a *poenae latae sententiae,* it appears more probable, and more in keeping with the spirit of the law, that a heretic or schismatic against whom no such sentence has been passed, is not included in the category of excommunicated persons whose burial would desecrate a church[90] The consequence is that most of our present-day heretics, so called, are not touched by this canon.

As four kinds of acts only are specified, no analogy or extension may be admitted.

Furthermore, these acts must be certain, *de iure* or *de facto. De iure* certain is desecration if homicide was committed; uncertain *de iure* would be the amount of blood shed. *De facto* certain is desecration if the burial of an infidel took place; *de facto* uncertain is when the

87 Cfr. can 2259, § 2.

88 S. Rit C, April 23, 1875 (*Dec. Auth*, n. 3344); Gasparri, *l. c*, n. 254.

89 Can. 2223, § 4

90 This was, as Gasparri owns, the *sententia communis* before the promulgation of the Code

fact of infidelity is doubtful, because he may have secretly been baptized. The general rule is that in doubtful circumstances the minimum is taken.[91] However, provisional reconciliation would not be out of place.[92]

The acts inducing desecration must be *notorious, i. e.* known and committed under circumstances that make it impossible to hide them for any length of time.[93]

Lastly, these acts must be commited *in the church itself*. If a man would shoot through a window of the church and kill a person outside, the church would not be defiled. But if the person were killed in the church by a shot fired from outside, desecration would take place. The martyrdom of St. Thomas à Becket implied desecration.[94]

Is any church liable to desecration, or *only a consecrated* or *blessed church?* It seems the more probable and, we may say, the more common opinion, that only a consecrated or blessed church is to be understood.[95] This would seem to be the more natural interpretation if we compare can. 1165, § 1, and the following one. A building is dedicated to divine worship by consecration or blessing, and no divine services can be held in it before this ceremony has taken place. Now the effect of desecration, as stated in can. 1173, consists precisely in the prohibition of divine services. What then would be the effect of desecration with regard to churches that are neither consecrated nor blessed?

Finally, by church is to be understood the body of the internal church, exclusive of the roof, tower, sacristy, vestibule and adjoining rooms. The crypt or basement is included if it is internally connected with the upper part of the church building.[96]

91 Reg. Iuris 30 in 6°.
92 S. Rit. C., Feb. 27, 1847 (Dec. Auth., n. 2938).
93 Can. 2197.
94 Gasparri, *l. c.,* n. 250.
95 Thus Gasparri, *l. c.,* n. 247.
96 Gasparri, *l. c.,* n. 250; Many, *l. c.,* p. 80 f.

§ 2 corrects the old law [97] and admits no connection between the desecration of a church and that of a cemetery, even though the latter adjoins the former, and *vice versa.*

CAN. 1173

§ 1. In violata ecclesia, antequam reconcilietur, nefas est divina celebrare officia, Sacramenta ministrare, mortuos sepelire.

§ 2. Si violatio accidat tempore divinorum officiorum, haec statim cessent; si ante Missae canonem vel post communionem, Missa dimittatur; secus sacerdos Missam prosequatur usque ad communionem.

The consequences of desecration are twofold: cessation of divine services and obligation of reconciliation. Until reconciliation is effected, it would be unlawful to hold divine services in a desecrated church or to administer the sacraments or bury the dead there.[98] Hence all liturgical services which have been instituted by divine or ecclesiastical law and are performed exclusively by the clergy,[99] are strictly forbidden in a desecrated church. However, though the injunction is grievous, yet no penalty, either of censure or irregularity, is attached to the transgression.[1]

If the desecration happens *during the divine offices, these must cease immediately.* Thus the canonical hours, or preaching, or any function should be immediately stopped. Yet we believe that Baptism might be finished if the ceremony had progressed nearly to the act of pour-

---

[97] C. un. 6°, III, 21.

[98] Cfr. cc. 27, 28, Dist. 1, *de cons.;* c. 10, x, III, 40.

[99] Can. 2256, n. 1.

[1] Neither was a penalty contained in the Constit. *"Apostolicae Sedis."*

ing the water. If the desecration happens before the Canon of the Mass, or after Communion, the Mass must be discontinued. If it happens between the beginning of the Canon and Communion, Mass must be continued until Communion, *viz.*, until the *Corpus tuum*. This is the rule of the Missal.[2]

Canonists generally hold that if there is no church in a place besides the one desecrated, and reconciliation cannot be promptly effected, the Ordinary may permit the celebration of Mass therein for the people. In case of necessity, for instance, for administering the Viaticum, if no other church is available, Mass may be said in a desecrated church without consulting the bishop, if he cannot be approached.[3]   Can. 1176 provides for emergencies.

THE RECONCILIATION OF CHURCHES

CAN. 1174

§ 1. Ecclesia violata reconcilietur, quam citissime poterit, secundum ritus in probatis liturgicis libris descriptos.

§ 2. Si dubitetur num ecclesia sit violata, reconciliari potest ad cautelam.

CAN. 1175

Ecclesia violata ob sepulturam excommunicati vel infidelis ne reconcilietur, antequam cadaver exinde removeatur, si remotio sine gravi incommodo fieri possit.

---

2 *Missale Romanum*, tit. *De De-fectibus*, c X, n. 2

3 Gasparri, *l. c.*, 243; Many, *l. c.*, p. 83.

Can. 1176

§ 1. Ecclesiam benedictam reconciliare potest rector eiusdem vel quilibet sacerdos de consensu saltem praesumpto rectoris.

§ 2. Ecclesiae consecratae valida reconciliatio ad eos spectat de quibus in can. 1156.

§ 3. In casu tamen gravis et urgentis necessitatis, si Ordinarius adiri nequeat, rectori ecclesiae consecratae eandem reconciliare fas est, certiore facto postea Ordinario.

Can. 1177

Reconciliatio ecclesiae benedictae fieri potest aqua lustrali communi; reconciliatio vero ecclesiae consecratae fiat aqua ad hoc benedicta secundum leges liturgicas; quam tamen non solum Episcopi, sed etiam presbyteri qui ecclesiam reconciliant, benedicere possunt.

The first of these four canons, all of which refer to the matter of reconciling a desecrated church, demands, like the old law,[4] that reconciliation be performed as soon as possible, according to the rites described in the approved liturgical books. If the fact of the desecration is doubtful, a provisional (*ad cautelam*) reconciliation *may* take place. The books referred to are the Roman Pontifical and Ritual (tit. viii, c. 28). Priests and bishops should beware of the assumption that a church is reconciled if Mass was said therein after desecration. Hence, even in case Mass has been said in a desecrated church reconciliation is required as a matter of necessity.[5]

Can. 1175 takes up the fourth case of can. 1172, *viz.*,

4 C. 10, X, III, 10.
5 S. Rit. C., Aug. 19, 1634, ad II (*Dec. Auth.*, n. 611).

when a church has been desecrated by the burial of an infidel or excommunicated person. Before reconciliation *the body must be removed* if it can be done without great inconvenience. It may be difficult to recognize the remains, especially if many were buried in the church. Prudence is required under such circumstances.[6] But if the expense caused by the calling of experts and witnesses would be too great, removal would not be required.

Can. 1176 determines *the ministers of reconciliation*. A church which was only *blessed* may be reconciled by its rector or by any other priest with the (at least) presumed consent of the rector. Former decisions required that a dignitary,[7] or at least one especially appointed by the Ordinary,[8] should perform the ceremony of reconciliation. Our text requires neither dignity nor faculty. Any priest may lawfully presume the consent of the rector, unless positively forbidden by the latter, or convinced of the intention of the rector to perform the rite himself.

A consecrated church can be validly reconciled only by those mentioned in can. 1156. Hence the Ordinary of the diocese is entitled to reconcile consecrated churches of his own territory, which belong to the secular clergy or non-exempt religious or laymen; and the higher superior of exempt religious can reconcile churches belonging to his order.

However, says § 3 of can. 1176, in *cases of serious and urgent* necessity, if the Ordinary cannot be reached, the rector of a consecrated church may reconcile it and inform the Ordinary afterwards. This is a liberal extension unknown before. A grave and urgent case would be the celebration of a festival which could not be post-

---

6 S. Rit. C., April 23, 1875 (n. 3344).
7 S. Rit. C., Feb. 9, 1608 (n. 246).
8 S. Rit. C., March 3, 1821 (n. 2612).

poned, for instance, first Holy Communion, or a wedding, or a funeral. In that case the Ordinary should be called either by telephone or telegraph; but if it is foreseen that he could not reach the place in time, it would be useless to send a message. Hence the bishop or major exempt religious superior, respectively, must simply be notified of the fact of reconciliation. It goes without saying that this information is not required for the validity of the reconciliation.

The rite to be followed by the rector of the desecrated church is that of the Roman Pontifical.

Can. 1177 says that reconciliation of a *blessed church* may be effected with ordinary holy water, whereas for a *consecrated church* water blessed according to the liturgical laws should be used. However, not only bishops, but also priests who perform the act of reconciliation, may bless this water. The Roman Ritual [9] states that a priest endowed with the faculty of reconciling a consecrated church, hence also the rector of the church in case of necessity, must wear amice, alb, cincture, stole and cope of white color. He must follow the rite prescribed in the Pontifical, and consequently use the water blessed by the bishop. If he blesses the water himself, he must follow the Roman Pontifical, at the beginning of Pars II: *De Benedictione et Impositione Primarii Lapidis.* After the water has been blessed he is to proceed according to the formulary of the Pontifical *De Ecclesiae et Coemeterii Reconciliatione,* and follow the rubrics there given. If the desecrated church was only *blessed,* the priest dresses as above, uses ordinary holy water (blessed, for instance, on Sunday before Mass), and proceeds according to the

[9] Tit III, c 28 (ed Pustet, 1913, p 247 ff). But the faculty mentioned there is no longer needed in case of necessity; nor is any faculty required for reconciling a church only blessed.

Ritual, title viii, c. 28: *Ritus Reconciliandi Ecclesiam Violatam.*

CAN. 1178

Curent omnes ad quos pertinet, ut in ecclesiis illa munditia servetur, quae domum Dei decet; ab iisdem arceantur negotiationes et nundinae, quanquam ad finem pium habitae; et generatim quidquid a sanctitate loci absonum sit.

All to whom it pertains shall take care that the churches are kept neat, as becomes the house of God; business and fairs, even though for a pious purpose, must not be held in them, and in general everything that is incompatible with the holiness of the place.

It is unnecessary to recall all the Decretals [10] and papal constitutions which refer to this matter. The very fact that a church is a sacred place, in which tremendous mysteries are celebrated, ought to suffice to keep it neat. Luxury or magnificence, says Benedict XIV, are not required, but neatness and cleanliness are possible everywhere, even in the poorest church.[11] The Pontiff adds: You will find well-furnished and neatly adorned residences, but squalid and barren churches lacking the most necessary furniture. Lack of neatness betrays a lack of interest and perhaps of faith on the part of the priest.

Those immediately concerned are the congregation, especially the trustees and altar society, the clergy and the Ordinary. The latter should make the condition of the church a subject of examination at the time of his canonical visit and issue regulations from which no

10 C 2, X, I, 27, c. 12, X, III, 1; cc. 1, 5, X, III, 49.

11 Const. "*Annus qui,*" Feb. 19, 1749, § 1.

appeal is admissible.   He may inflict penalties against incorrigible pastors.[12]   Fairs and markets are not usually held in the churches of our country; but even the vestibule and other places connected with the church should be kept free of them.

CAN. 1179

Ecclesia iure asyli gaudet ita ut rei, qui ad illam confugerint, inde non sint extrahendi, nisi necessitas urgeat, sine assensu Ordinarii, vel saltem rectoris ecclesiae.

Churches enjoy the right of asylum, which implies that criminals seeking refuge therein may, except in case of urgent necessity, not be taken out without the consent of the Ordinary or at least of the rector of the church.

As the Greek term *asylos* indicates, an asylum was understood to be an inviolable place.   Such in the old law was the altar of holocausts, the horns of which were held by the one who fled to the tabernacle or temple to seek safety from revenge or escape being killed without due trial.[13]   The Greeks, too, had their statues, temples, and marked off districts which offered safety to criminals.[14]   Roman temples, if consecrated, were endowed with the same privilege.[15]   Christian churches claimed the *ius asyli* before the Christian emperors enacted the same into law.[16]   The *Codex Iustinianus* (lib. I, tit. 12) contains a

---

12 Bened XIV, "*Ad militantis*," March 30, 1742, § 6, cfr. can 2182–2184.

13 Ex. 21, 28, III Ki 1, 50, 2, 28 ff. Besides, there were cities of refuge; Jos 20, 4, 21, 3

14 The space of asylum in the temple of Artemis at Ephesus extended to one stadion or 600 feet, cfr Stengel, *Die Griech. Kultusaltertumer*, 1898, p 29 f

15 Wissova, *Religion u. Kultur der Romer*, 1902, p. 405

16 S Ambrose, *Ep* 20, *ad Marcell*, n. 20 (Migne, 16, 997); *Cod. Theod.*, IX, 45

title: "*De his qui ad ecclesias confugiunt vel ibi excla-
mant*," forbidding extradition or violent seizure of
criminals and reserving the judgment to the bishop.   The
Decree and the Decretals [17] largely follow the Roman
law.   Later enactments, especially in papal constitutions,
either modified or determined the extent of the right of
refuge.   According to a Constitution of Gregory XIV
("*Cum alias*," May 24, 1591) highway robbers and
thieves who plundered the fields, those who committed
cold-blooded murder or wantonly shed blood, those guilty
of lèse majesté in the person of the ruler, and those who
prevented the application of the *ius asyli* were excluded
from the benefit of the privilege.[18]

Our text excludes no one, but limits the right of refuge
somewhat, as not only the Ordinary (*i. e.*, the bishop)
can give permission to extradite, but the rector of the
church also.   In cases of urgent necessity no permission is
required.   Such a case would be that of threatening mob
violence, from which the officials might save the criminal
by quick action.

The churches which enjoy this privilege are those consecrated or blessed, as all authors teach and the text
plainly intimates.   Common jurisprudence [19] would extend it to churches and public oratories not yet blessed,
but dedicated to divine worship.   This view may be accepted, as the *ius asyli* is a favor and consequently liable
to a broad interpretation.

No penalties against violators of this right are stated in
the Code.

17 Cc. 8–10, 19, 35, C. 17, q. 4;
X, III, 49

18 Benedict XIV., "*Officii Nostri*," March 15, 1750, § 12, reserved
the grant strictly to bishops, excluding even the prelates *nullius*.

19 Cfr. Many, *l. c*, p. 101.

THE TITLE OF BASILICA

CAN. 1180

Nulla ecclesia potest basilicae titulo decorari, nisi ex apostolica concessione aut inmemorabili consuetudine; cuiusque vero privilegia ex alterutro capite colligantur.

No church enjoys the title of basilica, except it has been given to it by the Apostolic See or by immemorable custom. The privileges of each church are to be determined either from the concessions of the Apostolic See or from immemorable custom.

Originally the term basilica indicated the architectural style of the structure. However, the name also implied a royal or stately building characterized by great splendor or prominence. Hence the more illustrious churches, especially those dedicated to renowned martyrs or saints, became known as basilicas. Later a distinction was introduced between *basilicae majores* and *minores*. The four major basilicas are: St. John Lateran, in which the Roman Pontiff used to be enthroned and which is the proper See of Rome; St. Peter's on the Vatican, which represents Constantinople; St. Paul's on the Via Ostiense, which designates the See of Alexandria, and S. Maria Maggiore, as representative of the See of Antioch. These four are also called patriarchal basilicas. Besides these there are many minor basilicas, for instance, S. Maria in Trastevere, Monte Cassino, St. Francis of Assisi, Lourdes, etc. These *minor* basilicas came to be called thus either by the renown of their clergy or because of important events or mere antiquity or splendor.[20] But

20 S. Rit. C , Aug 26, 1836 (*Dec. Auth,* n. 2744, and Vol. IV, p. 357 ff.).

unless an immemorable custom has borne constant witness to the existence of the title, it now requires a papal grant. The privileges, or rather decorative insignia, are the use of the canopaeum, the tintinnabulum, the palmatoria or bugia, and some vestments for the clergy.

ENTRANCE FEES NOT ALLOWED

CAN. 1181

Ingressus in ecclesiam ad sacros ritus sit omnino gratuitus, reprobata qualibet contraria consuetudine.

Admission to divine service must be entirely free, and every contrary custom is hereby reprobated.

Rome, and especially the S. C. Propaganda, was inexorable in rejecting the custom of demanding admission fees of any kind at the doors of churches. The Provincial Council of Cincinnati, held in 1861, thought it could permit the custom in three cities of the then Cleveland diocese. But the Prefect of the Propaganda demanded that the custom be abolished within two years. A similar amendment was prescribed for the acts of the II Plenary Council of Baltimore, in 1866, and finally for the acts of the Provincial Council of Australia, in 1869. From the last-named letter of the Propaganda our text has passed into the Code,[21] which has made the law even more emphatic by adding the reprobation clause. This renders the custom existing in many parts of our country juridically impossible, but it will take some time to eliminate it and to find other sources of revenue. The decree above mentioned forbids the placing of ushers (*collectores*) at the gate for collecting money from the faithful coming to

21 *Coll. Lac.*, t. III, coll. 220, 230, 506, 1085, 1086; S C P. F., Aug. 15 1869 (Coll n 1345).

attend divine service and to hear the word of God. But the S. Congregation does not intend to forbid spontaneous oblations at the Offertory, nor to abolish seat or pew rent.

THE ADMINISTRATION OF CHURCHES

CAN 1182

§ 1. Firmo praescripto can. 1519–1528, administratio bonorum quae destinata sunt reparandae decorandaeque ecclesiae divinoque in eadem cultui exercendo, pertinet, nisi aliud ex speciali titulo vel legitima consuetudine constet, ad Episcopum cum Capitulo, si de ecclesia cathedrali agatur; ad Capitulum ecclesiae collegiatae, si de collegiata; ad rectorem, si de alia ecclesia.

§ 2. Etiam oblationes factas in commodum paroeciae aut missionis, aut ecclesiae sitae intra paroeciae vel missionis fines, administrat parochus vel missionarius, nisi agatur de ecclesia propriam administrationem habente, distinctam ab administratione paroeciae vel missionis, aut nisi aliud ferat ius peculiare aut legitima consuetudo.

§ 3. Parochus, missionarius, rector saecularis ecclesiae, sive saecularis is sit sive religiosus, debet huiusmodi oblationes administrare ad normam sacrorum canonum, deque eis rationem loci Ordinario reddere ad normam can. 1525.

§ 1. This canon first safeguards the administration of church property in general, as governed by can. 1519–1528, and then states *to whom* pertains the administration of the *goods destined for the repair and embellishment of churches* and of divine service in cathedral, collegiate, and other churches. In cathedral churches it belongs to the bishop and the chapter conjointly; in collegiate churches, to the chapter; in all other churches, to the rector.

Wherever there is a diocesan chapter, in the canonical and full sense of the term, the administration of the funds destined for the repair and adornment of the cathedral church lies with the bishop and the chapter conjointly. Hence neither the bishop nor the chapter may proceed alone in matters pertaining to the cathedral church.[22] But what if there are no cathedral chapters, as in most of our dioceses,[23] or if they are not established along the lines of the law, as in England? After having perused the *Acta et Decreta* of our plenary councils we could perceive nothing that would be strictly to the point in our case. The third Council mentions (n. 266) a so-called Apostolic canon, which in substance commits the whole temporal affair to the bishop and then describes the mode in which church property may be held: — by fee simple, in trust, as corporation sole, or as personal property. In treating of diocesan consultors (n. 20) the Council demands the *consilium* (*sic!*) of the consultors for any alienation of church property the value of which exceeds $5000. However, this applies to ecclesiastical or diocesan property in general, and does not *per se* touch cathedral funds. Who, then, is responsible for the repair and decoration of the cathedrals in our country? Since there are no chapters, properly so-called, and the diocesan consultors certainly cannot claim any title to the administration of cathedral funds, it follows that the bishop himself is responsible. He may entrust the cathedral pastor with this important matter, but the ultimate responsibility

22 S. C. EE. et RR., May 23, 1662 (Bizzarri, *Collectanea*, p. 258).

23 There are honorary canons in the archdiocese of New Orleans, but their rights are unknown to the author.

is the bishop's. This is more clearly enunciated in the ruling of the first Westminster Provincial Council, 1852, n. 24: "The right to the temporal and spiritual administration of the cathedral church remains with the bishop, unless the Holy See shall have provided otherwise." [24] We could not find a contrary proviso. Neither is the Code opposed to our view, for the present canon is plainly intended for chapters which measure up to all requirements of the law. However, we hardly believe this holds of English chapters.

The care for *collegiate churches,* our text says, belongs to the chapter, not to the provost or pastor. The same may justly be said concerning abbey churches, whilst churches in care of exempt religious must be taken care of by the respective rector, as is the case with all other churches not in possession of a chapter or corporation. For if a corporation (a confraternity, for instance) is in possession of a church, the oblations of which it receives and administers, the right and duty of taking care of that church belongs to the confraternity, under the supervision of the Ordinary of the diocese.[25]

§ 2. Offerings made in favor of a parish church or mission, or of a church located within the boundaries of a parish or mission, are administered by the respective pastor or missionary, unless the church in question has its own separate administration, distinct from the administration of the parish church or mission, or unless a particular law or lawful custom rules differently.

There is no difficulty to be apprehended from this regulation in our country. The only trouble that might arise would be from a sodality or confraternity. How-

---

[24] *Coll. Lac.,* III, col. 948. The cathedral of Newport is an exception, for it has a monastic cathedral chapter (*Coll. Lac.,* III, 957 f.).

[25] S. C. EE. et RR., Feb. 11, 1842 (Bizz, *l. c.,* p. 478).

ever, these are generally ruled by the pastor or missionary. Besides, if they form a corporation acknowledged
by the civil law, they have a solid basis, provided they
give an account to the Ordinary. For an independent
confraternity can hardly be imagined.[26] Churches or
chapels governed by religious have their own administration and are dependent on the bishop only as far as the
law states.

§ 3. The pastor, the missionary, the rector of a secular
church, be he a secular priest or a religious, must administer these offerings according to church law and render an
account to the Ordinary, as provided in can. 1525.

Those who are obliged to render an account are: (a)
pastors, no matter whether they belong to the secular or
religious clergy; (b) missionaries, whether secular or religious; (c) rectors of churches which by right belong to
the secular clergy, although they are subject to religious.

A reasonable doubt might arise from can. 630, § 4,
where the religious superior is said to administer the
offerings of a church that belongs *pleno iure* to a religious
community. We stated what we think of that enactment
under the respective canon, *viz.:* It is impracticable for
a community which has many *expositi*. But our canon
speaks of all pastors alike and draws no distinction. All,
it says, must administer the offerings made to their
churches, all must render an account to the Ordinary. In
order not to go out of the way we assume it as the logical
consequence that the pastor, and not the religious superior, should administer these offerings, for which he is
responsible to the Ordinary. Otherwise, if we follow
can. 630, § 4, the religious superior would have to administer these offerings and render the account. There

---

[26] S. C. C., July 7, 1736; July 27, 1737 (Richter, *Trid.*, p. 170, nn. 8 f.
and *pluries*).

seems to be a contradiction here. The natural explana-
tion would seem to be that the pastor actually administers
those funds, and the religious superior has the supervision, if he cares to exercise it.

Which are the offerings spoken of in our canon? The
description of these may safely be taken from the IInd
Provincial Council of Westminster, and the IIIrd
Plenary Council of Baltimore.[27] They are: pew-rent,
collections at the Offertory, seat-money, and funds raised
by lectures and house collections. Of all these, therefore,
the administrators, as far as repair and embellishment of
the church and divine service are concerned, must give an
account to the Ordinary every year.[28]

TRUSTEES

Can. 1183

§ 1. Si alii quoque, sive clerici sive laici, in administrationem bonorum alicuius ecclesiae cooptentur,
iidem omnes una cum administratore ecclesiastico, de
quo in can. 1182, aut eius vicem gerente, eoque
praeside, constituunt Consilium fabricae ecclesiae.

§ 2. Huius Consilii sodales, nisi aliter legitime constitutum fuerit, nominantur ab Ordinario eiusve delegato et ab eodem possunt ob gravem causam re-
moveri.

Can. 1184

Consilium fabricae curare debet rectam bonorum
ecclesiae administrationem, servato praescripto can.

---

27 Tit. VIII, n X (*Coll*, *Lac* III, col. 982); *Acta et Decreta Com* *Baltim III*, n 90 (ed. 1886, p 48 f; p. 231 f).

28 See can. 1525. § 1.

1522, 1523; sed nullatenus sese ingerat in ea omnia quae ad spirituale munus pertinent, praesertim:

1°. In exercitium cultus in ecclesia;

2°. In modum et tempus pulsandi campanas et in curam tuendi ordinis in ecclesia atque in coemeterio;

3°. In definiendam rationem qua collectae, denuntiationes aliique actus ad divinum cultum ornatumque ecclesiae quoquo modo spectantes in ecclesia fieri possint;

4°. In dispositionem materialem altarium, mensae pro distributione sanctissimae Eucharistiae, cathedrae sive suggestus e quo ad populum verba fiunt, organorum, loci cantoribus assignati, sedilium, scamnorum, capsularum oblationibus recipiendis, aliarumque quae ad exercitium religiosi cultus spectent;

5°. In admissionem vel reiectionem sacrorum utensilium aliarumque rerum quae sive ad usum, sive ad cultum, sive ad ornatum in ecclesia vel sacrario destinentur;

6°. In scriptionem, dispositionem, custodiam librorum paroecialium aliorumque documentorum quae ad archivum paroeciale pertineant.

CAN. 1185

Sacrista, cantores, organorum moderator, pueri chorales, campanae pulsator, sepulcrorum fossores, ceterique inservientes a solo ecclesiae rectore, salvis legitimis consuetudinibus et conventionibus et Ordinarii auctoritate, nominantur, pendent, dimittuntur.

Canon 1183 says that if other administrators, either clerical or lay, are chosen, these together with, and under the presidency of, the ecclesiastical administrator, constitute the board of trustees or council of the church fabric.

The members of this committee, unless otherwise legally provided, are appointed by the Ordinary or his delegate and may be removed by him for weighty reasons.

The law does not command the appointment of trustees, but only says, *if*. Hence though prudence may dictate the measure, as the IIIrd Baltimore Council states,[29] a bishop or pastor would by no means act contrary to the law by not choosing any trustees. It cannot be denied that trustees have at various times in the past acted despotically and with little deference to the spirit and laws of the Church.[30] Hence the Code desires that they be appointed and removed by the Ordinary or his delegate, who in this case may properly be the pastor. But the text admits another lawful way of choosing trustees, and hence the enactments of the IIIrd Council of Baltimore[32] are in perfect keeping with the present law and may be followed as a safe guide.

Can. 1184 commands the trustees to take due care of the church funds, according to can. 1522 and 1523, and not to interfere with the spiritual administration. They are especially forbidden to meddle:

1. With the functions of divine worship in church;

2. With the manner and time of ringing the bells or the order of services in the church and cemetery;

3. With determining the manner of taking up collections, making announcements, and other acts which refer to divine worship or the adornment of the church, and are performed in church.

4. With the arrangement of the altars, communion rails, pulpit, organ and organ loft, seats and benches, col-

29 *Acta et Decreta*, n. 284 (*ed. cit.*, p. 163).

30 Conc. Prov. Balt. I (*Coll. Lac.*,

III, 20); Farley, *Life of Card. McClosky*, 1917.

lection boxes and other things belonging to divine service.

5. With the admission or rejection (because of unfitness according to traditional usage or the laws of the Church) of sacred utensils and other things which are destined either for divine worship or the embellishment of church or sacristy.

6. With the manner of writing, arranging or keeping the parochial books and other documents which belong to the archives of the parish.

It may be added, from the Instruction of the S. C. Propaganda [31] from which our text is substantially taken, that in these matters the pastor is to follow the laws of the Church, the diocesan statutes, and episcopal rulings. If the church funds must be used for buying or preserving things required for the adornment of the church, the board of trustees is obliged to see to it that the work is properly done. Should a dispute arise about the necessity of an expenditure, the bishop shall settle it.

Can. 1185 says that the sexton, the singers, the organist, the choir boys, the bell-ringer, the grave-diggers, and all other servers are to be appointed by, depend on, and are to be dismissed by the rector of the church, with due regard to lawful customs, concordats, and the authority of the Ordinary.

REPAIR OF CHURCHES

CAN. 1186

Salvis peculiaribus legitimisque consuetudinibus et conventionibus, et firma obligatione quae ad aliquem spectet etiam ex constituto legis civilis:

[31] S. C. P F, July 21, 1856, n. 21 (*Collectanea S C. P F.* ed 1917, Vol. I, n. 1127, p. 603).

1°. Onus reficiendi ecclesiam cathedralem incumbit ordine qui sequitur:

Bonis fabricae, salva ea parte quae necessaria est ad cultum divinum celebrandum et ad ordinariam ecclesiae administrationem;

Episcopo et canonicis pro rata proventuum, detractis necessariis ad honestam sustentationem;

Dioecesanis, quos tamen Ordinarius loci suasione magis quam coactione inducat ad sumptus necessarios, pro eorum viribus, praestandos;

2°. Onus reficiendi ecclesiam paroecialem incumbit ordine qui sequitur:

Bonis fabricae ecclesiae, ut supra;

Patrono;

Iis qui fructus aliquos ex ecclesia provenientes percipiunt secundum taxam pro rata redituum ab Ordinario statuendam;

Paroecianis, quos tamen Ordinarius loci, ut supra, magis hortetur quam cogat;

3°. Haec cum debita proportione serventur etiam quod attinet ad alias ecclesias.

CAN. 1187

Si qua ecclesia nullo modo ad cultum divinum adhiberi possit et omnes aditus interclusi sint ad eam reficiendam, in usum profanum non sordidum ab Ordinario loci redigi potest, et onera cum reditibus titulusque paroeciae, si ecclesia sit paroecialis, in aliam ecclesiam ab eodem Ordinario transferantur.

With due regard to special and lawful customs and concordats, and to the duty imposed by civil law:

I. The duty of repairing the *cathedral church* rests on the following in the order named:

a) On the *church funds* after deduction of the expenses necessary for the upkeep of divine worship and the ordinary administration of the church;

b) On the *bishops and canons* according to their respective income, after deducting the necessary support;

c) On the *faithful of the diocese,* whom, however, the Ordinary should induce by persuasion rather than compulsion to contribute to the necessary expenses according to their means.

It is well known that formerly one of the three or four parts of which the church revenues consisted [32] was reserved for the maintenance and repair of the sacred edifices. However, in course of time the different parts were no longer distinguished and the material care of the church devolved either upon the beneficiary or together with him on all those who derived either spiritual or temporary benefit from the church funds. Besides the right of advowson involved a duty which was borne by the advowee or patron. And since this could be a corporation, it followed that the corporation or community who enjoyed the right of presentation had the obligation to provide for the material support of the church.

That local or special *customs* played and still play a part in countries where the separation of Church and State is not in effect is quite intelligible and natural. Besides, in some countries the *civil law* provides for a special board of ecclesiastical administrators. Lastly, conventions or *concordats* may regulate the obligations of the government concerning church repairs. Thus, *e. g.,* the concordats between the Holy See and Prussia (1822)

[32] See cc. 23–30, C. 12, q. 2. These four parts were divided as follows· one for the bishop, one for the support of the clergy, one for the poor and orphans, one for the maintenance of the building and divine service. In Spain, however, the revenues were divided only into three portions, see c. 10, C. 10, q. 1; c. 1–3, C. 10, q 10.

and Russia (1847) embody regulations to that effect.[33] (By the way it may be said that such concordats bind also the new rulers.) These, then,— customs, concordats, and civil laws — are acknowledged by our Code and may be followed where they are in force. In our country the order according to which the obligation of repairing the cathedral church devolves on the various beneficiaries is: church fabric, bishop and canons, the faithful.

1. *Church funds* are moneys accruing from dowry, ordinary income, and extraordinary revenues. From these, first and above all, the expenses for the celebration of divine service[34] and for the ordinary or routine administration,— in other words,[35] the current expenses,— must be defrayed. What is left is to be employed for repairs of whatever description to be made on the cathedral church.

2. If, after deducting the necessary expenses, the church funds prove insufficient, the *bishop and the canons* must contribute to the necessary repairs, proportionately, *i. e.*, so that the salary of each is taxed *pro rata*, but the necessary support must not suffer. By this support is understood the personal maintenance of the bishop and canons, to the exclusion of relatives, for their salary is not given, as Benedict XIV says,[36] for the alimentation of the *consanguinei* or the upkeep of titles and the so-called social status. Benedict XIII allowed the so-called *media annata* or half of the income of the first year to be collected from all benefices, except such as belonged to col-

---

33 Cfr Nussi, *Conventiones*, 1870, p 206, p 277 f , where the Russian government appears to be favorable to the Church

34 This would include church and altar utensils, bread and wine, sanctuary oil, flowers, etc.

35 Includes the priest's salary, the support of janitor, organist, choir, the expenses for water, heating, light, insurance.

36 *Inst.*, 100, n XIII.

legiate chapters, parishes, benefices reserved to the Holy See and benefices which paid the same at any rate.[37] In our country the way is rather simple, because voluntary contributions or subscriptions generally cover expenses. But the bishop is not simply exempted from this duty if his income is sufficient and the cathedraticum "*sat pingue.*" Diocesan consultors cannot in justice be obliged to contribute, unless the clergy as such is taxed.

3. As to the *faithful,* we need not add anything, except that formerly the S. Congregation taxed all the cathedral members who lived in or had property within the district. This was called *per aes et libram.*[38]

II. The duty of repairing the *parish church* rests upon the following in the order named:

1. On the church funds, as described above;

2. On the advowson or *patron;*

3. On those who receive some income from the church, in proportion to the rate of such income, to be fixed by the Ordinary;

4. On the parishioners, whom the Ordinary should exhort rather than compel to contribute.

III. The rules given above also apply to other churches, with due regard to circumstances.

We will add that it would be unjust simply to call on the Ordinary for the means of repairing a church. For, as Benedict XIV says, such a procedure is unheard of in law.[39] But what we have said concerning the obligation of the bishop to contribute to the repair of the cathedral church also applies to pastors. The salary of a pastor is church money, not intended for his relatives. As to lay-

---

[37] "*Pius et misericors,*" May 25, 1725; Gasparri, *De SSma Euch,* n. 132.

[38] S. C. C, Sept 5, 1783, Jan. 10, 1784 *et plures* (Richter, *Trid.,* p.

121, n. 8 f.), July 20, 1895 (*A S. S.,* 28, 298 ff.)

[39] *Inst,* 100, n I f Therefore a well-to-do pastor might well think of his church in his last will.

men or clergymen who receive some sort of pension from the church funds, these are certainly bound to contribute to the repairs.[40] If a monastery or university should possess a parish or other church incorporated *quoad temporalia tantum,* it would be obliged to help keep it in good repair.[41] On the other hand it must also be stated that the obligation arises only from benefices, salaries, pensions, and revenues which are derived from the respective church. Hence neither the bishop, nor pastors, nor beneficiaries are obliged to defray such expenses from their private means or patrimony, nor are they bound to share the burden of repairing other churches than their own. The *parishioners,* as stated above, are treated very leniently in our Code.[42]

Can. 1187, following the tenor of a Tridentine decree,[43] permits a dilapidated church, which is unfit for sacred use and has absolutely no funds from which repairs might be made, to be used for decent profane purposes by the Ordinary. Whenever this happens, all liabilities and revenues are to be transferred to another church by the Ordinary, and if the abandoned church was a parish church, its title, too, must be transferred.

In usum profanum non sordidum means that the secular purpose to which a church is put should be honest or decent. If the church is sold, it should first be execrated. If it is torn down, profanation is hardly possible. But even in the latter hypothesis the title, if the church was a parish church, should be transferred to another church, which may assume it as a secondary title.[44] The obliga-

---

40 *Trid.,* Sess. 21, c. 7 de ref.; Bened. XIV, *Instit.,* 100, n. XIII.

41 S. C. C., March 11, 1711 (Richter, *Trid.,* p. 121, n. 6).

42 Cfr. S. C. EE. et RR., Dec. 10, 1841 (Bizzarri, p. 477 f.).

43 Sess. 21, c. 7, *de ref.*

44 S. C. C., May 22, 1841; March 31, 1708 (Richter, *l. c.,* p. 121, n. 12 f).

tions referred to in the text consist in taking over the foundation Masses and the celebration of the titular feast.[45]

45 S C C, May 22, 1841 (*l. c.*). The canons were obligated to assist at the solemn Mass.

TITLE X

ORATORIES

DEFINITION AND DIVISION

CAN. 1188

§ 1. Oratorium est locus divino cultui destinatus, non tamen eo potissimum fine ut universo fidelium populo usui sit ad religionem publice colendam.

§ 2. Est vero oratorium;

1°. *Publicum,* si praecipue erectum sit in commodum alicuius collegii aut etiam privatorum, ita tamen ut omnibus fidelibus, tempore saltem divinorum officiorum, ius sit, legitime comprobatum, illud adeundi;

2°. *Semi-publicum,* si in commodum alicuius communitatis vel coetus fidelium eo convenientium erectum sit, neque liberum cuique sit illud adire;

3°. *Privatum* seu *domesticum,* si in privatis aedibus in commodum alicuius tantum familiae vel personae privatae erectum sit.

§ 1. An oratory is a place destined for divine worship, not, however, principally for the purpose of having all the faithful worship there publicly.

The term oratory occurs in the fourth century and signifies *a house of prayer* (οἶκος εὐκτέριος). Later it was restricted to small or private chapels.[1] However, mere size is not the distinctive feature. Our Code insists, like

---

1 Cfr. Many, *l c*, p. 9.

former decisions,[2] upon another characteristic: *non uni-verso fidelium populo usui,* it must not be destined for the use of all the faithful. This is the specific purpose of a church in the technical sense of the term. An oratory is limited to a certain class or group of people. We would also stress the term *publice colendam,* although the phrase " public service " can have only a secondary meaning.

§ 2. Distinguishes three kinds of oratories, public, semi-public, and private.

1. A *public oratory* is one built for the benefit of a certain corporation, or of private individuals, but in such a manner that *all the faithful have the right* to frequent it, at least at the time when divine services are held there.

A founder may have had the intention of constructing a private oratory for his family, say at a summer resort, yet it has become public in the course of time, either by common use or by opening an entrance into it from a public street. *Public* here means the right of the public[3] to make use of a chapel for divine service. What are the signs or marks of publicity? The Code answers: the right of the public must be *lawfully proved.* This proof may be given legally in various ways. In one case a chapel had been built in the atrium of a baron's palace. It had a belfry with a bell, a fixed marble altar and other marks of a public oratory, and was declared to be such by the S Congregation, although there was no entrance from a public street.[4] If an oratory has been erected as a perpetual benefice, it is considered a public oratory.[5] Also if it has an entrance from a public street and is open to all

2 S. C. C, Sept 9, 1724, S. Rit C., Dec. 4, 1896, June 5, 1899 (*Dec. Auth*, nn. 3934, 4025).

3 Cfr. fr. 72, Dig 18, 1: "Si quid sacri aut religiosi aut publici est," etc.

4 S. C. C, May 31, 1704 (Richter, *Trid.,* p. 130, n 6), Gasparri, *l c.,* n. 192.

5 S. C. C, Feb 19, 1619, Many, *l. c,* p. 129.

the faithful. Summing up the Roman decisions we may say: A gate opening upon a public street or road used by the faithful; an immemorable custom or authentic document issued by the founder or owner of the chapel, even though it has no public entrance; or the title of benefice permanently attached to an oratory, are considered sufficient and evident proofs that an oratory is public. It goes without saying that prescription, say of thirty years,[6] may force a public way or entrance, for instance, upon the grounds or possessions of a landlord. But a mere public entrance or opening upon a public street could hardly be styled sufficient proof that an oratory is public,[7] unless the people are accustomed to frequent it. A legal proof would also be furnished by an express document to that effect issued at the time of the consecration or blessing of the oratory. It would be well for the ecclesiastical authorities to issue such documents. Finally, a legal proof that an oratory is a public one would be the erection or existence in it of a baptismal font, in accordance with can. 774, § 2.

2. *Semi-public oratories* are such as are built for the convenience of a certain community or class of people, but are not open to all the faithful indiscriminately Here stress is laid on the *corporate or specified class of faithful* who make up the ordinary attendance of a chapel. The rest of the faithful cannot set up a claim to be admitted, and if they are admitted, it is by mere favor, which should prejudice neither the community itself nor the parish at large. Such oratories, says a decree of the S. Rit. C., of Jan. 23, 1899, are those attached to seminaries and colleges, pious institutes living under a rule or constitution, houses of retreat, boarding schools and hos-

---

6 Can. 1511, § 2; Many, *l. c*, p. 129.

7 Such a public entrance may also be made in a semi-public oratory.

pices destined for the young, hospitals and orphanages, garrisons and prisons.

3. *Private or domestic oratories* are those erected in private homes for the convenience of a family or private individuals. The term *family* must here be taken in its strict sense, and excludes artificial persons and corporations. But it includes all the inhabitants of a house living under the authority of the same *paterfamilias*.[8] Private oratories exist in *private homes,* which signifies exclusive ownership, so that no public servitude or easement can deprive them of their private character. We find such oratories in the homes of wealthy citizens, in villas, castles, and summer resorts.

CHAPELS OF CARDINALS AND BISHOPS

CAN. 1189

Oratoria S. R. E. Cardinalium et Episcoporum sive residentialium sive titularium, licet privata, fruuntur tamen omnibus iuribus et privilegiis quibus oratoria semi-publica gaudent.

The oratories of resident or titular Cardinals and bishops, even though they be private, enjoy all the rights and privileges of semi-public oratories.

Benedict XIV solemnly declared that oratories of Cardinals and bishops were not included in the decree of the Council of Trent.[9] He said that the homes of these dignitaries cannot be considered as private dwellings and consequently the Tridentine decree forbidding seculars and regulars to say Mass in private houses does not apply to them.[10] This, however, does not mean, as our text says,

---

8 Becker-Metcalf, *Gallus, or Roman Scenes of the Time of Augustus,* 1898, p 151

9 Sess 22, *de observandis,* etc.

10 " *Magno cum animi,*" June 2, 1757, §§ 1, 2.

that such chapels are not private oratories in the modern sense. They *are* private, but enjoy the rights and privileges of semi-public oratories. Among these privileges is this that other priests, especially the Vicar General, may, even during the absence of the bishop or during the vacancy of the episcopal see, say Mass there either on week-days or holydays of obligation, and those who attend comply with the obligation of hearing Mass.[11] If the episcopal palace maintains a school, all the children and teachers may hear Mass in the chapel, said by any priest, and thereby satisfy their Sunday duty.[12] This privilege was extended to the chapels of all bishops, even though they were only titular bishops.[13] Other functions and offices are mentioned under can. 1193.

PRIVATE CEMETERY CHAPELS

Can. 1190

Aediculae in coemeterio a familiis seu personis privatis ad suam sepulturam erectae, sunt oratoria privata.

Chapels erected on cemeteries by families or private individuals for their burial place, are private oratories.

Tourists in Italy may have noticed such chapels in the magnificent grave-yards of Milan and Genoa.

In a different class are the chapels erected for the whole cemetery, *e. g.*, in memory of a pioneer priest or a benefactor. If they serve the purpose of a grave-yard chapel in general, the name private oratory cannot be applied to them.

11 S Rit. C, July 2, 1661 (n. 1196)

12 S. Rit. C, April 8, 1854 (n. 3021).

13 S. Rit C., June 8, 1896 (n. 3906).

CAN. 1191

§ 1. Oratoria publica eodem iure quo ecclesiae reguntur.

§ 2. Quare in oratorio publico, dummodo auctoritate Ordinarii ad publicum Dei cultum perpetuo per benedictionem vel consecrationem, ad norman can. 1155, 1156, dedicatum fuerit, omnes sacrae functiones celebrari possunt, salvo contrario rubricarum praescripto.

§ 1. Public oratories are governed by the same law as churches.

§ 2. In a public oratory, therefore, provided it has been dedicated for permanent divine worship by the authority of the Ordinary through blessing or consecration, all sacred functions may be held which are not forbidden by the rubrics.

The *rules* laid down for the building, consecration or blessing, execration, desecration and reconciliation, rights and privileges, administration and repairs of churches also apply to public oratories.

The *ecclesiastical functions* which may be performed in public oratories are those mentioned in can. 1171, to wit:

a) All *priestly functions,* such as high and low Mass, the blessing of candles, ashes, palms, the churching of women, etc.;

b) *All the Sacraments,* Baptism [14] not excepted, may be administered;

c) All *indulgences* that can be gained by a visit to a

---

14 Many, *l. c.,* p 387, excepts Baptism, but can 774 f. leave no doubt as to the correctness of the statement in our text

church, can be gained also in a public oratory. The public oratories in the residences and hospices of the Capuchins enjoy the same right as the churches of their order.[15]

d) As to *burial,* it is certain that the Ordinary may grant permission to bury in these oratories, as this was authentically decided.[16]

The last-named decree calls for a remark in view of the demand of can 1171, that the *parochial rights* should be safeguarded. If canon 1191, § 2, says that all ecclesiastical functions may be performed in public oratories, it means only those which do not clash with the strictly parochial rights described in can. 462. Can. 464, § 2, must also be considered, which permits the Ordinary to exempt some religious families from the pastor's jurisdiction. Again the local Ordinary, according to can. 1171, may determine the hours of divine service in these oratories, unless they belong to exempt religious This power he may exercise not only at the time of consecration or blessing, but at any time and for any sound reason, provided, as stated, the oratories do not belong to exempt religious.[17] If exempt religious should cause a disturbance by holding services that trench upon parochial rights or conflict with good order, recourse may be had to the Holy See (S. C. Conc. or Rel.).

Public oratories must be *blessed* or *consecrated* and thus forever dedicated to the service of God. Roman practice requires that they be either consecrated according to the Roman Pontifical or blessed according to the Roman Ritual.[18] An oratory so consecrated or blessed is a

---

15 S C. Indulg , June 11, 1732 (Prinzivalli, *l c.,* n. 69)

16 S. Rit. C , Jan. 13, 1704, ad 20 (n. 2123).

17 Bened. XIV, "*Etsi minime,*" Feb 7, 1741, § 14.

18 S. Rit. C., June 5, 1899 (n. 4025).

strictly sacred place, which may not be used for profane purposes and is endowed with the *ius asyli*.

Lastly, the Code states: *salvo contrario rubricarum praescripto*. The only contrary rubrical laws we could discover touch the celebration of the titular feast and the feast of dedication. If the oratory is only blessed, no dedication feast is permitted, but only the titular feast. The calendar of a public oratory must be followed by the secular as well as the religious clergy, and the clergy attached to the oratory, or living in the house to which it is attached, must commemorate the title of the same.[19]

If the oratory is consecrated, the feast of the dedication must be celebrated with octave

It may not be amiss to draw attention to the phrase, *auctoritate Ordinarii*. Can. 1155 and 1156 declare that the term Ordinary means not only the diocesan bishop, but also the superior of exempt religious. The diocesan bishop has the right to *consecrate* a public oratory, either personally or by a delegate; the superior of exempt religious may *bless* a public oratory in the same way.

SEMI-PUBLIC ORATORIES

CAN. 1192

§ 1. Oratoria semi-publica erigi nequeunt sine Ordinarii licentia.

§ 2. Ordinarius hanc licentiam ne concedat, nisi prius per se vel per alium ecclesiasticum virum oratorium visitaverit et decenter instructum repererit.

§ 3. Data autem licentia, oratorium ad usus profanos converti nequit sine eiusdem Ordinarii auctoritate.

§ 4. In collegiis aut convictibus iuventuti insti-

---

19 S Rit C., Sept 28, 1872; June 27, 1899 (nn. 3279, 4043).

tuendae, in gymnasiis, lyceis, arcibus, praesidiis militum, carceribus, xenodochiis, etc., praeter oratorium principale alia minora ne erigantur, nisi, Ordinarii iudicio, necessitas aut magna utilitas id exigat.

§ 1 forbids the erection of semi-public oratories without the permission of the Ordinary. This is in conformity with the Council of Trent.[20] Anyone may build a semi-public oratory, but only for private devotion, not for the purpose of having public services held there, especially Mass. This is the meaning of the Tridentine decree as well as of later enactments.[21] The local Ordinary may give permission to pontifical as well as diocesan institutes of non-exempt religious to found and open a semi-public oratory.[22] The superior of exempt religious may permit such an oratory to be erected for the convenience of his subjects.

§ 2. The Ordinary shall not grant this permission before he has inspected the oratory either personally or through an ecclesiastical delegate, and found it properly fitted.

§ 3. After the permission has been granted, the oratory may not be put to private uses without the authority of the same Ordinary.

Since the distinction between a semi-public and a private oratory was developed, within the last three decades (owing undoubtedly to the growth of religious communities) it became necessary to define the requisites of both more strictly. Yet it is difficult to find, either in the Roman practice or in the works of canonists, a clear-cut line

20 Sess 22, *de observ. et evit. in celeb. Missae*

21 Benedict XIV, "*Ad militantis*," March 30, 1742, § 6.

22 Leo XIII, "*Conditae*," Dec. 8, 1900, II, n. 3. The faculties mentioned in S. C P. F., Feb 29, 1836 (*Coll*, n 846), are still valid for countries subject to that S. Congregation

of demarcation. We surely interpret the mind of the legislator correctly if we apply the general requisites for a private oratory also to the semi-public. The Code, partly rehearsing the Tridentine decree [23] concerning private oratories, requires *inspection,* but leaves the designation of the place to the owner of the chapel. The inspection must comprise (a) the *building,* which should be such as to represent a sacred edifice and be constructed of solid materials,[24] or at least plastered; (b) the *furniture and utensils* which are required for the sacred functions, also the neatness and cleanliness of the place; (c) the *surroundings* of the oratory and its destination. § 3 clearly states that the chapel must not be used for profane purposes. The S. Congregation has in more than one instance insisted that there should be no dormitory immediately above the oratory or, if this can not be avoided, that a canopy (*baldachino*) be placed over the altar.[25] Furthermore, the chapel must not contain wardrobes, chests, or trunks for profane use, nor must it be allowed to serve as a parlor or recreation or work room; nor as a hallway, infirmary,[26] or dormitory.[27]

All these things, then, should be looked into by the Ordinary or his delegate, who may be any *vir ecclesiasticus* (not a *mulier*), even if he be only in minor orders, provided he has read the title on oratories.

§ 4. In colleges and boarding schools for the young, in high schools and lyceums (intermediate classical schools),[28] in fortresses and barracks (garrisons), in

23 Sess. *22, cit.*

24 Private oratories must have at least three walls of stone or brick; the fourth may be supplied by a curtain or tapestry

25 S Rit. C , May 11, 1641; Sept. 12, 1840, Nov. 23, 1880 (nn 756, 2812, 3525).

26 An epidemic might excuse from the observance of this rule.

27 Cfr Many, *l. c*, p. 157 f.

28 This is the Italian classification of schools, gymnasium standing for a five years' high school, lyceum for a three years' collegiate course.

prisons and asylums, etc., but one principal oratory may be erected, unless the Ordinary should judge that need or great usefulness demand more. According to a decision of the S. Congregation of Rites a special faculty imparted by the Holy See was required to erect other chapels, besides the principal one, in the places mentioned.[29] The Code dispenses with this faculty and leaves the matter to the prudent judgment of the Ordinary. The Ordinary in this case is the diocesan bishop for oratories belonging to secular or non-exempt religious, and the higher superior for oratories belonging to exempt religious.[30]

The decision quoted above also mentions some reasons of *need* and *utility* that may prompt the Ordinary to grant permission to erect some minor or accessory oratories besides the principal one. Such a reason, says the S. Congr., would be a great number of priests who would have to say Mass, say in a college or hospital, or the convenience of sick persons unable to visit the main chapel. To this might be reasonably added the cost of fuel.[31] A small chapel requires less coal, and would not only diminish expenses, but increase the comfort, especially of children and persons in delicate health.

A word may also be said concerning oratories of religious erected on their farms or summer resorts, which in Latin go by the name of *grangiae*,[32] *i.e.*, houses or villas built on the property of religious for sheltering the *oeconomus* or farm boss and his subordinates, hired hands or servants. A laybrother was generally set up as superintendent, and sometimes a priest resided there to say

---

29 S. Rit C, March 8, 1878, ad II (n. 3484).

30 For the text throughout this canon only speaks of the Ordinary, not the local Ordinary, and hence can. 198 may be applied

31 When there is a coal famine this amounts to a solid reason.

32 Cfr c. 27, X, III, 39.

Mass. In modern terms such an oratory would be semi-public, as it serves the convenience of a least a portion of a religious community.[33] Then there are religious institutions which own a college or hospital or university with a chapel insufficient to hold the number of attendants or to permit many priests to say Mass at a convenient hour. May the superior of these religious grant permission to erect, besides the principal chapel, another accessory one? If the place is owned by the exempt religious their major superior, *i.e.*, the general, provincial, or conventual prior may grant this permission. If the place is owned by non-exempt religious, the Ordinary in whose diocese the chapel is to be erected, must be asked for permission. It is no longer necessary to have recourse to a privilege granted to the Jesuits,[34] or a communication of privileges. Exempt religious superiors are "Ordinaries" for the purposes of this canon.[35] Besides, can. 1156 dispels any misgiving in this matter. But superiors must inspect the oratory before granting the desired permission.

CAN. 1193

In oratoriis semi-publicis, legitime erectis, omnia divina officia functionesve ecclesiasticae celebrari possunt, nisi obstent rubricae aut Ordinarius aliqua exceperit.

Can. 1193 provides that in semi-public oratories, lawfully erected, all divine offices and ecclesiastical functions may be held, as far as the rubrics and the rulings of the Ordinary permit.

---

[33] Sometimes these *grangiae* or *granciae* served as summer-resorts for a vacation colony.

[34] Gregory XIII, "*Decet Romanum*," May 3, 1575.

[35] See can 198.

The *lawful erection* of a semi-public oratory implies, as we have stated, inspection and permission by the Ordinary. Is consecration or blessing required? There is no text which prescribes either. It would be somewhat hazardous to consecrate a semi-public oratory, unless its stability and perpetuity were guaranteed. However, the blessing *may* be imparted, according to the Roman Ritual, although the simple blessing (*Benedictio loci*) is sufficient.[36]

Concerning the *divine offices* and *ecclesiastical functions* that may be held in semi-public oratories, we have only to repeat what was said under can. 1191. For, as the text implies, the same rules hold for both public and semi-public oratories. But the Ordinary may *except* some functions, and the members of such communities must abide by his ruling. (Remember that the Ordinary for exempt religious is their own superior.)

The *rubrics* which must be observed are those of the calendar prescribed for the principal chapel or semi-public oratory.[37] There is no restriction as to the number of Masses allowed in such chapels, or in regard to the priests who wish to say Mass there [38] The office may be chanted in such chapels, and Mass be said on a fixed or portable altar, even by sick or elderly priests.[39]

If a semi-public oratory has been solemnly blessed, the titular feast must be duly observed,[40] and the oration,

---

36 For the solemn blessing see *Rit. Rom.*, tit VIII, c 27, the *benedictio loci*, *ibid*, tit VIII, cc 6, 7 (ed Pustet, 1913, p 243 ff ; p 224 f).

37 S. Rit C , May 22, 1876 (n 3910).

38 S. Rit C , March 8, 1879, ad I, 1, 2; July 2, 1661 (nn. 3484, 1196).

39 S Rit C , Nov. 10, 1906, II (n. 4190); this decision ad II does not upset our contention for the *grangiae* of regulars, because can. 1192, § 4, is later than said declaration.

40 S Rit C., Nov. 29, 1878 (n. 3471).

or at least the name of the titular saint, recited in the office.

CAN. 1194

In privatis coemeteriorum aediculis, de quibus in can. 1190, Ordinarius loci permittere habitualiter potest etiam plurium Missarum celebrationem; in aliis oratoriis domesticis, nonnisi unius Missae, per modum actus, in casu aliquo extraordinario, iusta et rationabili de causa; Ordinarius autem has permissiones ne elargiatur, nisi ad norman can. 1192, § 2.

CAN. 1195

§ 1. In oratoriis domesticis ex indulto Apostolicae Sedis, nisi aliud in eodem indulto expresse caveatur, celebrari potest, postquam Ordinarius oratorium visitaverit et probaverit ad norman can. 1152, § 2, unica Missa, eaque lecta, singulis diebus, exceptis festis sollemnioribus; sed aliae functiones ecclesiasticae ibidem ne fiant.

§ 2. Ordinarius vero, dummodo iustae adsint et rationabiles causae, diversae ab eis ob quas indultum concessum fuit, etiam sollemnioribus festis permittere potest per modum actus Missae celebrationem.

CAN. 1196

§ 1. Oratoria domestica nec consecrari nec benedici possunt more ecclesiarum.

§ 2. Licet oratoria domestica et semi-publica communi locorum domorumve benedictione aut nulla benedictione donentur, debent tamen esse divino tan-

tum cultui reservata et ab omnibus domesticis usibus libera.

Canon 1194 says, first, that in *private cemetery chapels,* mentioned under can. 1190, the *Ordinary of the diocese* may grant permission for several Masses to be said habitually. This clause marks an extension of the former law and of the Roman practice, which required a special faculty for the bishop from the Apostolic See.[41] The term *Ordinarius loci* here excludes exempt religious superiors.

In other *domestic oratories,* continues can. 1194, the local Ordinary may permit one Mass to be said, not habitually, but upon occasion, in some extraordinary case, and provided there be a just and reasonable cause. This permission presupposes that the Ordinary has inspected said oratory and found it fit. This, too, is a mitigation of the former practice. The only conditions are: (a) that only *one Mass* may be said on the occasion or day for which the petition was granted; (b) that this permission *be not a habitual* or perpetual grant, but effective only for the time being and as long the reason exists; (c) that the occasion be an extraordinary one, for instance, a first Mass, or a jubilee, or a temporary necessity as that caused by an epidemic or quarantine; (d) that the *cause* be *just* and *reasonable, i.e.,* not detrimental to others, especially to the parish organization; (e) that the Ordinary first inspect the oratory, as required by can. 1192, § 2.

Can. 1195 refers to *domestic oratories* erected by virtue of a *papal indult.* Any one may build or construct an oratory for private devotion, but to have Mass said there

---

41 *Trid*, Sess. 22, S. C. C, Dec.   1836 (*Coll.,* n. 846); S. Rit. C, Sept.
20, 1856; S. C. P. F., Feb. 29,   20, 1749 ad 5 (n. 2404).

requires a papal indult, ever since the Tridentine Council   Therefore, says our canon, unless expressly provided otherwise in said indult, only one low Mass may
be said daily in such oratories, except on the more solemn
feastdays, and no other ecclesiastical functions are allowed. Before the indult takes effect the Ordinary must
inspect and approve the oratory, as required by can.
1192, § 2. He may also, for just and reasonable causes,
other than those for which the indult was granted, permit a Mass to be said there even on higher feastdays,
but only *per modum actus.*

This canon distinguishes between the right of having
Mass said daily and the right of having Mass said
habitually in private oratories. The Council of Trent
took away the right of the bishops to permit Mass in
private oratories *per modum habitus,* but left them the
power of granting the permission *per modum actus* for
weighty and urgent reasons.[42] The Code requires only
a just and reasonable cause.

Can. 1195 speaks of a *papal indult,* granted by the S. C.
of Sacraments. Such indults are almost invariably addressed to the local Ordinary, who is therefore obliged
to read the document carefully and note the *clausulae.*
The Ordinary in this case is an *executor mixtus, i.e.,* he
is obliged to investigate the truth of the reasons alleged
by the petitioner — *constito tibi de narratis* — and the
condition of the oratory, as required by can. 1192, § 2;
but he cannot withhold execution if he finds everything to
be as required by law.[43]

The text further says that *only one low* Mass may be
said *daily* in such oratories, even on Sundays, not, however, on the more solemn feastdays. This restriction was

42 S C. C., Dec 20, 1856, Many,
l. c , p. 151 f

43 Cfr Gasparri, *De SSma Eucharistia,* n 235, p 163 f.

no doubt made for the purpose of insinuating to the grantee that he should attend his parish church on those days. After the reorganization of feasts by Pius X and the S. C. of Rites,[44] the question naturally arose on *which feasts it was forbidden to have Mass in private oratories.* The answer was that on the feasts of the Commemoration of St. Joseph, the Annunciation of the B. V. Mary, Corpus Christi, the feast of the Blessed Trinity, the Sunday within the octave of Corpus Christi, and the Sunday on which the feast of St. John the Baptist was celebrated, Mass may be said in private oratories.[45] From this decision it may safely be deduced that the term "more solemn feasts" means the holydays of obligation, which do not fall on a Sunday. The indult may read otherwise, excepting no feastday or restricting the number of other days (*nisi aliud in eodem indulto expresse caveatur*).

Under § 2 of can. 1195 the Ordinary may permit a low Mass to be said in private oratories even on more solemn feasts, under two conditions: (a) that there be a just and reasonable cause not identical with the one expressed in the indult; (b) that the grant be made *per modum actus.* If, for instance, the reason for which the indult was given was the merit of the petitioner, old age or physical weakness may be alleged for obtaining from the Ordinary the favor of having a Mass said also on the more solemn feasts This instance also explains the second condition. Thus, if old age was the reason given, the petition may be granted until age has been turned into eternity, *i.e.,* until death. This is not stretching the tenor of the indult, for it must be remem-

---

44 Pius X, " *Supremi disciplinae,*" July 2, 1911; S Rit. C, July 24, 1911 (*A. Ap. S.,* III, 305 ff.; 350 f).

45 S C Sacr , April 11, 1913 (*A. Ap S,* V, 183 f)

bered that the grantee or principal *indultarius* must be present in the chapel, in order that the members of his household or family may enjoy the privilege of assisting at Mass and complying with the obligation of hearing Mass on the days prescribed. Besides, the indult lasts only as long as the person in whose name it was issued lives and can enjoy it. Finally, according to canonists, the phrase *modus actus* means as long as the reason exists (*durante causa*).[46]

Having mentioned the principal grantee and his family, the rescript may mention also the *consanguinei* and *affines*, those related by blood and affinity, which is understood to extend to the fourth degree.[47] In former rescripts, issued under Leo XIII, *noble guests* were also mentioned. This term, strictly speaking, excludes all who are not of noble rank; but we hardly believe that such a rigorous interpretation could be applied to a rescript issued for our country. Hence if guests are mentioned, they too are benefited by the indult. *Familiares* are servants employed in actual service at the time of Mass, *e g.*, those who wait upon the Master or Lady of the house at Mass, either as honorary ladies and gentlemen, or by helping a feeble lady or gentleman. Cooks, chauffeurs, or hired men in barn or field, janitors, etc, are not benefited by the indult.[48]

No other ecclesiastical functions are permissible in private oratories. This excludes all strictly parochial and other priestly or ecclesiastical functions, preaching (though a brief exhortation would not be forbidden), the administration of the Sacraments and sacramentals.

What about holy Communion? No matter what can-

46 Many, *l. c.*, p. 153.
47 *Ibid*
48 Benedict XIV, "*Magno cum*
animi," June 2, 1751, §§ 11, 12, 19,
Gasparri, *l. c.*, n. 236, p. 168.

onists formerly held, we believe that, since frequent communion is so strongly urged, the distribution of the Eucharist would not be forbidden. At any rate, the permission of the bishop would suffice.[49]

Can. 1196 forbids domestic oratories to be consecrated or blessed like churches. They may, however, and should receive the so-called *benedictio loci* or *domus novae*, as contained in the Roman Ritual.[50]

Notwithstanding this defect of consecration or blessing, domestic oratories must be exclusively reserved for divine service and not be used for domestic purposes, as explained under can. 1192, § 3. Nevertheless, a private oratory is, properly speaking, not a sacred, but a profane place, and hence not liable to desecration, nor does it enjoy the *ius asyli*. It also remains the private property of the owner of the house.[51]

49 Cfr. Bened. XIV *l c*, § 23 f.; *Institut*, 34, n 11 f; Gasparri, *l. c.*, n. 1088, II, p 332.

50 Tit. VIII, c. 6 f. (ed. Pustet, 1913, p. 224 f.); S. Rit. C., June 5, 1899, VI (n. 4025).

51 Many, *l. c.*, p. 174.

TITLE XI

ALTARS

CAN. 1197

§ 1. Sensu liturgico intelligitur:

1°. Nomine altaris *immobilis* seu *fixi,* mensa superior una cum stipitibus per modum unius cum eadem consecratis;

2°. Nomine altaris *mobilis* seu *portatilis,* petra, ut plurimum, parva, quae sola consecratur, quaeque dicitur etiam *ara portatilis* seu *petra sacra;* vel eadem petra cum stipite qui tamen non fuit una cum eadem consecratus.

§ 2. In ecclesia consecrata saltem unum altare, praesertim maius, debet esse immobile; in ecclesia autem benedicta omnia altaria possunt esse mobilia.

§ 1. In the liturgical sense of the word an *immovable* or a *fixed* altar means the upper table with its supports, consecrated together as a whole with the table. A movable or *portable* altar is a stone, generally of small size, which is consecrated alone, and called portable altar or sacred stone; or the same stone with its support, though the latter was not consecrated together with the table.

§ 2. In every consecrated church at least one, preferably the main, altar must be immovable; but in

84

churches that are only blessed all altars may be movable.

The earliest altar was a mere table copied after secular patterns. It consisted of a rectangular and slightly oblong top, supported by one, four, or occasionally five, legs. This simple and natural shape was retained until well into the fifth century. From the beginning, stone as well as wooden altars were employed. Gradually the Church came to discriminate in favor of stone, on account of its monumental character and greater durability. A change in the form of the altar was brought about in the sixth century by the new impetus given to the veneration of *relics*. The Holy Eucharist was brought into close relation with the tombs of the martyrs and it was regarded as a matter of prime importance that the altar be brought into the closest possible relation with the tomb, or at least be located directly above it. This was done by building a "*confessio*," *i.e.*, a chamber surrounding the tomb and connected by a shaft or gallery with the altar. The next stage in the development of the altar arose from the custom, which grew rapidly during the sixth century, of depositing the bodies of the martyrs within the churches. This often led to the construction of a true *confessio* or crypt; but more often the relics were deposited immediately beneath the plate of the altar and inclosed with a stone *cippus* or block, roughly cubical in form, hollow within, and ornamented on the front by a doorway, like a miniature tomb. Finally the altar was enclosed on all four sides by plates of stone and became a mere chest for the preservation of relics. Sometimes a sarcophagus or fully extended body was enclosed. The custom of erecting more than one altar in the same church grew out of the cult of relics. Such secondary altars came into use about the beginning of the fifth century, at first in side chapels, later in the main church, nay even in the nave.[1]

These brief remarks seemed necessary to explain the structure of the altar and the importance of relics for the same.

REQUISITES

CAN. 1198

§ 1. Tum mensa altaris immobilis tum petra sacra ex unico constent lapide naturali, integro et non friabili.

§2. In altari immobili tabula seu mensa lapidea ad integrum altare protendi debet, et apte cum stipite cohaerere; stipes autem sit lapideus vel saltem latera seu columellae quibus mensa sustentatur sint ex lapide.

§ 3. Petra sacra sit tam ampla ut saltem hostiam et maiorem partem calicis capiat.

§ 4. Tum in altari immobili tum in petra sacra sit, ad norman legum liturgicarum, sepulcrum continens reliquias Sanctorum, lapide clausum.

§ 1. The *table* of an immovable altar as well as a sacred stone must consist of one natural stone, whole and not easily crumbled. The altar stone is to be *one* single slab, which excludes several parts.[2] Even if the several parts should be compactly cemented together so as to appear as one stone, the altar cannot be validly consecrated.[3] A *natural* or pure stone is one that corresponds to the mineralogical definition of a stone. Any hard and compact stone is admissible, as, *e.g.*, marble, sandstone, travertine, etc. Even slate or schist is allowed, but

---

1 Cfr. Lowrie, *Monuments of the Early Church*, 1901, p. 159 ff.

2 S Rit C, June 17, 1843; Nov. 10, 1906 (nn. 2861, 4191).

3 S. Rit. C, Sept. 28, 1872; June 8, 1896, Nov. 10, 1906, ad I, II (nn. 3286, 3907, 4191), but the church would be validly consecrated

pumice-stone or gypsum have been rejected.[4]   Because of their composite nature cement plates or blocks must be considered forbidden.   The S. Congregation has always refused to admit a marble or wooden cornice or orna-ment surrounding the table like a wreath.[5]   An altar, the nucleus of which is of stone but covered with bricks over-laid with a marble crust, has also been declared uncon-secrable.[6]   *Integer* means that the stone should be of one piece, without fractures or crevices.   Should the stone have been perforated by cutting or chiseling the reposi-tory for relics into it, it would be sufficient to place a piece of marble or other solid slab on the part below, so that the *capsula* with the relics could be laid on it.[7] That the stone should be of a sort that will *not easily crumble (friabilis)* follows from the nature of stone.   If it were so fragile that the fourth part or more would break off in the act of consecration, the latter would be invalid.[8]

§ 2   In an *immovable altar* the table or stone plate must extend over the whole altar and be properly joined to the support; the support itself must be of stone, or at least the side props or columns which support the table must be of stone.

§ 3.   The *sacred stone* (portable altar) must be so large that at least the host and the larger part of the base of the chalice may find room thereon.

No dimensions for an altar are prescribed by the rubrics or the S. Congregation of Rites.   It ought, how-ever, to be large enough to allow a priest conveniently

4 S Rit. C , April 29, 1887; June 13, 1899 (nn 3675, 4032)

5 S Rit. C., Aug. 29, 1885; April 23, 1893 (nn 3640, 3797).

6 S Rit. C., Dec 14, 1888 (n. 3698), but the invalidity of consecra-tion is not clearly pronounced.

7 S. Rit. C., .Feb. 8, 1896 (n. 3884)

8 S. Rit. C , June 8, 1894, n. II (n. 3829)

to celebrate the holy sacrifice upon it, in such a manner that all the ceremonies can be decorously observed.[9]   But the S. Congregation has insisted, as does our text, that the altar-stone should cover the whole length and width of the fixed altar, without an ornamental addition.[10] If, for instance, the length of the whole fixed altar is ten feet, and its width from the tabernacle to the front twenty-two inches, the altar-stone must have the same dimensions.

It is absolutely required that the table or *mensa* be placed immediately upon the support so as to form one whole with it.   In one case the S. Congregation de-manded that if no connection between the altar-stone and the *stipes* had been made, stone *stipites* should be added. The consecration was declared valid, yet only by a spe-cial favor was the addition and separate anointing of these *stipites* granted.[11]   From this it is evident that only a moral, though material, conjunction is required, at least for licitness.[12]   But the connection must be one of stone with stone.

The support, therefore, (*stipes*) must be of stone.   It may be one solid mass of granite, marble, etc., or it may consist of four or more columns.   But it is absolutely necessary that these sides, columns, or small piers be of stone.[13]   Columns of copper, brass, or other metal are not allowed.   If the bases are of metal, the shaft, and more especially the capitals, must be of stone, or a stone layer must be placed between the columns and the table,

9 Cfr. Schulte, *Consecranda*, 1907, p 6

10 S. Rit C., Aug. 29, 1885 (n. 3640); the altar was only 2 27 me-ters in length and o 57 meters in width, wherefore they put a marble cornice around it.

11 S Rit. C , June 8, 1894; July 5, 1901 (nn 3829, 4075).

12 Many, *l c.*, p 204.

13 S. Rit. C , Aug 7, 1875; Dec. 14, 1888 (nn. 3364, 3698)

otherwise it cannot be consecrated as a fixed altar.[14]
The spaces between the side walls (columns or piers)
may be left open, or the spaces on the sides and back
be filled with any kind of stone, brick, or cement; but
the space between the two columns in front should be
left open, so that a reliquary can be placed beneath the
table.[15]

The portable altar is sometimes also called *altare viaticum*. Its dimensions are approximately pointed out in
§ 3, where it is said that the table must be large enough
to hold the sacred host and the greater part of the base
of the chalice.[16] Besides, as liturgists reasonably state,
it should have room enough for the ciborium. In general the dimensions may range between 12 x 12, or 14 x
16 inches.[17]

§ 4. In an immovable altar as well as in an altar
stone there must be, according to the rubrical prescriptions, a *sepulchre* containing relics of saints and closed
with a stone.

The historical remarks made above explain this venerable custom. The sixth synod of Carthage (401) enacted that no *memoriae martyrum* should be tolerated
without their relics being present or at least without
some historical reminiscence connected with the place.[18]
In this canon only the chapels of martyrs are mentioned.
Yet, as seen above, the custom of placing relics in the
altars soon extended to all churches and altars. When
some missionaries in South America claimed the privilege
of consecrating altars without relics, the Holy Office,[19]

14 S Rit. C , May 24, 1901 (n
4073)

15 S Rit C , Sept. 28, 1872; Dec.
20, 1864 (nn. 3282, 3126).

16 S C. Indulg , March 20, 1846
(Prinzivalli, n. 574).

17 Schulte, *l c* , p 232 f

18 Can 17 = c. 26, Dist 1, *de
cons* (Hefele, *Concil -Gesch.*, II,
72).

19 Jan. 17, 1900 (*Coll. P. F.*, n.
2076).

without entering into an historical discussion, insisted that relics be placed in the altars, but allowed Mass to be said on altars consecrated without relics. Gregory XVI, in a time of persecution, granted to the Vicars Apostolic of the Chinese empire and adjoining realms the faculty of consecrating altars without relics.[20] Consecration without relics would certainly be invalid[21] if no faculty to the contrary had been obtained.

The *sepulchrum* is a small square or oblong opening made in the table or solid support of the altar, in which the relics are placed. In a fixed or immovable altar the *sepulchrum* may be placed either *behind the altar* or midway between its table and foot; or at the *front;* or midway between its table and foot, or *in the table* at its centre, somewhat towards the front edge, if its base be solid or hollow; or in the *centre on the top* of the support, if it be solid.[22]

In *portable altars* the *sepulchrum* is located on top of the stone, usually towards its front edge.[23] A portable altar described as consisting of two parts, the upper one of which was of stone, whereas the lower was of wood, with a hollow space between both for the relics, which thus touched both the stone and wooden parts of which the *sepulchrum* was formed, was declared inadmissible. The *sepulchrum* must be of natural stone, not of metal, or brass, or cement; the lid, too, must be of stone, though cement may be used for closing it.[24] If cement was employed for the whole *sepulchrum* the altar must be recon-

20 S. C. P. F., July 8, 1838 (*Coll.,* n. 869).

21 S. Rit C., *Rhedon*, Oct 6, 1837; April 29, 1887 (nn. 2777, 3674)

22 Schulte, *Consecranda*, p 7 ff.

23 S Rit C, Aug 31, 1867 (n 3162).

24 S. Rit. C., Sept. 16, 1881; Dec. 15, 1882 ad I; July 28, 1883 (nn. 3532, 3567, 3585). Portable altars may not be of pumice-stone or gypsum; S. Rit C., June 13, 1899 (n. 4032).

secrated; but the S. Congregation granted faculties to use the short formula and have it done by a delegated priest.[25] The *cement* to be used for closing the sepulchre must be blessed by the bishop according to the formula prescribed for fixed altars. The bishop must lay the cement on the sepulchre and close it, but not place his seal on it.[26]

As to the *relics* to be placed in the sepulchre, it is understood that only *authenticated* ones are admitted. If they are authenticated, it matters not whether they are of nameless Saints.[27] Doubtful or uncertain relics are not to be mixed with authenticated ones.[28] If relics lie open and no attestation of their authenticity can be found, they must be replaced by authentic ones and re-enclosed in the sepulchre.[29]

The *quality* of relics is not determined, except that they must be of *Saints*. However, it is the general practice, confirmed by official decisions, that they should be relics of at least one *martyr*, to which relics of confessors and virgins may be added.[30] Whether these relics must be taken from the body (direct relics) or may be obtained from objects connected with the Saint (indirect relics), is nowhere stated, although some writers, like Gardellini, insist on direct relics.[31]

CONSECRATION OF ALTARS

CAN. 1199

§ 1. Ut Missae sacrificium super illud celebrari possit, altare debet esse, secundum liturgicas leges,

25 S. Rit C , Aug. 30, 1901 (n 4082).

26 S. Rit. C , May 10, 1890 (n 3726)

27 S. Rit. C , Sept. 7, 1630 (n. 542)

28 S Rit. C , Dec. 5, 1851 (n. 2991 ad I).

29 S Rit. C., Feb. 27, 1847 (n. 2941) *S. C. sanavit defectus*

30 S Rit C., Oct 6, 1837; Feb 16, 1906 (nn 2777, 4180).

31 Cfr Many, *l. c* , p 208; Schulte, *l c* , p. 10, also rejects indirect relics; but c. 26, Dist 1, *de cons* , admits them.

consecratum; idest vel totum, si agatur de immobili, vel ara tantum portatilis, si de mobili.

§ 2. Aras portatiles, salvis peculiaribus privilegiis, omnes Episcopi consecrare possunt; quod vero spectat ad altaria immobilia, servetur praescriptum can. 1155.

§ 3. Consecratio altaris immobilis, quae fit sine ecclesiae dedicatione, quamvis omni die fieri possit, magis tamen decet ut fiat die dominico aliove festo de praecepto.

§ 1. In order that the Sacrifice of the Mass may be celebrated upon an altar, it must be consecrated according to the liturgical laws; that is to say, if the altar is fixed, the whole must be consecrated, if it is portable, the altar table.

The resp. rites are contained in the Roman Pontifical, and no deviation from, or abbreviation of them is admissible; not even from the fast (on the day itself) when a portable altar is to be consecrated.[32] However, in forming the crosses from incense and putting on the candles, the consecrator may be assisted by priests.[33]

Fixed altars may be consecrated even in a church which is only blessed, as a church is consecrated even if the altar was not validly consecrated.[34] The vigils must also be observed before the consecration of an altar, as is evident from the Roman Pontifical.

§ 2. Besides those especially privileged, all bishops may consecrate portable altars; as to fixed altars can. 1155 must be observed.

Those *specially privileged* are the Cardinals, vicars

---

[32] S Rit C, May 22, 1841 (n. 2826).

[33] S. Rit. C., Jan. 14, 1910 (4244).

[34] S. Rit C, Sept. 12, 1857, ad XV; June 17, 1843 (nn. 3059, 2862).

Apostolic and prefects Apostolic, as well as their pro-vicars and pro-prefects during the time of vacancy, abbots and prelates *nullius*.[35] (For the rest, see can. 625 and 1147.) Besides these all bishops, whether resi-dential or titular, may consecrate portable altars. But fixed altars can be consecrated only by bishops and pre-lates or abbots *nullius,* if the latter have received the blessing required.

§ 3. The consecration of a fixed altar, if performed apart from the dedication of the church in which it is stationed, may take place on *any day,* but it is becoming that this ceremony should be performed on a Sunday or holyday of obligation.

LOSS OF CONSECRATION

CAN. 1200

§ 1. Altare immobile amittit consecrationem, si tabula seu mensa a stipite, etiam per temporis mo-mentum, separetur; quo in casu Ordinarius potest permittere ut presbyter altaris consecrationem rursus perficiat ritu formulaque breviore.

§ 2. Tum altare immobile tum petra sacra amittunt consecrationem:

1°. Si frangantur enormiter sive ratione quantitatis fractionis sive ratione loci unctionis;

2°. Si amoveantur reliquiae aut frangatur vel amoveatur sepulcri operculum, excepto casu quo ipse Episcopus vel eius delegatus operculum amoveat ad

---

35 Cfr can 239, § 1, n. 20; can. 294, § 2; can 310, §2; can 323, § 2; Bened XIV, "*Ex sublimi,*" Jan 26, 1753, § 2; "*Quam er sublimi,*" Aug. 8, 1755, § 1. The decree of S Rit. C, Sept 27, 1659 (n 1131), mentions no right of other abbots in this respect, and therefore only one resource remains: a directly granted privilege This is the Roman juris-prudence, not merely our individual and subjective view.

illud firmandum vel reparandum vel subrogandum, aut ad visitandas reliquias.

§ 3. Levis fractio operculi non inducit exsecrationem et quilibet sacerdos potest rimulam cemento firmare.

§ 4. Exsecratio ecclesiae non secumfert exsecrationem altarium sive immobilium sive mobilium; et viceversa.

§ 1. An *immovable altar* loses its consecration if the table or *mensa* is removed from its support, even if only for a moment; but in this case the Ordinary may grant permission to a priest to reconsecrate the altar with the short rite and formula.

Note that the support of a fixed altar is consecrated together with the table, as a whole, and therefore any removal, no matter for whatever reason, of the *mensa* from its support, necessitates reconsecration.[36] But if only the images, or titles, or ornaments are removed, whilst the support and the *mensa* remain united, reconsecration is not required.[37]

§ 2. A fixed as well as a portable altar loses its consecration:

1.° By a fracture which is regarded as very considerable by reason either of the break itself or of the anointed place;

2.° If the relics are removed, or the lid of the sepulchre is broken or removed, unless it be done by the bishop or his delegate for the purpose of fastening, repairing, or replacing it, or for the purpose of inspecting the relics.

The Code adopts the decision of S. Rit. C. concerning

36 S. Rit. C., May 15, 1819 (n. 2599), *et pluries.*   37 S. Rit. C., July 7, 1759 (n. 2450)

the definition of a *fractura enormis*.[38] Two reasons determine the character of a fracture: its extent and the
place where it occurs. If the *mensa* itself were split into
two, three, or four pieces, especially if it touched the sepulchre, the fracture would be " enormous " in the sense
of the law [39] If an anointed corner or cross would crack,
the fissure would be sufficient to require reconsecration,[40]
provided of course the cross itself would be cracked.
For if only a corner would break off, with the cross intact, we hardly believe that the whole altar would have
to be reconsecrated. The mere breaking of the seal
which is attached to the reliquary of the sepulchre would
not entail loss of consecration.[41] If the removal of the
stone covering the sepulchre is *doubtful,* reconsecration must take place, but the S. Congregation, upon request, may grant the use of the short formula.[42] If the
stone covering the reliquary was loosened, but the sepulchre was not laid bare, and the sacristan (lay brother)
applied lime or cement to fasten it, the consecration is
not lost.[43] But if a priest would open the sepulchre and
close it again, the consecration would be lost.[44] However, this last statement now requires a modification. If
the pastor acted in the name of the bishop, as his delegate,
for the purpose of fastening, or repairing, or replacing
the lid of the sepulchre, or of inspecting it, no loss of
consecration would be entailed. The fact of delegation,
however, would have to be expressed, either habitually or
per modum actus.

[38] S. Rit C., Oct. 6, 1837 (n.
2777).

[39] S Rit C., June 23, 1879 (n.
3497)

[40] S. Rit. C., Oct 6, 1837 (n.
2777).

[41] S. Rit. C , Dec 5, 1851, n. I
(n. 2991).

[42] S. Rit. C , May 18, 1883 (n.
3575)

[43] S Rit. C , Sept. 30, 1875 (n.
3379).

[44] S. Rit C., Aug. 31, 1857, ad V
(n 3162).

§ 3. A slight fracture of the cover of the sepulchre does not involve desecration, and any priest may fill it up with cement.

§ 4. The desecration of a church does not involve desecration of either its fixed or portable altars, and conversely Thus, if soldiers had desecrated a church, but left the altars untouched, the latter would not need reconsecration.[45]

TITLES OF ALTARS

CAN. 1201

§ 1. Sicut ecclesia, ita quodlibet etiam ecclesiae altare, saltem immobile, proprium sibi titulum habeat.

§ 2. Titulus primarius altaris maioris idem debet esse ac titulus ecclesiae.

§ 3. De Ordinarii licentia mutari quidem potest altaris mobilis, non autem altaris immobilis titulus.

§ 4. Altaria Beatis etiam in ecclesiis et oratoriis quibus eorum officium et Missa concessa sunt, dedicari nequeunt sine Sedis Apostolicae indulto.

§ 1. Like the church, so also the altars of a church, at least those that are fixed, must have each its own title.

§ 2. The principal title of the main altar must be the same as that of the church. For instance, if the church is dedicated to the Immaculate Conception, this must also be the title of the high altar. Besides this, the altar may also bear the name of a Saint, e.g., St. Columbkill.

§ 3. With the permission of the Ordinary [46] the title of a portable altar may be changed, but not the title of

---

45 S Rit. C , March 3, 1821 (n. 2612)

46 The Ordinary for exempt religious is their superior major.

a *fixed* altar. The latter requires a papal indult.[47] Thus, for instance, if a new religious congregation obtains a church that formerly belonged to an order, the old title of the altar, or church, respectively, must be retained for the main altar, and even on the side altar, if this is a fixed one, the former title under which the altar was dedicated must be placed, although a new title or image, *e.g.*, of the founder of the congregation, may also be placed there.[48]

Altars may not *be dedicated to the Blessed* without an Apostolic indult, even in churches and oratories for which the office and Mass of the resp. *Beatus* has been granted. This law binds also exempt religious, who are therefore not allowed to erect an altar in honor of a Blessed of their order without a papal indult.[49]

PROFANE USES NOT TOLERATED

CAN. 1202

§ 1. Altare tum immobile tum mobile debet esse divinis tantum officiis et praesertim Missae celebrationi reservatum, quolibet profano usu prorsus excluso.

§ 2. Subtus altare nullum sit reconditum cadaver; cadavera autem quae prope altare sepulta forte sunt, distent ab eo saltem spatio unius metri; secus Missam in altari celebrare non licet, donec cadaver removeatur.

§ 1. Immovable as well as portable altars are exclusively reserved for divine service, and every profane use must be excluded.

---

47 S. Rit. C., Nov. 10, 1906, ad III (n. 4191).

48 S. Rit. C., Aug. 27, 1836, ad V, VII (n. 2752).

49 S. Rit. C., April 17, 1660 (n. 1156).

§ 2. No corpses are to be entombed beneath the altar; if corpses are buried near the altar, a space of one metre [50] at least must intervene, otherwise Mass may not be celebrated on the altar until the body is removed.

A quaint custom prevailed in the archdiocese of Durazzo. Mohammedan women, when sick, took refuge under the antipendium of the altar on which Mass was said. This was promptly forbidden by the S. Congregation.[51] A less offensive though also rejected custom is that of leaving the altar cover rolled up on a stick on the altar during Mass.[52]

Altars should not be used as store-rooms, as this is forbidden by the general rubrics.

§ 2 forbids the saying of Mass on an altar which is too near a tomb or grave which contains the corpse or body of a person not canonized or beatified. The distance of one meter (39 inches) must be taken in the full, though not strictly in the mathematical [53] sense, and the dimensions are to be measured in every direction,— height, length, width, depth, including the *predella*.[54] If an altar is separated from the tomb by a stone chamber, although the distance is less than one meter, Mass may be said.[55] This distance must be observed also in cemeteries, vaults, and subterranean chapels, no matter whether they belong to religious or seculars.[56] Removal is necessary if morally possible. The S. Congregations have permitted bodies to remain if the re-

50 One metre is equal to 39 inches. The movement for introducing the metric system into the U. S and England can only be welcomed

51 S. C. P. F., Feb. 25, 1837 (*Coll*, n 854).

52 S Rit. C, June 2, 1883, ad II (n 3576).

53 S Rit. C., Jan 12, 1897, ad II; Aug. 3, 1901 (nn 3944, 4082).

54 S Rit. C, Feb 13, 1666, n. 5; July 7, 1766 (nn. 1333, 2479)

55 S Rit C, July 27, 1878 ad II; July 18, 1902 (nn. 3460, 4100).

56 S Rit C, Sept 28, 1872; April 21, 1873 (nn. 3283, 3294).

moval could be effected only with difficulty.[57]   One decision reads: " If it can be done conveniently." [58]
Piety and expenses should also be taken into consideration.

57 S. C. P. F., Nov. 22, 1790, ad
3 (*Coll.* n. 603).

58 S. Rit. C, 2, 1875 (n. 3339):
" *si commode fieri potest.*"

TITLE XII

ECCLESIASTICAL BURIAL

BURIAL VS. CREMATION

CAN. 1203

§ 1. Fidelium defunctorum corpora sepelienda sunt, reprobata eorundem crematione.

§ 2. Si quis quovis modo mandaverit ut corpus suum cremetur, illicitum est hanc exsequi voluntatem; quae si adiecta fuerit contractui, testamento aut alii cuilibet actui, tanquam non adiecta habeatur.

§ 1. The bodies of the faithful must be buried, cremation being reprobated.

§ 2. Should any one in any way order his body to be cremated, this order cannot lawfully be carried out, and any stipulation, will, or disposition to that effect must be disregarded

These canons embody a constant, time-honored tradition, which, while it does not directly involve a dogma, has been repeatedly enforced, especially against the Masons. Jews, Greeks, and Romans, various as their customs were at various time, nearly always buried their dead.[1] When, towards the end of the XIIIth century, the custom was introduced of boiling the corpses of those who had died in foreign lands, in order to render them

---

1 Cfr *Cath Encycl*, Vol IV, *s v*, "Cremation"

more easily transportable, Pope Boniface VIII strictly
forbade this abuse, which he styled abominable.[2]   It remained for the Freemasons who gathered at Naples, in
1869, to promote cremation and make it part and parcel
of their programme.   Cremation is frequently practiced
in missionary countries because of various difficulties.
The Vicar Apostolic of Vizagapatam in Hindustan solic-
ited an answer to the following question·   When a dying pagan asks to be baptized, the missionary baptizes
him without bothering himself whether the body may
be cremated or interred, being convinced that his family would not heed the desire of the deceased, even if
he insisted on burial.   Is this allowable?   The answer
was that the missionary should not approve of cremation,
but remain passive with regard to it, administer Baptism,
and instruct the people.[3]   Another pertinent decision is
that rendered by the Holy Office[4] to the effect that it is
forbidden to be enrolled in a lodge or society the purpose of which is to promote cremation without danger of
incurring the censures laid upon Masonic societies; and
that it is also forbidden to order one's own body or
the bodies of others to be cremated   The decision ex-
horts Ordinaries to instruct the faithful regarding the
abominable custom of cremating human bodies.   Another decision concerns *amputated limbs,* legs or arms.
The case was reported from a hospital in the U..S   The
answer was that the amputated limbs of non-Catholics
may be cremated, if the physician so advises, but those
of Catholics should be buried, if possible, in consecrated

2 Cfr c 1, Extrav. Comm, III,
6, *de sepulturis*
3 S. C P. F, Sept. 27, 1884
(*Coll.,* n. 1626). Instruction was
necessary because cremation was
considered a privilege of the caste
(*raiapont*), which the pagans
thought would be destroyed by the
Catholic religion
4 S. O, May 19, 1886 (*Coll P
F*, n. 1657); cf also S O., July
27, 1892 (*ibid*, 1808).

ground; else, anywhere. If the physician orders cremation, the sisters shall prudently and silently obey his command. The advice is added that a small consecrated lot
be kept in the garden adjoining the house for the purpose
of burying amputated limbs of Catholics.[5]

ECCLESIASTICAL BURIAL

CAN. 1204

Sepultura ecclesiastica consistit in cadaveris trans-
latione ad ecclesiam, exsequiis super illud in eadem
celebratis, illius depositione in loco legitime deputato
fidelibus defunctis condendis.

Ecclesiastical burial consists in bringing the body to
the church, holding the funeral service over the same in
the church, and entombing it in a place destined for the
burial of departed Catholics.

The Christian funeral rite differed greatly from the
pagan, as a passage from Minuctius Felix eloquently
demonstrates. The rules laid down in our canon were
observed conscientiously and religiously by the early
Christians. They embalmed or enshrouded the body,
accompanied the corpse with tapers or torches, singing
psalms and hymns, bringing an oblation, (*oblatio pro dor-
mitione*) and celebrating the love feast.[6] The whole
ceremony breathed belief in the resurrection of the body.
It is therefore not surprising to read of the insistence of
the Roman Court upon the full funeral rite. The custom of burying the bodies of the faithful from their

5 S O., Aug 3, 1897 (ibid. n. 1975)

6 "Nec mortuos coronamus, nos exequies adornamus eadem tranquilli-tate, qua vivimus; nec adnectimus arescentem coronam, sed a Deo aeternis floribus vividam sustine-mus;" cfr Armellini, Lezioni di Archeologia Cristiana, 1898, p. 89 f.

homes, without bringing them to church, is styled an abuse to be abolished.[7] Even in missionary countries, where superstitions are mingled with the Catholic rites, the Roman Ritual should be observed and funeral Mass be said *praesente cadavere,* if at all possible.[8] This service may also be held over human ashes or bones brought from foreign countries.[9] The Church does not abhor modern conveyances, and hence, no matter what means are used for carrying the dead to the cemetery, the pastor should accompany the funeral.[10]

Note well the *three parts of a Christian funeral, viz.:* transfer of the body to the church; funeral service in the church; interment in the graveyard. All three acts are accompanied by prayers.

The Roman Ritual [11] makes a distinction between the burial of adults and that of children.

The Code now proceeds to treat of cemeteries, of funeral services, and, lastly, of the refusal of ecclesiastical burial.

7 S. Rit. C., April 21, 1873 (n. 3291).

8 S. O , April 10, 1777, ad 2 (*Coll. P F.,* n 521).

9 S. Rit. C., Aug 11, 1883, ad I (n. 3693)· provided, of course, no voluntary or self-ordered cremation took place

10 S Rit. C , July 15, 1876 (n. 3405)

11 Tit. VI, c 3; c. 7.

23

CHAPTER I

CEMETERIES

BLESSED CEMETERIES

Can. 1205

§ 1. Cadavera fidelium sepelienda sunt in coemeterio quod, secundum ritus in probatis liturgicis libris traditos, sit benedictum, sive sollemni sive simplici benedictione ab iis data de quibus in can. 1155, 1156.

§ 2. In ecclesiis cadavera ne sepeliantur, nisi agatur de cadaveribus Episcoporum residentialium, Abbatum vel Praelatorum *nullius* in propria ecclesia sepeliendis vel Romani Pontificis, regalium personarum aut S. R. E. Cardinalium. *Bishop 1155*

§ 1. The bodies of the faithful must be buried in a *cemetery,* which may be solemnly or simply blessed according to the ritual books. The solemn blessing, as contained in the Roman Pontifical, can be imparted only by the Ordinary of the diocese, according to can. 1155; the simple blessing may be imparted by the local Ordinary, if the cemetery belongs to the secular or non-exempt religious clergy. However, the bishop may delegate any priest [1] for this function. If the cemetery belongs to exempt religious, the major superior or his delegate is competent.[2]

1 *Rit Rom*, tit. VIII, c. 29, can 1156; S Rit C, Feb 9, 1608 (n. 246)
2 Can. 1155

104

The necessity of burying the bodies of deceased Catholics in consecrated ground has been generally insisted upon, even for pagan provinces, where it was customary to bury infants, not in the family grave, but elsewhere.[3] In Mossul it was customary for Catholics as well as schismatics to be buried in one and the same family lot or vault. This custom was tolerated, as it could not be abolished without scandal[4]

The *cemetery must not be considered as blessed merely because the adjoining church was blessed.* These two blessings are entirely different rites.[5] If the whole cemetery was blessed, it is not necessary that the single graves be blessed again, and therefore the *benedicto tumuli* under the rubric: " when they have reached the grave, the priest shall bless it if it is not already blessed," should be omitted[6]

There is an apparent conflict between this and a decision of the same Congregation,[7] which orders all graves even in a cemetery already blessed to be blessed again if the grave is made of new material: *quoties agitur de sepulchro ex nova materia confecto* The contradiction is only apparent. For the last-mentioned decision regards a new grave made in the shape of a crypt or vault of stone or cement which has been newly added to the cemetery A simple grave (*fossa*) dug in the ground already blessed does not need to be reblessed.

§ 2. *No bodies shall be entombed in churches* except — if the civil laws permit it — the bodies of resident bish-

3 S O , Feb. 20, 1801 (*Coll P F,* n. 649). this was done because of the belief that infants and unmarried persons had no one to mourn or reverence them

4 S O , April 13, 1896 (*Coll. P. F,* n. 1089)

5 S Rit C , Feb 21, 1896 (n. 3888).

6 S Rit C., May 27, 1876, ad V (n 3400).

7 S. Rit. C., Sept 4, 1800, ad I (n. 3524).

ops and prelates or abbots *nullius*. These may be buried in their own church. The same privilege is accorded to the Roman Pontiff, royal personages and cardinals.

We said, "*if the civil laws permit it*," for it is a well-known fact that in Rome even Cardinals must be buried in the common city cemetery. Although this law is not in perfect keeping with the mind of the Church, yet it cannot be styled iniquitous as far as the mere prohibition of burial in churches is concerned, though in as far as it compels the promiscuous burial of baptized with non-baptized, and of criminals with distinguished prelates, it certainly is unjust and savors of intolerance. The first part of the law, to wit, forbidding burial in churches, would not be objected to by the ecclesiastical authorities, for, as will be seen from the following canon, the Code only demands free possession of cemeteries, whether situated inside or outside of church buildings. If a prelate mentioned in § 2, can. 1205, is buried in a church, his grave, though made in the middle of the choir, must be even with the floor and may not project over the altar of the *confessio*.[8] Besides, the distance of a meter from the altar must be observed, as prescribed in can. 1202, § 2.

RIGHTS OF THE CHURCH IN REGARD TO CEMETERIES

CAN. 1206

§ 1. Ius est catholicae Ecclesiae possidendi propria coemeteria.

§ 2. Sicubi hoc Ecclesiae ius violetur nec spes sit ut violatio reparetur, curent locorum Ordinarii ut coemeteria, societatis civilis propria, benedicantur, si, qui in eis condi solent, sint maiore ex parte catholici,

8 S Rit C , Feb 20, 1627 (n 433).

aut saltem ut in eis catholici spatium habeant, idque benedictum, sibi reservatum.

§ 3. Si ne hoc quidem obtineri possit, toties quoties benedicantur, secundum ritus in probatis liturgicis libris traditos, singuli tumuli.

§ 1. The Catholic Church has the right to possess her own cemeteries.

§ 2. Where this right of the Church has been violated, and there is no hope of recovering it, the local Ordinaries shall take care that the civil cemeteries be blessed, provided the majority of the persons to be buried in them belong to the Catholic faith, or at least that Catholics be granted a separate space, which should be blessed.

§ 3. If not even that much can be obtained, then the single graves must be blessed according to the liturgical books.

§ 1 is nothing else but a corollary from the doctrine of the corporate nature of the universal Church and its autonomous parts. Besides the sacred character of the burial grounds, the right of possessing them exclusively and independently of any outside corporation or society should be guaranteed to the Church. This right is evident from the principle of canon law: " With those with whom we have had no communion when living, we do not communicate when dead." [9] This right, inherent as it is in her very constitution, the Church can exercise effectively only if she possesses her own burial grounds.

§ 2 and § 3 are taken from an authentic answer of the Holy Office,[10] necessitated by the tendencies of the so-called Liberal school. A further declaration says that in common cemeteries, destined for Catholics and non-

[9] C 12, x, III, 28; Pius IX, "Nunquam certe," June 22, 1868. [10] S. O., Feb. 12, 1862 (Coll. P. F., n. 1227).

Catholics alike, a separate plot with a separate entrance should be obtained for Catholic burials.[11]

In the *United States* the Church has so far been allowed to possess her own cemeteries. "Rights of burial under churches or in cemeteries are so far public that private interests in them are subject to the control of the public authorities having charge of police regulations."[12] This, of course, also implies expropriation in case of public utility or health. Otherwise no state or county or municipal authority shall interfere with the right of the Church in matters of cemeteries and burial.[13]

INTERDICT, VIOLATION, ETC., OF CEMETERIES

CAN. 1207

Quae de interdicto, violatione, reconciliatione ecclesiarum canones praescribunt, etiam coemeteriis applicentur.

The regulations of canon law concerning the interdict, the desecration and reconciliation of churches also apply to cemeteries. Hence we refer to can. 1172 ff. Note well can. 1172, § 2, in order not to apply the old canons. What is to be said on interdicts will find its place under the respective heading.

OWNERS OF CEMETERIES

CAN. 1208

§ 1. Paroeciae suum quaeque coemeterium habeant, nisi unum pluribus commune ab Ordinario loci sit legitime constitutum.

---

11 S. C. P. F., March 29, 1830 (*ibid*, n. 812)
12 Zollmann,   *American   Civil*

Church Law, 1917, Ch. XVI, p. 439
13 *Ibid* " While thus the right

§ 2. Religiosi exempti possunt habere coemeterium proprium, a communi coemeterio distinctum.

§ 3. Etiam aliis personis moralibus vel familiis privatis permitti potest ab Ordinario loci peculiare sepulcrum, extra commune coemeterium positum, et ad instar coemeterii benedictum.

§ 3. Etiam infantium corpuscula, quatenus commode fieri potest, speciales et separatos ab aliis loculos et sepulturas habeant.

§ 1. Each parish should have its own cemetery, unless the local Ordinary assigns a common cemetery to several parishes.

and duty of a cemetery owner to vacate it in a proper case is perfectly plain, his right to determine who may be buried in it is equally clear Without such right, church societies might find their cemeteries interminable sources of trouble Not only might the peace of the society be disturbed by the burial of a person objectionable to its members, but the society itself might thereby actually be disrupted To prevent such a result religious organizations may not only establish cemeteries exclusively denominational, but may also guard and protect them by such rules and regulations as make effective the objects and purposes of their organization These rules and regulations will enter into and become a part of every contract for a lot in such cemetery, unless the proof is clear and convincing that a contract of a different kind was properly made with the lot owner by a duly authorized agent of the organization. When a party applies for a burial plot at the office of a distinctly Roman Catholic cemetery, it is with the tacit understanding that he is either a Roman Catholic, and as such eligible to burial, or at least that he applies on behalf of those who are in communion with the Church. The entire business is transacted on that basis. It follows that the mere payment of fees and charges confers the privilege of burial only 'in the mode used and permitted by the corporation.' While, therefore, the trustees of a church society who hold a cemetery as a 'free' burial ground cannot prevent the burial of a church member beside her husband where there is space left for that purpose; a person who has separated himself from the society, or who according to its decision had ceased to be a member of it, is not entitled as a matter of right to be buried in such cemetery, though he had contributed to it while still a member Nor may even a member of such organization bury his profligate son in such cemetery over the objection of the organization, nor be buried himself with ceremonies which are objectionable to it "

§ 2. ·Exempt *religious* may have their own cemetery, distinct from the common cemetery of the faithful.

§ 3. The Ordinary of the diocese may permit other corporations and private families to have their own burial places separate from the common one and blessed like a cemetery.

CAN. 1209

§ 1. Tum in coemeteriis paroecialibus, ex licentia scripta Ordinarii loci eiusve delegati, tum in coemeterio alius personae moralis, ex licentia scripta Superioris, fideles sibi suisque exstruere possunt sepulcra particularia; quae, de consensu eiusdem Ordinarii aut Superioris, possunt quoque alienare.

§ 2. Sepulcra sacerdotum et clericorum, ubi fieri potest, a sepulcris laicorum separata sint ac decentiore loco sita; praeterea, ubi id commodum fuerit, alia pro sacerdotibus, alia pro inferioris ordinis Ecclesiae ministris parentur.

§ 1 permits *lots or vaults* (*sepulchra particularia*) to be constructed with the written consent of the local Ordinary or his delegate on the parish cemetery. The same written consent may be given by the superior, either local or major, of the corporation on whose cemetery such a private sepulchre is chosen by the faithful. These private sepulchres, or graves, or lots may, with the consent of the Ordinary or Superior, be alienated. Alienation is, of course, here to be understood of a conveyance for burial purposes.

If suspicion of simony should arise from the term *alienation,* it may be observed that this is only an apparent difficulty, easily removed. If a certain sum would be charged for the grave itself, by reason of its being consecrated ground, there would indeed be simony. However, here there is question only of the exclusive right of usufruct, which is reserved to a determined person or family with regard to a specified lot. The cemetery itself or any part thereof is not sold or leased   But the exclusive right to a determined and honorable place has a material value and its sale, therefore, does not imply simony.[14]

§ 2. *Priests and clerics* should, if possible, have a special burial place, located in a more prominent part of the cemetery; the priests' lot should, if it can conveniently be done, be distinguished from that of the lower clerics.

§ 3. The burial place of infants should be separated from that of adults, as there is also a special rite for the burial of infants. Exempt religious, too, if they have plots for elective sepulture in their cemeteries, should set apart lots for the burial of children.[15]

KEEPING OF CEMETERIES

CAN. 1210

Quodlibet coemeterium sit undique apte clausum et caute custoditum.

CAN. 1211

Quodlibet coemeterium sit undique apte clausum et ad quos spectat, ne in coemeteriis epitaphia, laudationes funebres ornatusque monumentorum quidquam prae se ferant a catholica religione ac pietate absonum.

14 Cfr. Many, *l. c.*, p. 253 f.
15 S. Rit. C., Dec. 12, 1620 (n. 383).

Can. 1212

Praeter coemeterium benedictum alius, si haberi queat, sit locus, clausus item et custoditus, ubi ii humentur quibus sepultura ecclesiastica non conceditur.

Every cemetery shall be properly closed and carefully guarded.

The local Ordinaries, pastors and superiors, whom it concerns, shall take care that the inscriptions on the tombstones, eulogies, and adornments of the monuments be in keeping with Catholic faith and piety.

Besides the cemetery, or that part which is blessed, there should be a special plot, properly enclosed and guarded, to serve as burial-place for those who are denied ecclesiastical sepulture.

WAITING TIME

Can. 1213

Nullum corpus sepeliatur, praesertim si mors repentina fuerit, nisi post congruum temporis intervallum, quod satis sit ad omnem prorsus de vero obitu dubitationem tollendam.

No body should be buried, especially in case of sudden death, until sufficient time has elapsed to disperse all doubt as to death having really set in. This admonition was originally given to missionaries,[16] probably for lack of civil provisions on the subject. For where civil laws and the coroner attend to this matter, this canon is superfluous. For the rest, the process of embalming, properly

16 S. O., April 10, 1777 (*Coll. P. F.*, n. 321).

performed, will obviate the danger of burying anyone alive.

§ 1. Nullum cadaver perpetuae sepulturae ecclesiasticae ubivis traditum exhumare licet, nisi de licentia Ordinarii.

§ 2. Ordinarius licentiam nunquam concedat, si cadaver ab aliis corporibus certo discerni nequeat.

§ 1. No body that has been laid to final rest by ecclesiastical burial, can be exhumed without the permission of the Ordinary

§ 2. The Ordinary shall never grant this permission, if the corpse cannot with certainty be distinguished from other bodies.

This law is merely a corollary of the right of the Church to possess her own cemeteries. Difficulties may arise where the cemeteries belong to the municipality. Yet even there the Ordinary's permission is required, because a grave must be considered as sacred, since it has been blessed, and the Church is the quasi-custodian even of the bodies of the faithful

In closing this chapter it may be well to note briefly what rights the civil government may claim with regard to cemeteries and the burial of Catholics.

It has the right (1) to confine cemeteries to a district lying outside of the community of the living; (2) to determine the order of the graves and their depth, and to empty the graves after a certain lapse of time; (3) to establish a certain interval between death and burial, and to postpone burial in case of sudden death or crime, so as to ensure an autopsy; (4) to demand exhumation through the proper authority; (5) to ordain, through the proper authorities, that during epidemics, or the prevalence of contagious diseases, corpses be taken directly to the cemeteries.[17]

17 Cfr. Many, *l. c.*, p. 371.

CHAPTER II

FUNERAL SERVICES AND INTERMENT

CONVEYING BODIES TO CHURCH

CAN. 1215

Nisi gravis causa obstet, cadavera fidelium, antequam tumulentur, transferenda sunt e loco in quo reperiuntur, in ecclesiam, ubi funus, idest totus ordo exsequiarum quae in probatis liturgicis libris describuntur, persolvatur.

Unless there is a weighty reason for the contrary, the bodies of the faithful must, before interment, be taken from the place where they are (place of death) to a church, where the entire funeral service prescribed by the sacred liturgy shall be held.

The clergy of Brescia, Italy, had some doubts as to the admissibility of the ecclesiastical rites when a corpse was conveyed from the house to the church and from there to the cemetery by a vehicle. But the S. Congregation decided that the manner of conveyance does not interfere with the sacred liturgy and that the clergy should accompany the funeral to the graveyard,[1] as the people desired.

The text says: *nisi gravis causa obstet*. Since the sacred rites involve a grievous obligation, only a real, not an imaginary, reason can dispense from their observance,

---

1 S. Rit. C, March 5, 1870 (n. 3212).

though we do not wish to deny that a reasonable custom
may be admitted, especially in large cities. It is more
important to bring the body to church, than to accompany
it to the grave-yard, provided the grave has been blessed.

PAROCHIAL RIGHTS IN REGARD TO BURIAL

CAN. 1216

§ 1. Ecclesia in quam cadaver pro funere transferri
debet, ex iure ordinario est ecclesia propriae defuncti
paroeciae, nisi defunctus aliam funeris ecclesiam legitime elegerit.

§ 2. Si defunctus plures habuerit paroecias proprias, ecclesia funeris est ecclesia paroeciae in cuius
territorio decessit.

§ 1. By common law the corpse of a departed Catholic is to be brought to the parish church of the deceased,
unless he lawfully chose another church before his death.

§ 2. If the deceased belonged to several parishes, the
funeral should be held in the church of the parish within
which he died.

When the claim of another church is doubtful, the right
of the deceased's parish church must prevail.

The canon law formerly distinguished three reasons
which entitled a priest to bury a deceased person: elective sepulture, the family grave, and the parish burial.[2]
Our Code mentions but two: parish burial and elective
sepulture. But can. 1218, § 3, and 1229 admit the ancestral right, although only in a subordinate way, as is evident from the very position in our canon, which vindicates
the first, or at least general and ordinary right to the

---

2 Cfr c. 1, x, III, 28, c 3, 60,
III, 12, where the *sepulcrum maio-*
rum occupies the first place, because, says the text, this was the
custom of the patriarchs.

parish church of which the deceased was a member during life. However, the right of choosing his own burial or last resting place is acknowledged and granted to everyone not excluded by law, as determnied by can. 1223–1226. Provided, then, that no special church was designated before death by the persons who are allowed to choose either for themselves or for others, the body must be brought to the parish church, *i. e.*, the one to which the deceased belonged as a member when living, and of which he was a communicant.[3] This connection between church and parishioners is established by domicile or quasi-domicile, either being sufficient to render one a member of a parish. To *linguistically distinguished parishes* the same principle applies. The personal right of the parishioners prevails over territorial considerations.[4]

§ 2 of our canon provides for a case which may arise from the fact that one belongs to several parishes. Here a pertinent decision: A family had its domicile in the city and belonged to St. James' parish. The same family also had a summer villa in the parish of St. Mary, where the wife and mother lived every year for about eight months, and where she died, after having received the sacraments at the hands of St Mary's pastor, and was buried by him The S. Congregation decided that the pastor of St. Mary's was entitled to hold the funeral service and to receive the fee[5] This decision was perfectly natural One may have two domiciles or quasi-domiciles which suffice for contracting parish rights, and

---

3 Reiffenstuel (III, 28, n 6) justly remarks: " *ss. canones in ordine ad sepulturam non attendunt locum, ubi quis in extremis reficitur, sed ubi in vivis coelesti pabulo refici consuevit* "

4 Pignatelli, *Consultationes Canonicae*, Vol. III, Cons 48, n 22.

5 S. C. C, March 12, 1881 (*A. S. S.*, t. XIV, 209 ff.).

servants, hired hands, soldiers, students, nurses, teachers, etc., may contract a quasi-domicile, although they retire to their homes several times each year, and have no intention of staying longer than necessary. If they reside anywhere continuously the greater part of the year this is sufficient to contract a quasi-domicile.[6]

CAN. 1217

In dubio de iure alius ecclesiae, ius propriae ecclesiae paroecialis semper praevalere debet.

In *doubtful cases,* says can. 1217, the right of one's own parish church prevails. The reason lies in the right of the pastor, which corresponds to his duty of administering the sacraments, and he should not be deprived of the honor and material advantage.[7] Therefore if either the fact or the right are doubtful, the deceased's own parish comes first. The *fact* is doubtful if it is uncertain where one died or was killed. The *right* is doubtful if membership in the one or the other parish cannot be clearly established, or the will of the deceased regarding sepulture cannot be proved.

TRANSFER TO ONE'S OWN CHURCH

CAN. 1218

§ 1. Licet mors acciderit extra propriam paroeciam, cadaver tamen in ecclesiam paroeciae propriae quae vicinior sit, ob funus transferendum est, si ad eam commode pedestri itinere asportari possit; secus in ecclesiam paroeciae in qua mors accidit.

§ 2. Ordinarii est pro suo territorio, inspectis pe-

---

6 *A. S. S , l c ,* p. 214.
7 Cfr. cc 2, 3, 6, x, III, 12, c 2, § *Verum ne,* Clem III, 7.

culiaribus circumstantiis, distantiam aliaque adiuncta designare, quae translationem cadaveris ad ecclesiam funeris aut locum sepulturae incommodam reddant; et si paroeciae ad diversas dioeceses pertineant, designatio attenditur Ordinarii dioecesis in qua defunctus supremum diem obiit.

§ 3. Licet translatio ad ecclesiam funeris aut ad locum sepulturae incommoda sit, semper tamen integrum est familiae, heredibus, aliisve quorum interest, cadaver illuc deferre, susceptis translationis expensis.

§ 1. Even though a person has died outside his own parish, the corpse must be brought for the funeral service to his own parish church, if it is the nearest, and the corpse can be conveniently carried there on foot (*pedestri itinere*); otherwise it is to be carried to the church of the parish in which the person died.

This section must be understood in the light of the old law, which exempted transportation to the parish church in case of danger.[8] Transport was by most canonists presumed to be dangerous when it took a day's journey. Others more reasonably held that the judgment regarding the existing danger must be left to the family of the deceased. In our country and day of automobiles and motor hearses this canon has little practical value. However, we believe that the term *iter pedestre* is here to be taken, not exclusively as the mode of conveyance, but as a conditional supposition, as if we should say: supposing or provided the funeral journey could be made on foot.[9]

§ 2 provides for a more practical mode of judging distance and inconvenience. The Ordinary may, after examining the special circumstances, determine — prefer-

8 C. 1, Extrav. Comm., III. 6.
9 In Rome the bodies of prisoners were brought on foot to the church; S. Rit. C., Jan. 15, 1667 (n. 1346).

ably at a synod and by means of diocesan statutes — when and under what conditions the transportation of the corpse to the church or place of burial is inconvenient. If the parishes belong to different dioceses, the decision lies with the bishop in whose diocese the person died. Supposing a man was accidentally killed in a parish of the Des Moines diocese, but belonged to a parish of the diocese of St. Joseph, if there were no one to defray the transportation expenses and to claim the body, we suppose the Ordinary of Des Moines would decide in favor of burial in that city — *recto tramite.*

§ 3 grants to the *family* of the deceased, his *heirs, or other interested persons,* the right of having the body conveyed to the church where the funeral services are to be held, or to the burial place. And this even if the transfer were quite inconvenient, provided the relatives or heirs are willing to pay the expenses.

BURIAL OF CARDINALS AND BISHOPS

CAN. 1219

§ 1. Si S. R. E. Cardinalis in Urbe decesserit, corpus transferendum est, funeris causa, in ecclesiam quam Romanus Pontifex designaverit; si extra Urbem, in ecclesiam insigniorem civitatis seu loci ubi mors accidit, nisi Cardinalis aliam elegerit.

§ 6. Defuncto Episcopo residentiali, etiam cardinalitia dignitate aucto, aut Abbate vel Praelato *nullius,* corpus, funeris causa, transferri debet in ecclesiam cathedralem, abbatialem vel praelatitiam, si id commode fieri possit; secus, in ecclesiam insigniorem civitatis seu loci, nisi in utroque defunctus aliam ecclesiam elegerit.

§ 1. If a *cardinal* dies *in* the city (of Rome), his body is to be brought for the funeral service to the church which the Roman Pontiff may designate for that purpose; if he dies *outside* the city, the corpse must be carried to the more prominent church of the city or town where the cardinal died, unless he chose another.

§ 2. On the death of a *residential bishop,* even if he was a cardinal, or an abbot or prelate *nullius,* the body must be brought for the funeral service to the cathedral or abbatial or prelatial church, if this can be done conveniently; if not, to the more prominent church of the city or town, unless the prelate chose another.

FUNERAL OF BENEFICIARIES

CAN. 1220

Beneficiarii residentiales ad ecclesiam sui beneficii transferendi sunt, nisi aliam sibi elegerint ecclesiam funeris.

The *bodies of resident beneficiaries* must be brought *to the church of their benefice,* unless they have selected another church for their funeral.

The burial of cathedral and collegiate canons and other beneficiaries, provided they are really resident, is to take place from the church where they held a benefice. If they had their domicile or quasi-domicile in another parish [10] of the city or town, the stole fee must be given to the pastor of that parish.[11]

Concerning the canons of cathedral churches in *Eng-*

10 *Resident* does not imply that the canons and beneficiaries must reside at the cathedral or collegiate church, because this may not be a parish church.

11 S. C. C., May 12, 1685 (Richter, *Trid,* p. 462, n. 10), S Rit. C, May 16, Dec. 18, 1756, ad 11 (n. 2441).

land, the provincial council of Westminster (1852) decided nothing about their funeral; but since these are not really canonical prebends, as a decree of the S. C. P. F., April 21, 1852, clearly states,[12] it follows that the present canon cannot be applied to them. It has in view only beneficiaries in the strict sense.

FUNERALS OF RELIGIOUS

CAN. 1221

§ 1. Professi religiosi ac novitii, defuncti cum sint, transferendi sunt, funeris causa, ad ecclesiam vel oratorium suae domus vel saltem suae religionis, nisi novitii aliam ecclesiam ad suum funus elegerint; ius autem levandi cadaver et illud deducendi ad ecclesiam funerantem pertinet semper ad Superiorem religiosum.

§ 2. Si longe moriantur a domo, ita ut in ecclesiam suae domus vel saltem suae religionis nequeant commode asportari, funerandi sunt in ecclesia paroeciae ubi decedunt, nisi novitius aliam ecclesiam ad funus elegerit, et salvo Superioribus iure de quo in can. 1218, § 3.

§ 3. Quae de novitiis dicta §§ 1, 2, valent quoque de famulis actu servientibus et intra domus septa stabiliter commorantibus, qui tamen, si extra religiosam domum decesserint, funerandi sunt ad normam can. 1216–1218.

§ 1. The bodies of professed religious and novices must be brought for the funeral service to the church or oratory of their house, or at least to a church of their institute, unless the deceased was a novice and selected another church.

12 *Coll. Lac.,* III, 956

The right to remove the body and accompany it to the church belongs to the religious superior. Hence the pastor in whose parish a religious or novice died, even though the house or hospital be under the pastor's jurisdiction, is not entitled to interfere or claim compensation.[13]

Note that the Code simply says " religious," without drawing a distinction between exempt and non-exempt. Not intended are those that are not religious in the sense of the Code.[14]

§ 2. If a professed religious or novice dies in a place so *far distant from his religious house* that the body cannot conveniently be conveyed to a church of his own house, or order, or congregation, he must be buried where he died, unless a novice has chosen another church for the funeral service. Here again distance is mentioned without further determination. According to canonists,[15] " distance " is one day's journey. But this term must be taken in a relative sense; expenses, means of transportation, and the condition of the corpse must be duly considered. If the corpse cannot be conveniently transported, it must be buried where death occurred and religious have no right to choose the burial place.[16] Novices, however, may choose.

Our canon refers to can. 1218, § 3, which permits the family to remove the body wherever they please, provided they defray the expenses. This right is here vindicated to the superior, either local or higher. If he should choose to have the body transferred from the place of

13 Cfr c 16, x, V, 31, c 5, 6°, III, 12, S C. EE et RR, July 21, 1848 (Bizzarri, *l c.,* p 563 f)

14 Can. 673; unless of course they enjoy a special privilege to that effect

15 Ferraris, *Prompta Bibliotheca,* s v. "*Sepultura,*" n. 41.

16 Formerly the choice was not denied; c. 5, 6°, III, 12

death to a church of his institute, he may do so without consulting or excusing himself to the pastor in whose parish the religious died.[17]

The pastor, even though he may have administered the last Sacraments to the deceased religious, is not entitled to any stole fees.[18]

Religious superiors are not exempt from this law, *i. e.,* they are not allowed to choose their own burial place,[19] but are to be treated just like ordinary religious.

§ 3. What has been established concerning novices also applies to *servants* actually employed by religious and living permanently within the premises of a religious house (farm hands, janitors, mechanics, teachers, etc.). To enjoy the privilege here granted they must be actually serving the religious *and* live within the precincts of the convent or religious house.[20] If they boarded outside, the second condition would be lacking; if they worked without being hired or employed, the former condition would not be verified.[21] If they die outside the religious house the privilege ceases.

GUESTS AND STUDENTS OF RELIGIOUS

CAN. 1222

Quod attinet ad defunctos qui in domo etiam regulari vel collegio degebant ratione hospitii, educationis vel infirmitatis, et ad defunctos in hospitali, standum est canonibus 1216–1218, nisi constet de iure particu-

---

17 S C. C , June 10, 1620, ad 10; Ferraris, *l. c ,* n. 35 f

18 S. C EE. et RR , May 22, 1615; Ferraris, *ibid.,* however, compensation would not be against either the letter or the spirit of the law.

19 Cfr. can. 1224, 2°.

20 Cfr. *Trid ,* Sess. 24, c. 11; Sess 25, c. 11, *de rég.: " subque eorum obedientia tivunt "*

21 S. C EE. et RR , July 21, 1848 (Bizzarri, *l. c.,* p 563 ff.) Cfr. Vol. III, p. 142 f of this Commentary.

lari aut privilegio; quod vero ad illos attinet qui in Seminario moriuntur, servetur praescriptum can. 1368.

Guests, students or sick persons who have lived in a religious house, even though this belong to regulars, or in a college, and die there, as well as those who die in a hospital, are to be buried like other secular persons, *i. e.,* according to can. 1216–1218, unless a particular law or privilege exempts them from the common law.

Seminarians are to be buried by the authorities of the seminary, unless the Holy See has ruled otherwise with regard to certain seminaries.

The favor granted these persons by virtue ot can. 514 may not be extended to the funeral service, as the S. Congregations have constantly decided.[22] Of course, these persons are allowed to choose burial in the church of religious, provided this church is capable of being selected (can 1125) and the person free to choose. But in that case the stole fees belong to the parish priest who would otherwise be entitled to perform the burial.[23]

The text admits exemption by reason of a particular law or privilege. A particular law would be one issued according to can. 464, § 2, *viz.:* when the Ordinary exempts a religious family from the parish organization. The Barnabites were granted a privilege permitting their guests and all those who died suddenly in their houses or colleges to be buried by these religious [24]

Our text requires that the privilege must be certain or evident (*nisi constet de privilegio*). All religious, therefore, who can claim neither a particular law nor a privi-

22 S. C EE et RR , Dec 1674; Dec. 14, 1753 (Bizzarri, *l c*, pp. 271 f; 379), S C. C., April 21, 1742 (Richter, *Trid.,* p. 462, n. 13).

23 S C C, *l. c*
24 Greg. XV, 1621, *apud* Bizzarri, *l. c.,* p 564

lege, must permit the pastor in whose parish their house is situated, to perform the funeral service.[25]

CAN. 1223

§ 1. Omnibus licet, nisi expresse iure prohibeantur, eligere ecclesiam sui funeris aut coemeterium sepulturae.

§ 2. Uxor et filii puberes in hac electione prorsus immunes sunt a maritali vel patria potestate.

CAN. 1224

Ecclesiam funeris aut sepulturae coemeterium eligere prohibentur:

1.° Impuberes; verum pro filio aut filia impubere, etiam post eorum mortem, hanc electionem facere possunt parentes vel tutor;

2.° Religiosi professi cuiuslibet gradus aut dignitatis, non tamen si sint Episcopi.

Canon 1223 ordains (§ 1) that all may freely choose their funeral church or burial place, unless they are expressly forbidden to do so by law. Those forbidden are boys who have not yet completed the fourteenth and girls who have not yet completed the twelfth year.[26] In their stead, even after their death, the parents or guardians may make the choice. Whether the mother alone may do so, was not quite certain hitherto, because a Constitution of Innocent X seems to debar her if there is no local custom in her favor.[27] Our text leaves no doubt that

---

25 S. C. C., April 21, 1742 (Richter, *l. c.*, nn. 4, 13).
26 See can 88, § 2

27 "*Ex injuncto*," Nov. 16, 1645 (Richter, *l. c*, p. 461, n. 6).

mothers, too, may choose burial church and burial place for their children.

If the parents have a family lot, the children should be buried there, otherwise, if no contrary choice is made, they are to be buried from the parish church and in the parish cemetery.[28]

According to § 2, can. 1223, the wife as well as boys and girls who have completed the age of fourteen or twelve, respectively, are free to make their choice, and are not hampered in this matter by marital or parental power.[29] If this be true, we cannot see, as stated above, why the mother should be debarred from choosing, provided, of course, the father eithers consents, or is dead, or does not care. *Guardians,* too, are admitted.

Professed religious of whatever rank or dignity, except *bishops,* are deprived of the right of choosing their funeral church or burial place. The reason is that religious have no power either to *"velle"* or *"nolle."*[30] Cardinals who are religious enjoy the right here denied by virtue of can. 1219, bishops, by virtue of can. 1224. As the text speaks of bishops in general, all, resident and titular, are included.

CAN. 1225

Ut electio ecclesiae funeris valeat, cadat necesse est vel in ecclesiam paroecialem, vel in ecclesiam regularium, non tamen monialium (nisi agatur de mulieribus quae famulatus, educationis, infirmitatis aut hospitii causa intra clausuram eiusdem monasterii non precario commorabantur), vel in ecclesiam iuris pa-

---

28 S. C. C., Nov 16, 1645; Feb 22, 1646 (Richter, *l c*, n 2 f)
29 S C EE et RR, June 8,
1731 (Bizzarri, *l c*, p 343); Many, *l. c*, p 267 f
30 C 5, 6°, III, 12.

tronatus, si agatur de patrono, vel in aliam ecclesiam funerandi iure praeditam.

Can 1225 determines *which churches* may be chosen for *funeral services*. They are parish churches and churches of regulars, churches of advowson in favor of the advowee, and any other church endowed with the *ius funerandi*.

The first class, *i. e.,* parish churches, were the exclusive possessors of this right before the thirteenth century, except where the Popes had granted a special privilege.[31]

The Friars Preachers and the Friars Minor obtained such a privilege, and it was extended to all regulars by way of communication.[32] Now it has ceased to be a mere privilege but is common law. However, this law favors only churches of *regulars* to the exclusion of other religious, even though exempt.

The third class consists of churches which are subject to the *ius patronatus,* but only in favor of the patron or advowee.

There is a fourth class consisting of such churches as are expressly endowed with the *ius funerandi*.

The Code distinguishes between a church for funeral services and a cemetery for sepulture. The two are not identical. *Ius funerandi,* sometimes called *jus sepeliendi,* or *tumulandi,* here means strictly the right to funeral services, without the burial place. This is apparent from the fact that the church is called *ecclesia funeris, i. e.,* the church where the funeral service takes place.

Which churches have the *ius funerandi* besides those mentioned in the text? Note two facts: (1) The burial right is a strictly parochial right, and (2) all eccle-

31 Cfr. c 3, X. III, 28; c. 3, 6°, III, 12.
32 Cfr. c 2, Clem III, 7.

siastical functions may be held in all public oratories and also in semi-public oratories, unless excepted by the Ordinary.[33] The funeral service is an ecclesiastical function. Hence, unless the Ordinary forbids this function to take place in semi-public oratories, funeral services may be held there as well as in public oratories. This does not interfere with strictly parochial rights because, as will be seen under can. 1230, § 4, these rights are safeguarded by law.

Churches of nuns (*monialium*) may not be used to hold funeral services for outsiders. This was the traditional practice of the Roman Court.[34] However, female[35] servants, women who lived habitually within the enclosure of the convent for the sake of study, or because of sickness, or as guests, may have their funeral services performed in the nuns' church. *Moniales* must here be taken in the strict sense, excluding female religious with simple vows only. This distinction is clearly based on the nature of enclosure. Hence the many decisions against the permissibility of funeral services and burial in such churches. If anyone is buried in such a church, the stole fees belong to the parish church.[36]

Here may be added a decision concerning *confraternities* in churches of regulars. The members of these pious societies must be buried from the parish church, unless they have lawfully chosen the church of the regulars for burial.[37] Neither are tertiaries or oblates to be buried from the church of the respective religious order, but

[33] Cfr. can. 462, 5°; can 1191, § 2; can. 1193.

[34] Ferraris, *Prompta Bibliotheca,* s v. "*Sepultura,*" n 137; Many, *l. c.,* p 301 f

[35] Male servants are to be buried from the parish church, S. C. C.,

Jan 21, 1723, *et pluries* (Richter, *Trid,* p. 462, n 14).

[36] S C. C., Nov. 28, 1711; July 28, 1731 (Richter, *l c,* nn 18 f)

[37] Innocent X, "*Ex injuncto,*" Feb. 22, 1645 (Richter, *l c,* n. 16); S. C EE et RR, March 13, 1744, ad 8 (Bizzarri, *l. c.,* p. 364).

their funeral services must be held in the parish church, unless they have chosen another, *i. e.,* the church of the regulars.[38]

Can. 1226

§ 1. Ecclesiam funeris aut coemeterium sepulturae quis eligere potest per se vel per alium cui legitimum mandatum dederit; factamque electionem aut mandati concessionem quolibet legitimo modo probare licet.

§ 2. Si electio fiat per alium, hic suum mandatum explere potest etiam post mortem mandantis.

Can. 1226 determines the *manner in which the choice of a funeral church or cemetery may be made,* and how it is to be proved. One may do this personally or through another commissioned for that purpose. This choice is similar to a last will.[39] Hence § 2 states that the *mandatarius* may carry out the mandate either before or after the death of the *mandans* or person who has made the commission. Of course the *mandatarius* must abide by the wording of the disposition.

The second clause of § 1 says that the choice made, and the fact of commission, may be *proved* in legal form. Thus the form which is required for a last will, in the presence of two witnesses and a notary public, would certainly be sufficient.[40] Even two witnesses without a notary public, provided they testify under oath before the parish priest, are admissible [41] In case the person should be speechless, signs and nods which indicate his desire shall not be rejected.[42] Even the pastor's testimony, if it is not in his own favor, is admissible. The Ordinary or

---

38 S. C. EE et RR, Dec 11, 1615 (Bizzarri, *l c*, p 245).

39 C. 13, x, III, 26.

40 S. C. C, Feb 13, 1666; April 24, 1723; July 4, 1722 (Richter, p. 461, n. 8).

41 S C. C, Dec. 19, 1739 (*ibid*, n 9).

42 S C. C., Feb 13, 1666, ad II (*l. c*)

the pastor may, if they wish, demand a document or proof of the choice made before burial takes place.[43] *Synodal* acts may more closely determine the requisites of proof, but if they contravene this canon, they have no force. Thus the S. Congregation sustained a choice made by a woman before her confessor, her father, and another witness, though the synodal law required the presence of the pastor, and the father of the woman was dead at the time of the trial.[44]

CAN. 1227

Religiosi et clerici saeculares districte vetantur ne quos ad vovendum, iurandum vel fide interposita seu aliter promittendum inducant ut apud ipsorum ecclesias funus aut apud ipsorum coemeterium sepulturam eligant, vel factam electionem non immutent; quod si contra factum fuerit, electio aut immutatio sit nulla.

Can. 1227 strictly forbids *all clergymen,* whether secular or religious, *to induce* any person to choose a particular church for funeral service or cemetery for burial, or to change his choice. If such an inducement was made, the choice is null and void. Note, however, that this influence or persuasion must be brought to bear on the person by vow or oath, by pledging his word of honor, or by simple promise. Our text is taken substantially from the Decretals and contains only one penalty, to wit, the nullity of the promise.[45] It may also be noticed that only clergymen are mentioned. This is done in order to procure the necessary liberty to laymen and to prevent jealousy and dissension among the clergy.

43 S. C. EE. et RR., Sept. 19, 1732, ad 2 (Bizzarri, p. 344 f.).
44 S. C. EE. et RR., Feb. 6, 1852 (*ibid.,* p. 602 f.).

45 C. 1, 6°, III, 12; C. 3, Clem. V, 8: also interdict and excommunication.

CAN. 1228

§ 1. Si electa fuerit sepultura in coemeterio diverso a coemeterio propriae defuncti paroeciae, cadaver in illo sepeliatur, dummodo nihil obstet ex parte eorum a quibus coemeterium pendet.

§ 2. Electa sepultura in coemeterio religiosorum, ut cadaver inibi sepeliri queat, requiritur et sufficit consensus Superioris religiosi, ad normam constitutionum cuiusque religionis.

Can. 1228 repeats in a somewhat different form the enactment of Boniface VIII, mentioned above, concerning the incineration or boiling of bodies.[46]   The text merely says that the body must be *buried* in the cemetery chosen by the person, even though it be different from the cemetery of the parish to which the deceased belonged.   However, the authorities of the cemetery chosen by the deceased must give their, at least negative, consent.   If the cemetery thus specially selected belongs to religious, the consent of the respective superior is required and suffices. The superior is the one whom the constitution of the religious point out as competent for giving the consent. If the constitutions contain nothing to the contrary, or no enactment at all on this subject, the local superior is certainly competent.

ANCESTRAL TOMBS

CAN. 1229

§ 1. Si quis, sepulcrum maiorum in aliquo coemeterio possidens, non electa alibi sepultura, decesserit, in eodem sepeliendus est, si illuc commode asportari possit, salvo praescripto can. 1218, § 3.

---

46 C 1, Extrav. Comm , III, 6.

§ 2. Pro uxore attenditur sepulcrum viri, et, si plures habuerit, sepulcrum ultimi.

§ 3. Plura si sint maiorum aut viri sepulcra, defuncti familia aut heredes sepulturae deligant.

§ 1. If a person who has an ancestral tomb or grave in some cemetery dies without having chosen a burial place somewhere else, the body, if it can be conveniently transferred, must be buried there. The same holds good if his family, heirs or friends insist upon burial in the ancestral grave, and defray the expenses

§ 2. A wife is to be buried in the ancestral tomb of her husband; and, if she had several husbands, in the ancestral tomb of her last husband,— always provided, of course, that she had not chosen another burial place.

§ 3. If there are several ancestral tombs or family tombs, the family or heirs of the deceased may choose his burial place. In Europe there used to be different ancestral graves or tombs: strictly *family* plots, where only members of the family were buried; *hereditary* tombs, in which only heirs were buried, and *mixed* tombs for both members of the family and heirs.[47] Our text allows the family to choose between these different kinds of tombs where they exist The right to be buried in the ancestral tomb also belongs to infants and children.[48] Hence can. 1209 cannot be urged in this case.

DUTIES AND RIGHTS OF PASTORS IN REGARD TO BURIALS

Can. 1230

§ 1. Proprius defuncti parochus non solum ius sed etiam officium habet, excepto gravi necessitatis casu,

47 Many, *l. c.*
48 S. C. C , Oct. 21, 1613 (Richter, p. 461, n 1).

levandi per se vel per alium cadaver, illud comitandi ad suam ecclesiam paroecialem ibique exsequias persolvendi, firmo praescripto can. 1216, § 2.

§ 2. Quod si mors acciderit in loco alienae paroeciae, et cadaver ad ecclesiam propriae paroeciae commode asportari possit, parochi proprii est, praemonito parocho loci, illud levare, comitari ad suam ecclesiam ibique exsequias peragere.

§ 3. Si ecclesia funeris sit ecclesia regularis aliave exempta a iurisdictione parochi, parochus, sub cruce ecclesiae funerantis, cadaver levat ac deducit ad ecclesiam; sed exsequias rector ecclesiae celebrat.

§ 4. Si vero ecclesia funeris non sit exempta a iurisdictione parochi, celebratio exsequiarum, salvo peculiari privilegio, pertinet non ad rectorem ecclesiae funerantis, sed ad parochum in cuius territorio ecclesia sita est, dummodo defunctus parocho subiectus fuerit.

§ 5. Religiosas et novitias, in religiosa domo defunctas, ad clausurae limen deferant aliae religiosae; indeque, si de religiosis agatur iurisdictioni parochi non obnoxiis, ad propriam religiosae domus ecclesiam vel oratorium deducit et exsequias peragit cappellanus; si de aliis religiosis, valet praescriptum § 1; quod vero ad religiosas attinet extra domum defunctas, serventur generalia canonum praescripta.

§ 6. Defuncto S. R. E. Cardinali aut Episcopo extra Urbem in civitate episcopali, servetur praescriptum can. 397, n. 3.

§ 7. Si cadaver mittatur ad locum ubi nec defunctus propriam paroeciam habebat, nec ecclesia funeris legitime fuerat electa, ius levandi cadaver, peragendi exsequias, si peragendae sint, et cadaver ad sepulturam deducendi, pertinet ad ecclesiam cathedralem eiusdem loci; quae si desit, ad ecclesiam paroeciae in

qua coemeterium situm est, nisi aliud ferant loci consuetudo aut dioecesana statuta.

§ 1. The pastor of a deceased Catholic is entitled and
obliged, unless excused by grave necessity, to go himself
or send a delegate (assistant priest, curate) to the house
to receive the body (*levare corpus*),[49] accompany it to
the parish church, and there to hold the exequies, with
due regard to can. 1216, § 2. Needless to say, this is not
customary in our country, where distance often renders
it impossible to comply with this ruling. Therefore the
law most reasonably adds: *excepto gravi necessitatis casu*.

§ 2. If a person has died in a strange parish, and the
body can be conveniently brought to his own parish, the
pastor has the right and duty to perform the ceremonies
described in § 1, after previously informing the pastor of
the parish where the person died. Thus, for instance, if
a person dies in a hospital or asylum located in a strange
parish, his or her pastor is entitled and obliged to perform
the sacred rites, unless, of course, the hospital or asylum
enjoys exemption from the jurisdiction of the pastor.[50]

§ 3 draws a distinction between exempt and non-
exempt churches. In exempt churches the *parochus
proprius* may take up the body and accompany it to the
exempt church; but the cross behind which the funeral
procession marches must be that of the exempt church,
and the rector of the latter is entitled to hold the funeral
service. It required a great many decisions to make this
rule clear. If a church in charge of regulars was chosen
for the funeral service, the regulars had to invite the
pastor or chapter, and even accompany them to the

49 *Levare corpus* properly means
to raise or take up the body
(compare: *levare e sacro fonte*),
and is used for the first funeral act
performed by sprinkling the coffin
with Holy Water.
50 S. C. C, June 22, 1907 (*Anal.
Eccl.*, XV, 284 ff).

church. But if the pastor or chapter made the fathers wait more than an hour, they could go to the house of the deceased and conduct the funeral. The pastor or chapter were allowed to sprinkle the body, but not to intone any antiphon or psalm, etc. In fact they had to remain outside the church whilst the exequies were performed.[51] This last-mentioned ruling might reasonably be revoked.

§ 4. In *non-exempt churches* the celebration of the funeral service belongs to the pastor in whose parish the church selected for the funeral is located, provided the deceased was a subject of his. Therefore the rector or chaplain of the church in which the exequies are held must make way for the *parochus proprius* of the deceased. If the latter refuses to perform the services the rector or chaplain of the *ecclesia funerans* may hold them [52] Thus, if a member of a *confraternity* which has a public oratory within the limits of a parish dies, the pastor of the parish is entitled to hold the funeral services in such public oratory, provided the deceased was his parishioner.[53] If the deceased was not a parishioner of the parish within the boundaries of which the *ecclesia funerans* is situated, the chaplain of the confraternity may perform the funeral rites [54] If the public oratory is situated within the limits of a collegiate or cathedral parish, the pastor, and not the first dignitary of the collegiate or cathedral church, is entitled to perform the services, unless the chaplain enjoys this right.[55] This may be by

51 S. C. EE et RR, Aug 22, 1670; Sept 23, 1735, April, 1717 (Bizzarri, *l c*, pp 263, 346 f, 304)

52 S. Rit C, Dec. 22, 1629 (n. 523)

53 S. Rit. C., Jan 12, 1704, ad 20 (n 2123)

54 S Rit C, July 9, 1718, ad 4, May 13, 1719, ad 7 (nn. 2251, 2263).

55 S Rit C, Sept 13, 1670, ad 1 (n 1409)

reason of exemption, or by a *special privilege* which is sometimes given, especially to arch-confraternities.

§ 5 treats of the *burial of female religious and their novices.* If *they die* in their religious house, their bodies must be brought to the threshold of the enclosure, whence the chaplain conducts the funeral procession to the church or oratory, where he holds the exequies. But the chaplain is entitled to this privilege only if the religious are exempt from the jurisdiction of the pastor. If they are subject to the pastor in whose parish the religious house is located, the latter is obliged and entitled to conduct the funeral.

If sisters or novices *die outside their religious house,* the common law takes effect. Canons appear to have taken a particular interest in the funeral of *moniales,* since the decisions, the substance of which is embodied in our text, chiefly regard them. The confessor or chaplain of nuns (with solemn vows) has the exclusive right of accompanying the corpse from the threshold of the enclosure into the outer church, to hold the funeral service there, and then to accompany the body to the grave-yard If it is a custom of long standing that canons or other priests are invited, they may continue to observe the custom, but without prejudice to the confessor or chaplain, who, on his part, should beware not to enter the papal enclosure under pretext of a funeral service.[56]

This, then, is the rule for all nuns or *moniales,* no matter whether they are subject immediately to the Holy See or to the bishops or prelates regular.[57] The local Ordinary, according to can. 464, § 2, may exempt certain *religious communities* from the pastor's jurisdiction and place

56 S. C EE. et RR, May 30, 1856, Sept 17, 1858 (Bizzarri, *l c,* pp. 648, 657); S. Rit. C., April 20, 1641; May 10, 1805 (nn. 751, 2559).

57 S C. C, Feb. 24, 1872 (*A. S. S.,* VII, 161 ff.).

them directly under a chaplain appointed by him.[58]   However, it must be plainly understood and maintained that the mere appointment of a chaplain does not derogate from the rights of the pastor in the matter of burial.   And this is true of every non-exempt religious institute of women, no matter whether approved by the Holy See or by the Ordinary only.[59]   The consequence is that unless the Ordinary formally exempts a religious community of women, or of men, which belongs to the class of non-clerical congregations, the pastor's rights in the matter of burial must be sustained.

The last clause of § 5, can. 1230, states that concerning female religious *who die outside their religious house* the common law must be observed.   What is the common law on this point?   No doubt that part of the present title which affects secular persons, otherwise the text would simply have referred to can. 1221, treating of male religious.   Therefore the pastor's rights are here still more evidently safeguarded   But the question may not be useless, whether such female religious are allowed to choose their burial places.   This, we believe, must be denied, for the reason that they do not have their own will.   But the parish church or parish cemetery as well as the ancestral tomb may safely be vindicated for them.   For the rest, a religious community may claim the right granted by can. 1218, § 3.

Here it may be permitted to add a note which might have been placed under can. 1221, but also fits here.   If a religious who has been pastor or teacher for years, were buried in the place of his activity, we believe it would not be reprimanded by the lawgiver, because "convenient conveyance" might suffer on account of discontent on the

58 Cfr. can 514, § 3, 4
59 Leo XIII, "*Conditae*," Dec. 8, 1900, II, n 8

part of the people. Piety also has its claims, provided, of course, that the distance between the religious house and the deceased person's last residence amounts to a good many miles, and the superior's permission is obtained.

§ 6. When a *cardinal* or *bishop* dies outside the city of Rome, in his episcopal city, the cathedral canons shall provide an appropriate funeral service and burial.[60] Note that any cardinal of the Holy Roman Church, whether he was bishop of the city or diocese in which he lived, or not, is entitled to this honor.

§ 7. If a corpse is sent to a place where the deceased person neither had parish rights nor had chosen a burial place, the conduct of the funeral belongs to the cathedral church of that place; — supposing, of course, the body was shipped to the episcopal city; for if the corpse is sent to another city, the clergy of the parish in which the cemetery is located must attend to the funeral, unless custom or diocesan statutes decide otherwise.

BURIAL

Can. 1231

§ 1. Expletis in ecclesia exsequiis, cadaver tumulandum est ad normam librorum liturgicorum in coemeterio ecclesiae funeris, salvis praescriptis can. 1228, 1229.

§ 2. Qui exsequias in ecclesia peregit, non solum ius, sed etiam officium habet, excepto gravi necessitatis casu, comitandi per se vel per alium sacerdotem cadaver ad locum sepulturae.

After the exequies held in church, the body must be buried in the cemetery of the church in which the service

60 Can 397, n 3

was held, unless the burial in another cemetery or the ancestral tomb was chosen by the deceased. The officiating priest or his substitute is entitled and obliged to accompany the casket to the grave-yard. The bishop cannot issue synodal acts or diocesan statutes forbidding the officiating clergy to accompany the funeral procession. Nor may the cemetery chaplain take care of all the bodies that are brought to the cemetery. The clergy should not discriminate between rich and poor, but accompany all alike, no matter what the distance,[61] provided, of course, the cemetery belongs to the parish. Exception is made in cases of grave necessity. Such a necessity would be physical indisposition of the clergyman or perhaps a long-standing tradition against accompanying funeral processions, based on the fact that they gave rise to disturbances If the clergy does go to the grave-yard, surplice and stole, or at least the stole, should be made use of [62]

We may add that religious who have lost their convent by suppression, but continue to officiate in their former church, have the right of performing the funeral service and conducting corpses to the grave.[63]

FUNERAL PROCESSIONS

Can. 1232

§ 1. Sacerdos qui cadaver comitetur ad ecclesiam funeris vel ad locum sepulturae, libere transire poterit, cum stola quoque et cruce elevata, per territorium

---

61 S. C. C , Jan 26, 1907 (*Anal Eccl* , XV, 12 ff).

62 S C. P F., Sept. 12, 1884, ad II (n. 3619) mentions stole and surplice, but S. Rit. C , April 23, 1895, ad II (n. 3854), only refers to the stole; the latter custom is therefore admissible

63 S. C EE. et RR , May 7, Sept. 17, 1880 (*A. S S* , XIII, 409 ff.); S. Rit. C , Sept. 12, 1884 (n. 3619)

alius paroeciae vel dioecesis, etiam sine parochi vel Ordinarii licentia.

§ 2. Si cadaver tumulandum sit in coemeterio ad quod commode asportari nequeat, parochus vel rector ecclesiae funeris nequit sibi vindicare ius illud comitandi extra fines civitatis vel loci.

§ 1. The priest who conducts a body to the funeral church or the grave-yard is entitled to pass with stole and raised cross through a strange parish or diocese, without the permission of either pastor or Ordinary. The term "*cruce elevata*" is chosen in order to do away with the presumption that when passing through strange territory, the cross had to be lowered, to show subordination or at least tacit acknowledgment of the jurisdiction of the pastor through whose district the procession wended its way. This right belongs also to regulars when they conduct a funeral through strange territory.[64] The pastor has the same right, even when the cathedral chapter is present. If the funeral procession has to pass through strange territory, the shortest route should be taken,[65] in order not to provoke others or " make a show."

§ 2. The right of accompanying the body outside the city or town limits cannot be claimed in case the corpse is to be buried in a cemetery to which it cannot conveniently be transported, for in that case the whole funeral procession might easily turn into a farce.

MOURNERS AND EMBLEMS

CAN. 1233

§ 1. Nequit parochus, sine iusta et gravi causa ab

64 S. C. EE. et RR., Nov. 24, 1713 (Bizzarri, *l. c.*, p. 301); Sept. 17, 1880 (*A. S. S.*, XIII, 410).

65 S. Rit. C., April 23, 1895 (n. 3854).

Ordinario probata, excludere clericos saeculares, religiosos ac pia sodalitia quae familia vel heredes advocare velint ad deducendum cadaver ad ecclesiam funeris et ad sepulturam, et assistendum funeri; clerici tamen ipsi ecclesiae addicti a familia vel heredibus prae aliis omnibus invitari debent.

§ 2. Nunquam admittantur societates vel insignia religioni catholicae manifeste hostilia.

§ 3. Associantes cadaver tenentur morem gerere parocho circa ductum funeris, salvis uniuscuiusque praecedentiae iuribus.

§ 4. Laici cadaver, generis aut dignitatis cuiusvis ille fuerit, clerici ne deferant.

§ 1. Except for a weighty and just reason approved by the Ordinary, the pastor has no right to prevent secular or religious clerics, or pious societies whom the family or the heirs wish to invite, from accompanying the body to the church and grave-yard and assisting at the funeral. But the clergy of the respective church should be invited above all others by the family of the deceased or his heirs.

Confraternities and regulars, in particular the Friars Minor, had often to recur to the Roman Court to defend the right enunciated in our text. The pastor must consult the Ordinary to judge whether reasons for non-compliance are just and weighty. But the Ordinary has no right to issue synodal decrees forbidding either confraternities or regulars to accompany the funeral procession, if (at least implicitly) invited by the family of the deceased.[66] Even if the cathedral chapter should not have been invited, the members of a confraternity may be

---

[66] S. C. EE. et RR, Nov. 24, 1713; May 13, 1744 (Bizzarri, l. c, p. 307, 363), S. Rit. C., Aug. 18, 1629; April 22, 1633; Jan 14, 1640; Dec. 7, 1641 (nn. 516, 604, 696, 784).

called and assist.[67]   The invitation to regulars or members of a fraternity may be issued by the family or heirs without the pastor's knowledge.[68]   No definite or proportionate number of regulars, seculars and confraternity members is prescribed.[69]   Nor is it required that the secular clergy should be invited before the regulars.[70]   When the regulars are called by the family to accompany a funeral which is to take place in the cathedral church, they are allowed to enter it.[71]   These are the most important decisions rendered in this matter.   A timely admonition is that of the last clause of our section to show respect to one's own clergy.

§ 2.   No *societies* or *emblems* manifestly *inimical to the Catholic religion* are to be admitted.   Concerning the emblems of Masonic lodges — for these are here chiefly intended — the Holy Office has decided as follows: Ecclesiastical sepulture may be given only to such members of a condemned sect as have received the sacraments and have not, after receiving them, demanded to be buried with or under these insignia, or have formally retracted their desire.   If such emblems are placed on the coffin against the will of the deceased, they must be removed before the funeral starts (*ante associationem cadaveris*).[72]   The same rule applies to banners or standards.

§ 3.   Those who accompany the funeral must obey the orders of the pastor concerning the arrangement of the funeral cortège, with due regard, of course, to the rights

67 S. Rit C., June 8, 1630 (n 533).

68 S C. EE. et RR., Dec 10, 1729 (Bizzarri, *l c*, p. 340).

69 S. C EE. et RR., Nov. 24, 1713; May 13, 1744 (Bizzarri, *l. c*, pp. 301, 363).

70 S Rit. C, Nov. 22, 1643 (n 852)

71 S. C. EE. et RR., April 13, 1723 (Bizzarri, *l. c*, p 313).

72 S O, Dec 2, 1840, July 5, 1878 (*Coll. P. F.*, nn 915, 1495).

of precedence. The pastor may decide in which direction or through which streets the funeral procession should march.[73] Concerning regulars and members of confraternities, it has often been decided that they should not join the funeral procession at some corner, but should meet 'at the church and join the rest of the clergy and march together with them.[74]

As to *precedence,* the general rule is that the pastor " precedes," *i. e.,* takes the last place in the procession.[75] However, if the cathedral chapter or, where custom admits, the collegiate chapter assists in a body, it marches behind the pastor. In that case the first dignitary of the chapter should wear stole and cope, whilst the pastor wears only the stole (and surplice).[76] With regard to the rest of the clergy, secular and religious, the general rules of precedence, as laid down and explained under can. 106 and 491, must be observed.

§ 4. Clerics shall never act as pall-bearers for a defunct layman, no matter what his rank or dignity may have been. The reason is because the clerical dignity transcends every secular rank and degree.

FUNERAL FEES

CAN. 1234

§ 1. Locorum Ordinarii indicem funeralium taxarum seu eleemosynarum, si non exsistat, pro suo territorio, de consilio Capituli cathedralis, ac, si opportunum duxerint, vicariorum foraneorum dioecesis et parochorum civitatis episcopalis, conficiant, attentis legitimis consuetudinibus particularibus et omnibus

---

73 S Rit C, Dec 19, 1671, ad 5 (n. 1440)

74 S. Rit C, Sept 7, 1670; April 8, 1854 (nn. 1408, 3080).

75 S C C, May 12, 1635; May 14, 1644 (*Coll. P F*, nn. 82, 111).

76 S Rit C, April 23, 1895, ad III (n. 3854).

personarum et locorum circumstantiis; in eoque pro diversis casibus iura singulorum moderate determinent, ita ut quaelibet contentionum et scandali removeatur occasio.

§ 2. Si in indice plures classes enumerentur, liberum est iis quorum interest classem eligere.

Can. 1235

§ 1. Districte prohibetur ne quis, sepulturae vel exsequiarum seu anniversarii mortuorum causa, quidquam exigat ultra id quod in dioecesano taxarum indice statuitur.

§ 2. Pauperes gratis omnino ac decenter funerentur et sepeliantur, cum exsequiis, secundum liturgicas leges et dioecesana statuta, praescriptis.

§ 1 of can. 1234 provides that the local Ordinaries shall, each one for his own territory, draw up a list of funeral fees, if none such exists, with the advice [not consent] of the Cathedral chapter, and, if deemed advisable, with the coöperation of the rural deans and pastors of the episcopal city. In drawing up this list they shall take into account the lawful customs of the district as well as the circumstances of persons and times. The stole fees should be moderate and so determined that every occasion for quarrel and scandal is removed

§ 2. If the list contains several classes of funeral services, arranged by degrees, those interested may choose any of these.

But, says can 1235, § 1, no clergyman may demand more than is officially allowed for burial or funeral services or anniversaries.

§ 2. The poor shall by all means be given a decent funeral and burial, inclusive of the exequies, free of charge, according to the sacred liturgy and the diocesan statutes. Alexander VII and Clement X enjoined especially on the missionaries of the East Indies, that they should bury the poor gratis, and not go about among the neighbors and relatives to beg alms for this purpose.[77]

PORTIO PAROECIALIS

CAN. 1236

§ 1. Salvo iure particulari, quoties fidelis non funeratur in ecclesia paroeciali propria, proprio defuncti parocho debetur portio paroecialis, excepto casu quo cadaver in ecclesiam propriae paroeciae commode asportari nequeat.

§ 2. Si quis habeat plures paroecias proprias ad quas cadaver commode deferri posset, et alibi funeretur, portio paroecialis dividenda est inter omnes parochos proprios.

CAN. 1237

§ 1. Detrahi debet portio paroecialis ex omnibus et solis emolumentis, quae statuta sunt pro funere et tumulatione in taxa dioecesana.

§ 2. Si quacunque de causa primum sollemne officium funebre non statim, sed intra mensem completum a die tumulationis fiat, licet hoc die non defuerint minora publica officia, portio tamen paroecialis ex huius etiam funeris emolumentis debetur.

§ 3. Quantitas portionis paroecialis determinetur in taxa dioecesana; et si ecclesia paroecialis et ecclesia funerans ad diversas dioeceses pertineant, quantitas

---

77 Alexander VII, " *Sacrosancti*," Jan 18, 1658, § 2, n. 19; Clement IX," *In excelso*," Sept. 13, 1669, n. 19.

portionis paroecialis attenditur secundum taxam ecclesiae funerantis.

§ 1.   The *quarta funeris,* or pastor's portion, must be
given to the deceased's pastor if the funeral is not held in
the parish church.   There is no exception to this rule unless a particular law provides otherwise or unless the body
cannot conveniently be brought to the deceased's own
parish church.

§ 2.   If the deceased had several parish churches, to
which his body might be carried, yet is buried elsewhere,
the pastor's portion must be divided among the different pastors.

Our Code calls the portion due to the pastor *portio
paroecialis.*   Formerly it went by the name of *portio
canonica,*[78] because established by the canons, or *quarta
funeris,*[79] because one-fourth of all funeral offerings,
either in alms or candles, belonged to the *parochus proprius.*   It was justly considered meet that he who nur-
tured the deceased whilst living, should also receive his
due on the occasion of his funeral.[80]   The pastor's portion, therefore, is nothing but a material token of gratitude and respect.

The text says, *quoties, i. e.,* whenever a deceased parishioner is buried in or from a church other than his
own parish church, no matter whether he himself made
the choice or the family had him buried in the ancestral
chapel or tomb.[81]   Even the canons of cathedrals and
collegiate churches owe the *portio canonica* to their own
church within the boundaries of which they had their
domicile or quasi-domicile, though they may be buried in

78 C. 4, x, III, 28; c. 2, 6°, III,
12.
79 *Trid.* Sess. 25, c. 13, *de ref.*

80 Cfr. cc. 1, X, III, 28; c. 2,
Clem., III, 7.
81 C. 1, X, III, 28.

their own cemeteries.[82] But no pastor's portion is to be paid by male religious or nuns whose superior or confessor performs the funeral service.[83] Nor does it appear proper that female religious should pay the *quarta*, even though their members die outside the religious house. Yet the law would seem to permit the pastor to demand it, because can. 1230, § 5, provides no exception for them.

§ 2 says that if one had several parishes, all the pastors concerned are entitled to an equal share of the *portio paroecialis*. If *vagi* are buried, the *quarta* need not be paid [84]

Can 1237, § 1, determines the offerings, and the quantity of the same, from which the pastor's portion is to be deducted. *All the fees* established by synodal decree for funerals and burials are to be rated for subtracting the pastor's portion. The question is reduced to simple terms where the funeral fees are clearly fixed. Note the term for funeral and burial (*pro funere et tumulatione*). We generally include both in the name *funeral service,* to wit, the service in church and at the grave. No doubt this is the intention of the lawgiver. Hence it is not customary to make an itemized statement for the use of candles, torches, utensils, etc. Neither is the pastor's share to be deducted from the celebration of the third or seventh day, or the " month's mind." [85] Nor is any free offering which the family may make to the priest who accompanies the body to the grave, to be taxed or shared by the pastor.[86] Nor are pastors to demand a larger share if the burial

---

82 S C C, Sept 12, 1699; 1 and 22 March, 1766.

83 Cfr Many, *l c*, p 322

84 C. 2, 6°, III, 12; S. C C., Nov 29, 1851; Many, *l. c*, p. 324.

85 S Rit. C, July 24, 1638 (n. 649).

86 S. C EE. et RR, Sept 17, 1880 (*A S S.*, XIII, 421).

takes place in or from a church of regulars, than when it is held from a church in charge of secular clergy.[87]

§ 2.   If, for any reason, the solemn funeral service is held, not immediately, but within a month from the date of the burial, the pastor's share must be paid from the fees received for that solemn, though belated, service. Suppose a man dies on Sept. 1, and his body is taken either to the door of the church, or directly to the cemetery, where the grave is blessed by the priest because the civil authority for some reason or other would not permit the corpse to be taken into the church.   On Oct. 1, the exequies are held, with Mass and *absolutio ad tumbam*.   Now, if these exequies are held in a church which was not the deceased's parish church, and by a priest who was not his pastor, and the regular stole fee is paid, the pastor would be entitled to his share[88]   But the stole fee was supposed to have been offered only for the solemn function, which means not a sung Mass, but the funeral service, with either low or high Mass, and the absolution or *Libera*.   For *minor* services, such as accompanying the body to the grave and blessing it, or even a private Mass, are not liable to the *portio paroecialis*.   The meaning of the text, therefore, is that the pastor is entitled to his share of the fees even if the full funeral service is held a month from the date of burial.

§ 4.   The *quantity of the pastor's portion* should be determined by the synodal tax.   If the parish church and the funeral church are different and belong to different dioceses, the *portio poroecialis* must be refunded according to the tax established in the funeral church.

It may not be amiss to add here a decision which is

[87] S. C. C, April 3, 1745 (Richter, *l c*, 463, n 27).
[88] S. C. C, July 29, 1905; Feb. 23, 1907 (*Anal Eccl.*, XII, 330; XV, 58 ff.).

very appropriate, and we dare say, very reasonable. It is to the effect that where there is an immemorable custom between parish churches of not demanding the *quarta funeris,* it should be observed.[89]   This permits us to say that the Code is not against such a custom, as is evident from the clause placed in § 1, can. 1236: "*salvo iure particulari,*" and we believe it would be conducive to peace and charity if this *quarta funeris* would be relaxed, especially with regard to religious, because they, too, work for the benefit of the diocese and religion in general and help the secular clergy.

RECORDING OF DEATHS

CAN. 1238

Expleta tumulatione, minister in libro defunctorum describat nomen et aetatem defuncti, nomen parentum vel coniugis, tempus mortis, quis et quae Sacramenta ministraverit, locum et tempus tumulationis.

After the funeral services the minister shall enter in the book of the dead the name and age of the deceased, the name of the parents or consort, the date of death, who administered the Sacraments, what Sacraments, and the place and date of the funeral.[90]

---

[89] S   C   C., Feb   9,   1732 (Richter, *l. c.,* p. 463, n. 28)

[90] The   formula   in   the   *Rituale Rom.,* tit. X, c. 2, n. 7.

CHAPTER III

ECCLESIASTICAL BURIAL, TO WHOM GRANTED OR DENIED

TO WHOM GRANTED

CAN. 1239

§ 1.   Ad sepulturam ecclesiasticam non sunt admit‑
tendi qui sine baptismo decesserint.

§ 2.   Catechumeni qui nulla sua culpa sine baptismo
moriantur, baptizatis accensendi sunt.

§ 3.   Omnes baptizati sepultura ecclesiastica do‑
nandi sunt, nisi eadem a iure expresse priventur.

§ 1.   Baptism, being the Sacrament of initiation and
sign of communion with the Church and membership in
the same, is the fundamental condition of receiving a
Catholic burial.   Baptism may be received by desire —
baptismus flaminis — and this is generally supposed in
those who had received instructions in the faith (catechu‑
mens).   Hence our canon in its first section states that *no
person who has died without Baptism* may be admitted to
ecclesiastical burial.   This includes even unbaptized in‑
fants, though it is generally admitted that a child not yet
born may be buried together with the mother in conse‑
crated ground.[1]   Besides, it appears, at least to many,
very awkward and offensive if this law should be applied
to burial in the ancestral grave.   Yet, unless non-compli-

---

1 Cfr. Many, *l. c.,* p 353

ance must be tolerated in order to avoid greater evils, the law should be enforced.[2]

§ 2. *Catechumens,* or such as are preparing to embrace the Catholic faith, may be given ecclesiastical burial, if they have died without baptism through no fault of their own. For they are to be compared to baptized persons.[3] Thus if a would-be convert would die suddenly, with no priest at hand, as may happen in places which missionaries seldom visit, he could receive ecclesiastical burial.

§ 3 says that, although one may be baptized, he must be *deprived of ecclesiastical burial if he has been expressly declared worthy of that penalty in law.* For ecclesiastical burial is a sign of honor and respect given by the Church to her dead children, and a consolation and favor to the living   Denial of that favor must be looked upon as a *post mortem* penalty for the dead, and a warning to the living.

However, being a penalty, the denial of ecclesiastical burial must be strictly interpreted, and not extended beyond the cases stated in the law. These now follow.

TO WHOM ECCLESIASTICAL BURIAL MUST BE DENIED

CAN. 1240

§ 1. Ecclesiastica sepultura privantur, nisi ante mortem aliqua dederint poenitentiae signa:

1.° Notorii apostatae a christiana fide, aut sectae haereticae vel schismaticae aut sectae massonicae aliisve eiusdem generis societatibus notorie addicti;

---

[2] S O., Jan. 4, 1888, where n. 389 of Conc Balt II is explained as mere tolerance *ad praecavenda maiora mala;* S. O , March 30, 1859 (*Coll P. F.,* n. 1173).
[3] Cfr c 2, x, III, 43

2.° Excommunicati vel interdicti post sententiam condemnatoriam vel declaratoriam;

3.° Qui se ipsi occiderint deliberato consilio;

4.° Mortui in duello aut ex vulnere inde relato;

5.° Qui mandaverint suum corpus cremationi tradi;

6.° Alii peccatores publici et manifesti.

§ 2. Occurrente praedictis in casibus aliquo dubio, consulatur, si tempus sinat, Ordinarius; permanente dubio, cadaver sepulturae ecclesiasticae tradatur, ita tamen ut removeatur scandalum.

§ 1. Unless they have given signs of repentance before death, the following are deprived of ecclesiastical burial:

1.° *Notorious apostates from the Christian faith and persons who notoriously belonged to a heretical or schismatical sect, or to the Masonic sect, or to other societies of the same kind.*

The term *apostates* evidently includes pagans and Jews as well as infidels or unbelievers who have fallen away from the Christian faith and whose defection is notorious. A Catholic who was an unbeliever, but not known as such to others, because he kept his unbelief to himself, or expressed himself only to the one or other friend, who kept the secret, could be buried ecclesiastically. For notoriety implies public knowledge, or such as could not be concealed by any artifice.[4]

Heretics and schismatics are those who have pertinaciously forsaken the Catholic faith or abjured obedience to the Pope.[5] Heresy and schism, too, must be notorious to have the effect here under consideration. What was said of apostates applies also to heretics and schismatics.

4 Can 2197, 30; Cfr. c 12, x, III, 28.
5 Can. 1325, § 2.

Thus a non-Catholic may be taken for a Catholic, because he acts like one, although he is not convinced of the truth of every Catholic dogma. Such a one might be given ecclesiastical burial, provided, of course, that his heresy was not notorious and he desired such a burial. The reason lies in the fact that by Baptism he belonged to the body of the Church, and in his mind may even have belonged to the soul of the Church.

The next class is that of members of *Masonic sects*. The adjective "*damnatae*" being omitted, it appears that *all* Masonic rites are included. *Eiusdem generis* means all societies whose principal purpose is to promote cremation,[6] or which have tendencies similar to those of Freemasonry.

What is to be done if the relatives or friends of such a person insist upon his receiving ecclesiastical burial? If the priest was called and found the patient unconscious or speechless, the relatives or friends must tell the priest that the sick man had desired to see a priest and gave signs of repentance.[7] Besides, the body of the deceased must not be carried into the Masonic hall or temple. If this was desired by the deceased himself, ecclesiastical burial must be denied, but if the Masons carry the coffin against the will of the defunct, ecclesiastical burial may be granted.[8]

2.° Persons *excommunicated and interdicted after a condemnatory or declaratory sentence*. The text requires that a sentence of excommunication or interdict has been pronounced. Whether this sentence be one declaring that the person had *de facto* incurred excommunication, or one directly inflicted by the ecclesiastical judge, is of no

6 S O , Dec. 15, 1886 (*Coll P.   8 S. O., Aug. 1, 1855 (*ibid.*, n.
F , n. 1665)   1116).
7 S O , Sept 19, 1877 (*ibid ,
n. 1483)

importance. It is also immaterial whether the *excommunicatus* be *vitandus* or only *tolerandus*. Stress, however, is laid on the sentence.[9] The *interdict* is here to be understood of the personal interdict, which requires a declaratory or condemnatory sentence and is generally accompanied by a personal sentence.[10]

3.° *Those who have deliberately killed themselves.* As a rule, says the Holy Office,[11] those who commit suicide from despair or in wrath (*desperatione vel iracundia*) cannot be given ecclesiastical burial. But when insanity has been proved, or was evident, and attested by the verdict of a conscientious physician, ecclesiastical sepulture is permitted with all its ceremonies. When there is a doubt as to the suicide's mental state, ecclesiastical burial may be granted, but all pomp and solemn exequies must be avoided. This would mean that the funeral service may be held from the church, but that the Requiem Mass should be omitted, as well as preaching, for this is certainly a species of "pomp." A private Mass may be said.

4.° *Those who died in a duel or from a wound received in a duel.* The term duel (*duellum, monomachia*) signifies a contest with deadly weapons which takes place by agreement between two persons on account of some private quarrel.[12] Hence our prize-fights, in which no deadly weapons are used, and bull-fights, cannot be styled duels. It is otherwise with the so-called "*Mensuren*" of students and officers, as practiced chiefly in Austria and Germany.[13] This "detestable custom," as it

9 "*Ad evitanda,*" of Martin V, 1418, cannot be interpreted, as Many does (*l. c., p.* 354), so as to admit *tolerandi;* see can 2259 f.

10 C. 1, Clem. III, 7

11 S O, May 16, 1866 (*Coll P F,* n. 1290).

12 Cfr *Cath. Encycl.,* V, 184 ff.

13 S C C, Aug 9, 1890 (*Coll. P. F.,* n. 1739).

is called by the Council of Trent and Benedict XIV,[14] was and still is wide-spread, especially in Teutonic countries, where it also had its origin in pagan times. The Church tried to eradicate this savage custom and inflicted severe penalties on the perpetrators.[15] One of these is precisely the denial of ecclesiastical burial.

Our text says that only those who died in the act of duelling, or from a wound received in a duel, are to be deprived of ecclesiastical burial. Benedict XIV, in a well-known Constitution, uses a similar expression: "*a decedente quoque extra conflictus locum ex vulnere ibidem accepto.*" Therefore a connection between cause and effect must be maintained. In other words, the wound received in a duel must be the cause of death. And it seems that a *direct* cause is required, for it may be that a wound received in a duel causes some other disease, after a time, and in this case we hardly believe that the penalty could be sustained.

5.° *Those who ordered their body to be cremated.* Of this enough has been said under can. 1203, § 2. Such persons must have retracted their order before death, otherwise they cannot receive ecclesiastical burial.

6.° *Other public and manifest sinners.* This phrase is rather wide, but may be contracted to a few categories in the light of former legislation. By sin must here be understood a *delictum publicum,* or crime, which is such intrinsically as well as in the eyes of sensible persons. To this class belong: (a) manifest and public *usurers and robbers,* unless they have made restitution;[16] public profiteers and bank or train robbers; (b) those who ac-

---

14 Sess 25, c. 19, *de ref* ; Bened. XIV, "*Detestabilem,*" Nov. 10, 1752.

15 Cfr. cc. 1, 2, x, V, 13; Gregory XIII "*Ad tollendum,*" Dec.

5, 1582; Clement VIII, "*Illius vices,*" Aug. 17, 1592.

16 Cfr cc 3, 5, x, V, 19; c. 2, x, V, 17; c. 2, 6°, V, 5.

tually *live a sinful and scandalous life, e. g.,* in public concubinage, or conduct a notoriously meretricious trade, or panderage;[17] (c) those who have *habitually violated the precepts of annual confession and communion.* As to the last-named class of persons the Roman Ritual[18] says that their fault must be evident, which means that they must have omitted their Easter duty for several years and be known to the faithful as having been guilty of serious neglect.[19]

Note that all the persons mentioned under n. 1–6 are deprived of ecclesiastical burial only if they *have given no signs of repentance.* If they have given such signs, they may be buried like faithful Catholics, because it is the desire of the Church that all should return to God's grace by contrition and be restored to communion with the mystic body of Christ.[20]

Signs of repentance would be kissing the crucifix, acts of devotion, oral prayers, etc. But these signs, especially in case of public sinners, must be known and divulged to the bystanders and the faithful. If this has been done, ecclesiastical burial may be given; but if possible, pomp and solemn exequies should be omitted.[21]

Benedict XIV excluded duellists from ecclesiastical burial, even when they had given certain signs of penance.[22] This too rigorous clause has been softened in our code, as is manifest from the position of the phrase, "*nisi ante mortem aliqua dederint signa poenitentiae.*"

§ 2. It may be in the six cases mentioned that the pastor has a doubt, for instance, concerning a suicide, or a wound received in a duel, whether it was the direct cause

---

17 Cfr. Many, *l c*, p 361
18 Tit. II, c. 2, n 6, c 12, x, V, 38.
19 Many, *l. c*, p 360

20 S O, Aug 1, 1855 (*Coll. P. F* n. 1116).
21 S. O, July 6, 1898 *ibid*. n. 2007).
22 "*Detestabilem,*" § 9.

of death. If time permits, he should inform the Ordinary and abide by his decision.[23] If the doubt remains even after the pastor has been advised by the Ordinary, ecclesiastical burial may be granted, provided no scandal is given. Scandal may be removed by divulging the fact that the deceased gave public signs of repentance, or that, for instance, the suicide was committed in a moment of mental aberration according to the physician's verdict.

CAN. 1241

Excluso ab ecclesiastica sepultura deneganda quoque sunt tum quaelibet Missa exsequialis, etiam anniversaria, tum alia publica officia funebria.

For those who have been deprived of ecclesiastical burial no [public] Requiem Mass, no anniversary, or other public funeral service may be held.

We enclose the word "public" within brackets, but it no doubt expresses the intention of the legislator. For private Masses may be said for any of the persons mentioned under n. 1–6, provided there be no *communicatio in sacris*. Thus it has been decided that a private Mass may be said for one who ordered his body to be cremated.[24] In cases of doubt the Ordinary, who has to be consulted in the matter, may grant permission to have solemn funeral services if he deems it expedient.[25]

23 S. O, July 6, 1898 (*l c*); Sept. 19, 1877 (*l c*, n 1483)
24 S. O, July 27, 1892 ad II (*Coll. P. F*, n 1808).
25 S. O, Sept. 19, 1877; Dec. 15, 1886; July 6, 1898 (*ibid*, nn. 1483, 1665, 2007).

EXHUMATION OF CORPSES

Can. 1242

Si fieri sine gravi incommodo queat, cadaver excommunicati vitandi qui, contra canonum statuta, sepulturam in loco sacro obtinuit, exhumandum est, servato
praescripto can. 1214, § 1, et in loco profano de quo in
can. 1212, reponendum. *[block - said ———— -]*

If it can be done without great inconvenience, the body
of an *excommunicatus vitandus*, who obtained burial in
sacred ground against the law, should be exhumed, with
the permission of the bishop,[26] and be buried in a lot
especially assigned for that purpose.[27]

26 Can. 1214, § 1
27 Can. 1212; see c 12, x, III, 28.

SECTION II

HOLY SEASONS

Can. 1243

Tempora sacra sunt dies festi; iisque accensentur dies abstinentiae et ieiunii.

Holy seasons are feastdays; to them must be added days of abstinence and fast.

Already in remote antiquity civilized people found a call to the worship of God in the changing seasons. Sacred times and places are common to all religions. The change of seasons, bringing with it changes in nature, made a religious impression upon mankind. Man sanctified certain seasons and dedicated them to God. The days thus consecrated to God were known as festivals. They were marked by two features: rest from labor or worldly affairs, and consecration to the worship of God. The first was expressed in the ancient Roman term *feria*. Both ideas are contained in the Hebrew word *sabbath*, which means a day of rest and sanctification. The Church did not at first change the Sabbath of the Jewish calendar, at least we have no evidence thereof. But gradually the *prima sabbati* or first day of the Jewish week commenced to be held in honor as the day of the resurrection of Christ and was called the Lord's Day [1] (*dies dominica*). Besides these weekly recurring festivals there were others to commemorate the chief events

1 Cfr Apoc. 1, 10.

in the life of the Lord. Among these in the order of time, Easter holds the first place. Gradually were developed all the feasts as we have them now, forming that rich and carefully thought out system of feasts which is proper to the Catholic Church.[2] The old Canon Law contains two lists of festivals, the one presenting the state of things in the twelfth,[3] the other that in the thirteenth century.[4] In the course of centuries the number of feasts increased, so much so, in fact that their multitude led to a reaction on the part not only of civil governments but also of bishops. Pope Urban VIII revised the list.[5] The present arrangement was made by Pius X.[6]

As to days of *fast and abstinence* it must be said that the fast before Easter seems to be the most ancient of all. But its duration varied according to localities. Some fasted one day, others two, and yet others many days, whilst some simply observed a fast of forty hours. The *forty days' fast* became the rule at Rome in the seventh century, and was soon adopted throughout the West, except at Milan In the eighth and ninth centuries an increase took place in the number of fasting vigils, nearly all the feasts, especially those of the Apostles,[7] obtaining the dignity of a vigil. The *embertides* were said to be of Apostolic origin by Leo the Great, but there is no document testifying to the *feriae* observed as embertides earlier than the *Liber Pontificalis*.[8] There were originally three. In St. Leo's day four embertides were observed. The present arrangement was made by Gregory VII and is distinctly Roman [9]

[2] See Kellner, *Heortology* (Eng tr.) 1918, Introduction.

[3] C. 1, Dist 3 *de cons*

[4] C. 5, X, II, 9 *de feriis*.

[5] "*Universa*," Sept. 13, 1642.

[6] Motu proprio "*Supremi disciplinae*," July 2, 1911.

[7] Funk, *Manual of Church History*, 1913, Vol. I, pp 74, 296 f.; II, 164.

[8] *Liber Pontificalis*, ed. Duchesne, I, 141.

[9] Kellner, *l. c*, p. 183 ff.

CAN. 1244

§ 1. Dies festos itemque dies abstinentiae et ieiunii, universae Ecclesiae communes, constituere, transferre, abolere, unius est supremae ecclesiasticae auctoritatis.

§ 2. Ordinarii locorum peculiares suis diœcesibus seu locis dies festos aut dies abstinentiae et ieiunii possunt, per modum tantum actus, indicere.

The *supreme authority of the Church* alone can establish, transfer, or abolish holydays as well as days of abstinence and fasting. This rule, as may be seen from the historical note, was impressed upon the Christian people ever since the Council of Trent[10] Hence not even a chapter, be it cathedral or collegiate, can impose a holyday of obligation not observed by the Roman Church, whereas the feastdays appointed by the latter oblige everywhere,[11] unless, of course, otherwise provided. Nor can a synod or *conciliabulum* transfer movable feasts to a Sunday.[12]

But the *local Ordinaries* may, *per modum tantum actus* (i. e., for a transient reason and for the time being, but not forever or habitually), prescribe the observance of a feastday or of a day of fast and abstinence. Thus, for instance, the Ordinary is not entitled to establish the feast of the patron saint of the main or episcopal city as a holyday of obligation for the whole diocese.[13] Nor can the Ordinary make a feastday which is *ex voto* obligatory for an exempt religious community, *de praecepto* for them if the feast is not found in the list of feasts of obli-

10 Urban VIII, " *Universa*," Sept. 13, 1642, § 3 (*Dec. Auth*, n. 812).

11 S. Rit C., June 8, 1630 (n. 535)

12 *Prop. 74 damn. per " Auctorem*

fidei," Aug 28, 1794 (Denzinger, n. 1437).

13 S. Rit. C., Aug. 18, 1725 (n. 2277).

gation prescribed for the universal Church. Feasts which have been introduced by exempt religious by reason of a vow oblige only the persons bound by the latter.[14] Of course, since the vow of a community lasts as long as the community itself who made the vow, these feasts must be observed that long; as to later generations see can. 1310.

It may not be superfluous to add that our text mentions *local* Ordinaries, which term does not include religious superiors. The latter are, therefore, not entitled to impose a feastday upon their communities   The vow mentioned in the last paragraph concerns the community as such.

DISPENSATIONS

CAN. 1245

§ 1. Non solum Ordinarii locorum, sed etiam parochi, in casibus singularibus iustaque de causa, possunt subjectos sibi singulos fideles singulasve familias, etiam extra territorium, atque in suo territorio etiam peregrinos, a lege communi de observantia festorum itemque de observantia abstinentiae et ieiunii vel etiam utriusque dispensare.

§ 2. Ordinarii, ex causa peculiari magni populi concursus aut publicae valetudinis, possunt totam quoque dioecesim seu locum a ieiunio et ab abstinentia vel etiam ab utraque simul lege dispensare.

§ 3. In religione clericali exempta eandem dispensandi potestatem habent Superiores ad modum parochi, quod attinet ad personas, de quibus in can, 514, § 1.

§ 1.   Not only the local *Ordinaries,* but also pastors, may in individual cases and for a just cause dispense their

---

14 S. Rit. C., June 23, 1703 (n., 2113).

subjects from the common law of keeping feasts and from
the observance of abstinence and fast, or from both fast
and abstinence at the same time. Ordinaries could always dispense in certain circumstances and cases by law,[15]
but the right of the pastor to dispense rested on custom [16]
rather than on written law. Now it has become part of
the general law. But in order to act licitly, they must
observe the conditions laid down in this canon, which is
partly a repetition of the old law.

a) They can dispense only in *individual cases* as they
occur. Hence Ordinaries cannot issue synodal acts dispensing persons and families from the common law, or
grant a habitual dispensation. Each case stands for itself
and none can establish a precedent; [17] each must be examined like a physician makes his diagnosis.

b) They may dispense only *single individuals* and *single families subject* to their jurisdiction by reason either
of domicile or quasi-domicile, or by actual residence in the
territory over which their jurisdiction extends. Subjects
by reason of domicile or quasi-domicile may make use of
such a dispensation also outside of the territory of the
grantor. But *peregrini* or transient residents are benefited by the dispensation only as long as they reside in the
district of the grantor.

c) Finally there must be a *just reason* for dispensing,
since every dispensation involves a violation of the common law. Such a cause would be sickness [18] and impossibility of obtaining abstinence food, although the higher
cost of such was not deemed a sufficient reason by Benedict XIV.[19] The climate, the nature of one's work, and

---

15 Urban VIII, " *Universa*," § 3.
16 Cfr. Putzer, *Comment. in
Facult Apost* , p 36, n 24.
17 *Reg Iuris 28* in 6° This is
called " *toties quoties opus fuerit*

concedenda " by Bened. XIV, " *Non
ambigimus*," May 30, 1741, § 3
18 C 2, X, III, 46
19 " *Libentissime*," June 10, 1745,
§ 18.

physical debility must be taken into consideration. The grantor himself is the judge of the sufficiency of the reasons advanced.[20]

§ 2. The Ordinaries may, because of a great concourse of people, or for reasons of public health, also dispense the *whole diocese* or any place therein from the law of fasting and abstinence, or from both combined. This liberal concession renders special faculties (not particular indults; see can. 1253) superfluous. What is meant by a *great concourse of people* has been authentically explained by the Holy Office.[21] It is not necessary that people from other towns or cities are present, but a multitude of inhabitants of the same city or town assembled for an occasion suffices. Of course, the occasion should be Catholic and religious, for instance, a centenary, a pilgrimage, a large meeting of Catholic societies, etc. As our county and State fairs offer a serious occasion for violating the law of fast and abstinence, such a one would constitute a sufficient reason for dispensing the participants. Our Code is not against this authentic interpretation, for it simply says: a great concourse of people. The danger of violating the law must be general, which is often the case on great festivals.

We may add that another decision of the Holy Office[22] requires for a dispensation from the law of abstinence on a holyday proper, that the abstinence be anticipated. The Code is silent about anticipation, and therefore this rule may be considered as abolished. It was, in fact, already abrogated by decree of the S. C. C., which directed the Ordinaries to make ample use of dispensation for the

20 S. C. P. F., Aug. 2, 1781 (*Coll.,* n. 548).

21 S. O., March 28, 1896 (*Coll., P. F.,* n. 1922).

22 S. O., Dec. 5, 1894 (*ibid.,* n. 1884), where *nundinae* (fairs), are especially mentioned.

holydays suppressed by Pius X, without mentioning anticipation at all.[23]

The other reason mentioned in § 2 of can. 1245 is the *public health*. An example which recalls the influenza is given by Benedict XIV in his Constitution *"Libentissime."* The disease, to justify a dispensation, must affect the people or territory, not merely a few individuals, in other words, it must be epidemic, as is explained in the same Constitution. Benedict XIV requires the testimony of physicians to verify the existence of an epidemic. The local or State Board of Health would be the proper adviser in our country.[24]

Note that these are the only two general cases in which the Ordinaries may grant a general dispensation: a great concourse of people and reasons of public health. Beyond those they should not stretch the power now granted to them by the common law, which was formerly given only in the form of a "faculty" with the significant clause: *"non tamen per generale indultum, sed in casibus particularibus."* [25] The Code has removed this restriction, but, as stated above, only for two general reasons, which cannot be extended at random.

It may be asked: *How far does the power of dispensing* in individual as well as in general cases *extend?* Benedict XIV, in three Constitutions,[26] drew certain limits, to wit, (a) that only one full meal of flesh meat could be taken a day; (b) that no mixing of meat and fish was permitted; (c) that the meal hours be not inverted, e. g., dinner substituted for supper or lunch and

---

23 May 3, 1912 (*A. Ap S.*, IV, 341).

24 June 10, 1745, § 23, *inflammatio pectoris*, which was raging in 1730, 1733, 1740.

25 S O., March 17, 1883 (*Coll.*

P. F., n. 1594), Facult I, art. 27 (Putzer, *l c*, p 292, n 169).

26 "*Non ambigimus,*" May 30, 1741; "*In suprema,*" Aug. 22, 1741; "*Libentissime,*" June 10, 1745.

vice versa. Restrictions (b) and (c) are certainly removed by can. 1251, § 2. But how about the *unica comestio,* upon which Benedict XIV insisted so emphatically? The difficulty may be solved, not by recourse to special faculties, which have ceased *in foro externo* since the decree of April 25, 1918, but by interpretation   The Code grants the ordinaries power to dispense from both fasting and abstinence.   Hence the petitioner must clearly state the extent of his demand, and if the grantor fulfils his wishes to their full extent, there can be no doubt that the petitioner may eat fleshmeat more than once a day. Everything, therefore, depends upon the tenor of the dispensation.   The grantor can restrict the use of flesh meat to one meal a day; see can. 1251.

§ 3. *Religious superiors of exempt clerical institutes enjoy the same powers as pastors with regard to all the persons mentioned in can. 514, §1.* A difficulty may perhaps arise from can. 1253, which says that by these canons nothing is changed in the constitutions and rules of the various religious organizations. Elsewhere [27] we have stated that exempt superiors may dispense the whole community from fasting and abstinence. This statement must be restricted to the days prescribed by the rule or constitutions, since the religious superior of exempt institutes can dispense only *ad modum parochi, i. e.,* like a pastor, and a pastor can dispense only single individuals and families. Hence the superior cannot dispense the whole community as such from the duty of fasting or abstinence as prescribed by the common law.   However, provided no vow is involved, we believe that the exempt superiors may, in urgent cases, unless the constitutions expressly forbid it, dispense the whole community by

[27] Vol. III, p. 300, of this Commentary

virtue of § 2, can. 1245, for reasons of public health. For the text simply says " ordinaries," and this term includes the exempt religious superiors. The diocesan Ordinary could not grant that dispensation to exempt religious by reason of exemption, and why exempt religious should be worse off in such extraordinary circumstances than other people is not easily intelligible. *Religious* who are employed *in the missions,* even as prefects apostolic, and are entitled to dispense their subjects from the law of fasting and abstinence, must apply to their superiors for a dispensation.[28]   However, this applies only to exempt religious; for non-exempt religious, as well as exempt religious belonging to lay institutes, the competent superior is the local Ordinary.   Besides, it is evident that exempt religious who are vicars apostolic or bishops, are not bound to apply to their religious superiors for dispensation.   To do so would contravene can. 627, § 2, and be unworthy of their rank.   But the rule applies to exempt religious who are pastors or assistants (curates), who, therefore, must have recourse to their superiors, either local or higher, according to the constitutions, in order to obtain a dispensation from fasting and abstinence which they themselves need, though, as pastors, they may by law dispense single individuals or families without having recourse to their superiors.

RECKONING OF FEASTS AND FAST DAYS

CAN. 1246

Supputatio diei festi, itemque diei abstinentiae et ieiunii, facienda est a media nocte usque ad mediam noctem, salvo praescripto can. 923.

28 S O , April 12, 1742 (*Coll P F.,* n. 337).

Feastdays as well as the days of fasting and abstinence run from midnight to midnight, *i. e.,* twenty-four hours, counting from midnight to twelve o'clock of the following night, according to the time in vogue at the time of cele- bration. If the new time has been adopted, this is to be followed; if the old time was retained, it may be taken as standard. The time for gaining indulgences is regu- lated in can. 923.

TITLE XIII

HOLY-DAYS

CAN. 1247

§ 1. Dies festi sub praecepto in universa Ecclesia sunt tantum: Omnes et singuli dies dominici, festa Nativitatis, Circumcisionis, Epiphaniae, Ascensionis et sanctissimi Corporis Christi, Immaculatae Conceptionis et Assumptionis Almae Genitricis Dei Mariae, sancti Ioseph eius sponsi, Beatorum Petri et Pauli Apostolorum, Omnium denique Sanctorum.

§ 2. Ecclesiastico praecepto dies festi Patronorum non subiacent; locorum autem Ordinarii possunt sollemnitatem exteriorem transferre ad dominicam proxime sequentem.

§ 3. Sicubi aliquod festum ex enumeratis legitime sit abolitum vel translatum, nihil inconsulta Sede Apostolica innovetur.

§ 1. *Feastdays of obligation for the universal Church are:* All Sundays; Christmas (Dec. 25th); the Circumcision of our Lord (New Year's Day, Jan. 1st); Epiphany (Jan. 6th); the Ascension of Our Lord; Corpus Christi (Thursday after Trinity Sunday); the Immaculate Conception of the B. V. M. (Dec. 8th); the Assumption of the B. V. M. (Aug. 15th); St. Joseph's day (March 19th); the festival of SS. Peter and Paul (June 29th), and All Saints' Day (Nov. 1st).

The holy-days of obligation for the universal Church, therefore, are ten in number, and no Ordinary or religious community may introduce others with equal obligation for all the faithful.

Hence § 2 provides that the patron feast of a diocese, or city, or town does not oblige by ecclesiastical precept, though the Ordinaries may transfer the external celebration of the same to the following Sunday.

The custom of calling a church after a saint, or dedicating it to his honor, grew out of the old *martyria*. The faithful were wont to observe the feast of a prominent martyr as a general festival, whether it fell on a weekday or on a Sunday. In the ninth century diocesan statutes command this celebration. But the obligation of celebrating the festivals of patron saints was not imposed by the decretal of Gregory IX. Urban VIII, in his Constitution " *Universa*," of Sept. 13, 1642, directed that the feast of the principal patron of every kingdom, province, city or town be observed as a holyday of obligation. The people at large were not pleased with the sweeping innovation caused by the French revolution, and consoled themselves by transferring the abrogated holydays to the following Sunday.[1] This transfer is permitted by the Code as far as the external celebration is concerned; the *officium chori* must be celebrated on the proper or occurring day, but the *officium fori,* or the celebration with solemn Mass and ceremonies, decoration of the Saint's picture, etc., may be transferred to a Sunday.

§ 3. If any of the above named (ten) holydays (of obligation) has been anywhere abolished or transferred, nothing shall be changed without the advice of the Apostolic See.

[1] See Kellner, *Heortology*, p. 194 ff.

In the United States, under a decree of the S. C. Propaganda Fide of Nov. 25, 1885, there are *six* holydays of obligation, namely, the feast of the Immaculate Conception, Christmas, New Year's Day (the Circumcision), the Ascension, the Assumption of the B. V. M., and All Saints' Day.[2]

In *Canada* the provincial council of Quebec (1854) asked for an arrangement of feasts similar to that made for the United States. The S Congregation answered affirmatively, but commanded to retain the feast of the Epiphany and to omit the Assumption.[3] Hence they, too, have six holydays of obligation; but instead of the Assumption they observe Epiphany.

On the islands of *Trinidad* and *Dominica* (dioceses of Port of Spain and Roseau, or Charlottetown) the feasts of the Assumption and of SS. Peter and Paul are transferred to the following Sunday, but the office and ceremonies must be held on the day proper.[4]

These examples may suffice to interpret the meaning of § 3, can. 1247.

OBLIGATIONS CONNECTED WITH HOLYDAYS

CAN. 1248

Festis de praecepto diebus Missa audienda est; et abstinendum ab operibus servilibus, actibus forensibus, itemque, nisi aliud ferant legitimae consuetudines aut peculiaria indulta, publico mercatu, nundinis, aliisque emptionibus et venditionibus.

---

2 Cfr. *Acta et Decreta Conc. Balt. III*, 1886, p. CV f.

3 S C. P. F., May 25, 1855 (*Coll. Lac.*, III, 614, 664).

4 S C. P. F., March 1, 1868 (*Coll.*

Lac, III, 1112, 1116). Regarding other English-speaking countries, Great Britain, Ireland, etc., we could find nothing special

As stated in the historical note, every holyday of obligation is a day of rest and worship. Hence on these days *Mass must be heard.* This obligation obliges all the faithful of the Latin Church and the inhabitants of China and other missionary countries under the S. C. P. F.[5] The obligation is grievous, binding under mortal sin. One does not comply with this precept by hearing two or even four parts of Masses said simultaneously by different priests.[6] It may not be amiss to set forth here what the S. C. P. F. answered the Vicar Apostolic of Ueskub in Servia; for it has a general bearing. Not only distance, but also the condition of roads, as well as age, sex, and mental attitude of the faithful must be taken into consideration where there is question of excusing them from the obligation of attending Mass on holydays of obligation. If going to church would cause a great inconvenience, one may be freed from the duty; but if the distance is not great, or the fatigue would be but small, the obligation does not cease.[7] The decision refers to the theories of the moralists, who may therefore be consulted.[8]

The second obligation is to *abstain from servile work,* including all kinds of forensic acts (unless lawful custom or a particular indult permits them), the holding of public markets, fairs, sales, etc. *Servile works* are such as are performed by the bodily faculties and destined chiefly for the use and support of the body. Some think that the element of slavery or drudgery might have been added.[9] But now-a-days there is no reason why this ele-

5 S. O., March 23, 1656 ad 1; Nov. 13, 1669; S. C. P. F., Sept. 12, 1645 (*Coll.*, nn. 126, 189, 114).

6 S. O., propp. 52, 53 damn., March 4, 1679 (Denzinger, n. 1069 f.).

7 S. C. P. F., Sept. 26, 1840, dub. 16 (*Coll.*, n. 914).

8 See Sabetti-Barrett, *Theol. Moralis*, ed. 27a, 1919, p. 240, n. 240 ff.

9 Thus most moralists (see Sabetti-Barrett, *l. c.*, n. 252, p. 248). The ancient Roman idea that such menial labors were performed only by slaves had its influence upon theologians.

ment should be introduced into the definition of servile work. Farm work, such as ploughing, planting, harvesting, is certainly servile; but a farmer would object to being called a slave or mercenary. The same is true of professional labors.

Forensic acts are all trials held in civil as well as criminal (even ecclesiastical) courts and the routine business of administration conducted therein. Extraordinary and urgent acts of administration may be excepted. The term _forensic,_ at least in ecclesiastical language, also includes military operations.[10] This does not mean that the cleaning of barracks and polishing of arms or an hour of gymnastic exercise could not be permitted or at least tolerated. _Public markets and fairs_ or sales, for instance, of stock or produce, are not allowed by the civil law in our country, and a check issued on a Sunday is invalid. Benedict XIV had to deal chiefly with Italians, who were and still are wont to hold fairs (_fiere_) on holydays. These fairs were more leniently dealt with than public markets, which the Pope forbade.[11] Hence the clause: " unless lawful custom and special indults permit." There is nothing in the text which would forbid _baseball or athletic games or sports._ Neither can the Constitution of Benedict XIV be invoked against them,[12] for it forbids such games and plays — our " movie " shows would perhaps deserve a severer censure [13] for the reason of indecency and lasciviousness. Athletic games, if properly conducted, _i. e.,_ with due regard to Christian modesty, belong rather to the liberal arts and cannot be condemned. The S. Congregation has instructed missionaries to be

10 S. C. EE et RR , Dec. 14, 1674 (Bizzarri, _l. c_ , p 272): " _militaribus praesidus aliisque forensibus._"

11 " _Paternae charitatis,_" Aug. 24, 1744; " _Ab eo tempore,_" Nov. 5, 1745.

12 " _Nihil profecto,_" Aug. 12, 1742.

13 See Koch-Preuss, _Moral Theology,_ Vol III, St Louis, 1919, pp. 52 sqq.

more lenient towards servants and bakers who have to work on holydays and therefore can not assist at Mass.[14] Equal leniency is admissible for workingmen engaged in the service of public utilities, such as railroads, fire departments, light, power, and heat plants, etc.[15]

WHERE MASS MAY BE HEARD

CAN. 1249

Legi de audiendo Sacro satisfacit qui Missae adest quocunque catholico ritu celebretur sub dio aut in quacunque ecclesia vel oratorio publico aut semi-publico et in privatis coemeteriorum aediculis de quibus in can. 1190, non vero in aliis oratoriis privatis, nisi hoc privilegium a Sede Apostolica concessum fuerit.

The law of hearing Mass may be complied with by attending a Mass said in any Catholic rite. (Latin, Greek, Syriac, Coptic, or Armenian). Hence Ordinaries or priests are not allowed to forbid the faithful to frequent a church of another rite, although they may exhort them to come to their own church, especially on holydays.[16] One restriction, or rather natural condition, must, however, be added. The law requires that Mass be *heard*. If a Catholic of the Latin rite would enter a Greek Church, not knowing what kind of celebration or function he was attending, he certainly could *not* be said to hear Mass, although we readily admit that external attention only is required.

The second clause of our canon states that one may

14 There is a great deal of servile work connected with running machines which require constant attention. There is, from this point of view, more excuse for a decent theatre than for the psychologically, physiologically and morally objectionable " movies."

15 S. C. P. F., Sept 26, 1840, *ad dub.* 15 (*Coll*, n 914).

16 S. C. P. F, April 30, 1862, ad 1 (*Coll*, n. 1228).

hear Mass in the *open air, or in a church or a public or semi-public oratory.* In such oratories, according to our Code,[17] all ecclesiastical functions may be held. One may also hear Mass and fulfill the obligation in a *private cemetery chapel,* as described in can. 1190.

Domestic or *private chapels erected with an indult of the Apostolic See* are only for the benefit of the grantee and those mentioned in the indult, as explained under can. 1195, and hence others do not comply with the law by hearing Mass in them.

As to *chapels on ships or vessels,* the S. Congregation has decided that these must have a fixed or permanent place, *i. e.,* they must be dedicated for the purpose of divine worship, and form, as it were, a special and separate compartment for that sole purpose, as long as the vessel lasts. If this is the case, the chapel is to be considered a public oratory, and all who assist at Mass therein, even while the ship is in port, comply with the precept of hearing Mass. If the chapel has no permanent place, it is to be regarded as a portable altar.[18]

---

17 See can. 1191, § 2; can. 1193.

18 S. Rit. C., March 4, 1901; May

10, 1901 (n. 4069); Many, *l. c.,* p. 132.

TITLE XIV

ABSTINENCE AND FASTING

Can. 1250

Abstinentiae lex vetat carne iureque ex carne vesci, non autem ovis, lacticiniis et quibuslibet condimentis etiam ex adipe animalium.

The law of *abstinence* forbids the eating of flesh meat and broth or soup made of meat; but it does not forbid eggs, *lacticinia,* and seasoning with fat of animals. The new law here is milder than the old, for *lacticinia* were not always permitted by the Church, as may be seen from some Constitutions of Benedict XIV.[1] The term *lacticinia* includes everything that is produced from milk, as well as the milk itself,— cheese, butter, margarine, etc. These, therefore, may be used even on days of abstinence.[2] *Fat of animals* was defined as the fat, grease, or lard of any animal, not only of hogs.[3]

THE LAW OF FASTING

Can. 1251

§ 1. **Lex ieiunii praescribit ut nonnisi unica per diem comestio fiat; sed non vetat aliquid cibi mane et**

---

1 "*Non ambigimus*"; "*In suprema*"; "*Libentissme.*" Cooking with oil only was permitted.

2 S. O., May 13, 1896; Sept. 1899 (*Coll. P. F.,* nn. 1928, 2067).

3 S. O., May 1, 1889 (*ibid.,* n. 1704).

vespere sumere, servata tamen circa ciborum quantitatem probata locorum consuetudine.

§. 2. Nec vetitum est carnes ac pisces in eadem refectione permiscere; nec serotinam refectionem cum prandio permutare.

The law of fasting permits *only one full meal a day,* but it does not forbid the taking of some food for breakfast and supper.

The quantity and quality of this repast is left to local custom. Care must be taken that one does not take " something " between meals too often on days of fast, as this might eventually constitute a considerable quantity or amount almost to a full meal.[4]

Those who are not obliged to fast on the days prescribed, and have received either a general or a particular indult to eat meat, may eat flesh meat every time they take a meal.[5] Thus aged or sickly persons or laborers, who are dispensed from observing the fast, may eat flesh meat three times or oftener a day. This, too, is a modification of former papal constitutions.[6] Besides, the S. Penitentiary has decided that if the head of the family (*pater familias*) is dispensed from the law of abstinence, all members of the family subject to him (*quae sunt in potestate patris familias*) may also eat flesh meat. However, those who are bound to fast may use flesh meat only once a day, at the principal or full meal.[7] If a son or daughter, or other member of the family is lawfully dispensed from abstinence on account of sickness, the head of the family may extend that favor to the other members, under the same condition as stated above, *viz.,*

4 S. O., prop. 29 damn. March 18, 1666 (Denzinger, n. 1000).

5 S. Poenit., Feb. 24, 1819; March 16, 1882 (*Coll. P. F.,* nn. 734, 1569).

6 Especially of those of Benedict XIV, quoted above.

7 S. Poenit., Jan. 10, Jan. 16, 1834 (*Coll. P. F.,* n. 832).

that flesh meat may be used only once a day by those who are otherwise obliged to fast.[8]

Another mitigation of the law of fasting is here generalized: Flesh meat and fish may be taken at the same meal, and dinner and supper may be interchanged. Thus, for instance, if one, because of his studies, or for any other reason, should prefer to take lunch at about 10 or 11 o'clock, and dinner at 5, there could be no reasonable objection.[9] Note also canon 1252.

DAYS OF ABSTINENCE AND FASTING

CAN. 1252

§ 1. Lex solius abstinentiae servanda est singulis sextis feriis.

§ 2. Lex abstinentiae simul et ieiunii servanda est feria quarta Cinerum, feriis sextis et sabbatis Quadragesimae et feriis Quatuor Temporum, pervigiliis Pentecostes, Deiparae in caelum assumptae, Omnium Sanctorum et Nativitatis Domini.

§ 3. Lex solius ieiunii servanda est reliquis omnibus Quadragesimae diebus.

§ 4. Diebus dominicis vel festis de praecepto lex abstinentiae, vel abstinentiae et ieiunii, vel ieiunii tantum cessat, nec pervigilia anticipantur; item cessat Sabbato Sancto post meridiem.

§ 1. The law of *abstinence only* must be observed on all Fridays.

§ 2. The law of *abstinence and fasting* must be observed on Ash Wednesday, on the Fridays and Saturdays

---

[8] *Ibid.*, the reason why this favor may be used is not the indult, but the physical inability of the *filia familias* to procure other food

[9] S. O , July 29, 1859; Sept. 17, 1862 (*Coll. P F*, un 1146, 1230); cfr. *Eccl. Review*, 1920, Vol. 62, p. 309 f.

of Lent, on the emberdays, on the vigils of Pentecost, the Assumption, All Saints' Day, and Christmas.

§ 3. The law of *fasting only* must be observed on all other days of Lent.

§ 4. On Sundays and holydays of obligation (except holydays in Lent) the laws of fasting and abstinence do not bind; nor must vigils of holydays of obligation, which fall on a Sunday, be observed on the preceding day. Thus if the feast of the Assumption or All Saints or Christmas should fall on a Monday, the vigil need not be observed on the preceding Saturday or Sunday. Not on Saturday, because, as the text says, *"nec pervigilia anticipantur";* not on Sunday, because there is no fast. Only holydays of obligation are thus favored.

The Lenten fast and abstinence cease at noon on Holy Saturday, that is to say, at 12 o'clock.

PARTICULAR LAWS

CAN. 1253

His canonibus nihil immutatur de indultis particu-laribus, de votis cuiuslibet personae physicae vel mo-ralis, de constitutionibus ac regulis cuiusvis religionis vel instituti approbati sive virorum sive mulierum in communi viventium etiam sine votis.

These canons leave unchanged particular indults, the vows relating to fasting and abstinence made by individ-uals or corporations, and the constitutions and rules of approved orders or congregations of religious, male as well as female, and of those who live in common without vows.

I. As regards *particular indults of the Apostolic See,* it must first of all be observed that the decree of the S. C. Consistorialis of April 25, 1918, cannot simply be applied to particular indults, because it refers to habitual faculties of Ordinaries granted for the external forum. Indults are not identical with faculties, as the latter comprehend various kinds of concessions or favors, whilst indults are given for specific purposes, generally designated very minutely, and to individual persons. It must, however, be admitted that these two terms are frequently employed synonymously. But there is a more stringent reason: it would be absurd to hold that the S. Congregation would nullify a canon without as much as specifying it in its decree. Canon 1253 distinctly maintains and upholds particular indults. The adjective *particular* must be explained according to the significance of a particular law, which implies local or provincial legislation, or such as differs from universal legislation. Hence a particular indult may affect a diocese or province, or even a nation, in contradistinction to the whole Church. These considerations premised, the following indults may concern the United States.[10]

1. The indult of July 25, 1858, which permits the eating of flesh meat on Saturdays when the law of fasting does not oblige. This indult is out of date,[11] for these Saturdays are now abolished by general law, and unless a vow is in the way, they need not be observed.

2. The indult granting the use of flesh meat on *Wednesdays of Advent,* given Sept. 2, 1837, is partly out of date,[12] for the law of abstinence no longer obliges in Advent, except on Wednesday of embertide. However, since the S. C. P. F. granted permission to use flesh meat on all Wednesdays of Advent, including the Wednesday

10 Concerning Great Britain we were unable to find any particular indults.

11 *Coll Lac.,* III, 17; it ceases

also for the province of St. Louis (*ibid ,* III, 319, 321)

12 *Coll. Lac.,* III, 61

of the emberdays, we believe that this part of the indult still holds. But as this day is not included in the indult of Aug. 3, 1887, given by the Holy Office [13] and ratified by Leo XIII, it would seem to follow that the latter must be considered binding, especially since Saturday was accepted as exempt from abstinence.

3. The indult of Aug. 3, 1887, granted by the Holy Office reads: (a) The use of flesh meat, eggs, and *lacticinia* is allowed on every Sunday of Lent, at every meal, and on every Monday, Tuesday, Thursday, and Saturday of Lent at the principal meal, except on the Saturdays of Ember week and Holy Week. There is added a clause forbidding the promiscuous use of meat and fish; this clause is now abolished by can. 1251, § 2. (b) *Lacticinia* and eggs are permitted on every day of Lent on which no flesh meat is allowed at the main meal and lunch (supper). (c) Some bread may be taken, together with coffee, tea or chocolate. (d) Where the principal meal cannot be taken at noon, the order of lunch and dinner may be inverted. For this no indult is now needed. (e) Lard or fat may be used for cooking. No indult required. (f) Those exempt from the law of fasting may eat flesh meat, eggs, and *lacticinia* several times a day on all days on which their use is permitted to all the faithful (as on the Sundays of Lent).

This indult was given for ten years, and express mention of it must be made each year in the Lenten regulations. We suppose it has been renewed, and thus remains in force. Of practical value are only points (a) and (f), and the latter only *ad quietem conscientiae*. Under this indult in Lent the Wednesdays are observed instead of the Saturdays, with the exception of Ember week and

13 Cfr. Putzer, *Comment in Fac. Ap.,* p 295.

Holy Week, when Wednesday, Friday, and Saturday must be observed as days of abstinence.

One more remark: the indult of Aug. 3, 1887, in the very beginning mentions the fact that the favors it grants are intended for *Lent only*. What then of the other Ember days? Must all three days of the other three Ember weeks be kept? Custom, we are told,[14] has extended this favor to all the other fast days. But certainly not by virtue of the indult; for although we are allowed to interpret favors broadly, we have no right to extend a favor beyond the tenor of the indult by which it is granted.[15] We do not deny the force of custom in the matter, nor are we obstinately bent on enforcing the "magro." Since even the last Plenary Council of Baltimore (n. 1112) had to confess that uniformity in the discipline of fasting was impossible, we fear that the conditions of custom are verified. Recourse to the Holy See would certainly be safer.

4. The indult granted by Pius IX to *our soldiers and sailors* is still in force. In virtue of this indult they are obliged to abstain from flesh meat only on six days of the year: Ash Wednesday, the three last days of Holy Week (or now rather only Good Friday and Holy Saturday to twelve o'clock), on the vigils of the Assumption and of Christmas. This favor is granted to all who are in active service, but not when they are on leave of absence. The families who eat with these soldiers at the same table, enjoy the same favor. The special faculties granted to our army bishop were given only for the time of war.

II. *Vows* are not affected by these canons. The Minims have a special vow of perpetual abstinence. A municipality or government may vow to observe the fast

---

14 Putzer, *l. c*, p. 297, according to Konings and Kenrick
15 *Ibid.*

or abstinence on a certain day, for instance, on account of an epidemic or earthquake.[16]

III. The *constitutions and rules* of religious institutes may prescribe days of fasting and abstinence besides those appointed in the Code. If nothing specific is determined on this head, the members are allowed to observe the days mentioned in can. 1252. Besides, the superiors may grant dispensations, as far as can. 1245, § 3, permits, and provided the constitutions do not forbid. A declaration of the S. C. Rel., of Sept 1, 1912, says: The mitigations and dispensations of fasting and abstinence prescribed by the general law of the Church also benefit religious, but fasts and abstinence prescribed by their rule and constitutions are not mitigated by a general indult or law, unless such indult or law expressly includes religious. Our Code emphatically states that the approved rules and constitutions of religious institutes are *not* changed by the general law. Those religious, therefore, who do not observe their peculiar laws concerning fasting and abstinence transgress their rule, but not the law of the Church, and therefore are liable to punishment only in so far as their constitutions declare them guilty and punishable.[17] Most constitutions do not bind under pain of sin.

WHO IS OBLIGED TO FAST AND ABSTAIN

CAN. 1254

§ 1. Abstinentiae lege tenentur omnes qui septimum aetatis annum expleverint.

§ 2. Lege ieiunii adstringuntur omnes ab expleto vicesimo primo aetatis anno ad inceptum sexagesimum.

---

16 See can. 1310.   17 *A. Ap S*, IV, 626 f.

The law of *abstinence* binds all who have completed the seventh year of age. This law obliges even on the vigils of suppressed feasts if these vigils were observed by reason of a particular precept or vow.[18]

The law of *fasting* obliges all Catholics from the twenty-first year of age, completed, until the beginning of the sixtieth year. The general tenor of this law, from which no one in the Latin Church is exempt, was explained above.[19] Here two condemned propositions may be mentioned: (1) All officials employed by the State in physical labor are excused from the law of fasting, nor is it necessary to be morally certainly whether fasting and work are compatible. (2) All those riding on horseback, whether the journey be necessary or not, even if it lasts only one day, are absolutely excused from fasting.[20]

Concerning working men, professional men, builders, servants, etc., employed by non-Catholics or lax Catholics, the Holy Office has decreed that they may eat meat on forbidden days, provided it is not purposely served to spite the Catholic Church, and provided also they can find no other employment.[21] For the rest the moralists should be consulted.

18 S C C, Sept. 18, 1911 (*A. Ap. S.*, III, 480), see can 1310.

19 See S. O, March 23, 1656; S. C. P F, Sept. 12, 1645 (*Coll.*, nn. 126, 114).

20 Propp. 30, 31 damn. March 18, 1666 (Denzinger, n. 1001 f).

21 S. O, May 27, 1671, Dec. 14, 1482 (*Coll. P. F.*, nn. 195, 960).

PART III

DIVINE WORSHIP

Divine worship is an essential feature of the Church, originating in the relation of the creature to the Creator. Foremost, of course, in this worship is God himself. But as the Second Person of the Blessed Trinity is, as it were, more closely connected with the Church, in whose temples He dwells, the Blessed Eucharist and all that is related to it deserves closer consideration. Around the Divinity there clusters a crown of Saints, to whom men pay homage. Hence a special section of the Code is devoted to the worship of the Saints. The worship of God being the outcome of the virtue of religion, may show itself in external acts, and the same is true of the veneration of the saints. Hence mention is made of processions. Lastly, man may bind himself more immediately to the worship of God by vows and the solemn invocation of the Divine Name.

The Code deals with Divine Worship logically after treating of sacred places and seasons, because these latter form the setting or frame of the interior picture, or, as we might say, the *continens* of the *contentum*. We must again remind the reader that dogmatic exposition is not the purpose of these canons, although they offer matter for lengthy elucidation.

CAN. 1255

§ 1. Sanctissimae Trinitati, singulis eiusdem Personis, Christo Domino, etiam sub speciebus sacramentalibus, debetur cultus latriae; Beatae Mariae Virgini cultus hyperduliae; aliis cum Christo in caelo regnantibus cultus duliae.

§ 2. Sacris quoque reliquiis atque imaginibus veneratio et cultus debetur relativus personae ad quam reliquiae imaginesque referuntur.

§ 1. To the Blessed Trinity as well as to each of the three Persons, to Christ our Lord, also under the sacramental species, is due the cult of *latria;* to the Blessed Virgin Mary, the cult of *hyperdulia;* to the other Saints reigning with Christ in heaven, the cult of *dulia.*

Latria, from the Greek word λατρεύω, means service, worship; *dulia,* from δουλεία, also signifies service. From this it may be seen that the original etymology hardly indicates an essential distinction between the two terms. It was the theologians who introduced this well-known distinction.

The difference between *dulia* (including *hyperdulia*) and *latria* is as vast as the gulf that separates the creature from its Creator. The relation between *dulia* and *latria,* like that between creature and Creator, is purely analogical. Their formal objects are separate and distinct. The formal object of *latria* is the *virtus religionis,* or virtue of religion, which is based upon justice; that of *dulia* the *virtus observantiae,* as St. Thomas says.[1] This distinction is sufficient to disprove the odious charge, sometimes made against Catholics, that they *adore* the Virgin Mary and the Saints. Of its very nature the

[1] *Summa Theol.,* II–II, q 102 sq

worship we give to the Saints has nothing in common with idolatry.[2]

§ 2. To the sacred *relics and images* a relative veneration and worship are due, in as far as these relics and images refer to persons. The *dulia* which we exhibit to the person of a Saint is absolute, in contradistinction to the merely relative worship which we give to relics and images. Another essential difference is that relics and images, being inanimate objects, may be venerated but not invoked. " Honor or reverence," says St. Thomas, " is due solely to rational creatures; those devoid of reason can be honored or reverenced only with respect to some rational nature." [3] Thus it would not be impious or unlawful to venerate the image of God the Father seated on a throne, which may be placed in a Christian temple.[4] For the veneration or worship is exhibited not to the image as such — this would be sheer idolatry or fetichism — but to the Sacred Person of God the Father.

Here a few rules may be given concerning the veneration of the Holy Cross and other instruments of the Passion and death of our Lord. If a relic of the *true Cross* is exposed publicly and in a visible or perceptible way, a genuflection on one knee is made *in accessu et recessu*, as often as the faithful or clergy pass by the middle of the altar. The priest who incenses the sacred relics also makes the genuflection on one knee, but incenses it standing. If the sacred relic is hidden in a tabernacle or custody, the head is bowed.[5] Sacred *thorns* receive the same signs of veneration as relics of the Holy Cross.[6]

---

2 Pohle-Preuss, *Mariology*, 1914, p. 140.

3 *Summa Theol*, III, q 25, art. 4; Pohle-Preuss, *l. c.*, p 141

4 Prop. 25 damn , Dec. 7, 1690 (Denzinger, n. 1182).

5 S. Rit C , May 7, 1846; March 29, 1869; May 23, 1835 (nn. 2391, 3201, 2722).

6 S Rit. C, Sept 7, 1897 (n. 3966).

Before the *Crucifix* (without relics of the Holy Cross) a bow is sufficient (*inclinatio profunda*), but from the *adoratio crucis* on Good Friday to the None of Holy Saturday, inclusively, a genuflection on one knee is made.[7] To *sacred linens* miraculously soaked with the species of the sacred blood, the same signs of veneration are paid as to the relics of the true Cross, and to the same extent.[8] The image of the *Infant Jesus* (Bambin' Gesu), exposed on the main altar during Christmas time, is incensed like the Cross.[9]

PUBLIC AND PRIVATE WORSHIP

Can. 1256

Cultus, si deferatur nomine Ecclesiae a personis legitime ad hoc deputatis et per actus ex Ecclesiae institutione Deo, Sanctis ac Beatis tantum exhibendos, dicitur *publicus;* sin minus, *privatus.*

Worship exhibited to God, the Saints, and the Blessed Virgin in the name of the Church, by ministers lawfully appointed for that purpose and through acts established by the Church, is called *public;* otherwise it is *private.*

Note here three requisites for public worship: it must be offered (1) in the name of the Church, (2) by her ministers (3) by acts established by her. For instance, veneration may be paid to a person who died in the odor of sanctity by pious persons, but it cannot be called a public cult before the person has been declared a Saint or Blessed;[10] such a cult would be purely private and of very doubtful merit. Again prayers may be publicly re-

7 S. Rit. C., May 9, 1857 (n. 3049).

8 S. Rit C., June 27, 1868 (n. 3176).

9 S Rit. C., Feb. 15, 1873 (n. 3288).

10 Cfr. Bened. XIV, "*Quamvis justo,*" April 30, 1749, § 12.

cited, but if they are not approved by the Church, they have a private character.

APPROBATION OF THE LITURGY

CAN. 1257

Unius Apostolicae Sedis est tum sacram ordinare liturgiam, tum liturgicos approbare libros.

The Apostolic See alone has the right to prescribe the sacred liturgy and to approve liturgical books.

Hence neither patriarchal nor cathedral nor collegiate chapters may change or add anything to the liturgical books.[11]   Neither archbishops nor bishops — still less, of course, inferior prelates — may act as judges in answering doubts concerning sacred rites and ceremonies.[12] This, of course, must be understood of authentic answers.   If one has consulted the rubrics and looked up the authentic decrees of the S. Congregation of Rites, he may state what in his opinion has been authentically decided.   A bishop cannot extend to the whole diocese the office of a Saint who is venerated in the cathedral church.[13]

Concerning the *liturgical books,* the following general decree [14] serves as a guide.

1. The liturgical books, as far as they require official approbation, are: the Roman Breviary, the Missal, the Ritual, the Pontifical and excerpts from them, as well as the Roman martyrology.   Then, the *Caeremoniale Episcoporum,* the *propria* of the Breviary and the Missal of a diocese, a religious order or a congregation, the *Memo-*

---

11 S. Rit C., May 2, 1612 (n. 297).

12 S Rit C., June 11, 1605 ad 1 (n. 179).

13 S. Rit. C., Jan 16, 1607 (n. 225).

14 S. Rit. C., May 17, 1911 (n. 4266).

riale of Benedict XIII for smaller churches, the *Instructio Clementina* for Forty Hours' Devotion, the *Collectio Decretorum S Rit. C.*

2. The editions of these books are either *typicae* or *iuxta typicas.* The typical editions may be printed only by the Vatican Press or by publishers who have obtained that privilege from the S. Congregation of Rites. The same Congregation revises every single sheet of the typical edition, and every typical edition must contain the decree of the S. Rit. C., certifying that this edition is a typical one and that editors must conform their editions to it.

Editors, after issuing a typical edition, must send two copies thereof to the S. Rit. C., in whose archives they are preserved.

3. *Any publisher* may, with the consent and approval of the Ordinary, print editions called *iuxta typicas,* provided they agree perfectly with the typical edition. To make sure of this the Ordinaries shall appoint a revisor or censor, who shall carefully compare each edition with the *typica* and grant the *imprimatur* only after it is found a faithful copy thereof.

4. If there is no typical edition of the *propria Missarum* or *Officiorum* of a diocese, the local Ordinary in whose diocese they are printed, shall declare them conformable to the original and give the *imprimatur.* As to the *propria* of a strange diocese, and those of religious orders and congregations, the local Ordinaries to whose jurisdiction the editors (*typographi*) belong, shall give the imprimatur, after the Ordinary of the strange diocese or the religious superior to whom the *propria* pertain, shall have declared that the edition is conformable to the original.

The rules for publishers of typical editions as well as

reprints of liturgical books are laid down in the Constitutions of Pius V, Clement VIII, and Urban VIII, which are contained in the preface to every Roman Breviary. These rules must be accurately followed even as to punctuation, grammatical rules, position and sequence of hymns, chapters, and so forth.[15]

Manuals of sisterhoods which are used for the investiture of novices and for making the religious profession must be approved by the Holy See, or at least by the Ordinary.[16] The formula of profession must be contained in the Constitutions.

COMMUNICATIO IN SACRIS

CAN. 1258

§ 1. Haud licitum est fidelibus quovis modo active assistere seu partem habere in sacris acatholicorum.

§ 2. Tolerari potest praesentia passiva seu materialis, civilis officii vel honoris causa, ob gravem rationem ab Episcopo in casu dubii probandam, in acatholicorum funeribus, nuptiis similibusque sollemniis, dummodo perversionis et scandali periculum absit.

It is unlawful for Catholics to assist actively in any way at, or to take part in, the religious services of non-Catholics A passive or merely material presence may be tolerated, for reasons of civil duty or honor, at funerals, weddings, and similar celebrations, provided no danger of perversion or scandal arises from this assistance. In doubtful cases the reason for assisting must be grave, and recognized as such by the bishop.

15 S. Rit C., April 26, 1834; March 11, 1871 (nn 2716, 3241).

16 S. Rit. C., Sept. 12, 1857, ad XVI (n 3059) — which proves the necessity of uniformity; the Sisters changed Ps. 19: *Exaudiat te Dominus in die professionis*," instead of *tribulationis*, in the *Libera* they sang: "*Tremens facta sum.*"

This is the so-called *communicatio in sacris activa cum acatholicis*. The reason why the Church has always forbidden such participation in the religious services of non-Catholics is the intimate conviction that she herself is the only true Church of Christ. Secondary reasons for this prohibition are: the *quasi-approbation* of *non-Catholic* worship which lies in a Catholic's participation therein and which at the same time is an external profession of faith. The other reason is *scandal*, which may be given to Catholics who see the mixture of worship and the deference paid to non-Catholic ministers and functions. Finally there is the *danger of perversion*, or of gradually increasing religious indifference when the faithful freely and indiscriminately participate in heretical religious services. Even the simulation of false religion is incompatible with the purity of the Catholic faith.[17] Hence:

(a) The Sacrament of *Baptism* can never be lawfully received from a non-Catholic minister; nor is it allowed to offer a child for baptism to such a minister, even if the child was first baptized by a Catholic minister and the heretical ceremony is admitted in order to avoid a fine.[18] Neither are Catholics allowed to assist as sponsors, either personally or by proxy, at a baptism conferred by a non-Catholic minister.[19]

(b) *Confirmation* may not be administered to such as are compelled by a non-Catholic parent to assist at heretical services.[20]

(c) The *Holy 'Eucharist* may not be received at the hands or in the temples of non-Catholics, nor are Catholics allowed to assist at the Mass of schismatics; if they

17 S. O , Aug. 28, 1780; S. C P. F., 1729 (*Coll*, nn 546, 311).
18 S. O , Sept. 26, 1668; Nov 29, 1672 (*ibid*, nn. 169, 205).
19 S. O., May 10, 1770; Jan. 3, 1871 (nn. 478, 1362).
20 S. O , Aug. 28, 1780 (*ibid.*, n. 546)

have no church of their own, they are not bound to hear
Mass on the days prescribed.[21]   Concerning the visiting
of churches of non-Catholics, the Holy Office has decided
as follows: Catholics may enter non-Catholic temples
merely from curiosity, without participating in the services and provided they have no evil intention.   An evil
intention would exist if a Catholic would visit a Protestant church for the purpose of assisting at a religious
function, or of participating *in sacris,* or if the government had commanded such visits as a sign of religious
indifference, or if the public would regard such a visit as
a sign of an interior conviction that there is no distinction between Catholics and non-Catholics.[22]   To the point
is another decision of the same Holy Office regarding
former conditions in schismatical Russia, where officials
compelled pupils to assist at schismatical functions.
Their assistance was declared an unlawful *participatio in
sacris,* which teachers of religion cannot tolerate in silence.   Therefore they must warn the children and parents of the wrong, and only in case of their being in good
faith may they omit a second warning, and grant them
absolution, provided always that there is no scandal.[23]

(d) *Confession* may be made to a heretical or schismatic minister only when there is danger of death, provided that no scandal be given, that no other priest be
present, that there be no danger of perversion, and that
the non-Catholic administer the sacrament in valid form,
i. e., *secundum ritus Ecclesiae.*[24]

(e) Under no conditions is it permitted to receive *holy
orders* from a non-Catholic minister.[25]

21 S O., Dec. 5, 1668 (n. 171).

22 S O , Jan 13, 1818 (*ib ,* n. 727,
ad 2).

23 S. O , April 26, 1894 (*ib.,* n.
1868).

24 S. O , July 7, 1864, ad 6 (n.
1257)

25 S O., Nov 21, 1709 (n. 278):
"*Alias sunt irregulares et sus-
pensi*", suspension is stated in can.

(f) Concerning *marriage* enough has been said under can. 1063.

(g) An *oath* imposed by the government may be administered by a non-Catholic minister and be taken by Catholics if said minister acts merely as an official and wears no stole or insignia of his creed.[26]

(h) Here an instruction [27] of practical value, not so much in our country, as in countries where the government compels officials and also bishops to assist at religious ceremonies conducted by non-Catholics, or to hold services in Catholic churches. It is never allowed for any bishop to go to a schismatical church to take part in the sacred functions or to chant the doxology. Government officials are not to be disturbed if they go to these churches, provided no Mass is said, and they take no part in the doxology. Catholic bishops if invited by the governor to have a celebration in the Catholic churches shall content themselves with singing the " *Te Deum* " and holding benediction of the Blessed Sacrament. This may be done with the intention of praying for the spiritual and temporal welfare of people and ruler. But the bishops shall abstain from Pontificals or singing Mass, lest the non-Catholic civil authorities should assist and incense and the " pax " should have to be offered them, which is by no means allowed.

§ 2 permits a *passive or merely material assist-*

2372, and irregularity follows suspension if can 985, n 7 is verified

26 S. O , April 1, 1857 (n. 1133). In the province of Quebec (Canada) *Protestant bibles* were used in administering oaths, only the clergy were permitted to give oath by holding the hand to the breast. The Holy Office declared that the faithful should not be disturbed; Feb 23, 1820 On an-

other occasion (for British India) the S C. P F asked that the ecclesiastical authorities should demand freedom to swear on the Catholic Bible, but as long as this could not be obtained, they should keep silent; Sept. 8, 1869 (*Coll.*, nn 739, 1346); somewhat different Sabetti-Barrett, *Theol Moral*, ed. 27a, pp 226 f.

27 S. O , May 12, 1841 (n. 921).

ance at funerals, weddings and similar festivals. What does that assistance involve or admit? Concerning *funerals* the decisions are quite distinct. No religious act or ritual participation is permitted. Hence Catholics are not supposed to recite public prayers or carry torches or candles, etc., for the souls of deceased non-Catholics.[28] At *weddings* there is hardly more than a mere passive assistance, even for witnesses.[29] In Japan and other pagan countries, where at funerals the pagan priests are first called in to perform their rites, the faithful must abstain from any participation in these ceremonies, but may bury their dead according to their own ritual.[30]

Civilis officii vel honoris causa means civil duty or respect due to the dead or to the person who is the object of the ceremony at a wedding or similar festivity, for instance, the birthday of a ruler's son or a thanksgiving celebration. When a non-Catholic ruler dies, the clergy may assist in a body, outside the church, at the funeral procession, but without sacred vestments, *i. e.,* without stole and surplice, although in cassock, when no scandal is given or when it may be removed.[31] At the coronation of King Edward VII his Catholic subjects were allowed to enter Westminster Abbey because of the personal presence of the King, but in India Catholics were not permitted to enter the temples of non-Catholics because the King was not present. Besides, Catholics were permitted to sing the *Te Deum,* but not the solemn Mass,[32] in their own churches. If a non-Catholic relative or a good friend of a Catholic pastor dies, is the latter allowed to assist at the funeral? He may do so, but is not allowed

28 S. O , Jan 13, 1818; June 30, July 7, 1864 (*Coll P. F.,* nn. 727; 1257 ad 1)

29 S. O , June 22, 1859 (n. 1176).

30 S. O., March 11, 1868 (n. 1328).

31 S O , Aug. 1, 1900 (n. 2089).

32 S. C. P. F , April 25, 1902 (n. 2136).

to wear the insignia, *i. e.,* surplice and stole, and must take no active part in the ceremonies of the non-Catholic rite.[33]

Difficulties may arise concerning coöperation in the divine services of Catholics who are employed by non-Catholics as *singers or organists.* Although we could find no specific decision with regard to Catholic singers at non-Catholic services, it is evident that the Church cannot tolerate such a formal coöperation, for to that it would certainly amount. Besides, if it is forbidden for a Catholic to play the organ at non-Catholic services — which has been formally decided [34]— it naturally follows that Catholics may not sing at such functions. The Church has been more lenient lately with regard to admitting non-Catholics as singers and organists at Catholic services. Thus, in 1889, the Holy Office wished the abuse to be eliminated as soon as possible, in 1906 it made a concession for Bulgaria, in favor of sisterhoods whose non-Catholic pupils were admitted to sing in their chapels.[35]

The present canon only forbids active assistance at, or participation in, the religious services of non-Catholics. Therefore those who contribute to the building of non-Catholic churches or help to erect them as architects, contractors, or workingmen are not concerned here. The Holy Office [36] has indeed declared that no such contributions are allowed, but at the same time urged that those who build synagogues and heretical temples are not to be

---

33 S. O , May 8, 1889 (n. 1705).

34 S. C. P. F., July 8, 1889 (n 1713): " *Cum ibi falsum cultum exercent."* Exception might be made for school exercises or purely civil celebrations held in non-Catholic churches, provided they have no religious feature attached; for in that case there would be no " exercise of false worship "

35 S. O , May 1, 1889; Jan. 24, 1906 (*Coll P. F ,* n 1703, 2227).

36 S O., June 30, July 7, 1864, ad 8–10 (ib , n. 1257) Stricter is the instruction of the *Card. Vic Urbis,* of July 12, 1878, but this concerns Rome only and cannot be generalized, because conditions are different elsewhere.

disquieted, provided such edifices are not erected to spite or provoke Catholics. But, as stated, even contributions are not excluded by our canon. Besides it would be almost impossible, in our country at least, to carry such a prohibition into effect. Business men especially cannot be expected to ignore or offend their non-Catholic patrons.

APPROBATION OF DEVOTIONS AND LITANIES

Can. 1259

§ 1. Orationes et pietatis exercitia ne permittantur in ecclesiis vel oratoriis sine revisione et expressa Ordinarii loci licentia, qui in casibus difficilioribus rem totam Sedi Apostolicae subiiciat.

§ 2. Loci Ordinarius nequit novas litanias approbare publice recitandas.

Prayers and devotions are not to be permitted in churches and oratories without previous revision by, and express permission of, the local Ordinary, who shall report more difficult cases to the Apostolic See. The local Ordinaries cannot approve new litanies which are to be publicly recited. A bishop must and may revise all kinds of devotions, and if there is doubt whether the prayers or invocations comply with the dogmatic and traditional requirements, he shall refer the matter to the Holy Office,[37] which, if merely ritual doubts exist, shall report to the S. Congregation of Rites. Concerning litanies, first and above all, *no new ones are allowed.* Only those may be recited publicly which are contained in the Breviary or in the new edition of the Roman Ritual, approved by the Holy See.[38]

[37] The veneration of the Holy Face of our Saviour is given to the traditional representation, and no special pictures are preferred, S. O., May 4, 1892 (n 1792).

[38] S Rit. C, March 6, 1894 (*Dec.*

To these approved litanies *no additions* can lawfully be made. Thus neither new " Saints," even though they be titular or patron saints, nor versicles or other prayers not contained in said additions are to be added.[39]   Religious are allowed to add the name of the founder or patriarch, but the name of no other Saint of their order or congregation.[40]   Nor is the addition of special invocations allowed in the litany of the Blessed Virgin.[41]   Neither is the name of any saint or invocation, as contained in the approved editions to be omitted in the recitation.[42]   Even quasi-invocations recited in the form of a Litany are forbidden.[43]

§ 2 of our canon says: *publice recitandas,* to be recited publicly.   This term was, especially after the decree of March 6, 1894, made the object of doubts, which were dispersed by the S. Congregation.   Thus it would be a public recitation if several of the faithful would gather in a church or public oratory to recite together a litany, although the minister of the Church would assist only as a private person, not as a minister.   Thus to recite a non-approved litany is, therefore, forbidden.[44]   Neither are Sisters or nuns allowed to recite such litanies in common in their choir, even though this be separated from the church by a grate.[45]   Single religious may recite or chant

Auth., n. 3820); no litany of St. Anthony, or of the Holy Family, or of La Salette has so far been approved; S. Rit. C., Jan. 29, 1656; Feb. 11, 1898; May 12, 1877 (*ibid.*, nn. 995, 3980, 3419).

39 S. Rit. C., March 8, 1631; May 31, 1821, ad 7 (nn. 562, 2613).

40 S. Rit. C., June 16, 1674; Feb. 11, 1702; Aug. 2, 1631 (nn. 1518, 2093, 576).

41 S. Rit. C., Aug. 2, 1631 (n. 576); additions approved are: *auxi-*

lium christianorum (S. Rit. C., Sept. 15, 1815); *Regina SSmi Rosarii* (Dec. 10, 1883, nn. 2566, 3598); *Regina pacis* (May 5, 1917).

42 S. Rit. C., Sept. 11, 1847 n. 1 (n. 2956).

43 S. Rit. C., Aug. 24, 1880 (n. 3523).

44 S. Rit. C., June 1, 1896 (n. 3916).

45 S. Rit. C., June 20, 1896 (n, 3917).

such litanies for their private devotion, but not in common.[46]

The *approved litanies are:* the Litany of All Saints, according to the general tenor and the formula for the Forty Hours' Devotion; the Litany of the Holy Name of Jesus [47]; the Litany of the Sacred Heart, approved April 2, 1899; the Litany of the Blessed Virgin Mary, known as that of Loreto; the Litany of St. Joseph, and the Litany for the Dying (*in ordine commendationis animae*).

INDEPENDENCE FROM SECULAR INTERFERENCE

CAN. 1260

Ecclesiae ministri in cultu exercendo unice a Superioribus ecclesiasticis dependere debent.

This canon is a well deserved rebuke of the arrogant bearing of the regalists, as well as of the modern oppressors of ecclesiastical liberty in matters of divine worship. Benedict XIV, although prone to make concessions, admonished the hierarchy of his time never to allow the lay power to command public prayers to be said for them, either as a thanksgiving or in case of necessity. And he exhorted the bishops to speak like Hosius of Corduba to the emperor Constantius: "Do not interfere in things ecclesiastical, nor command in that kind; but rather learn from us. God gave you the reins of government, but to us He has entrusted what pertains to the Church." [48] The government may ask, but not command. Neither are pastors allowed simply to comply with the

---

46 S. Rit C, Feb 11, 1898 (n. 3981).

47 With the addition: "*Per SSmae Eucharistiae institutionem tuam libera nos, Jesu,*" after "*Per*

ascensionem tuam", S. Rit. C., Feb. 8, 1905 (n. 4153)

48 "*Quemadmodum,*" March 23, 1743.

arrogant edicts of an ignorant board of health, or city council, or mayor, or governor, or even president. Everything must be done through the proper channels. The hierarchy shall comply with the reasonable wishes of the public or civil authorities. Authority to decide whether and what kind of prayers are to be said, belongs to those who are ordained in the things that appertain to God, to offer gifts and sacrifices.[49]   Pius X had to complain of Portugal, the so-called republic, which severed the tie that connected it with the Church.   How iniquitous was the law concerning the " associations of cult " is evident, for it entrusted the whole care of divine worship to associations of laymen, from which clergymen were rigidly excluded.[50]   There are two societies, the spiritual and the temporal, with entirely different spheres, rights, and claims.   What is purely spiritual, as divine worship, appertains solely to the society set up for religious purposes.

DUTY OF THE ORDINARY

CAN. 1261 ·

§ 1. Locorum Ordinarii advigilent ut sacrorum canonum praescripta de divino cultu sedulo observentur, et praesertim ne in cultum divinum sive publicum sive privatum aut in quotidianam fidelium vitam superstitiosa ulla praxis inducatur, aut quidquam admittatur a fide alienum vel ab ecclesiastica traditione absonum vel turpis quaestus speciem praeseferens.

§ 2. Si loci Ordinarius leges pro suo territorio hac in re tulerit, etiam religiosi omnes, exempti quoque, obligatione tenentur easdem servandi; et Ordinarius pot-

---

49 Heb. 5, 1
50 " Iamdudum," May 24, 1911 (A. Ap. S , III, 219).

est eorundem ecclesias vel publica oratoria in hunc finem visitare.

The local Ordinaries should carefully see to it (1) that the regulations laid down in the *sacred canons* on divine worship are properly *observed;* especially (2) that no *superstitious practices* be introduced into the public or private divine worship or into the daily life of the faithful; (3) that nothing be admitted which is contrary to *faith or ecclesiastical tradition,* or which savors of shameful money-making.

The remark concerning superstitious practices is intended especially for missionary countries, as is manifest from the fact that most of the papal Constitutions[51] as well as the decisions of the Roman Congregations adduced here have in view the aforesaid countries. "Superstition," says St. Thomas,[52] "is a vice opposed to religion by excess, not as if it would offer more worship to God, but because it offers worship to those to whom it is not due, or in an unlawful manner." This is the case with ancestor worship[53] in China and other superstitious practices mentioned in the Constitution of Benedict XIV, "*Omnium sollicitudinum,*" Sept. 12, 1744. There is always danger that missionaries will connive at such practices in order to swell the number of converts. The essence of all these practices is formal and willful coöperation in idolatry. The faithful may be present when the pagans perform their rites for the dead, provided they take no active part in them and protest as much as they can.[54] They may eat of the food prepared for idols if it is dished up with other foods, and the banquet takes place

---

[51] Cfr. *Coll P F.*, nn. 347, 349.
[52] *Summa Theol*, II–II, q 92, art. 1.
[53] S. C. P. F., Jan. 14, 1753 (n. 386).
[54] S. O, March 23, 1656 (*ibid.,* n 126).

far away from any pagan place of worship.[55]   But they are not allowed to assist at the meals of gentiles prepared in commemoration of the dead.[56]   Catholics may sell chickens, eggs, plots for cemeteries, etc., provided the sale is not strictly and knowingly made for superstitious purposes or with superstitious rites.[57]   But they are not allowed to contribute to, or aid in, the building of pagan temples, even though they protest against compulsion and comply in order to avoid persecution.[58]

But pagan countries are not the only ones which are in danger of superstitious practices.   There are so-called pious superstitions even in Christian communities.   Thus it is irreverent, to say the least, and unbecoming, to throw relics of the true Cross, or other relics, even if included in a reliquary, into the river, or to moisten them, in order to obtain rain.[59]   New and non-approved devotions are the cult of the heart of St. Joseph and the veneration of the B. V. Mary under the title of the Cross.[60]

Omitting other silly practices,[61] which abound among Southern people more than in the sober North, we must mention *Spiritism*.   It would be disastrous to regard this serious menace as a joke   Newspapers, magazines, and books are now making a regular propaganda for the dangerous new sect.   Hence the Holy Office has justly forbidden Catholics to assist at spiritistic séances, whether with or without a medium or the use of hypnotism, even though the sittings have an honest purpose or bear the semblance of piety, no matter whether the souls or spirits

---

55 S O , Dec. 15, 1768 (n 470)
56 S C P. F , Jan 14, 1753 (n. 386).
57 S C. P F , Jan 21, 1778, April 5, 1785 (nn 526, 575)
58 S O , Sept 5, 1736 (n 320)
59 S. Rit C., Jan 16, 1619; Sept.

12, 1769 (*Dec. Auth.*, nn 369, 2486).
60 S Rit. C , June 14, 1873, Feb 23, 1894 (*ibid ,* nn. 3304, 3818)
61 S. O., Aug. 3, 1903 (*Coll P. F ,* n 2173)· to dissolve paper pictures of the B V Mary in water or form them into pills to obtain health.

of the dead are invoked or whether the answers are simply heard, or even if the parties simply look on and protest either tacitly or explicitly that they will have nothing to do with evil spirits.[62]   Fortune telling and clairvoyance are also strictly forbidden.

§ 2 obliges *religious,* no matter how *exempt* they may be, to abide by the laws which the local Ordinary makes for his territory.   The same Ordinary is entitled to visit their churches and public oratories for the purpose of this canon.   We have here an old law, enforced by the Council of Trent,[63] and no appeal is permissible.[64]

SEPARATE SEATS FOR MEN AND WOMEN IN CHURCH

CAN. 1262

§ 1. **Optandum ut, congruenter antiquae disciplinae, mulieres in ecclesia separatae sint a viris.**

§ 2. **Viri in ecclesia vel extra ecclesiam, dum sacris ritibus assistunt, nudo capite sint, nisi aliud ferant probati populorum mores aut peculiaria rerum adiuncta; mulieres autem, capite cooperto et modeste vestitae, maxime quum ad mensam Dominicam accedunt.**

§ 1.   Conformable to ancient discipline, it is desirable that the women should be separated from the men in church.   The very division of the ancient basilica singled out the vestibule for the penitents; the catechumens were usually admitted to the rear of the nave; the faithful occupied the side aisles, the *men on the right side of the entrance, the women on the left.*   Those who were held in

---

62 S. O., April 24, 1917 (*A. Ap. S.,* IX, 268); for further literature see Raupert, *The New Black Magic,* 1919; Liljencrants, *Spiritism and Religion,* 1918.

63 Sess. 21, c. 8 *de ref.;* sess. 22 *de observ. et evit.*

64 Benedict XIV, "*Ad militantis,*" March 30, 1742, § 6.

special honor by the congregation, as widows and virgins, and those who, on account of age or social position, were entitled to peculiar regard, had their place in the forward end of the aisles or in the transept.   The different orders of the clergy were in turn distinguished, the bishop had his seat in the middle of the apsidal circle, while the presbyters were seated on either side of him, but at a lower level, the deacons stood near the altar and the inferior clergy had their place with the choir in the nave.[65]   In this country it will, we fear, be difficult to carry out this "desire" of the Church, on account of our custom of family pews.

§ 2.   The *men* should assist at sacred functions, either in or outside of the church, with their *heads uncovered,* unless a reasonable national custom or special circumstances justify a departure from this rule.   The *women,* on the other hand, should cover their heads and be dressed modestly, especially when they approach the Lord's table.

Those especially who, like our trustees, carry the canopy over the Blessed Sacrament, or reliquaries, or sacred statues, should walk bareheaded.[66]

In China the wearing of a cap or hat is a sign of respect and honor, and therefore the Church does not insist upon this disciplinary rule there.[67]   An old-fashioned blizzard on the prairies may constitute a " special circumstance," justifying the wearing of a warm cap in church.   The rule that women should cover their heads is doubtless taken from St. Paul's Epistle.[68]   It applies whenever they attend sacred functions, even from a window which separates them from the place of worship[69]   Concerning

---

65 Lowrie, *Monuments of the Early Church*, 1901, p. 105 f.

66 S. Rit. C , Sept. 25, 1688; June 18, 1689; Sept. 2, 1690 (nn 1800, 1810, 1841)

67 S. C. P. F , Oct 18, 1883, nn. XV f (*Coll* , n. 1606).

68 1 Cor 11, 4 ff.

69 S. Rit. C , July 7, 1876, ad IV.

decency of dress nothing need be said, since the general rules of Christian modesty suffice.

CAN. 1263

§ 1. Potest magistratibus, pro eorum dignitate et gradu, locus in ecclesia esse distinctus, ad normam legum liturgicarum.

§ 2. Sine expresso Ordinarii loci consensu nemo fidelis locum habeat in ecclesia sibi suisque reservatum; Ordinarius autem consensum ne praebeat, nisi ceterorum fidelium commoditati sit sufficienter consultum.

§ 3. Ea semper factis in concessionibus inest tacita conditio, ut Ordinarius possit, ex iusta causa, concessionem revocare, non obstante quolibet temporis decursu.

§ 1. A distinguished place or seat in the church may be reserved for the civil magistrates, according to their dignity and rank. However, the liturgical laws must never be disregarded. These laws are summed up in the *Cæremoniale Episcoporum*.[70] There we read that the seats reserved for nobles and illustrious laymen, magistrates and princes, no matter whether of the highest or the lowest rank, should be placed outside the sanctuary or presbytery. Some princes and governors were very arrogant in this matter, and some bishops too lenient. The S. Congregation of Rites has always referred to the *Cæremoniale*. Princes, magistrates, etc., may have a *predella* or kneeling bench and a special seat covered with a tapestry or upholstered, but always outside the choir or sanc-

___

70 Lib 1, c XIII, n 13 (ed Pustet, 1886, p 58).

tuary, and no canopy is allowed[71]   They may also, in
their proper place, be given the *" pax cum instrumento "*
and two swings of the censer, but these must not be offered by the minister of the Holy Sacrifice, but by a chaplain dressed in surplice.[72]   If the magistrates wish to have
a seat and kneeling bench in the choir, they must obtain a
special papal indult.[73]   A concordat not ratified by the
Holy See can not confer this privilege.[74]   It is an intoler-
able abuse for laymen to occupy the choir stalls of the
canons during divine service.[75]   All these laws must be
observed also by *exempt religious,* and should they dare to
violate them, the bishop may proceed against them by
censures.[76]

§ 2.   *No Catholic may,* without the express consent of
the diocesan Ordinary, *have a seat reserved for himself
and his family in church,* and the Ordinary shall not give
his consent unless he is certain that the rest of the faithful can be conveniently seated.   This, of course, does not
mean that the renting of pews is forbidden.   For the
source whence this law is taken, speaks of a citizen who
occupies two, or three, or more pews (*scamna*), while
others have to stand.   This decision gives the bishop the
right to see to it that such unqualified disregard for the
rights of others is prevented.[77]   From this it is clear that
pastors need not worry about the lawfulness of pew-rent,
which is common in our country, but they should see to it
that all the faithful are conveniently seated.

§ 3.   All these concessions contain the tacit condition

71 S. Rit C , May 23, 1639, Dec.
15, 1640 (*Dec Auth ,* nn. 680, 726)

72 S. Rit C., Jan 15, 1661 (n.
1187).

73 S. Rit. C., July 8 and 18, 1654
(n 959 f)

74 S. Rit. C., March 12, 1689 (n.
1808).

75 S. Rit C , Feb 21, 1604 (n.
157).

76 S. Rit C., March 13, 1688;
April 22, 1690 (nn 1792, 1831).

77 S. Rit C., Dec. 11, 1604 (n.
174).

that the Ordinary may revoke them for a just cause and that no prescription confers a permanent right. For laymen, even by paying pew-rent for a number of years, acquire no personal right to pews or seats.[78]

Conformable to this canon are most *statute laws* of this country. Pew rights are all "a matter of bargain, and entirely conventional between the trustees and those individuals who wish to become hearers or members of the society and to have seats in the church." [79] The pewholder's rights are not absolute, but subordinate to, and limited by, the superior rights of the owner of the building, and may even be affected by by-laws passed after he has acquired his right. It follows that the civil courts cannot decide otherwise than according to the church law.

CHURCH MUSIC

CAN. 1264

§ 1. Musicae in quibus sive organo aliisve instrumentis sive cantu lascivum aut impurum aliquid misceatur, ab ecclesiis omnino arceantur; et leges liturgicae circa musicam sacram serventur.

§ 2. Religiosae mulieres, si eisdem liceat, ad normam suarum constitutionum vel legum liturgicarum ac de venia Ordinarii loci, in propria ecclesia aut oratorio publico canere, tali e loco canant, ubi a populo conspici nequeant.

§ 1. All kinds of lascivious or impure music, whether accompanied by the organ or other instruments, or rendered vocally, must be entirely eliminated from the

---

78 S. Rit. C., Nov. 22, 1642 (n. 816).   79 Cfr. Zollmann, *American Civil Church Law*, 1917, p. 414 ff.

churches; and the liturgical laws concerning sacred music must be observed.

This is a repetition of an enactment of the Council of Trent [80] as well as of later papal constitutions. It is not within the sphere of a canonist to dwell upon the development of Church music, much less upon the finer " nuances " between the different kinds of music, Gregorian [81] or Plain Chant and polyphonic renderings. Suffice it to say that the Church has never condemned Polyphony, which began to come into being in the fourteenth century, when the Plain Chant commenced to decline. [82]

What is menat by *lascivious and impure music?* According to a decree of Alexander VII, of April 23, 1657, it signifies music which suggests the dance or profane rather than ecclesiastical ideas. [83] Benedict XIV complains that what is lawfully permitted to be sung is often treated theatrically and operatically, like a stage play. [84] The same Constitution permits the following musical instruments: violoncello and double bass, bassoon, viola and violins; but excludes drums, hunting horns, trumpets, oboes, [85] flutes and picolos, piano, mandolins and such like, which savor of the theatre. Instruments are allowed only to strengthen the voice parts, so as to lead the mind more forcibly to the contemplation of divine things and the love of God. Finally, the *sensuous* and *improper qualities* of church music are negatively described in the well known "*Motu proprio*" of Pius X, Nov. 22, 1903. There the

80 Sess. 22, *de observ. et evit.*

81 We leave the question open as to whether St Gregory the Great may fully claim the title of " Father of the Plain Chant "; — *adhuc sub-iudice lis est.*

82 Cfr R. R Terry, *Catholic Church Music*, London, 1907, p 55.

83 Terry, *l c.*, p. 21.

84 "*Annus qui,*" Feb 19, 1749, § 2 ff.

85 However, oboes and clarinettes are moderately permitted; S Rit. C, Nov 13, 1908 (*Dec. Auth*, n 4226); not allowed are chimes or peals together with the organ for liturgical service, S. Rit C, May 18, 1917 (*A Ap S.*, IX, 352).

great restorer of Christian ideals says: " Nothing, therefore, should have place in the temple that is calculated to
disturb, or even merely to diminish, the piety and devotion
of the faithful; nothing that may give reasonable cause
for disgust or scandal: nothing, above all, which directly
offends the decorum and the sanctity of the sacred functions, and is thus unworthy of the House of Prayer and
the Majesty of God." [86]

Church music must be *sacred* music, and therefore exclude all profanity, not only in itself, but in the manner in
which it is presented [87]   The whole instruction is note-
worthy.   We cull from it one more sentence (n. 22):
" It is not lawful to keep the priest at the altar waiting on
account of the chant or the music for a length of time not
allowed by the liturgy."

The *typical Vatican edition* of the *Graduale* was approved Aug. 7, 1907, and all editors have to conform to
that edition.[88]   This edition must be used in the churches
exclusively, even to the exclusion of the Medicæa.[89]   Various other decrees were issued to give weight to the
Motu proprio of Pius X.   The quintessence of these is
that the Vatican edition of the *Graduale Romanum* is *the*
typical one, with which all others must agree, since the
rhythmic signs (*signa rythmica*) are fully contained in
said edition.[90]   Other editions which, though accurately
presenting the melodies of the *Vaticana,* have special
rhythmic signs appended by private authority, may be
used as subsidiary aids by the singers, and for these the

---

86 *Dec Auth*, n 4121, Terry, *l.
c*, p 9.

87 Terry, *l c*, p 12.

88 *Dec Auth*, n 4203, see also
nn. 4166, 4168, 4229

89 S. Rit. C., April 8, 1908 (n.
4217).

90 S Rit C, Jan 25, 1911 (n.
4259): the Vatican edition represents
the signs, although not especially
printed, by the distance of the
neums, and thus indicates what is
called the *mora vocis.*

Ordinaries may give their *imprimatur*, provided the other rules laid down in the decrees referring to Plain Chant are complied with.[91] In 1912 was approved the *Antiphonale Diurnum Sacrosanctae Ecclesiae Romanae* and edited by the Vatican Press the same year. To this also the liturgical rules and decrees referring to the Gradual must be applied.[92]

§ 2. *Religious women*, if their Constitutions or the liturgical laws and the local Ordinary permit them to do so, may sing in their own church or public oratory, but only in a place where they cannot be seen by the public.

It is hardly probable that nuns will again sing together with canons and monks, as was the case at the time of Innocent II, who complained [93] of this abuse, but certain regulations have been made concerning women singers in church choirs, which must be applied with discretion. Thus congregational singing by all the people, who thus take, as it were, the place of the choir (*schola cantorum*), does not exclude women and girls, provided they occupy a place distinct from that of the men, as far as possible.[94] Sisters or nuns are not supposed to mix with the congregation, but if they sing with the children entrusted to their care, there can be no reasonable objection to the practice. However, since mixed choirs, *i. e*, choirs composed of men and women, have not found favor with the S Congregation,[95] it is perhaps not too much to say that Sisters should not take part in such choir singing.

Besides, according to the Instruction of Nov. 22, 1903,

91 S. Rit. C., April 11, 1911 (n 4263), June 23, 1917 (*A. Ap S*, IX, 396 f) These private editions are generally printed in modern notation

92 S. Rit. C, Dec. 8, 1912 (*A. Ap. S*, IV, 727)

93 Cfr c 25, § 1, C 18, q. 2

94 S Rit. C , Jan. 17, 1908, ad II (n 4216)

95 S Rit C., Dec. 18, 1908 (n. 4231). We notice that Card Gasparri has not quoted the two decisions just mentioned Is it perhaps because they are impossible of execution?

n. 12–13, since the singers in church take the place of the ecclesiastical choir, women cannot be admitted to form part of the choir or of the musical chapel. Their place should be taken by boys, provided of course this regulation can be carried into effect. It takes time to train men and boys and to fill up the gaps caused by the dismissal of women. Some of our country churches would be as silent as a grave without the voices of women singers.

TITLE XV

RESERVATION AND WORSHIP OF THE BLESSED SACRAMENT

CAN. 1265

§ 1. Sanctissima Eucharistia, dummodo adsit qui eius curam habeat et regulariter sacerdos semel saltem in hebdomada Missam in sacro loco celebret:

1.° Custodiri debet in ecclesia cathedrali, in ecclesia principe Abbatiae vel Praelaturae *nullius*, Vicariatus et Praefecturae Apostolicae, in qualibet ecclesia paroeciali vel quasi-paroeciali et in ecclesia adnexa domui religiosorum exemptorum sive virorum sive mulierum;

2.° Custodiri potest, de licentia Ordinarii loci, in ecclesia collegiata et in oratorio principali sive publico sive semi-publico tum domus piae aut religiosae, tum collegii ecclesiastici quod a clericis saecularibus vel a religiosis regatur.

§ 2. Ut in aliis ecclesiis seu oratoriis custodiri possit, necessarium est indultum apostolicum; loci Ordinarius hanc licentiam concedere potest tantummodo ecclesiae aut oratorio publico ex iusta causa et per modum actus.

§ 3. Nemini licet sanctissimam Eucharistiam apud se retinere aut secum in itinere deferre.

Provided there is a guard, and provided a priest says Mass regularly at least once a week in the sacred place:

1.⁰ The Holy Eucharist *must* be kept in the cathedral church, the main church of an abbatial or prelatical territory *nullius*, of a Vicariate and Prefecture apostolic, in every parish and quasi-parish church, and in the church adjoining the house of exempt religious, either male or female.

2.⁰ The Holy Eucharist *may* be kept, with the permission of the local Ordinary, in collegiate churches, in the principal public or semi-public oratories of charitable or religious houses, as well as in those of ecclesiastical colleges, in charge of either the secular or religious clergy.

In the earliest centuries, as ancient documents testify, the Holy Eucharist was kept by private persons and in private houses. But this custom ceased when the churches were no longer exposed to persecution and communities of faithful gathered around the cathedral as well as parish churches. The foremost reason for keeping the Blessed Sacrament is the necessity of administering it as viaticum to the sick. But the living also are entitled, especially now-a-days, to the privilege of receiving the Holy Eucharist. Lastly, the Real Presence naturally implies adoration.[1] The present legislation mitigates the former rigid laws or at least decisions,[2] which required papal indults.

A distinction is made between obligation and permission. The first paragraph of § 1 says: *debet,* the second, *potest.* The reason for this distinction is clear from the purpose of reservation, as stated above. Among the churches which *must* keep the Blessed Eucharist are those of exempt religious of both sexes, because they are parish churches for the members. However, it should be noted that canonical erection is required before a church

1 Cfr. Gasparri, *De SSma Euch.*, n. 972.

2 S. C. C., quoted by Gasparri, *l. c.* n. 980.

is allowed to keep the Blessed Sacrament.[3] Note, also, that the *cathedral* church is mentioned in general terms. This means that every cathedral church, even though it is not a parish church, must keep the Blessed Sacrament. Hence it may no longer be looked upon as a privilege,[4] but as an obligation This is, to say the least, becoming because the cathedral church is, as it were, *the* parish church of the whole diocese.

Among the churches in which the Blessed Sacrament *may* be kept without special papal indult, and with the sole consent, either written or oral, explicit or tacit, of the *local Ordinary,* are the *principal* oratories of religious and charitable institutions. In each religious institution or house, therefore, one chapel, *i. e.,* the main public or semi-public oratory, may keep the Holy Eucharist Infirmary chapels or private oratories, even of prelates inferior to bishops, cannot preserve the Holy Eucharist without a special papal indult. Nor are religious allowed to keep the Blessed Sacrament in their rural chapels without an indult [5]

Charitable institutions in whose principal chapels the Blessed Sacrament may be kept are, of course, those which are under ecclesiastical government [6]

Observe the term *local Ordinary.* Hence the permission must be obtained, not from the prelate regular under whose jurisdiction or direction a sisterhood or brotherhood is placed, but from the diocesan Ordinary, by which name also the Vicar General may be understood.

The canon mentions *two preliminary conditions:* a guard and a priest who says Mass at least once a week, as a rule. It is not required that the one who keeps

3 Cfr. can ,496 f and our Commentary, Vol III, 82 ff , S Rit C., April 16, 1644 (n. 860).

4 As formerly, see Gasparri, *l c.*

5 S C C , Sept 3, 1703, Gasparri, *l c ,* n 978

6 Cfr. can. 1489.

watch at the church or chapel be a priest. He may be a
layman,[7] and in religious communities no special guards
are required because the community itself is the guard.
But it is always required that a priest say Mass once a
week, unless he is prevented by an accident. This rule
was made in order to provide for the renewal of the
sacred species and to safeguard the observation of the
rubrics. Where the church is not adapted for the reservation of the Blessed Sacrament, either for lack of doors
or windows, or want of safety, the S. C. has decided that
the Blessed Sacrament should, on account of the sick, be
kept in the parish residence or in the house of another
priest.[8]

§ 2. To keep the Holy Eucharist in any other church
or oratory besides those mentioned requires a papal indult.
The local Ordinary may grant this permission only for
churches and public oratories, for a just cause, and *per
modum actus.*

Petitions asking for this privilege must be sent to the
S. C. of Sacraments. Religious may address the S. C. of
Religious, though the grant is always made by the former
Congregation.

Which are the *" other churches "* mentioned in the text?
They are, negatively, all churches not of the classes mentioned in § 1, 1°, and the collegiate churches named in
§ 1, n. 2. The term therefore comprises the churches of
confraternities which are not erected in parish churches
or in churches of exempt religious orders or which do not
serve a charitable purpose, *v. g.,* hospital or school work.[9]

The *" other oratories "* are all private oratories, with

7 S. Rit. C., Feb. 17, 1881 (n.
3517).

8 S. C. P. F., Aug. 23, 1852, ad 2
(*Coll.,* n. 1079).

9 S. Rit. C., Sept. 12, 1626; June
14, 1646; Jan. 12, 1704 n. 26 (nn.
420, 895, 2123).

the exception of course of those located in the residences of cardinals or bishops, all semi-public oratories which do not serve as main chapel of a religious community or charitable institute, and all public oratories which belong to confraternities or sodalities; not, however, the oratories of pious associations, because these may reasonably claim the favor of § 1, n. 2.

The papal indult generally contains the clause: "provided that the chapel be decently furnished, that the Blessed Sacrament be safely kept, that a light be always kept burning before it, and that a priest says Mass there at least once a week."[10]

The *Ordinary* may grant this permission only to churches and public oratories, not to semi-public or private oratories. Besides he must demand a just reason, and can give the permission only *per modum actus* (see can. 1195). Such a reason for, and transient manner of, granting this permission would be repair work on the main church, or deficient seating capacity of the parish church, or some temporary physical impediment, like a flood, a fire, or an epidemic.

§ 3. No one is allowed to keep the Blessed Sacrament in his home or to carry it with him when travelling. If one would keep the Blessed Sacrament in his home for sinister purposes, such as magic, he would be open to the suspicion of heresy and liable to be denounced to the Holy Office.[11]

The custom of carrying the sacred host when travelling has long been given up, and the practice declared unlawful, even for missionaries.[12]

---

10 S. Rit. C., May 23, 1593 (n. 31) 1. Sometimes has been added the clause: "*absque parochi, intra cuius parochiae fines existit, praeiu-*dicio." May 14, 1889 (n. 3706).

11 S. C. P. F., Feb. 25, 1859 (*Coll.*, n. 1171).

12 Gasparri, *l. c.*, n. 971.

CAN. 1266

Ecclesiae in quibus sanctissima Eucharistia asservatur, praesertim paroeciales, quotidie per aliquot saltem horas fidelibus pateant.

Churches in which the Blessed Sacrament is kept, especially parish churches, should be open a few hours daily to the faithful   For one purpose of reservation is adoration of the Eucharistic Christ.

CAN. 1267

Revocato quolibet contrario privilegio, in ipsa religiosa vel pia domo sanctissima Eucharistia custodiri nequit, nisi vel in ecclesia vel in principali oratorio; nec apud moniales intra chorum vel septa monasterii.

In religious houses or charitable institutions the Holy Eucharist may be kept only in the church or principal oratory, and nowhere else; nuns are not allowed to keep it within the choir or convent enclosure. Every privilege to the contrary is hereby revoked.

THE BLESSED SACRAMENT ALTAR

CAN. 1268

§ 1. Sanctissima Eucharistia continuo seu habitualiter custodiri nequit, nisi in uno tantum eiusdem ecclesiae altari.

§ 2. Custodiatur in praecellentissimo ac nobilissimo ecclesiae loco ac proinde regulariter in altari maiore, nisi aliud venerationi et cultui tanti sacramenti commodius et decentius videatur, servato praescripto legum liturgicarum quod ad ultimos dies hebdomadae maioris attinet.

§ 3. Sed in ecclesiis cathedralibus, collegiatis aut conventualibus in quibus ad altare maius chorales functiones persolvendae sunt, ne ecclesiasticis officiis impedimentum afferatur, opportunum est ut sanctissima Eucharistia regulariter non custodiatur in altari maiore, sed in alio sacello seu altari.

§ 4. Curent ecclesiarum rectores ut altare in quo sanctissimum Sacramentum asservatur sit prae omnibus aliis ornatum, ita ut suo ipso apparatu magis moveat fidelium pietatem ac devotionem.

§ 1. The Blessed Sacrament cannot be kept habitually on more than *one* altar of the same church.

This altar should be designated by the Ordinary,[13] and the rule laid down in this canon also binds regulars.[14] But an exception is made in favor of churches of *perpetual adoration,* which must have another tabernacle on another altar, where holy Communion may be distributed to the faithful.[15] Note the word *habitually.* During the Forty Hours' Devotion the Blessed Sacrament must also be kept on another, for instance, a side altar for the distribution of holy Communion. On this altar must be placed a movable tabernacle, and if no railing surrounds the altar, benches may be placed round about it to mark it off.[16] Of course, where there is no other altar, this expedient will not work, and the best thing to do is to have the other kind of Forty Hours' which permits of reposition every day, or else to construct a temporary altar with a movable tabernacle. The term habitually

13 S Rit C , July 21, 1696 (*Dec. Auth*, n 1946).

14 S Rit. C , March 14, 1861 (n. 3104).

15 S. Rit C , May 18, 1878 (n 3449)

16 S. Rit. C , Nov. 23, 1880 (n. 3525).

admits of another departure from the general rule. Thus it is permitted to transfer the Blessed Sacrament from the usual to another altar during a triduum or novena, and in the months of May and June, and, we suppose, also in October, for the distribution of Holy Communion and Benediction.[17]

§ 2. The Blessed Sacrament should be kept in the most *prominent place of honor,* and therefore generally on the main altar, unless there is one more conveniently located and better suited for the veneration and cult of this holy Sacrament. But the rules regarding the last three days of Holy Week must be observed. The Blessed Sacrament may not be kept continually on the altar in the choir (*altare chori*), but it may be kept on side altars or in side chapels.[18]

The *liturgical laws* referred to are the rubrics and certain decrees concerning the *triduum* of Holy Week. One of these says that no sacred particles may be placed in the repository together with the Host to be used for the *Missa Praesanctificatorum on Good Friday.*[19] For the rest we must refer the student to the general rubrics.

§ 3. In cathedral, collegiate, and conventual churches in which the choir functions are held at the main altar, the Blessed Sacrament may as a rule be kept in another chapel or on another than the high altar, in order not to interfere with the services. The text says "*opportunum,*" which *per se* does not imply a strict law. However, the S. Congregation, in one instance at least, refused to allow the Blessed Sacrament to be kept on the high altar of the cathedral church.[20] The *Cæremoniale Epis-*

17 S. Rit. C., June 2, 1883 (n. 3576).

18 S. Rit. C., April 26, 1901 (n. 4071).

19 S. Rit. C., Dec. 9, 1899, ad IV (n. 4049).

20 S. Rit. C., Feb. 6, 1875 (n. 3335).

coporum prescribes removal of the Blessed Sacrament from the altar on which the bishop solemnly pontificates.[21]

§ 4. The rectors of churches shall take care that the altar on which the Blessed Sacrament is kept, be more elaborately decorated than the other altars, so that its very appearance may move the faithful to devotion.

We know of no special rules for the decoration of the sacramental altar, except that a light should burn before it [22] and the tabernacle be curtained. The *Cæremoniale Episcoporum* (1. I, c. 12, n. 8, 12) has in view pontifical functions. It certainly is becoming that the sacramental altar should be more elaborately decorated than the others. More candlesticks, more steps, flowers (when permitted), an antipendium, and similar ornaments permitted by the rubrics will help to draw the attention of the faithful to their Eucharistic Lord. The sacramental altar should be clearly distinguished from the altar of the Blessed Virgin, for the Hidden God must not stand back before even His noblest creature.

THE TABERNACLE

CAN. 1269

§ 1. Sanctissima Eucharistia servari debet in tabernaculo inamovibili in media parte altaris posito.

§ 2. Tabernaculum sit affabre exstructum, undequaque solide clausum, decenter ornatum ad normam legum liturgicarum, ab omni alia re vacuum, ac tam

21 Tit 1, c 12, n 8. The reason for this rule lies in the ceremonies to be performed before the Pontiff. But if a cathedral church serves as parish church, it certainly is more convenient for the people that the Bl. Sacrament be kept on the main altar, neither is the law against this practice, because it is " opportune "

22 A canopy or curtain should be over the tabernacle; Rit Rom, tit IV, c. 1, n 6. But it may frankly be stated that an artistic tabernacle often suffers from a cover.

sedulo custodiatur ut periculum cuiusvis sacrilegae profanationis arceatur.

§ 3. Gravi aliqua suadente causa ab Ordinario loci probata, non est vetitum sanctissimam Eucharistiam nocturno tempore extra altare, super corporali tamen, in loco tutiore et decenti, asservari, servato praescripto can. 1271.

§ 4. Clavis tabernaculi, in quo sanctissimum Sacramentum asservatur, diligentissime custodiri debet, onerata graviter conscientia sacerdotis qui ecclesiae vel oratorii curam habet.

§ 1. The Blessed Sacrament must be kept in an immovable tabernacle in the middle of the altar.

§ 2. The tabernacle must be skilfully constructed and safely locked, appropriately decorated according to the liturgical rules, be empty, and so carefully guarded that there is no danger of sacrilegious profanation.

Concerning the material of which the tabernacle is to be made, there are no rigid rules.[23]   But the more precious the metal or stone, the more becoming it will be. Inside the tabernacle may be draped with white cloth, or simply gilded.   On the outside [24] it must be covered with a veil or curtain.   No veil is required on the inside, though this custom may be tolerated.[25]   The material of the outside cover or veil may be silk, cotton, wool, hemp, etc.   The color of the veil (called *conopaeum*, because it is supposed to be thrown over the whole tabernacle) has not been determined.   The S. Congregation has admitted two opinions: the one which holds that the color must always be white, the other (Gavante) that it must change

23 The Capuchins may have a wooden tabernacle without any special painting outside, S. Rit. C., Dec 7, 1888, ad XIII (n. 3697).

24 S Rit. C , Aug. 7, 1871; June 5, 1889 (nn 3454, 3709).

25 S. Rit. C , April 28, 1866 (n 3150)

according to the office and the seasons   This latter opinion was favored by the S. Congregation,[26] but no strict rule can be deduced from its answer.   Hence a white veil is certainly admissible.   However, since at funeral masses, exequies and on All Souls' Day, the antipendium and the drapery are of black, the veil of the tabernacle should also be, not black, but purple.[27]

§ 3.   For any weighty reason which the Ordinary deems sufficient, it is permitted to keep the Blessed Sacrament *at night* away from the altar, in a more secure and decent place, but always on a corporal and with due regard to can. 1271.   This would undoubtedly be permitted in case of churches [28] used by Catholics and Protestants alternately, and also in case a missionary lives far away from the church, especially for administering the Viaticum.[29]

§ 4.   The *key of the tabernacle,* in which the Blessed Sacrament is kept, must be *carefully guarded;* the responsibility for carrying out this law rests with the priest who has charge of the church or oratory.

In order to prevent sacrilegious theft or irreverence, the priest, *i. e.,* the pastor, or rector, or canon sacristan, should keep the key in his pocket or put it with other keys in a cupboard or drawer, so that strangers cannot discover and abuse it [30]   It is especially forbidden to hand the key of the sepulchre on Holy Thursday to a layman, or to a confraternity or sodality; and no custom to the contrary is tolerated.[31]   How serious this obligation is may be

26 S. Rit C, July 21, 1855 (n. 3035)

27 S. Rit C, Dec. 1, 1882 (n. 3562)

28 S. C. P. F., March 7, 1805 (*Coll*, n 681): "*in aedibus parochi*"

29 S Rit, C, Feb. 10, 1871, ad V, 1 (n 3234).

30 S C EE. et RR, Feb 9, 1751 (Bizzarri, *l. c.,* p 31 f)

31 S Rit. C., Dec 6, 1631; Dec 7, 1737; May 22, 1841 (nn. 579, 2335, 2833).

judged from the penalties threatened in the decretals and in one letter of the S. Congregation: Imprisonment, privation of the active and passive vote, and suspension. The bishop together with the superior may proceed thus against exempt religious.[32]

THE PYX

CAN. 1270

Particulae consecratae, eo numero qui infirmorum et aliorum fidelium communioni satis esse possit, perpetuo conserventur in pyxide ex solida decentique materia, eaque munda et suo operculo bene clausa, cooperta albo velo serico et, quantum res feret, ornato.

A number of consecrated particles, sufficient for the communion of the sick and other faithful, must always be kept in a pyx or ciborium made of some solid and suitable material, kept neat and well closed, covered with a veil of silk, which may be artistically ornamented as far as the rubrics allow.

This text is taken almost verbally from the Roman Ritual, and is also intended for the Orientals, who should, like the Latins, preserve the particles in a pyx, not in a dried or unbecoming form, as if they were mere bread.[33] The pyx should be made of metal, not of glass or some similar substance, even though there be danger that it be stolen.[34] Copper is admissible,[35] if gilded.

The particles may never be kept on the corporal, even though there be danger of theft.[36] They must be pre-

32 S. C. EE. et RR., *l. c.*

33 *Rit. Rom.*, tit. IV, c. 1, n. 5; Bened. XIV, "*Praeclaris,*" March 18, 1746 (*Coll. P. F.*, n. 356).

34 S. Rit. C., Jan. 30, 1880 (*Dec. Auth.*, n. 3511).

35 S. Rit. C., Aug. 31, 1867, ad VI (n. 3162).

36 S. Rit. C., Feb. 17, 1881 (n. 3527).

served *perpetuo, i. e.,* always, even during the Corpus Christi procession.[37]

The veil or cover of the ciborium may be embroidered or bear some suitable emblems having reference to the Holy Eucharist; but it must not be overloaded or so heavy that it is difficult to open the lid.

The ciborium itself must be kept clean, especially from rust and verdigris.

THE TABERNACLE LIGHT

CAN. 1271

Coram tabernaculo, in quo sanctissimum Sacramentum asservatur, una saltem lampas diu noctuque continenter luceat, nutrienda oleo olivarum vel cera apum; ubi vero oleum olivarum haberi nequeat, Ordinarii loci prudentiae permittitur ut aliis oleis commutetur, quantum fieri potest, vegetabilibus.

At least one lamp must burn day and night before the tabernacle in which the Blessed Sacrament is kept. For this lamp olive oil or beeswax should be used; if no olive oil is available, other oils may be used, according to the prudent judgment of the Ordinary, but they should be vegetable oils, if possible.

This is a grave obligation, as may be seen from the constant insistence with which it was forced upon the rectors of churches. The sanctuary lamp must be reserved for the sole purpose for which it is prescribed, and not serve other purposes, for instance, illumining a dormitory.[38] The lamp may be attached to the side wall, like a bracket or cornucopia, provided that the light burns

37 S. Rit. C., Aug. 13, 1667, ad 2 (n. 1357).

38 S. Rit. C., Aug. 22, 1669 (n. 2033).

towards and before the altar (*infra et ante altare*).[39]

Olive oil best serves the mystic significance of the sanctuary lamp, as expressed in the liturgy of Palm Sunday [40] However, beeswax, the significance of which is pointed out on Candlemas Day, is also permitted. So, too, is a mixture of olive oil and beeswax.[41] Vegetable oils (linseed, sesame, etc) may be used where olive oil is unavailable. Note well that the text does not admit the use of electric light for the sanctuary lamp, as a decree of the S. Rit. C. permitted about four years ago, " on account of war conditions." [42] On the other hand it is safe to say that this decree seems to pave the way for the use of electric or gaslight as an aid to reading and for ornamental purposes, even on the altar. Hence the former rigorous decisions [43] may be taken with a goodly dose of discretion.

ALTAR BREADS

Can. 1272

Hostiae consecratae, sive propter fidelium communionem, sive propter expositionem sanctissimi Sacramenti, et recentes sint et frequenter renoventur, veteribus rite consumptis, ita ut nullum sit periculum corruptionis, sedulo servatis instructionibus quas Ordinarius loci hac de re dederit.

The consecrated hosts reserved for the communion of the faithful or for the exposition of the Blessed Sacrament must be fresh and should be frequently renewed, the

---

39 S Rit. C., June 2, 1883 ad IV (n 3578).

40 S Rit C., July 9, 1864 (n. 3121).

41 S. Rit C., Nov. 8, 1907 (n. 4205).

42 S Rit. C., Nov 22, 1907 (n. 4206), Nov. 23, 1916 (A Ap. S., VIII, 72 f)

43 S Rit. C, Nov 29, 1901, May 16, 1902, Nov 22, 1907 (nn. 4086, 4097, 4206).

old ones having been duly consumed, so that there is no danger of corruption. Upon this matter the instructions given by the local Ordinaries should be scrupulously observed. See can. 815. Attention may be drawn to the decisions of the S. Congregation of Rites, which insist upon weekly renewal of the sacred species according to the *Cæremoniale Episcoporum*.[44]

FREQUENT ASSISTANCE AT MASS AND VISITS TO THE BLESSED SACRAMENT

CAN. 1273

Qui in religiosam fidelium institutionem incumbunt, nihil omittant ut pietatem erga sanctissimam Eucharistiam in eorum animis excitent, eosque praesertim hortentur ut, non modo diebus dominicis et festis de praecepto, sed etiam diebus ferialibus intra hebdomadam, frequenter, quantum fieri potest, Missae sacrificio assistant et sanctissimum Sacramentum visitent.

Those who have charge of the religious instruction of the faithful, should endeavor to foster in their hearts devotion to the Holy Eucharist, and exhort them to assist at Mass not only on Sundays and holydays of obligation, but also as often as possible on weekdays, and to visit the Blessed Sacrament.

EXPOSITION OF THE BLESSED SACRAMENT

CAN. 1274

§ 1. In ecclesiis aut oratoriis quibus datum est asservare sanctissimam Eucharistiam, fieri potest expositio privata seu cum pyxide ex qualibet iusta causa sine Ordinarii licentia; expositio vero publica seu cum

44 Lib. I, c. VI, n. 2; S. Rit. C., Sept. 12, 1884, n. II (n. 3624).

ostensorio die festo Corporis Christi et intra octavam fieri potest in omnibus ecclesiis inter Missarum sollemnia et ad Vesperas; aliis vero temporibus nonnisi ex iusta et gravi causa praesertim publica et de Ordinarii loci licentia, licet ecclesia ad religionem exemptam pertineat.

§ 2. Minister expositionis et repositionis sanctissimi Sacramenti est sacerdos vel diaconus; minister vero benedictionis Eucharisticae est solus sacerdos, nec eam impertire diaconus potest, nisi in casu quo, ad normam can. 845, § 2, Viaticum ad infirmum detulerit.

§ 1. *Private* exposition of the Blessed Sacrament, *i. e.,* with the ciborium, may be held for any reasonable cause without the permission of the Ordinary in churches and oratories in which the Blessed Sacrament is lawfully kept. This sounds partly like a definition and is no doubt intended as such, to distinguish private from public exposition, which is mentioned in the next clause. But the definition is not complete and should be supplemented by a decision of the S. Congregation of Rites.[45] Private exposition (*ex causa privata*) takes place if the Blessed Sacrament is not taken out of the tabernacle, but remains hidden, so that the Host cannot be seen. Hence the tabernacle is opened and the ciborium is placed near the opening.[46] Private exposition excludes placing the ciborium or pyx, as it is called in the decisions,[47] upon a throne or movable tabernacle. Benediction with the ciborium is not forbidden where there is a long-standing custom authorizing it.[48] In fact, says Cardinal Gasparri,[49] if this less

---

[45] May 31, 1642 (n. 800).

[46] Bened. XIV, *Instit.*, 30, n. XVI; Gasparri, *De SSma Euch.*, n. 1022.

[47] S. Rit. C., May 23, 1835; April 28, 1902 (nn. 2725, 4096).

[48] S. Rit. C., Sept. 11, 1847; March 16, 1876 (nn. 2957, 3394).

[49] *L. c.*, n. 1034; Bened. XIV, *Instit.*, 30, n. VI f., where the pros

solemn benediction can be imparted *pro causa tum pub-lica tum privata,* the Ordinary should not permit solemn and visible benediction with the ostensorium except for a *causa publica.* This appears to us a very reasonable rule. Thus during the month of October this private benediction, we believe, would be amply justified and sufficient on weekdays.

What is a *causa privata?* A case of sickness or the mere desire of pious persons or of a religious community would be a private cause sufficient to justify private exposition.[50]

The *mode* of holding this kind of exposition and imparting the benediction is as follows: The priest wears stole and surplice, also, if he wishes, a cope. At least six candles must be lighted, but the incensation is omitted, since this is not in keeping with the Roman practice.[51] Praying and singing are allowed, and the *Tantum ergo* with versicle and oration may be said or sung. After the blessing is given the tabernacle should again be closed.[52]

Such an exposition requires no permission from the Ordinary, and is permitted in all churches and oratories which are entitled, either by law or by an indult, to keep the Blessed Sacrament, according to can. 1265.

Public exposition, i. e., with the *ostensorium* or monstrance, may be held in all churches on the feast of Corpus Christi and every day within its octave, at Mass and Vespers, but not on other occasions except for a just and weighty reason, especially of a public character, *and* with the permission of the diocesan Ordinary, which is required also for churches which belong to exempt religious.

and cons of frequent exposition are set forth.

50 Bened. XIV, *l. c.,* n. XVI.

51 S. Rit. C., Sept. 11, 1847 (n. 2957).

52 Gasparri, *l. c.,* n. 1027.

The difference between private and public exposition lies in the manner of exhibiting the Blessed Sacrament as well as in the reason for which it is permitted. The prescribed vessel here is the *ostensorium* with the *lunula*.[53] This is generally placed under a canopy on a throne, on which is spread a palla or corporal. It is becoming that twenty candles, or at least twelve,[54] be burning on the altar during the exposition. The color of the antipendium as well as of the canopy and the vestments worn by the ministers is white. However, if the exposition is connected with the office of the day, for instance, Pentecost, the antipendium and the vestments worn by the ministers must be of the color of the day, *i. e.*, red in the case supposed, whilst the canopy may be white. But this is required only if the priest does not leave the altar before the exposition. If he goes to the sacristy after Mass or Vespers are said, he may vest in white. White is also the color of the *velum* or *humerale* thrown over the shoulders.[55] Black is not allowed under any circumstance at the altar or in the chapel of exposition, even though the rest of the church still bears signs of mourning[56] All relics must be removed from the altar of exposition.[57]

The Mass of exposition should as a rule be at least a *missa cantata* or *solemnis*, although the term *inter Missarum sollemnia* does not strictly require a sung Mass.[58] When the Blessed Sacrament is exposed after Communion

---

53 A so called *custodia* is not necessary for the lunula The material for the ostensorium and lunula is not determined by law, but should be the same as for the ciborium; Gasparri, *l. c.*, n 1030 f.

54 S Rit. C., Feb. 8, 1879 (n. 3480); in this case the churches were poor.

55 Gasparri, *l. c.*, n 1040.

56 S. Rit C., March 13, 1804 (n. 2558), not even if a ruler dies.

57 S. Rit. C., Sept. 2, 1741, ad 1 (n. 2365).

58 S. Rit C, Sept. 25, 1882 (n. 3558) has permitted the custom of exposing the Bl Sacr with a low Mass early in the morning.

at Mass, the ostensorium should not be covered with a velum.[59]

The genuflections are to be made by bending both knees at private as well as public expositions.[60]

Public exposition is permitted on the feast of Corpus Christi and within its Octave, but only in churches. which term includes public oratories. But what about semi-public oratories which, according to can. 1265, § 1, n. 2, are allowed to keep the Blessed Sacrament habitually? The text of our canon would seem to exclude them. Cardinal Gasparri simply says: It is evident that exposition can only be held in a church which is entitled to keep the Blessed Sacrament. This would apply also to semi-public oratories, and we believe that the term *in ecclesiis* here should not be taken too strictly, provided, of course, the functions can be carried out according to the rubrics. At any rate, it would only require a permission from the Ordinary to authorize public exposition in pious institutions.[61]

The last clause of § 1, can. 1274, mentions "*other times*" at which public exposition may be held for a just and reasonable, especially a *public cause*. What is a *causa publica?* It is one that concerns the whole commonwealth, or municipality, or parish, or diocese, or country. But it may also be a reason of less extent, according to approved authors.[62] Such a reason would be the eradication of vice and fostering of virtue, public peace and tranquillity, impending disasters, etc., or any other reason which in one way or another, according to the judgment of the Ordinary, affects a community, or at least the larger part thereof. *Other times* are all those days which do not fall within the Octave of Corpus Christi. On no other

59 Gasparri, *l c*, n. 1036.
60 *Ibid.*, a 1023
61 Gasparri, *l. c.*, n. 1038.
62 *Ibid*, n 1034

day of the year, except, of course, the last three days of Holy Week, is public exposition forbidden, although Benedict XIV refused to permit it on the feastdays of Saints, when these are celebrated with more or less worldly pomp.[63] But custom may admit also those days.[64] Note that a weighty and public reason is required and, besides, the *express permission of the Ordinary* must be obtained. From this rule the S. Congregation would dispense neither in favor of exempt religious, no matter how many privileges they may claim, nor in favor of confraternities.[65] The latter may have an exposition, provided episcopal permission was given, without asking or notifying the pastor.[66] Hence the faculty of keeping the Blessed Sacrament does not include that of having an exposition of it outside the feast and octave of Corpus Christi.[67]

§ 2. The *minister* of exposition is the priest or deacon; but a priest may give the benediction, whereas a deacon may only impart the blessing according to can. 845, § 2, *viz.*, when administering the viaticum.

Note that no mechanism is allowed for exposing the Blessed Sacrament, but the minister must expose it with his hands.[68] The rather quaint manner of exposition mentioned in one decision, where the ostensorium was placed on the right arm of the statue of a Saint, was forbidden.[69]

63 *Institt*, 30, n. XIV.

64 S. Rit. C, Sept 27, 1864, ad 5 (n 3124)

65 This is the tenor of all the decisions quoted by Card. Gasparri in his edition; cfr. Bened XIV, *Inst.*, 30, n. IX f.

66 S. Rit. C, March 18, 1679 (n. 1622).

67 S Rit. C, Jan. 12, 1704 ad 27 (n. 2123).

68 S Rit C, April 3, 1873 (Gasparri, *l. c.*, n. 1041); not contained in *Dec. Auth*

69 S. Rit. C., Aug. 2, 1884 (n. 3615).

THE FORTY HOURS' DEVOTION

CAN. 1275

Supplicatio Quadraginta Horarum in omnibus ecclesiis paroecialibus aliisque, in quibus sanctissimum
Sacramentum habitualiter asservatur, statutis de consensu Ordinarii loci diebus, maiore qua fieri potest
sollemnitate quotannis habeatur; et sicubi ob peculiaria rerum adiuncta nequeat sine gravi incommodo et
cum reverentia tanto sacramento debita fieri, curet ·
loci Ordinarius ut saltem per aliquot continuas horas,
statis diebus, sanctissimum Sacramentum sollemniore
ritu exponatur.

The Forty Hours' Devotion should be held every year,
on the days established, with the consent of the local Ordinary, in all parochial and other churches in which the
Blessed Sacrament is habitually kept, and with the greatest possible solemnity. When special circumstances permit the exposition of the Blessed Sacrament only with
great inconvenience or danger of irreverence, the local
Ordinary shall see to it that it be exposed solemnly at
least for a number of consecutive hours on stated days.

The consent of the Ordinary may be given once for all,
especially when definite churches are assigned for holding
the devotion on certain days. This consent is required also
for churches of regulars and confraternities,[70] nor may
the pastor or first dignitary of the cathedral church prescribe the devotion without the permission of the bishop.[71]
During Holy Week, i. e., from the morning of Holy

[70] S. Rit. C., Sept. 12, 1642 (n. 814).

[71] S. Rit. C., June 4, 1644 (n. 869).

Thursday until early on Holy Saturday, the devotion must be stopped.[72]

The Forty Hours' Devotion began in the sixteenth century. It was at first held on the days preceding Lent, which custom was approved by the Roman Pontiffs.[73] Clement VIII ordered the Forty Hours' Devotion as we know it. Clement XI not only approved it, but prescribed perpetual exposition on the same occasion and issued the so-called *Clementina*. The privileges and favors granted by this document are attached only to perpetual exposition, unless a special indult is obtained.[74]

[72] S. Rit. C., March 12, 1661 (n. 1190).

[73] Bened XIV, Jan 1, 1748.

[74] *Instructio*, 21, 1705; S. Rit. C., May 27, 1911, ad III (n. 4268).

TITLE XVI

WORSHIP OF THE SAINTS, SACRED IMAGES, AND RELICS

CAN. 1276

Bonum atque utile est Dei Servos, una cum Christo regnantes, suppliciter invocare eorumque reliquias atque imagines venerari; sed prae ceteris filiali devotione Beatissimam Virginem Mariam fideles universi prosequantur.

This canon, taken substantially from the dogmatic canons of the Council of Trent,[1] embodies the time-honored practice of the Catholic Church and voices a rebuke against ancient and modern image-breakers. It lays it down as a good and useful practice to invoke the intercession of the servants of God who reign with Christ, above all the Blessed Virgin Mary, and to venerate their relics and images. The *hyperdulia* paid to the Mother of God is not in vain,[2] although she is a creature. Nor is it imposture, as the so-called reformers maintained, to say Mass in honor of the Saints and to obtain their intercession with God.[3] It would be rash and pernicious to reprove the faithful for showing particular veneration and attributing special titles of honor to miraculous images of the Saints, especially those of the Blessed Virgin Mary.[4]

1 Sess. 25, *de invoc.*
2 *Prop. 26 damn. a S. O.*, Dec. 7, 1690 (Denzinger, n. 1183).
3 *Trid.*, Sess. 22, can. 5, *de Sacrif. Missae.*
4 *Propp. 70, 71 damn. per " Auc-*

There is not the slightest danger that, in venerating the Saints and their images, we shall fail to adore God in spirit and in truth, or that the memory of the Saints will dislodge God from the hearts of the faithful.[5] For the rest, the reasonableness of the veneration of the Saints is a matter for theologians.

PUBLIC WORSHIP OF THE SAINTS

CAN. 1277

§ 1. Cultu publico eos tantum Dei Servos venerari licet, qui auctoritate Ecclesiae inter Sanctos vel Beatos relati sint.

§ 2. In album Sanctorum canonice relatis cultus duliae debetur; Sancti coli possunt ubique et quovis actu eius generis cultus; Beati vero non possunt, nisi loco et modo quo Romanus Pontifex concesserit.

§ 1. Only those servants of God may be publicly worshiped who are counted among the Saints and Blessed by the authority of the Church.

The history of beatification and canonization may be studied in the classic work of Benedict XIV.[6] Since the XIIth century this function is reserved to the Holy See as a *causa maior*. (See P. II, Book IV.)

Urban VIII, in his Constitution "*Caelestis Hierusalem,*" of July 25, 1634, ruled that no images or votive tablets should be permitted in churches and oratories of persons who had not yet been declared Saints or Blessed by the Apostolic See, except such as had been venerated

---

lorem fidei," Aug. 28, 1794 (Denzinger, n. 1433 f.).

[5] *Propp 18, 35, 36 damn. Nov. 20, 1687* (*ibid.*, nn 1105, 1122 f).

[6] *De Servorum Dei Beatificatione et Canonizatione,* ed Prati, 1839, Vols. 7. We may also refer to Part II, Book IV of this Commentary.

either "by common consent of the Church, or by immemorable custom or in the writings of the Holy Fathers and holy men." From this ruling it was but natural to conclude that there was a *casus exceptus* from the general rule of beatification and canonization, *viz.*, the cult attributed to a distinguished servant of God and proved by means described in the Constitution of Urban VIII, quoted above.

Pending the *Causa*, or after the Commission for the trial has been assigned, it is strictly forbidden to call a servant of God "Venerable" and to hold any service of thanksgiving for the *introductio causae* or to deliver any panegyrics.

A person may be called "Venerable" only after a formal decree to this effect has been published.[7] Besides it must be understood that, although Saints or Blessed were venerated publicly with Office and Mass, it is required that their worship be approved and ratified by the Church before a Mass or a proper office in their honor is permitted. For the general rule is that such *propria* and Mass are accorded only to such Saints and Blessed who are mentioned in the Roman Martyrology or have enjoyed a public cult which has been either formally decreed or ratified by the Holy See.[8] Sometimes Saints and Blessed are inserted in diocesan calendars (ordo) who are neither found in the Martyrology nor endowed with a decree of the Holy See. This insertion in diocesan calendars or *propria* of a diocese or order can never produce the effect or create the presumption of a formal or *aequipollens* beatification, but leaves both title and cult in *statu quo ante*.[9]

7 S Rit. C , Aug. 26, 1913 (*A. Ap. S.*, V, 436 ff)
8 S. Rit C , July 13, 1896 (n. 3926).
9 S. Rit C , April 28, 1914 (*A. Ap.* S , VI, 235 f.)

Above a *prohibition of exhibiting the images or statues of Saints or Blessed not approved as such by the Holy See,* was mentioned. This prohibition includes any public veneration either outside or inside of the church or altar.[10] But it is not forbidden to paint the pictures and events from the life of pious servants of God upon the walls of a church, or on the stained windows, provided these representations contain no *nimbus* or halo that would indicate canonization, beatification or a cult.[11]

§ 2. To those who have been canonically inserted in the catalogue of Saints is due the worship called *dulia.* *Saints* may be worshipped everywhere and by any act of *dulia,* but the *Blessed* may be worshipped only in the places and manner expressly granted by the Roman Pontiff.

A *canonical* insertion is made either by a formal or by an equivalent (*aequipollens*) decree issued by the Church, ratifying the cult offered to a Saint or Blessed person either by a long-standing tradition, or the common consent of the Church, or the writings of Holy Fathers and saintly men. These Saints, then, may receive the worship of *dulia,* as explained in can. 1255.

There is a difference between *Saints* in the strict sense and *Blessed,* although the distinction of cult is hardly perceptible. Benedict XIV [12] states three characteristics which distinguish Saints from Blessed:

(1) Beatification *permits,* canonization *prescribes* worship; at least this is the rule, though the Pontiff admits exceptions.

(2) The worship of a Blessed is confined to a certain

---

10 S. Rit C, Sept 28, 1658 (n. 1097).

11 S. Rit C., Aug. 27, 1894 (n. 3835).

12 *De Servorum Dei Beat. etc.,* l. I, c. 39, nn 12 ff.

province, diocese, city, or religious institute, whereas the Saints may, though they need not, be worshipped everywhere throughout the whole Church.

(3) Canonization is the definitive and ultimate sentence of the Sovereign Pontiff, by which the worship of a Saint is prescribed for the whole Church, whilst beatification is a less definitive pronouncement.[13] This latter feature, according to Benedict XIV, marks the real difference between Saints and Blessed.

The general rules which must be observed concerning the *worship* of the *Blessed* are the following:

1. *Mass* and *Office* must be especially granted by the Roman Pontiff in honor of the Blessed. This indult is not included in the grant of erecting an altar in honor of the Blessed, nor is the public recitation of the Office permitted by the act which permits worship. Devotions, however, or *festa devotionis*, may be celebrated in honor of the Blessed, but not regular holydays with Mass and office, unless there be a special indult to this effect.[14]

If a Mass and office have been granted by special indult, the priests who celebrate Mass in chapels or churches for which the indult was given may and must conform to the rubrics, *i. e.*, they should say the Mass of the Blessed, if prescribed according to the approved calendar.[15]

2. As to *images,* votive tablets, statues, and pictures of the Blessed, these may be publicly exhibited for veneration in churches and oratories *if* the indult for Mass and office has been given, because this indult includes permission to exhibit said objects. Otherwise the images,

---

[13] Hence theologians are unanimous in stating the infallibility of the Pope with regard to canonization, whilst they are more or less divided concerning beatification, cfr. Mazzella, *De Rel & Eccl* n. 813.

[14] S Rit C., Sept. 27, 1659; April 17, 1660; July 24, 1915 (*Dec. Auth*, nn. 1136, 1156; *A Ap. S.,* VII, 389).

[15] See the decree of Dec 9, 1895 of the S. Rit. C.

etc., may only be placed on the walls of the church or chapel, but never on the altar; and the local Ordinary is entitled to have them removed.

3. The *names* of the Blessed may not be inserted in the general calendar, but only in the one used for the particular place or institute; nor may it be recited in the *suffragium Sanctorum,* or in other prayers, except those approved by the Holy See.

4. If the worship of a Blessed has been granted for a *certain place,* it cannot be extended to another without a papal indult.

5. These rules must also be observed by *exempt religious,* no matter what their name or privileges may be or have been.

PATRON SAINTS

Can. 1278

Laudabiliter quoque, servatis servandis, Sancti nationum, dioecesium, provinciarum, confraternitatum, familiarum religiosarum aliorumque locorum et moralium personarum eliguntur et, accedente confirmatione Sedis Apostolicae, constituuntur Patroni; Beati non item, sine peculiari eiusdem Sedis Apostolicae indulto.

It is praiseworthy that nations, dioceses, provinces, confraternities, religious institutes, places and corporations should choose patron *saints* with the approval of the Apostolic See. But the *Blessed* can be chosen patrons only with a special indult of the same Holy See.

The approval of the Apostolic See is also required when a new patron Saint is chosen instead of an old one.[16] Thus it may happen that a revolution sweeps away religious communities and the new occupants of a church

---

16 S. Rit. C., March 23, 1630 (n. 526).

choose another patron saint.   Such a change may be made
with the consent of the S. Rit. C.[17]   The patron-saint of
a place or community may differ from the one in whose
name a church is dedicated.   In a large city, for instance,
there may be many patron or titular saints of different
churches, but only one patron of the city, or diocese, or
province.[18]

PICTURES OF SAINTS

Can. 1279

§ 1. Nemini liceat in ecclesiis, etiam exemptis,
aliisve locis sacris ullam insolitam ponere vel ponen-
dam curare imaginem, nisi ab Ordinario loci sit approbata.

§ 2. Ordinarius autem sacras imagines publice ad
fidelium venerationem exponendas ne approbet, quae
cum probato Ecclesiae usu non congruant.

§ 3. Nunquam sinat Ordinarius in ecclesiis aliisve
locis sacris exhiberi falsi dogmatis imagines vel quae
debitam decentiam et honestatem non praeseferant, aut
rudibus periculosi erroris occasionem praebeant.

§ 4. Si imagines, publicae venerationi expositae,
sollemniter benedicantur, haec benedictio Ordinario
reservatur, qui tamen potest eam cuilibet sacerdoti
committere.

§ 1 repeats almost verbally the strict prohibition of the
Council of Trent [19] against exhibiting *unusual images,* in
churches or sacred places, even of exempt religious, unless
the approval of the local Ordinary has first been obtained.

§ 2. The Ordinaries shall never allow any sacred im-

17 S. Rit C , June 1, 1876, ad VI   18 S. Rit. C , May 1, 1857 (n.
(n. 3400).   3048).

19 Sess 25, *de invocat.*

ages to be publicly exhibited to the veneration of the faithful, unless these images are in keeping with the approved
usage of the Church.

From this paragraph may be negatively deduced what
an unusual image (*insolita imago*) is, namely, an image
that represents persons or events in a manner which has
no justification in either Holy Scripture or tradition.
Thus to represent the Holy Ghost in the form of a young
man has never been sanctioned, but rather reprobated, by
the Church.   The Blessed Trinity may not be represented
in the shape of a man with three heads, or of one man
with two heads with a dove between them.[20]   A statue or
painting similarly representing the Sorrowful Mother
dressed in black and holding a crucifix in the left hand
would be an unusual picture.[21]   Pictures of the Sacred
Heart of Jesus representing the Heart alone, without the
rest of the body, are not allowed to be exhibited publicly
on altars, but may be used for private devotion.[22]   The
title " *Cor Jesu Eucharisticum* " is neither canonical nor
liturgical, and hence no pictures of it may be exhibited to
the veneration of the faithful.[23]   Chinese Christians sometimes depict our Saviour with a Chinese beard and shoes.
This custom is not strictly forbidden, but should be dis-
couraged.

Note that the term *images* comprises all kinds of representations : statues, pictures, medals, etc.

§ 3. The Ordinary shall never permit the exhibition, in
churches or sacred places, of images which offend against
dogma or lack decency and propriety, or are apt to lead

[20] Bened. XIV, " *Sollicitudini*,"
Oct. 1, 1745, §§ 10 ff

[21] S. Rit. C, Feb. 23, 1894 (n.
3818).

[22] S. O., Aug. 26, 1891 (*Coll. P.
F*, n. 1767). The S. Heart of Mary
is to be represented according to the
decree of April 26, 1875; Nov. 29,
1878 (n 3470).

[23] S. Rit C., March 28, July 15,
1914 (*A. Ap. S.*, VI, 146, 382 f.).

the ignorant into error. Undogmatic are the above-mentioned representations of the Holy Ghost and the Blessed Trinity. Decency is also required in the garb or dress given to statues, which only too often offend against good taste.[24] Danger might arise from the veneration of images if ignorant persons would be permitted to worship one who has never been declared or acknowledged as a saint,[25] or if fetichism were attached to their devotion.

§ 4. The *solemn* blessing of images which are to be exhibited for public veneration is *reserved to the Ordinary,* who may, however, delegate this function to any priest. There is no rule or law prescribing the blessing of images.

RESTORATION OF STATUES AND PAINTINGS

CAN. 1280

Imagines pretiosae, idest vetustate, arte, aut cultu praestantes, in ecclesiis vel oratoriis publicis fidelium venerationi expositae, si quando reparatione indigeant, nunquam restaurentur sine dato scriptis consensu ab Ordinario; qui, antequam licentiam concedat, prudentes ac peritos viros consulat.

Images which possess great value by reason of their antiquity, artistic finish or the veneration given to them, and which have been exhibited to the worship of the faithful in churches and public oratories, if in need of repairs, must not be restored without the written consent of the Ordinary, who shall seek advice from wise and experienced men before he grants such a permission. This is a very timely law which should have been enforced in the seventeenth and eighteenth centuries when ecclesiastical

24 S. Rit. C., March 15, 1888 (n. 3690).

25 S. Rit. C., Aug. 31, 1889 (n. 3715).

dignitaries often " restored " fine romanesque chuiches of Gothic or Moorish architecture and converted them into whitewashed Barocco edifices [26]

We may also be permitted to add that some modern statues savor very much of the " salon." Take, for example, a good many representations of St. Francis of Assisi and St. Antony, which are anything but dignified in their fancy costumes. Ecclesiastical statuaries should be inspected before they are ecclesiastically approved.

ALIENATION OF RELICS AND IMAGES

CAN. 1281

§ 1. Insignes reliquiae aut imagines pretiosae itemque aliae reliquiae aut imagines quae in aliqua ecclesia magna populi veneratione honorentur, nequeunt valide alienari neque in aliam ecclesiam perpetuo transferri sine Apostolicae Sedis permissu.

§ 2. Insignes Sanctorum vel Beatorum reliquiae sunt corpus, caput, brachium, antibrachium, cor, lingua, manus, crus aut illa pars corporis in qua passus est martyr, dummodo sit integra et non parva.

§ 1 prohibits the alienation of important relics or images of great value, as well as of such relics and images as are held in great honor by the people in some church. To alienate such without an apostolic indul is void of effect in the ecclesiastical external forum as well as in the court of conscience. Nor may such relics or images be permanently transferred to another church without permission from Rome.

In the eighth and ninth centuries, after many relics had

[26] Example: the cathedral of Amalfi in Italy

been transferred from the catacombs to the churches of Rome, a regular traffic in relics began which soon became a public scandal. A synod of Mayence, in 813, forbade the transfer of bodies of saints without the permission of the secular ruler, or bishop, or synod.[27] The fourth Lateran Council prohibited the exhibition of relics for sale as detrimental to religion and also commanded that all ancient relics should be enclosed in reliquaries and neither exposed nor sold without authority from the Sovereign Pontiff. Minor prelates in whose churches relics were venerated, were urged not to permit fraud by exhibiting false documents to allure the faithful — as, adds the council, had happened in several places, for the sake of gain.[28] Transfer from one altar to another of the same church may be permitted by the bishop.[29]

Temporary transfer is permissible because the Code uses the term *perpetuo*. Hence if repairs or other reasons would render a temporary transfer necessary, no recourse to the Holy See would be required, provided, of course, the relics or images are replaced.

§ 2 defines what an important relic (*insignis reliquia*) is. It is the entire body, head, arm, forearm, heart, tongue, hand, leg of a saint or blessed person, or that part of his body in which the martyr suffered death, provided it be entire and not a small part. This paragraph is verbally taken from a decree of the S. C. of Rites, which however, added: "duly approved by the Ordinary."[30] This clause is omitted in our text, probably on account of the following canon. There is a special reason for mentioning the different parts, namely, because on the

27 Can. 51, c. 37, Dist. 1 *de cons.;* Hefele, *Concil-Gesch.*, III, 711.
28 C. 2, X, III, 45.

29 S. C. Indulg., Nov. 17, 1676 (Prinzivalli, *l. c.*, n. 13).
30 S. Rit. C., April 8, 1628 (n. 460).

Feast of Relics the *Credo* is to be recited in churches where an important relic is preserved.

After the publication or the decree of 1628 doubts arose as to what parts of the body of a Saint were meant. Most of the answers given in reply to questions were negative. Thus, the *tibia* or shinbone, or *femoris ossa* or thighbone, or smaller parts of the same, or the foot with some toes on it, were not acknowledged to be an *insignis reliquia*, nor even part of the head.[31]   On the other hand, the forearm and the upper arm, from the elbow to the shoulder, were acknowledged as *insignia*.[32]

Integra or entire is that part of the body in which the martyr suffered, provided it be unmutilated; if it *is* mutilated, for instance, the cranium crushed, it could be gathered up and the parts reassembled so as to make one whole.[33]   Besides, it must be a considerable part, not a mere splinter (*non parva*).

Can. 1282

§ 1. Insignes Sanctorum vel Beatorum reliquiae nequeunt in aedibus vel oratoriis privatis asservari, sine expressa Ordinarii loci licentia.

§ 2. Reliquiae non insignes debito cum honore etiam in domibus privatis servari pieque a fidelibus gestari possunt.

Important relics of saints and blessed persons may not be preserved in *private homes and oratories* without the express permission of the local Ordinary. *Minor relics,* on the other hand, may be kept in private houses and rev-

---

31 S. Rit. C., Dec. 20, 1628; June 3, 1662 ad 2, Dec. 7, 1844 (nn 490, 1234, 2883); S C Indulg., June 12, 1822 (Prinzivalli, n. 430).

32 S. Rit C., June 27, 1899, ad II (n. 4041).

33 S. Rit. C., Dec. 3, 1672 (n. 1460).

erently carried about by the faithful. The first paragraph
is undoubtedly prompted by the desire that all the faithful should be benefitted by the presence of such sacred
objects, and that important sacred remains should receive
a greater reverence than they ordinarily receive if in
private possession.

AUTHENTICATION OF RELICS

CAN. 1283

§ 1. Publico cultu eae reliquiae in ecclesiis, quanquam exemptis, honorari possunt, quas genuinas esse
constet authentico documento alicuius S. R. E. Cardinalis, vel Ordinarii loci, vel alius viri ecclesiastici
cui facultas *authenticandi* indulto apostolico sit concessa.

§ 2. Vicarius Generalis nequit, sine mandato speciali, reliquias authenticas edicere.

CAN. 1284

Locorum Ordinarii reliquiam, quam certo non esse
authenticam norint, a fidelium cultu prudenter amo-
veant.

CAN. 1285

§ 1. Sacrae reliquiae, quarum authenticitatis documenta ob civiles perturbationes vel ob alium quemlibet casum interierint, publicae venerationi ne exponantur, nisi praecedat iudicium Ordinarii loci, non
autem Vicarii Generalis sine mandato speciali.

§ 2. Reliquiae tamen antiquae in ea veneratione qua
hactenus fuerunt, sunt retinendae, nisi in aliquo peculiari casu certis argumentis constet eas falsas vel
suppositicias esse.

CAN. 1286

Locorum Ordinarii ne sinant, maxime in sacris concionibus, libris, ephemeridibus vel commentariis fovendae pietati destinatis, ex meris coniecturis, ex solis probabilibus argumentis vel praeiudicatis opinionibus, praesertim verbis ludibrium aut despectum sapientibus, quaestiones agitari de sacrarum reliquiarum authenticitate.

Only genuine relics may be exhibited for public veneration in churches, even those of exempt religious. The genuineness of a relic is ascertained by an authentic document, issued either by a cardinal, or by the local Ordinary, or by a clergyman who has obtained an apostolic indult authorizing him to authenticate relics.

The Vicar General needs a special mandate to issue such a document.

The authentification of ancient relics is a delicate and difficult task, which requires a great deal of archaeological and palæographical knowledge. Hence the Cardinal Vicar of Rome supports a special department, called *lipsanotheca*, for the purpose of authenticating relics. This means was especially employed after 1870, when many churches and convents were suppressed, shrines and reliquaries scattered and sold without the knowledge of the proper authorities and imitations were not infrequently sold by unscrupulous persons for filthy lucre's sake. Hence the Vicariate of Rome warned bishops against being too credulous concerning bodies which purported to have been taken from the catacombs, even though they were "authenticated" by an Italian bishop, for these nefarious traders did not shrink from forging documents.[34]

34 Vicariatus Urbis litt. encycl., Jan. 17, 1881 (*Coll. P. F.*, n. 1546).

Absolute certainty in regard to the genuineness of relics, especially such as date back to a remote age, is next to impossible. It would, however, be wrong for that reason to reject all ancient relics. Many documents attesting the transfer or translation of relics have been preserved, and, besides, the immemorable custom of veneration must be admitted as a living proof which amounts at least to moral certainty. It may also be assumed that Divine Providence watches over these sacred objects with special care.[35] Finally, even if there be fraud or erroneous belief, the act of venerating a relic is always a religious act addressed ultimately to God, and hence can never be entirely void of effectiveness.

The ecclesiastical authority who has to authenticate relics must, if possible, investigate their origin or source, and therefore demand a document. This document must contain the signature and seal of the one who enclosed the relics in its container. The latter (capse) must be sealed with the same seal which is impressed on the document of authentification. Generally also the make of the capse, its artistic decoration and the material from which it is made are indications of authenticity. If the signature, seal and capse (or shrine) all point to some degree of certainty, the document may be accepted as genuine.[36] In the same way the bishop must proceed when relics are transferred from one church or country to another, provided, in the latter case, the Apostolic indult was obtained. If no authentic document or no immemorable custom can be shown, no document should be issued.[37]

Can. 1284 obliges the local Ordinaries to withdraw from public veneration all relics of which he knows for

---

[35] See Ps. 33, 2

[36] S. C. Indulg , Dec. 16, 1749 (Prinzivalli, n. 187).

[37] S. Rit. C , July 21, 1696, ad 4 (n. 1946).

certain that they are *not* genuine. As stated, the signature and seal on the document and capse may be considered sufficient authentication. However, the signature must be by hand, and not with a stamp (*colla stampiglia*), unless the prelate is notoriously prevented from writing by paralysis or other bodily infirmity.

Titular bishops are not empowered to authenticate relics.[38] This privilege is expressly reserved to cardinals and ordinaries in the strict sense of the term, though Vicars Capitular or Administrators are not excluded. Relics which are certainly spurious,[39] the Ordinaries would do well to withdraw and destroy.

However it may happen, as is evident from can. 1285, that the authenticating documents are lost. This has happened under the Huguenots' terror in Toulouse, during the French Revolution,[40] and in Italy after 1870. Such relics may be exposed to public veneration only if the local Ordinary deems it proper. The Vicar General is not competent to grant this permission without being specially commissioned to do so. If the faithful are deeply attached to certain, especially ancient, relics and have a special veneration for them, they may be retained and venerated, provided their spuriousness cannot be proved by solid arguments.[41]

The *public discussion of the authenticity of relics* should be avoided and may be forbidden by the local Ordinaries if the argument rests on mere conjectures, probabilities or prejudices, and if the methods employed are apt to cast ridicule and contempt on sacred relics or their

38 S. C. Indulg., Sept. 23, 1783 (Prinzivalli, n. 378).

39 For instance, relics of the Highpriest Melchisedek; S. Rit. C., Aug. 3, 1687 (n. 1977).

40 S. C. Indulg., Feb. 22, 1847 (Prinzivalli, n. 582); S. Rit. C., June 23, 1892 (n. 3779).

41 S. C. Indulg., Jan. 20, 1896; Pius X, "*Sacrorum Antistitum,*" Sept. 1, 1910, n. VI (*A. Ap. S.*, II, 664 f.).

veneration. Such discussions should not be conducted in sermons, or in books, magazines, and pamphlets intended to foster devotion rather than critical research. This well directed and carefully worded admonition, which is partly taken from the Motu proprio "*Sacrorum Antistitum*," of Sept. 1, 1910, warns writers against setting up merely probable statements for absolute truth, but it does not forbid sober and respectful criticism based upon scientific research. For the rule laid down in our canon applies to devotional books or periodical publications only, — not to critical disquisitions and scientific reviews. Besides, whilst it warns against the propagation of purely probable and subjective views, it leaves a large margin for solid arguments.[42] The language employed by critics should, of course, always be moderate and respectful.

EXPOSITION OF RELICS

Can. 1287

§ 1. Reliquiae, cum exponuntur, in thecis seu capsis clausae et obsignatae sint oportet.

§ 2. Reliquiae sanctissimae Crucis nunquam in eadem theca cum reliquiis Sanctorum publicae venerationi exhibeantur, sed propriam thecam separatam habeant.

§ 3. Beatorum reliquiae, sine peculiari indulto, in processionibus ne circumferantur, neve in ecclesiis exponantur, nisi ubi eorum officium et Missa celebretur ex Sedis Apostolicae concessione.

When relics are exposed, they should be *enclosed* in a shrine, case or capsule, and *sealed* with the seal of the authenticating prelate or official.

---

42 The Bollandists cannot be seriously accused of making exaggerated or unfounded statements.

Relics of the true Cross should never be exhibited to public veneration together with relics of Saints, *i. e.,* enclosed in the same chest or shrine, but in a separate case.[43]

Relics of the true Cross and of other instruments of Christ's Passion may be carried about in procession under a canopy; but no other relics of Saints or Blessed may on such occasions be carried in procession under the canopy at the same time.[44]

Relics of *Blessed* persons may not be carried about in procession without a special indult, nor may they be publicly exposed in churches except where the Mass and office is permitted by the Apostolic See.

RELICS IN THE BISHOP'S PECTORAL CROSS

CAN. 1288

Sanctissimae Crucis reliquiae, quas in cruce pectorali Episcopus forte defert, ecclesiae cathedrali, ipso defuncto, cedunt, Episcopo successori transmittendae; et si defunctus pluribus praefuerit dioecesibus, ecclesiae cathedrali dioecesis, in cuius territorio supremum diem obiit aut, si extra dioecesim mortuus est, ex qua ultimo discessit.

Relics of the true Cross which may be enclosed in the pectoral cross of a bishop, after his death belong to his cathedral church, which shall hand them to the bishop's successor. If the deceased bishop ruled several dioceses, the relics pass to the cathedral church of the one in which he died; if he dies outside the diocese, the relics belong to the cathedral church of the diocese in which he passed away. The reason for this enactment is to be sought

---

[43] S. C. Indulg., Feb. 22, 1847 (Prinzivalli, n. 589).

[44] S. Rit. C., May 27, 1826 (n. 2647) and *pluries.*

in the scarcity of these relics which bishops should carry about their person as a token of their dignity. But the law only touches the relic, not the pectoral cross, or the *theca* or capsule in which the relic is contained. The *theca* may, after the sacred relic has been withdrawn, be disposed of or sold, with due precaution, of course, against profanation.[45]

PRECAUTIONS AGAINST THE SALE AND PROFANATION
OF RELICS

CAN. 1289

§ 1. Sacras reliquias vendere nefas est; adeoque Ordinarii locorum, vicarii foranei, parochi aliive curam animarum habentes, sedulo caveant ne sacrae reliquiae, praesertim sanctissimae Crucis, occasione maxime hereditatum aut alienationis acervi bonorum, veneant, neve in acatholicorum manus transeant.

§ 2. Rectores ecclesiarum, ceterique ad quos spectat, sedulo invigilent ne sacrae reliquiae ullo modo profanentur, neve hominum incuria pereant, vel minus decenter custodiantur.

It is forbidden to sell relics, and hence the local ordinaries, rural deans, pastors, and all those who have charge of souls shall take proper precautions lest sacred relics, especially of the Holy Cross, be sold on the occasion of hereditary transfer or public auction, and see to it that they do not pass into the hands of non-Catholics.

· The rectors of churches, and others whom it concerns, (*e. g.*, the *custos sacrae supellectilis*) should also take great care lest sacred relics be exposed to profanation,

---

45 Vic. Urbis lit encycl., March 25, 1889 (*Coll. P. F.*, n. 1699).

or lost through carelessness, or preserved in an unbecoming manner.

As mentioned above, the impious custom of selling relics was practiced at times for gain. Often also well-meaning Catholics bought relics from traders in order to save them from profanation. But even this is forbidden because of the danger of simony and of aiding this impious traffic. All the faithful are in duty bound to denounce to the Ordinary any place where relics are exhibited for sale. He will then take such steps as he deems proper.[46]

46 S. C. Indulg., Dec. 21, 1878 (*Coll. P. F.,* n. 1505).

TITLE XVII

SACRED PROCESSIONS

CAN. 1290

§ 1. Nomine sacrarum processionum significantur sollemnes supplicationes quae a populo fideli, duce clero, fiunt eundo ordinatim de loco sacro ad locum sacrum, ad excitandam fidelium pietatem, ad commemoranda Dei beneficia eique gratias agendas, ad divinum auxilium implorandum.

§ 2. *Ordinariae* sunt quae statis diebus per annum fiunt ad normam librorum liturgicorum vel consuetudinum ecclesiarum; *extraordinariae,* quae aliis publicis de causis in alios dies indicuntur.

Sacred processions are solemn invocations made by the faithful people marching in an orderly manner, under the leadership of the clergy, from one sacred place to another, for the purpose of arousing devotion, praising God's benefits, thanking Him, and imploring His help.

Ordinary processions are those held on stated days throughout the year, according to the sacred liturgy or the custom of the churches; *extraordinary* processions are those held for some other public cause on other days.

Processions are a popular element in almost every form of religious worship.[1] The Roman Ritual specifies as *or-*

---

1 Cfr. *Cath Encycl.,* XII, 446 ff. *s. v.* " Procession "

dinary processions those held on Candlemas Day (Feb. 2), on Palm Sunday, the so-called greater Litanies of April 25, and the Rogation Days preceding the feast of the Ascension. Besides these, we may designate as ordinary the procession on Maundy Thursday, the return on Good Friday, and the procession for the holy fire on Holy Saturday. Funeral processions may also be called ordinary. Moreover, as the text also mentions as ordinary the processions introduced by ecclesiastical custom, it is evident that so-called *field processions,* as still in vogue in Switzerland, and *processions* from one church to another in honor of a special *patron,* must likewise be reckoned among the ordinary ones.

Extraordinary processions, according to the Roman Ritual, are all those held for the purpose of obtaining rain, or fair weather, of driving away storms, the three assigned for times of famine, plague, and war, one for the occasion of any calamity, one for thanksgiving, and one for the translation of relics.

The *essential* feature of a sacred procession certainly is that it is held under the leadership of the clergy. Hence a mere parade held for any purpose, even for the translation of sacred images from house to house, in which the clergy are mere participants without sacred vestments, cannot be called a procession in the liturgical sense.[2] Besides, even a religious procession if arranged and led by laymen, cannot be styled a sacred procession.

A sacred procession must be conducted in an *orderly* manner. This rule has a double meaning, of which one is described in can. 1295, and has reference to due reverence and becoming conduct, while the other is that the order of the participants be according to the rules of precedence, regarding which see can. 1295.

2 S. Rit C., Aug. 20, 1870 (*Dec. Auth.,* n. 3217).

CORPUS CHRISTI PROCESSIONS

CAN. 1291

§ 1. Nisi aliter ferat immemorabilis consuetudo, vel locorum circumstantiae, prudenti Episcopi iudicio, aliud exigant, die festo Corporis Christi unica tantum sollemnisque per publicas vias processio in uno eodemque loco fieri debet ab ecclesia digniore, eique clerici omnes religiosaeque virorum familiae, etiam exemptae, et laicorum confraternitates interesse debent, regularibus exceptis qui in strictiore clausura perpetuo vivant, aut a civitate ultra tria millia passuum distent.

§ 2. Ceterae paroeciae et ecclesiae etiam regulares possunt, intra octavam, proprias processiones extra ecclesiae ambitum agere; sed ubi plures sunt ecclesiae, Ordinarii loci est dies, horas ac vias praestituere quibus suam quaeque processionem agant.

§ 1. Unless there be an immemorial custom to the contrary, or unless local circumstances in the prudent judgment of the bishop demand a deviation from the rule here laid down, only *one solemn procession is permitted* in the same place through the public streets *on the feast* of *Corpus Christi.* This procession is to be arranged and led by the more prominent church of the respective city or town, and all the clergy and male religious orders, including the exempt, as well as the confraternities of laymen, must attend it. Only those regulars who live perpetually in strict enclosure, or dwell three thousand paces from the city, are excused from participation.

The solemn *Corpus Christi procession* is to be held on the following Sunday, if the feast is transferred to that day,[3] as is the case in our country. Therefore, even taking into consideration § 2 of our canon, it would clearly be against the intention of the Church to hold the principal procession on Corpus Christi Thursday and a less pompous one on Sunday.

There must be only one *public procession* in the same town or city, unless an immemorial custom or special circumstances should induce the bishop to permit more. There is not much danger in our country, especially in the large cities, of having too many processions.

The *dignior ecclesia,* i. e., the more distinguished church, should lead the procession. *Dignior* undoubtedly is the cathedral church, which follows the collegiate church, provided it is also a parochial church.[4] It appears but just that a parochial church should be preferred to a collegiate church if the latter is not a parish church. Among the parish churches the more ancient one takes the lead over those established later, according to the rule: *Prior in tempore prior in iure.*

In this public procession the entire *secular* and *regular clergy,* as well as all confraternities, of men as well as women, are bound to participate. Religious congregations and orders of women need not attend, though Sisters who do not live in enclosure *may* do so if they wish; — at least the text does not exclude them because it only mentions those who are obliged to assist (*interesse debent*). As to the *regulars,* whether exempt or not, the Council of Trent[5] had already made it obligatory for them to attend, with one exception, to be explained further down (see next paragraph). The Council employs the phrase, "*vocati accedant,*" which presupposes some

---

3 S. Rit. C., June 24, 1911 ad VI (n. 4273).

4 S. Rit C., Jan. 11, 1681 (n. 1657).

5 Sess. 25, c. 13, *de reg.*

kind of invitation. The Code discards this clause, and hence no invitation is required, though the leading church may reasonably be expected to indicate or announce the hour of holding the procession and the place where it is to start.

The *exception* for regulars is based upon enclosure and distance. The *enclosure,* of course, is to be understood of the so-called papal enclosure, as stated under can. 597. This was already enacted by the Council of Trent and confirmed by later interpretations, the substance of which is that all regulars, no matter how exempt they may be, must attend the Corpus Christi procession, unless they live under strict perpetual enclosure or can show a privilege granted after the Council of Trent, and directly, *i. e.,* not obtained by way of communication.[6] Such privileges were granted to the Society of Jesus, to the Discalced Carmelites, the Theatines and the Scolapii.[7] The Code does not annul these privileges by any contrary clause. The great Mendicant Orders of St. Francis and St. Dominic are obliged to attend the Corpus Christi procession,[8] as are also the Augustinians, *Calceati* as well *Discalceati,* and the Celestinians.[9] As to the Benedictines there are two decisions worthy of note: the Cassinese monks need not take part in any procession except that of Corpus Christi, which they *must* attend, even though there be but six monks living in the monastery.[10] Note that no communication of privileges avails in this case. But what about enclosure? The Benedictines have a papal

6 Urban VIII, " *Nuper,*" Nov. 17, 1638, § 1 f ; S. Rit. C, Sept. 28, 1658 (n. 1096).

7 Piatus M , *Praelectiones Juris Regul.,* II, p. 41.

8 S. Rit. C., May 10, 1594; May 9, 1693 (nn. 48, 1895).

9 S. Rit. C., Dec. 9, 1638; Sept. 2, 1602, Aug. 4, 1674 ad 1 (nn. 661, 1244, 1716).

10 S. Rit C., June 10, 1602; Oct. 2, 1683 (nn. 99, 1716).

enclosure, but no strict enclosure in the sense of the text, like the Carthusians and the Camaldolese Hermits. The decision concerning the Cassinese Benedictines mentions custom, but the Corpus Christi procession is expressly excepted   The same is true of the Celestinians and may safely be applied to other monastic bodies of regulars; because if the enclosure means something, it certainly must be applied to that case also, the Corpus Christi procession, as a special token of belief in that mystery and a public profession of the same against heresy.

The next reason for exception is *distance*. The general decree of Urban VIII, as restated by the S. Congregation, mentions " *Ultra medium milliare a civitate*," *i. e.*, over half a mile from the city. Our text has 300 *passus*. A passus, according to Roman reckoning, is 485 English or American feet, so that 3000 passus would be about 14,550 feet, or 1,290 feet less than three English statute miles [11] In round figures, therefore, we may say, three English (not geographical) miles, especially since the text says, *ultra,* above.

The point from which the distance must be reckoned is simply stated as " the city." But in a large city there may be a considerable difference between the different points from which distance may be measured. If the city limits are taken as the starting point, the three miles would be entirely outside the boundaries. This, we believe, is the meaning of the text, for it obliges the entire clergy of a city or town to attend the procession, and one decision says that all the Friars Preachers and Friars Minor *intra septa moenium civitatis* must be present.[12] Therefore not the church from which the procession

[11] Cfr   Ramsay-Lanciani, *Roman Antiquities*, 1901, p 462 f.   [12] S Rit. C , May 10, 1594 (n. 48).

starts, but the city limits, is the point from which the distance is to be calculated. The direction, of course, is intended in the direct or air line, *i. e.,* within a radius of three miles outside the city limits.

It may be added that the obligation of assisting at the Corpus Christi procession binds the secular and regular clergy only if the procession is held in the open air, *per publicas vias,* and the term *regular* must be taken in the strict sense, to the exclusion of such religious as are exempt by a special indult.

§ 2. The other parishes and churches, including those which are in charge of regulars, may have their own processions outside the church during the Octave of Corpus Christi; but the local Ordinary should assign the day, the hour and the route for each parish. This rule was established in order to avoid unpleasant encounters. In some cases even the side of the wall or street had to be determined [13] and pastors were ordered not to invade the boundaries of other parishes.[14]

OTHER PROCESSIONS

CAN. 1292

Ordinarius loci, audito Capitulo cathedrali, potest ex publica causa extraordinarias processiones indicere; quibus, sicut et ordinariis ac consuetis, ii omnes interesse debent de quibus in can. 1291, § 1.

The local Ordinary, after having heard the advice of his cathedral chapter, may for a public cause order extraordinary processions, which, like the customary and ordinary ones, must be attended by those mentioned in can. 1291, § 1.

---

13 S. Rit. C, June 11, 1594 (n. 49).

14 S. Rit C, Jan 11, 1681 (n. 1657).

If the Ordinary is obliged to hear the advice of the chapter and cannot lawfully order a procession without it, this is *a fortiori* true of the Vicar Capitular or administrator. Should a procession be ordered without their advice, the canons cannot be compelled to attend it.[15] This rule must also be followed in our country, where the consultors should be asked *collegialiter*. This does not, however, mean that the bishop cannot order a customary or extraordinary procession without first hearing the advice of the consultors. He may order a procession to be held in any parish; but he cannot oblige the whole clergy, secular and regular, to attend it if he has not previously asked the chapter or the consultors. However, it is sufficient to ask their advice; their consent is not required.[16] Besides the bishop no one else in the diocese is entitled to order a procession, but in the absence of the bishop the Vicar General may do so, provided he has asked the advice of the chapter.[17]

The *extraordinary* processions which the local Ordinary may order must be for a public cause, or, as is sometimes stated, [18] *pro bono publico et publico honore*. This means that the public interest or the welfare of the community must be at stake, as is evident from the enumeration of these extraordinary processions in the Ritual. They cannot be ordered for mere display. If a procession is customary on the occasion of the entrance of a new bishop, this may be ordered for all, including the regulars, though without threatening censures.[19] An extraordinary procession may also be ordered on the

15 S C EE. et RR , May 11, 1663 (Bizzarri, *l. c.*, p 261).

16 S Rit. C., March 28, 1626 (n. 394).

17 S Rit. C , Jan. 14, 1617, ad 1; Sept 28, 1630 (nn. 346, 545).

18 S. Rit C., July 27, 1609 (n. 272).

19 S C. C., July 11, 1750 (Richter, *Trid*, p 416, n. 9).

occasion of a Eucharistic Congress, or a Congress in honor of the Sacred Heart of Jesus, or an important meeting of Catholics.

Those obliged to participate in these extraordinary processions are the same as mentioned in can 1291; hence, first of all, the whole *secular clergy*, provided the Ordinary has duly intimated his intention to that effect. *Indicere,* to order, certainly implies a lawful summons. The *regular clergy,* too, must be present, under the same conditions as stated above. We will add that the monks, unless they can prove a legitimate contrary custom, must also be present. Thus it has been decided concerning the monks of St. Basil and St. Benedict in a case from the diocese of Paderborn.[20] The time or hour for the procession must be announced by the Ordinary, who may suit himself about it.[21] The lay *confraternities* also must attend these processions if they have been summoned by the Ordinary.[22]

RELIGIOUS NOT ALLOWED TO HOLD PUBLIC PROCESSIONS WITHOUT THE PERMISSION OF THE ORDINARY

CAN. 1293

Religiosi etiam exempti nequeunt extra suas ecclesias et claustra processiones ducere sine Ordinarii loci licentia, salvo praescripto can. 1291, § 2.

With the exception of the Octave of Corpus Christi, religious, even though exempt, are not allowed to hold processions outside their churches and cloisters without the permission of the local Ordinary, who may grant this

20 S. Rit. C, June 23, 1670; Dec. 22, 1770, ad 2 (nn 2116, 2490)

21 S. Rit. C, June 17, 1606 (n. 217).

22 S. Rit. C., Sept. 23, 1820 (n. 2608).

permission without asking the consent or advice of his chapter or consultors, nay, even against the will of the pastor or collegiate chapter,[23] and once for all. He may also prescribe or change the route the procession has to take.[24] If the religious have obtained a special papal indult, or can prove a legal custom, they do not need the permission of the Ordinary.[25] Also, if they have obtained a direct privilege, or can prove that the custom existed after the year 1628, no permission is required.[26] But if they have neither the Ordinary's permission, nor a privilege, nor an indult, nor a legitimate custom in their favor, they are allowed to hold processions only *within their church or cloister,* always excepting the Octave of Corpus Christi. However, a general decree of 1658, Sept. 28, states that if they have no cloister they may lead a procession even outside the church, provided they keep to the walls of the church and re-enter through the same or another door of the same (*non extra ambitum ecclesiae*).

PASTORS AND THE CLERGY IN RELATION TO PROCESSIONS

CAN. 1294

§ 1. Parochus vel quivis alius nequit processiones novas inducere aut consuetas transferre vel abolere sine Ordinarii loci licentia.

§ 2. Processionibus alicuius ecclesiae propriis interesse debent omnes clerici eidem ecclesiae adscripti.

§ 1. Neither the pastor nor anyone else can introduce new, or transfer or abolish the customary processions without the permission of the local Ordinary.

23 S. Rit. C., March 11, 1690; June 13, 1673; Aug 31, 1697; (nn 1824, 1573, 1980)

24 S. Rit C., Nov. 24, 1691 (n. 1859)

25 S Rit. C, Nov. 14, 1676, April 8, 1702 (n. 1581, 2099)

26 S. Rit. C., Sept 28, 1658, Dec. 19, 1671, ad 1 (nn 1096, 1440).

The term *quivis alius* includes cathedral and collegiate chapters, as well as confraternities, so that the prohibition also applies to them.[27]   If the Ordinary wishes to transfer a procession, for instance, on account of rain, the chapter would have to be asked.[28]   Our canon is silent about the advice of the chapter, we believe with good reason.   It goes without saying that also pastors or religious orders or congregations must abide by this law concerning processions.[29]

§ 2. At processions which are peculiar to any church, all the clergy belonging to the respective church must be present.   The term *adscripti* means ascribed or assigned, and, in canonical parlance, includes all the *beneficiaries* of a church.   All who hold a benefice in a church, unless they are *iubilati*, must attend the processions of that church.[30]   In our country all the clergy assigned to a church are under the same obligation.   However, the bishop may exempt such as are employed in other occupations, for instance, in mission work, teaching, etc. One who has been granted a vacation need not trouble his conscience concerning this obligation.

ORDER OF PROCESSIONS

CAN. 1295

Curent Ordinarii ut sacrae processiones, exstirpatis, si qui sint, malis usibus, ordinate procedant eaque modestia ac reverentia ab omnibus perficiantur, quae piis ac religiosis huiusmodi actibus maxime convenit.

27 S. Rit C., Nov 22, 1681, ad 2, 8, Jan 12, 1704, ad 22 (nn 1684, 2123).

28 S. Rit C , Sept. 3, 1695; July 21, 1696 (nn. 1932, 1947).

29 S. C. EE et RR., March 14, 1879 (*A S. S.*, XI, 595 ff.).

30 S C C , Feb. 27, 1677, Bened. XIV, *De Syn. Dioec* , III, 8, 9 f.

The Ordinaries shall take care that any abuses that may have crept in are eliminated and that the processions proceed in an orderly manner, with the modesty and reverence suited to such pious and religious acts.

An *orderly* procession presupposes an orderly arrangement according to rules.[31] The participants must walk two by two, with the Cross leading the procession. After the cross-bearer follow the girls and boys, then the women and men, then the confraternities according to rank, then the religious according to the rules of precedence set forth in can. 491, then the secular clergy, and finally the officiating minister, prelate or priest. Here may be supplied what has been omitted under canons 106 and 491. The cathedral chapter precedes, or rather, strictly speaking, follows the collegiate chapter, and the chapter or body of regulars with their abbot or prelate must walk among the religious.[32] Among the secular clergy priority of ordination decides the order of precedence, to which also the " doctors " must defer.[33] Each of the religious orders or congregations must march separately under its own cross, if it carries one, and not promiscuously with other religious or the secular clergy. This rule also binds *magistri*[34] (*i. e.,* doctors of divinity) in the order of Preachers.

There should be no dancing or fighting, no eating or drinking, and no unseemly noise.[35] For this reason processions should not last too long or cover a distance of more than six miles, especially if the roads are bad or walking is difficult.[36]

---

31 Cfr. *Pont. Rom.*, l. II, c. 32, n. 2; *Rit. Rom.*, tit. IX, c. 1.

32 S. Rit. C., Dec. 22, 1770 (n. 2490 ad 2).

33 S. Rit. C., April 4, 1626 (n. 397).

34 S. Rit. C., July 6, 1593; May 10, 1594; July 10, 1638 (nn. 33, 48, 647).

35 S. Rit. C., Jan. 21, 1690 n. 5 (n. 1821); *Rit. Rom., l. c.,* n. 6.

36 S. Rit. C., March 7, 1703 (n. 2109).

TITLE XVIII

SACRED VESSELS, UTENSILS, VESTMENTS ETC. (SACRA SUPELLEX)

The Latin term *sacra supellex* includes all sacred vessels, utensils, vestments, linens, and ornaments which are used for sacred functions, especially for the celebration of the Mass. The reader should not expect a canonist to go into details with regard to these objects, as they strictly belong to the domain of liturgical writers, who, however, curious to say, seem to evade a definition of the term *sacra supellex*.[1]

CARE AND MAINTENANCE

CAN. 1296

§ 1. Sacra supellex, praesertim quae, ad normam legum liturgicarum, benedicta aut consecrata esse debet quaeque publico in cultu adhibetur, caute custodiatur in ecclesiae sacrario aliove tuto ac decenti loco, nec ad usus profanos adhibeatur.

§ 2. Ad normam can. 1522 universae sacrae supellectilis inventarium fiat et accurate servetur.

§ 3. Circa materiam et formam sacrae supellectilis, serventur praescripta liturgica, ecclesiastica traditio et, meliore quo fieri potest modo, etiam artis sacrae leges.

---

1 We consulted De Herdt, Van der Stappen, Martinucci, Wapel- horst, and several books written in the vernacular.

\

CAN. 1297

Nisi aliter sit provisum, qui officio tenentur reparandae ecclesiae ad normam can. 1186, debent quoque ei
providere de sacra supellectili ad cultum necessaria.

Articles of *sacra supellex*, especially when blessed or
consecrated as required by the liturgical rules, and used
for public worship must be *carefully guarded* in the
sacristy of the church or in some other safe and decent
place, and may not be used for profane purposes.

An inventory should be made of the whole stock and
diligently preserved.

As to the material and form of the *sacra supellex*, the
liturgical laws, ecclesiastical tradition, and, as far as
possible, the rules of sacred art should be observed.

Chalice and paten must be *consecrated* by the bishop,
or whoever is authorized to perform this function.

The following articles must be *blessed:* the ciborium·[2]
(and most probably also the *lunula*,[3] because it comes
into immediate contact with the Blessed Sacrament);
the *vestments* used by the priest at sacred functions,
particularly in saying Mass, to wit: amice, alb, cincture,
maniple, chasuble, palla, corporal and altar linens.

The following objects *may* be blessed, though it is
not prescribed by the rubrics: the ostensorium, the *custodia* or pyx for the *lunula;* dalmatics, cope, and surplice.

Not to be blessed are the purificators,[4] the chalice veil,

2 The formula is either that of the *Pontif. Rom*, tit *De Bened. Taber-naculi sive Vasculi pro SS. Euch. Conservanda*, or that of the *Rit Rom.*, tit VIII, c 23 (ed Pustet, 1913, p. 76*).

3 Gasparri, *De SSma Euch*, n. 1031; S Rit. C, Feb 4, 1871 (n. 3234, ad IV) forbids the use of *lunulae* which so enclose the S Host that the glass directly touches the sacred species. Yet, says Gasparri (*l c.*, n. 1029), the custom is wide-spread in France, we may add, also in the U S.

4 S. Rit·C., Sept. 7, 1816 ad 12 (n. 2572).

the burse, the antipendium, candlesticks, cruets, censers, etc.

Concerning the consecration of the chalice and paten it may be noted that the formula requires *three signs of the cross,* one at the word *consecrare,* the other at the word *sanctificare,* the third at the *benedictionem.* If the last were omitted, there might be a doubt as to the validity of the consecration, although the S. Congregation would not answer the question directly.[5] It is more probable that the consecration would be valid, for the act of consecration proper is completed by the two anointings with holy chrism, made with the twofold sign of the cross, and the same S. Congregation has declared that chalice and paten are validly consecrated even though but one sign of the cross was made on them with holy chrism, either at the *consecrare* or *sanctificare.*[6] From this it appears lawful to conclude that, even though the last or third sign of the cross were omitted, the consecration would be valid. If .the cup (*cuppa*) of the chalice be very deep, so that the consecrator cannot reach the bottom, which he should do when anointing from one rim through the center or bottom to the other rim, with the thumb, he may reach as far as possible with the thumb, rather than use the middle finger, and thus observe the rubric.[7]

The *sacerdotal vestments* require a *special blessing.* Therefore, if a priest should, in good faith, wear unblessed vestments, they would not become blessed by the mere act of wearing them at Mass.[8] *Priests* who are allowed to bless sacred vestments and linens must

5 S Rit. C., June 14, 1873 (n 3305): "*servetur rubrica Pont. Romani.*"

6 S. Rit. C, Dec. 2, 1882 (n. 3560).

7 S. Rit C., Sept. 12, 1884 (n. 3620).

8 S Rit. C, Aug. 31, 1867, ad VII (n. 3162).

use the formula given in the Roman Ritual, and are not allowed to use the *Pontificale* for single pieces.[9] Thus a palla and corporal should be blessed together, and if only one of them is to be blessed, the formula prescribed in the Roman Ritual should be used.[10]

For the rest we refer to the rubrics in the liturgical books and to the authors who have written on the subject.

Can. 1297 applies the rules concerning the obligation of repairing churches as laid down in can. 1186 also to the support of the *sacra supellex*, which is necessary for divine worship. Hence, unless other provisions have been made, the same persons are bound to provide for the upkeep and repair of the sacred vessels, utensils, and vestments. There is a good rule stated in one decision, viz., if the parishioners cannot afford to contribute money, they should contribute their labor.[11] This is often done by the women, especially where there is an Altar Society which busies itself with embellishing the house of God. If other means fail, the beneficiaries of the church are obliged to share the burden *pro rata*.[12] Finally, Catholic storekeepers and pawnbrokers are admonished not to buy or sell any sacred utensils, especially if there is reason to suspect theft.[13]

CARDINALITIAL, EPISCOPAL, AND CLERICAL SUPELLEX

In order to understand these canons it will be well to take a historical note from the Constitution of Benedict XIV, which directly refers to our subject.[14] Whilst at Avignon, the Popes erected a magnificent chapel in their

9 S. Rit. C, March 16, 1876; Dec. 2, 1881, ad 1 (nn. 3392, 3533)

10 S. Rit. C, Sept. 4, 1880 (n. 3524); *Rit. Rom*, tit. VIII, c. 22.

11 S. C. EE et RR, Dec. 10, 1841 (Bizzarri, *l. c.*, p 477 f)

12 S. C. C, March 13, 1657; Bened XIV, *Instit.*, 100, n. 13.

13 Bened XIV, *Instit.*, 69, n 3.

14 " *Inter arduas*," April 22, 1749.

palace, a.1d after their return to Rome, they retained this custom in the Vatican palace, often performing solemn functions there which were formerly held in the basilicas, assisted by the Cardinals and the whole papal chapel. The Cardinals, too, held pontifical ceremonies requiring a more than common *sacra supellex,* which was partly purchased by the prelates, partly by the papal treasurer. The former were from time immemorial accustomed either to leave or bequeathe their vestments, etc., to the papal chapel,[15] and thus established a precedent which might be called a juridical prescription. Urban VIII formulated the written law [16] which, in substance, has entered our Code.

CAN. 1298

§ 1. Defuncti S. R. E. Cardinalis, qui in Urbe domicilium habebat, quamvis Episcopus suburbicarius aut Abbas *nullius* esset, quaelibet sacra supellex, exceptis annulis et crucibus pectoralibus etiam cum sacris reliquiis, aliaeque res omnes stabiliter divino cultui destinatae, nulla habita ratione qualitatis et naturae redituum quibus comparatae sint, cedunt pontificio sacrario, nisi Cardinalis eas donaverit aut testamento reliquerit alicui ecclesiae vel oratorio publico vel loco pio vel alicui personae ecclesiasticae seu religiosae.

§ 2. Optandum ut Cardinalis, qui huiusmodi facultate uti velit, saltem ex parte praeferat illas ecclesias, quas in titulum, administrationem seu commendam obtinuerit.

This law commands: (1) that the entire *sacra supellex* and everything that was permanently destined for divine

---

15 Julius III, *" Cum sicut nobis,"* June 26, 1550

16 Urban VIII, *" Acquum est,"* July 19, 1642.

worship, found in the possession of a cardinal at the time of his death, if that cardinal had his domicile in Rome, even though he was a suburbicarian bishop or an abbot *nullius*, belongs to the *papal sacristy*. Urban VIII excepted some things, viz., one tunicella for each cardinal deacon, one chasuble for each cardinal priest, one cope for each cardinal bishop, candlesticks, ewer, and basin. But none of these things are excepted by the new Code, and consequently all may be claimed by the papal sacristan. (2) Rings and pectoral crosses, together with the sacred relics enclosed therein, must not, but may be ceded to the pontifical sacristy.[17] (3) The entire *sacra supellex*, with the exceptions mentioned, belongs to the papal sacristy, *without any regard as to the quality and nature of the pecuniary means* from which said *sacra supellex* was acquired, *i. e.*, it matters not whether the cardinal bought it from church revenues, or from his patrimonial income, or obtained it by donation or bequest. (4) But the Code permits cardinals *de curia* to donate or bequeathe their *sacra supellex* to a *church, or a public oratory, or a pious institution, or any ecclesiastical or religious person*. This was the point which gave occasion to the aforesaid constitution of Benedict XIV.

§ 2 expresses the wish that, when such a donation or bequest is made, *preference* be given to the church which the Cardinal held as titular possessor, administrator, or commendatory abbot.

Sacra supellex here comprises the following articles: mitres, chasubles, copes, tunics, dalmatics, sandals, gloves, sacerdotal vestments, chalices, patens, sacred vessels of every kind (pyx, ostensorium, thimble) especially those

17 Cfr. Pius IX, " *Quum illud,*" June 1, 1847 (*A. S. S*, III, 281).

consecrated or blessed, also oilstocks, ewer and basin, cruets, procession cross, candlesticks, crozier, faldstool; also the Missal, Pontifical, Canon, and Gradual.[18]

CAN. 1299

§ 1. Defuncti Episcopi residentialis, etiamsi cardinalitia dignitate fulserit, sacra supellex cedit ecclesiae cathedrali, exceptis annulis et crucibus pectoralibus etiam cum sacris reliquiis, salvo praescripto can. 1288, et iis omnibus utensilibus cuiusvis generis quae legitime probetur ab Episcopo defuncto comparata fuisse bonis ad ipsam ecclesiam non pertinentibus neque constet in ecclesiae proprietatem transiisse.

§ 2. Si quando Episcopus duas vel plures dioeceses successive rexerit aut simul praefuerit duabus vel pluribus dioecesibus unitis aut in perpetuam administrationem concessis, cathedralem ecclesiam habentibus propriam et distinctam, quae sacra utensilia constiterit reditibus unius tantum dioecesis fuisse comparata, ea eiusdem cathedrali ecclesiae cedunt; secus dividi debent, aequis partibus, inter singulas ecclesias cathedrales, dummodo dioecesium reditus ne sint divisi, sed unam episcopalem mensam perpetuo constituant; si vero reditus divisi sint ac separati, divisio fiat inter singulas ecclesias cathedrales pro ratione fructuum quos in singulis dioecesibus Episcopus perceperit ac temporis quo eisdem praefuerit.

§ 3. Episcopus obligatione tenetur inventarii sacrorum utensilium authentica forma conficiendi, in quo pro rei veritate quando acquisita sint, exprimat, distincteque describat si qua non ex ecclesiae reditibus ac proventibus, sed ex propriis bonis vel ex donatione

---

18 Pius IX, " *Quum illud,*" 3, III.

**sibi facta comparaverit; secus omnia reditibus eccle-
siae comparata praesumuntur.**

Can. 1299 lays down a rule concerning the *sacra supellex* left by a *residental bishop,* even though he may have
been a cardinal.   It excepts the rings and pectoral crosses,
but as to the relics contained therein, it refers to can.
1288, which concerns a relic of the Holy Cross.   Otherwise all articles of a bishop's *sacra supellex* belongs by
law to the deceased prelate's *cathedral church,* with the
exception, however, of such sacred appurtenances (*omnibus utensilibus*) which were bought by the deceased
bishop with his own money and such utensils as have not
passed into the possession of the church.   However, for
each of these two kinds of *sacra supellex* there must be
legal proof that the money was not church money and
that the ownership was acquired by the church.   How is
that proof to be furnished?

§ 3, following a letter of Pius IX, "*Quum aliud,*"
says that bishops are strictly obliged to draw up an
inventory faithfully describing their sacred utensils, both
as to the time when they were bought — because according to can. 1511, § 2, thirty years' possession suffices to
acquire such objects — and also as to the nature of the
revenues with which they were bought.   If this is done
conscientiously and accurately, there should be little difficulty to carry out the present law, which, be it said by
the way, involves a strict obligation.   If no inventory is
found, the presumption (*praesumptio iuris*) is that the
entire *sacra supellex* was purchased with church money.

§ 2 describes what is to be done in the case of a bishop
who ruled *several dioceses,* either as titular bishop or
perpetual administrator.   The supposition is, of course,
that each of these dioceses has its own cathedral church.

If the bishop has made the required inventory, it will be easy to decide which of the cathedral churches furnished the money for the *sacra supellex*. If only one of them furnished the money, it has an exclusive claim to the articles in question. If two or three dioceses contributed to the purchase, there are two possibilities: If no separate accounts are kept but all revenues go to constitute the income of the bishop (*mensa episcopalis*), then the *sacra supellex* accrues to the different cathedral churches in equal shares.[19] But if the different dioceses keep separate and distinct accounts of their revenues, then the *sacra supellex* is to be divided and apportioned according to the salary, cathedraticum, etc, the bishop received from each diocese, and according to the length of time he governed each diocese. Of course, unless books and records are carefully kept, there may be difficulties in making the division.

CAN. 1300

Quae in can. 1299 praescripta sunt, applicentur quoque clerico qui in aliqua ecclesia beneficium saeculare vel religiosum obtinuerit.

This canon applies the enactment of can. 1299 to *clergymen* who held either a secular or a religious benefice in any church during their lifetimes. It is a timely reminder to the clergy of their legal status with regard to the *sacra supellex*, which received attention from the earliest times and is frequently mentioned in the Decretals.[20] Thus Alexander III sanctioned a previous law which provided that all the goods appertaining to and acquired by a church must and may be claimed by said church. Pius V

19 We suppose this holds also with regard to pro-cathedrals

20 Cf *Can Apost*, 40; c. 12, X, III, 26

reiterated this regulation and explained to the papal collectors that they had no right to claim these goods for the *camera spoliorum,* but should leave them to the church whose beneficiary died.[21] The same rule applied to the canons and beneficiaries of St. Peter's basilica, no matter whether they still held their offices at the time of their death or not.[22]

This canon is, strictly speaking, applicable only to clergymen who held a church *benefice,* either secular or religious, but we venture to say that the mind of the legislator also includes those who, though not beneficiaries in the strictly canonical sense, have been employed either as pastors or curates (assistants), or otherwise. In other words, the law is applicable also to most clergymen of our country. The reasons are almost the same: the *sacra supellex* should not pass into profane hands and the churches should not be deprived of the necessary furniture. Besides, there is no doubt that many, perhaps most sacred vessels, utensils, vestments, etc., are bought with money contributed by the congregation or the members of the altar society, and such *supellex,* therefore, strictly belongs to the church. On the other hand, we would not deny that sometimes gifts are made for merely personal motives, for instance, by parents, relatives, friends. These could not in justice be claimed by the church. Care must always be taken, however, to avoid profanation.

21 S. Pius V, " *Romani Pontificis,*"
Aug. 30, 1567, § 11.

22 Benedict XIV, " *Ad honoran-
dum,*" March 27, 1752, § 27.

DUTY OF MAKING A VALID TESTAMENT

CAN. 1301

§ 1. S. R. E. Cardinalis, Episcopus residentialis aliique clerici beneficiarii obligatione tenentur curandi testamento vel alio instrumento in forma iuris civilis valido ut canonica praescripta, de quibus in can. 1298–1300, debitum effectum etiam in foro civili sortiantur.

§ 2. Quamobrem tempestive ac forma iure civili valida personam integrae famae designent ad normam can. 380, quae, adveniente ipsorum morte, non solum sacram supellectilem, sed etiam libros, documenta aliaque quae ad ecclesiam pertinent et in eorum domo reperiuntur, occupet et cui debentur, remittat.

Cardinals, residential bishops, and all other clerical beneficiaries are in duty bound to draw up a last will or other instrument in a form acknowledged as valid by civil law, in order that the regulations laid down in can. 1298–1300 may be made effective also in the civil courts. For this purpose they shall in due time and legal form appoint some person of good character who, at the approach of their death, shall take temporary possession not only of their *sacra supellex,* but also of books, documents, and other objects belonging to the church and found in their residence, and deliver them to the lawful claimants.

Since the decree of the S. C. of the Propaganda, Dec. 15, 1840,[23] substantial changes have been introduced in the laws of our country which render said decree largely superfluous. Church property is no longer held in fee simple, but other forms of tenure have developed, which

23 *Coll. P. F.,* n. 916

render the conveyance of church property more simple. There is no doubt that the " corporation sole " effectively serves the necessities of churches whose form of government is monarchical.[24] For the rest, the statute laws in the different States of the Union differ widely. In many States bishops are authorized to become corporations sole by complying with certain conditions, which are usually extremely simple, consisting merely of the filing of some statement, certificate, or affidavit with a certain officer of the law. Then there is the system of quasi-corporations, which are by statute declared corporations for the purpose of taking over property.[25]

[24] Cfr. K. Zollmann, *American Civil Church Law,* 1917, p. 63

[25] *Ibid ,* p 46. Here it may be well to allege the following passage from the same distinguished author's work, p 354 f :

" The Roman Catholic church in this country has been until recently on a missionary basis. With the exception of some parishes in the territory acquired by the Louisiana Purchase, there are therefore few Catholic parishes in the United States The theory was that the mission was conducted from abroad It followed that the property necessary for the purposes of the church must be subject to the control of the church in general, rather than to that of any individual congregation or congregations. To achieve this condition of affairs the aim has been to place all the property of all the churches in the name of the bishop or archbishop of the diocese to which the particular church belongs Consequently the property of Catholic churches is universally vested in some church dignitary either in his personal capacity or as a corporation sole. The question then arises as to the nature of this title. Is it legal or equitable or both? There can be no question that the bishop or archbishop is the holder of the legal title The property ordinarily stands absolutely in his name. It is customary, and in fact required by church regulation in at least some of the dioceses, to eliminate from deeds to bishops all words of trust and all words indicating the official character of the grantee. Where the bishop is not a corporation sole he is required to make a will by which he devises such property to certain persons with a direction to convey it to the person appointed as his successor. The devisee, under such circumstances, is not held responsible for any negligence of the devisor . . . It follows that money raised for the special purpose of building a local church and placed in the hands of the bishop does not pass absolutely to him, but is a trust fund which the congregation can reclaim at any time by action. It further follows that

CUSTODY OF THE SACRA SUPELLEX

CAN. 1302

Rectores ecclesiarum aliique quibus credita sit cura sacrae supellectilis, sedulo debent eiusdem conserva-tioni et decori prospicere.

Rectors of churches and others entrusted with the care of the articles known as *sacra supellex,* shall diligently preserve them and keep them clean and neat.

Chapter churches generally have a *custos* among their members.[26] Of course the Ordinary cannot be dispensed from the duty of vigilance, and this applies also to the churches of the Oriental Rite.[27] Everything connected with divine service should be clean, whole and decent.[28] The pastors are responsible in a particular manner for the condition of the *sacra supellex,* which must not be left exclusively in the hands of laymen or even Sisters. The pastor may, of course, entrust his curate or assistant with this duty.[29] Care must be bestowed not only on pontifical vestments and utensils, but also on the things that are worn or used by *simplices sacerdotes,* for the law draws no distinction between the two, and the sacred minister, when he celebrates the sacred mysteries, is not inferior to the pontiff, except by accident, because the

a voluntary assignment by a bishop for the benefit of creditors does not cover such property and that a deed or mortgage given to a purchaser who has notice of the facts (and who could purchase church property without such notice) passes no beneficial title. It further follows that on the death of the bishop the court may appoint a trustee in his stead " Parish corporations are recommended and corporations sole per-mitted, by the S C. C., July 29, 1911 (*Eccl. Review,* Vol. 45, p 585 f.).

26 C. 1, X, 27.

27 S C. P. F., April 13, 1807, III (n 692); S C EE. et. RR., Feb 9, 1751 (Bizzarri, *l. c,* p 31 ff.).

28 S C. EE et RR , *l. c.; Rit. Rom,* tit I, c un, n 9

29 *Rit. Rom., l. c., n. 3.*

vestments he wears refer chiefly to the sacred action, and not to the person who performs it.

FURTHER DIRECTIONS REGARDING THE SACRA SUPELLEX

Can. 1303

§ 1. Ecclesia cathedralis debet sacram supellectilem aliaque quae ad Missae sacrificium vel ad alias pontificales functiones necessaria sint, gratis Episcopo subministrare etiam privatim celebranti non solum in ecclesia cathedrali, sed in aliis quoque civitatis vel suburbii ecclesiis.

§ 2. Si qua ecclesia paupertate laboret, potest Ordinarius permittere ut a sacerdotibus qui in proprium commodum inibi celebrant, propter utensilia ceteraque ad Missae sacrificium necessaria, moderata stipes exigatur.

§ 3. Episcopi, non autem Vicarii Capitularis aut Vicarii Generalis sine speciali mandato, est eandem stipem definire, et nemini, etiam religiosis etsi exemptis, licet ea maiorem exigere.

§ 4. Episcopus pro tota dioecesi eiusmodi stipem in dioecesana Synodo, si fieri possit, definiat, aut extra Synodum, audito Capitulo.

§ 1. The *cathedral church* must furnish free of charge the *sacra supellex* and everything else that may be required for the celebration of Mass and other pontifical functions, no matter whether the bishop celebrates privately or solemnly, in the cathedral church or in any other church of the episcopal city or its suburbs. Hence if the bishop celebrates within the city limits or its suburbs he may take the pontifical vestments along with him, and the cathedral church cannot object.[30]   But this holds only for the episcopal city, not for the whole diocese.

§ 2. If a church is very poor, the Ordinary may permit that a moderate fee is paid by the priests who say Mass there for their own convenience, to defray the expense of the sacred utensils and other things required for the celebration of Mass. The S. Congregation has decided that beneficiaries who are compelled to say Mass in a church not their own should contribute something for the candles, bread, and wine, and for the use of the vestments.[31]

§ 3. The *bishop,* but not the Vicar Capitular nor the Vicar General without a special mandate, may fix the amount of said offering, and no one, not even exempt religious, may charge more.

§ 4. The bishop should fix this fee for the whole diocese at the diocesan synod, or else with the advice of the chapter or diocesan consultors.

BLESSING OF THE SACRA SUPELLEX

CAN. 1304

Benedictionem illius sacrae supellectilis quae ad normam legum liturgicarum benedici debet antequam ad usum sibi proprium adhibeatur, impertire possunt:

1.° S. R. E. Cardinales et Episcopi omnes;

2.° Locorum Ordinarii, charactere episcopali carentes, pro ecclesiis et oratoriis proprii territorii;

3.° Parochus pro ecclesiis et oratoriis in territorio suae paroeciae positis, et rectores ecclesiarum pro suis ecclesiis;

---

30 S. Rit. C , March 14, 1643, ad 4, 5 (n. 831).

31 S C. C., May 14, 1729 (Richter, *Trid.,* p. 137, n. 62).

4.° Sacerdotes a loci Ordinario delegati, intra fines delegationis et iurisdictionis delegantis;

5.° Superiores religiosi et sacerdotes eiusdem religionis ab ipsis delegati, pro propriis ecclesiis et oratoriis ac pro ecclesiis monialium sibi subiectarum.

The *sacra supellex* should be blessed before use, and it may be blessed by the following:

1.° By the cardinals and all bishops (hence also by titular bishops) ;

2.° By local Ordinaries not endowed with the episcopal character for the churches and oratories of their respective territory;

3.° By the pastors for the churches and oratories situated within their parishes, and the rectors of churches for their own churches;

4.° By priests delegated by the local Ordinary, within the limits of their delegation and the jurisdiction of the *delegans;*

5.° By religious superiors and by priests of the same institute delegated by the superior for their own churches and oratories and those of the nuns subject to them.

Notice that only *blessings in which no sacred anointing is required* are here understood. The consecration of chalices and patens is not included. The S. Congregation has clearly stated this in more than one decision, as may be seen from the references in the footnotes. What is said in no. 4, concerning delegation, may be deduced from the general rules on delegation.

The *finis delegationis* or purpose of delegation must be ascertained from the wording of the faculties. If the general term *sacra supellex* is used, it includes everything comprised under that name, also the *vasa sacra,* which only need to be blessed.[32] But if the faculty reads, *" benedicto sacerdotalium indumentorum,"* it excludes the blessing of altar linens, corporals, palls, and sacred vessels, which are all separate and distinct blessings given by means of special formulas.

Concerning *religious superiors* the text establishes nothing new, except perhaps that they require no privilege for blessing these things. Their power is, as it always was, restricted to their own *churches.* Thus abbots, priors (convenual not cloistral priors), guardians, rectors of the Society of Jesus, and all others who enjoy the privilege of blessing sacred vestments, cannot make use of this privilege except for the benefit of their convents and churches,— provided always that no sacred anointing is required.[33] When the S. C. was asked whether this faculty could be used also for blessing things pertaining to other churches than their own, in view of a standing custom (*stante eorum allegata consuetudine*), it replied: *non posse,* they cannot.[34] Hence the " awful " decree of Sept. 1659, decided nothing else but what was Roman jurisprudence.[35] The Cassinese abbots were also included in this decision.[36] If it is asked, which churches are meant by the term *propriae ecclesiae,* the answer is clearly contained in a decision[37] of the S. Rit. C., of May 16, 1744. They are the *pleno iure subiectae,* i, e., those churches which have been forever incorporated with the monasteries or religious organizations both as to temporal and spiritual matters by the Holy See. For the rest there is no need of stretching this power.

32 S. Rit C , Dec. 2, 1881, ad II (n. 3533).

33 S Rit. C., March 13, 1632 (n 587)

34 S. Rit. C , Aug. 18, 1629 (n 513).

35 S. Rit. C , n. 1131.

36 S. Rit C., July 30, 1689, ad II (n 1815).

37 S. Rit C , May 16, 1744, ad II (n. 2377).

If every pastor and every rector has the right to bless these articles, why should the religious superior trouble himself? An occasion for this assumption, and a reasonable one at that, would be if a religious community would distribute vestments to poor churches gratis. But not even in that case would the religious superior be authorized to bless the vestments to be distributed to churches outside of his jurisdiction.[38]

The *churches of nuns who are subject to religious,* are of course, those of such nuns as are subject to the prelates regular; therefore they are styled *moniales, i. e.,* Sisters with solemn vows. Tertiaries are not included. If these *moniales* (like the Sisters of the Visitation) are subject to the bishop, the *sacra supellex* of their churches must be blessed either by the Ordinary or the chaplain, provided the latter has received due delegation from the bishop. The same rule holds concerning the *sacra supellex* of ordinary sisterhoods. The chaplains should not imagine that they are rectors of the chapels or oratories of the religious whom they attend, for can. 479 gives a precise definition of a rector, in which they are not included.

LOSS OF BLESSING OR CONSECRATION

CAN. 1305

§ 1. Sacra supellex benedicta aut consecrata benedictionem aut consecrationem amittit:

1.° Si tales laesiones vel mutationes subierit ut pristinam amiserit formam, et iam ad suos usus non habeatur idonea;

2.° Si ad usus indecores adhibita vel publicae venditioni exposita fuerit.

---

[38] S. Rit. C, Aug. 31, 1867, ad XI (n. 3157).

§ 2. Calix et patena non amittunt consecrationem ob consumptionem vel renovationem auraturae, salva tamen, priore in casu, gravi obligatione rursum ea inaurandi.

§ 1. An article of *sacra supellex* that has been blessed or consecrated, loses its blessing or consecration:

1.° If it is so badly damaged or changed that its form is lost and it becomes unfit for its proper purpose;

2.° If it has been used for unsuitable purposes or exhibited for public sale.

The first case would be verified if a *chalice* sustained a slight break or split in the cup near the bottom. Not so however, if the break be near the upper part, so that consecration can take place in it without fear of spilling the contents.[39] The same rule applies, *mutatis mutandis*, to the paten, if it had holes in it. Concerning *vestments* a serious damage or injury would occur if a vestment were entirely taken apart and a relatively large portion renewed. The form of a corporal, or palla, etc., would be changed if, according to common parlance, the vestment could no longer be recognized as such, which would be the case, *e. g.*, if only rags remained.

Concerning *indecorous use* there is a synodal decree of Auvergne (536) which prohibits the use of sacred vestments for bridal or wedding purposes. The same synod also forbade covering corpses with altar linens (*pallia et ministeria divina*).[40] Zitelli refers to a decision according to which the consecration of a chalice would be lost if the sacred vessel was used for drinking purposes

---

39 Cfr. Schulte, *Consecranda,* 1907, p 272, who also says: If the cup can be detached from the stem by loosening the screw, consecration would not be lost.

40 Can. 43, Dist. 1, *de cons.* Hefele, *Conc.-Gesch.,* II, 739: *ministeria divina* here means sacred vestments.

by heretics.[41] There is no doubt that any profanation of a sinful character entails the loss of consecration. Exhibition for public sale or public auction also effects loss of consecration, no matter whether it is done by Catholics or non-Catholics.

§ 2 changes the former discipline or practice of the Roman congregations [42] when it states that *chalice and paten do not lose their consecration by the wearing away of the gilding, or by the process of regilding.* But if the gold plating wears away, there is a grave obligation to have the vessel replated. This new law undoubtedly presupposes, not only that the whole chalice is consecrated, but also that the consecration does not attach to the mere surface or gilding.

HANDLING SACRED VESSELS

CAN. 1306

§ 1. Curandum ne calix cum patena et ante lotionem purificatoria, pallae et corporalia, quae adhibita fuere in sacrificio Missae, tangantur, nisi a celericis vel ab iis qui eorum custodiam habent.

§ 2. Purificatoria, pallae et corporalia, in Missae sacrificio adhibita, ne tradantur lavanda laicis, etiam religiosis, nisi prius abluta fuerint a clerico in maioribus ordinibus constituto; aqua autem primae lotionis mittatur in sacrarium vel, si hoc desit, in ignem.

§ 1. Care must be taken that the chalice with the paten, as well as the purificators, palls, and corporals, before being washed, after having been used in the Sacrifice of the Mass are touched only by clerics or by those who have charge of these things.

41 *Apparatus Iuris Eccl*, 1886, p 433; Lib II, c III, art 1, § 5. 42 S. Rit C., June 14, 1845 (n. 2889)

Pseudo-Soter says nuns and consecrated virgins were not allowed to touch the sacred vessels and palls.[43] Another canon says subdeacons and acolythes are allowed to touch sacred utensils — *sacra ministeria,* as they were then called.[44] The janitors (*ostiarii*) were *not* allowed to wash or handle them, but had to watch that no one touched them.[45] The general name for all who were allowed to touch such objects was *sacrati Dominoque dedicati homines.*[46] That the old Testament played a part in this prohibition is evident.[47] According to present-day practice only those who have received the *clerical tonsure* are allowed to touch the sacred objects mentioned. A cleric may touch the chalice and prepare it for the holy Sacrifice in the sacristy.[48] One who has received the clerical tonsure may *act as chaplain* to a prelate saying low Mass, or as *quasi-master of ceremonies* to a priest singing high Mass without deacon and subdeacon. But in the latter case he has to observe the following rules: (a) he shall not wipe the chalice before the offertory, nor bring it to the altar uncovered; (b) he shall not pour wine and water into the chalice; (c) he shall not pass the paten with the host, nor the chalice to the celebrant; (d) he must not touch the chalice after the canon has started, nor remove the pall from it; (e) after the ablution he shall not clean the chalice, but may cover it with the veil and burse, and carry it to the credential. If a cleric who has received only the tonsure[49]

---

43 C 25, Dist. 1, — the manufacturer of this canon betrays himself as a forger, because *monachae* were unknown in Soter's time

44 C. 32, Dist. 1.

45 C. 40, Dist 1, *de cons.* (Pseudo-Clem.).

46 C. 41, Dist. 1, *de cons.* (Pseudo-Sixtus)

47 C. 42, Dist 1, *de cons*

48 S Rit. C., Nov. 23, 1906, ad I (n. 4194).

49 A reasonable or plausible cause is required that one in minor orders or simply tonsured be admitted as subdeacon, but one who is no cleric should not be admitted, S. Rit. C., March 10, 1906, ad I (n.

acts as *subdeacon*, dressed in amice, alb, cincture and tunic (without maniple), he has to observe these rules, but may carry the chalice to the altar. If an untonsured cleric is to assist a prelate at low Mass, the chalice must be placed on the altar before Mass, entirely covered and the cleric must act as if he were assisting a *simplex sacerdos*. He may, however, assist the prelate at the missal, turn the leaves, hold the candle, but he must not touch or wipe the chalice.[50]

§ 2. Purificators, palls, and corporals, which have been used in the Sacrifice of Mass, shall not be given to lay persons, even though they be religious, to be washed by them before they have been washed by a cleric in higher orders. The water of the first washing should be poured into the waste hole, called *sacrarium,* or if there is no *sacrarium,* into the fire.

Religious here means lay Brothers and Sisters. Even the Ordinary cannot grant these the permission here in question.[51] If, therefore, laymen, Sisters or Brothers, have to handle an object which they are forbidden by § 1 to touch, let them use a clean purificator.

Concerning the *ostensorium, ciborium,* and *custodia,* there is no prohibition of touching these objects, nor are laymen obliged to use a cloth in handling them.

4181); this is the general tenor of decisions

50 S. Rit. C., March 10, 1906, ad II–VII (*l c*).

51 S. Rit C., Sept 12, 1857 (n. 3059). "*Vel ab aliis qui eorum custodiam habeant*" may cause a doubt, as if laymen or Sisters were allowed to touch said articles. Yet it appears from can. 1302 that these cus-

todians are supposed to be of the clerical rank This is confirmed by the last quoted decision of S. Rit. C However, this seems to be understood of immediate touch; for a mediate touch, i. e., by means of a cloth, can hardly be forbidden. Neither should Sisters have scruples if they touch the sacred vessels transiently or inadvertently.

TITLE XIX

VOWS AND OATHS

CHAPTER I

CAN. 1307

§ 1. Votum, idest promissio deliberata ac libera Deo facta de bono possibili et meliore, ex virtute religionis impleri debet.

§ 2. Nisi iure prohibeantur, omnes congruenti rationis usu pollentes, sunt voti capaces.

§ 3. Votum metu gravi et iniusto emissum ipso iure nullum est.

§ 1. A vow is a deliberate and free promise made to God concerning something possible and better; it obliges by reason of the virtue of religion.

The promise [1] must be made to *God,* because He is the end of our actions, which ought indeed all to be directed to Him. A *promise* involves the obligation of keeping it, and hence differs from a mere resolution. A promise, to entail a lasting obligation, requires *full consent, freely given.* Every substantial error, therefore, in fact every error which is the cause of a vow, renders the latter

---

1 Cf. Suarez, *De Religione,* tract. VI, *De Voto* (ed Paris, 1859, t XIV, p 750 ff), S. Alphonsus, Lib IV, tr. II c. 3, *De Voto* (ed. Paris, 1875, Vol. II, p 120 ff.); Lehmkuhl, *Theol. Moralis,* I, n. 428 ff ; *Cath Enc,* Vol XV, 511 f. (by Vermeersch, S J).

null and void. This does not, however, imply that every circumstance or detail attending the vow must be known in advance.

Freedom excludes fear and compulsion, which may be brought to bear upon the will either from the outside or from within.

From the necessity of free and deliberate consent — because every vow is a human act — it naturally follows that the *material object* of the promise made must be something that lies in man's power, an object of which he is allowed to dispose and over which he has control. Hence it must be something *possible,* namely, attainable by his physical and moral faculties. Thus it would involve a physical impossibility to impose upon oneself a fast which were incompatible with the physical labor one has to do, or which would seriously impair one's health; and it would be morally impossible to avoid every sin.

The object of a vow must furthermore be a *bonum melius, i. e.,* something better than its omission, or something which does not impede or nullify a higher or better good. Hence no object which is sinful in itself (*ex parte rei votae*) can be made the object of a vow. Nor can anything useless or entirely indifferent be properly speaking intended in a vow. Thus a matter which would disturb the means of higher perfection or prevent the fulfillment of an ecclesiastical law, could not be made the object of a vow.

Lastly, the definition says that a vow obliges by reason of the *virtue of religion.* A vow is an act that refers to God as its immediate and proper end, and therefore is an act of that worship (*actus latriae*) which is due to God alone. If one " makes a vow to a saint," the meaning is that he makes the vow to God in honor of the saint, just as churches are dedicated. Such acts naturally spring from the virtue of religion, which regulates the relation between the Creator and His creature, the union between God and man.

§ 2. Unless prohibited by law, all who have the necessary use of reason, are capable of making a vow.

§ 3. A vow made under the influence of grave and unjust fear is null and void by law.

The general rule [2] is that everyone who has sufficient use of reason and free will may make a vow. However, as Suarez [3] says, for a vow to be valid before God there is required the necessary knowledge of God and of what the vow implies. If the latter knowledge were wanting, the subject would not enjoy that use of reason which is proportionate (*congruens*) to the object of the vow. On the other hand, although it may be said that the use of reason enlightened by faith is necessary, yet even a heretic who errs in certain doctrinal matters may pronounce a valid vow of chastity, provided he has the intention to make a vow and knows what it involves, at least substantially.[4] And substantial knowledge is generally supposed to exist in those who have sufficient use of reason to realize what a grievous sin is.

Some persons are *excluded* by law from making vows. Thus those who have not attained the required age, are forbidden to make a religious vow, and those who are subject to others in the matter of the vow are forbidden to do so. Bishops and clergymen should not take a vow to resign their offices or undertake a pilgrimage which would for a long time prevent them from fulfilling their duties.[5]

2 Cfr S. Thom , *Summa Theol.*, 2ᵃ 2ᵃᵉ q. 88, art 8 f.

3 *De Voto*, l. III, c. 2, n. 9 (*l. c* , p. 895).

4 S. Poenit , Nov. 29, 1842 (*Coll. P. F* , n 959).

5 Cfr. Suarez, *l. c.* l. III, c. 4.

Married women should not make vows incompatible with their state, religious should not, without the knowledge of their superiors, vow things which would clash with their ordinary duties.

Fear to render a vow invalid, must be *grave, i. e.,* such as is apt to influence a man of character and constancy. Such a fear would be that of torment or death.[6]   It must also be *unjust, viz.,* threatened by such as have no authority or right to do so, or entirely out of proportion to the matter of the vow.   The law which declares such a vow invalid is presumably the *ecclesiastical law,* for it would be difficult to prove that the natural law renders such a law invalid, since the *voluntarium* is not entirely wanting even under the pressure of grave fear.

KINDS OF VOWS

CAN. 1308

§ 1. Votum est *publicum,* si nomine Ecclesiae a legitimo Superiore ecclesiastico acceptetur; secus *privatum.*

§ 2. *Sollemne,* si ab Ecclesia uti tale fuerit agnitum; secus *simplex.*

§ 3. *Reservatum,* cuius dispensationem sola Sedes Apostolica concedere potest.

§ 4. *Personale,* quo actio voventis promittitur; *reale,* quo promittitur res aliqua; *mixtum,* quod personalis et realis naturam participat.

A vow is *public* when it is accepted by a lawful ecclesiastical superior in the name of the Church; all vows not so accepted are *private.*

Therefore, the intervention of the Church through her

---

6 C. 6, X, 40; Suarez, *De Voto,* 1 I, c. 8, n. 5, thought otherwise.

lawful representatives is necessary to make a vow public.

The term *superior* supposes authority *in foro externo,* at least this is the usual acceptation. Hence neither the pastor, as such, nor a confessor, as such, can accept a public vow or render a vow public.

Private vows, of course, may be made into the hands of pastor or confessor, nay without any intervention on the part of the Church.

A vow is *solemn* if it is acknowledged as such by the Church; otherwise it is *simple.* This distinction has been explained in Vol. III of this Commentary. A vow is *reserved* if dispensation from it can be granted only by the Apostolic See.

A vow is *personal* if the object of the promise is an act of the vowing person, for instance, to love another; it is *real* if an object other than the act itself is promised; it is *mixed* if it combines the elements both of a personal and of a real vow. A vow to make a pilgrimage, *e. g.,* is a personal vow, but if it includes giving an alms, it is mixed.

RESERVED VOWS

CAN. 1309

Vota privata Sedi Apostolicae reservata sunt tantummodo votum perfectae ac perpetuae castitatis et votum ingrediendi in religionem votorum sollemnium, quae emissa fuerint absolute et post completum decimum aetatis annum.

The only private vows which are reserved to the Apostolic See are that of perfect and perpetual chastity and that of entering a religious order with solemn vows, provided they are made unconditionally and after the eighteenth year of age has been completed.

St. Thomas knew two reserved vows: that of continence and that of a pilgrimage to the Holy Land. But the number was later increased, so that five were considered as reserved: to enter a religious order, to observe perpetual chastity, to make a pilgrimage to Jerusalem, St. James of Compostella (Spain), and to the tombs of St. Peter and Paul in Rome.[7] Now the three pilgrimages are taken away from the number of vows reserved to the Holy See, and only two are left. These two are explicitly defined, so that little doubt is left as to their extent.

The vow of perfect and perpetual chastity (*perfectae et perpetuale castitatis*) tends to an act that is perfect in itself and by reason of the matter intended. If the vow is taken from a motive lower than love of the virtue of chastity, it is imperfect. Such a lower motive may be vanity, physical imbecility, or even stubbornness. A vow of chastity would be imperfect on the part of the matter vowed, if only virginity, or integrity of the body, or not marrying, was contracted.[8]

A vow is perpetual if it is taken not for a limited time only, (for instance until a certain age), but forever.

The vow of " *entering a religious institute* " here refers to orders of regulars, *i. e.*, the religious state in which *solemn* vows are pronounced.

These private vows are not reserved to the Holy See unless made *unconditionally*. A condition would be, for instance, if I receive that favor, if I am restored to health; if the order is approved by the Holy See; if there is a convent of that order in such and such a country, etc.

Besides, the person who takes such a vow must have completed the *eighteenth year of age*. This is a higher

7 Bened. XIV, "*Inter praetcri-*   8 Cfr Lehmkuhl, I, n. 477.
tos," Dec. 3, 1749, § 42.

limit than was set before, in fact until now there was no definite limit set to age in this connection.

PERSONAL OBLIGATION

CAN. 1310

§ 1. Votum non obligat, ratione sui, nisi emittentem.

§ 2. Voti realis obligatio transit ad heredes, item obligatio voti mixti pro parte qua reale est.

§ 1. A vow, as such, obliges no one but the person who makes it, for the reason that a vow involves a strictly personal obligation, which can neither be assumed nor fulfilled except by the one who has offered this promise to God.

In the city of Rome the fastday of Feb. 1 was long ago introduced by reason of a vow. After the promulgation of the Constitution of Urban VIII, " *Universa,*" of Sept. 13, 1642, doubts were proposed to the S. Congregation of Rites as to whether the feasts suppressed by that constitution also included the feasts which had been kept merely by reason of a vow. The answer was that the feasts observed by reason of a vow, but now suppressed, oblige only those who made the vow, not their successors.[9] Why, then, is the 1st of February still observed in Rome? Because there was a law, or statute, or precept attached to the vow. Therefore it is not the vow as such (*ratione sui*), but the law attached to it, which obliges the successors of the one who made the original vow [10]; provided that law was accepted by the majority and was not abrogated by a later law or contrary custom.

§ 2. The obligation arising from a *real vow passes*

9 S C. Rit , April 18, 1043; Nov. 19, 1650; June 23, 1703, ad 1 (nn. 834, 932, 2113).

10 Suarez, *De Voto,* l. IV, c 9.

to the heirs, that arising from a *mixed vow* only in so far as the *real* part is concerned.

A personal vow expires with the death of the person who made it, and hence, for instance, the obligation of making a pilgrimage does not pass to the heirs. But if one vowed not only a pilgrimage, but also a certain sum of money to the sanctuary, the *real* part of the vow, respecting the donation, must be fulfilled by those who succeeded the deceased in the possession of his property. Why? Because an heir is, in virtue of justice and by reason of an at least implied or tacit contract, obliged to pay the debts of the one whose property he obtains either by last will and testament or by succession *ab intestato.* There is no reason why religious debts should not be paid, even though the civil law does not compel the heirs to pay them.[11] It is not necessary to recur to the religious aspect of the question, because, as Suarez truly says,[12] religious loyalty does not strictly oblige to restitution. Of course, if the vow was originally restricted to the lifetime of the *vovens,* or made conditional upon its acceptance by the heirs, it does not oblige the latter unless they accept the inheritance. It is evident that the heir must know of such a vow, one way or the other; if he does not, the inheritance must be considered free of encumbrance. A legacy or bequest left by vow must therefore, in virtue of justice, be delivered to the persons or pious institutes for whom it was intended by the *vovens.*

11 Cfr 1. 2, Dig. 50, 12 *"voti enim obligationem ad heredem transire constat"*

12 *De Voto,* l IV, c. 11, n. 8 f.

The older English law left it with the Ordinaries to dispose of goods left *ab intestato* for pious purposes. Cfr. Blackstone-Cooley, II, § 494.

CAN. 1311

Cessat votum lapsu temporis ad finiendam obligationem appositi, mutatione substantiali materiae prom-
issae, deficiente conditione a qua votum pendet aut
eiusdem causa finali, irritatione, dispensatione, commutatione.

A vow ceases to oblige:

(a) After the time conditionally set for its fulfillment
has expired; (b) If there is a substantial change in the
thing promised; (c) if some condition on which the vow
was made to depend, is not fulfilled; (d) if the cause or
object for which the vow was made ceases to exist; (e)
by nullification, dispensation, or commutation.

Before explaining these points we must premise that the
time when an obligation commences (*terminus a quo*),
differs according to the character of the vow, whether
it is negative (a promise to omit something) or positive
(a promise to perform a good work). If a vow is *negative* (for instance, not to play cards, not to gamble), it
obliges immediately (*statius ac pro statim*), unless it was
limited by the *vovens*. An affirmative vow, on the other
hand, *e. g.,* to enter a religious order, though it also begins to oblige from the time it was made, may reasonably
be postponed until a time which is more convenient according to one's own prudent judgment.[13]

Now as to *cessation*.

Ad 1. The lapse of time is here considered as *ad finiendam* which signifies that a precise term was set, beyond
which the *vovens* had no intention to oblige himself. For
instance, if one would take the "pledge" (to abstain from

---

13 See Suarez, *De Voto,* 1. IV, c. 12.

intoxicating drinks) in the form of a vow (in itself the
pledge implies no vow, but a mere resolution) for one
year, the obligation would cease after 365 days have
elapsed, even in a leap year. This rule holds good for
personal as well as real and mixed vows. If a vow was
made for a certain time, but the time limit was only
a secondary or accessory consideration, and not a condition proper, it is generally presumed that the vow, if
personal (for instance, of fasting), ceases after the lapse
of that period. Whereas if it is real, it does not cease to
oblige even after that time and must therefore be complied with even if the time limit has expired.[14] This, of
course, holds also of mixed vows, as to their material
object.

Ad 2. A *substantial change* of the thing promised also
renders a vow null and void. Such a change would occur,
e. g., if one had vowed to give substantial alms for a good
purpose, and later became poor; he would then be free of
his vow and need not beg to get the money.[15] The same
rule applies to a personal vow (for instance, of undertak-
ing a pilgrimage or of fasting) if one's health becomes so
gravely impaired that one cannot comply with one's promise. This holds even if the change has been brought
about by one's own fault.[16]

Ad. 3. A vow ceases to oblige, thirdly, if the *condition*
attached to it by the *vovens* is not fulfilled, for instance, if
one made a vow in order to obtain good health, and this
favor has not been restored; or if one vowed to enter religion, provided such and such a convent would receive
him or her. In the latter case he would not be obliged to
ask for admission to another convent.[17]

14 S. Alph , lib IV, tr II, c 3,
De Voto, n 220 (*ed cit* , p 132 f.)
15 *Ibid.,* n. 225, 3 ff.
16 *Ibid.*
17 Cfr. Suarez, *De Voto,* l. IV,
c 17.

Ad 4. By final cause (*causa finalis*) must be understood the main and primary reason that moves or prompts one to make a vow; for instance, if the poverty of a church caused one to vow a legacy to it, or if the sickness of a friend prompted one to vow a pilgrimage for his recovery. Besides this final cause, there may be impulsive reasons, which aided in impelling one to make the vow, but only accidentally or secondarily; these do *not* constitute the end or object for which the vow was made.[18] Now, if the final cause or purpose of a vow ceases to exist, as in the case of a poor institution becoming wealthy, the obligation ceases. But if the poverty of the institution was only a secondary or impelling cause (*" ad facilius donandum "*) the vow obliges even after the institution ceases to be poor. It is, therefore, somewhat similar to a condition.

Ad. 5. The nullification or irritation of vows as well as dispensation and commutation are treated in the following canons.

IRRITATION OF VOWS

CAN. 1312

§1. Qui potestatem dominativam in voluntatem voventis legitime exercet, potest eius vota valide et, ex iusta causa, etiam licite irrita reddere, ita ut nullo in casu obligatio postea reviviscat.

§ 2. Qui potestatem non quidem in voluntatem voventis, sed in voti materiam habet, potest voti obligationem tandiu suspendere, quandiu voti adimplementum sibi praeiudicium afferat.

§ 1. Whoever lawfully exercises controlling power over the will of the *vovens* may validly and, for a reasonable

18 Suarez, *De Voto*, lib. IV, c. 18, n 8

cause, also licitly nullify his vow, so that the obligation ceases, never to revive.

This is what is called irritation, and may be defined as an act by which either the object of the vow, or the act of the vowing person itself, ceases to oblige. When the matter of the vow (for instance, a pilgrimage) is immediately concerned, irritation is called *indirect* (see § 2). When the will, or, rather, the act of the *vovens,* is affected, irritation is called *direct,* because by it the act is revoked and, as it were, cancelled.[19]   This power may be exercised only by persons to whom the will of the *vovens* is subject by reason of governing or domestic power, as distinguished from the power of jurisdiction. The *dominative* or *domestic power,* like the paternal power, is radically based upon the natural law, but has its formal sanction in ecclesiastical law.

The *domestic authorities* here concerned are:

(1) The pope and religious superiors (and *superioresses*) with regard to vows made by their subjects after their religious profession. As to the pope, the question is solved in can. 499, § 1; as to the superiors, there can be no doubt, since all superiors, even the female, enjoy domestic power over their subjects by virtue of the vow of obedience. This certainly is true with respect to all those who rule and live in a community to which the name "religious" may be applied in the canonical sense. Hence the superiors, higher and local, of all orders and congregations, papal as well as diocesan, have the power of irritating vows made by their subjects after the simple profession, for it is by this profession that the members are really placed under domestic power.

The answer is different for religious societies which

19 Suarez, *De Voto,* l. VI, c. 1, n. 4.

pronounce no vows, or only the one or other. For the mere act of constituting a body or society does not yet give rise to the dominative power in its full sense. However, if the members are obliged to obey superiors who, in the constitutions, are said to enjoy dominative power,[20] there can be no doubt that their private vows can be nullified by these superiors. Vows of novices cannot be nullified by the religious superior in virtue of *direct* irritation.[21] Neither can the superiors, *per se,* irritate vows made before profession. Yet in virtue of the higher perfection attached to the religious state, and by reason of the ecclesiastical law, these private vows remain suspended, as will be seen under can. 1315.

(2) *Parents* and *tutors* or *guardians* may by direct irritation nullify the vows taken by boys who have not yet completed the fourteenth or by girls who have not yet completed the twelfth year of age.[22] Some authors[23] have extended this right to grandparents, which may be accepted as a benign interpretation, although can. 89 hardly warrants the extension.

(3) The *husband,* being the head of the wife according to divine and ecclesiastical law, *may nullify the vows of his helpmate made in the married state.* This rule most probably applies to all kinds of vows made by the wife, not only to such as are directly opposed to conjugal life.[24] The wife, on the other hand, cannot directly irritate any vow of her husband. What if the wife has taken a vow with the consent and approval of her husband? Even in

---

20 Thus the Constit. of the *Precious Blood Fathers, pro Praxi Americana* reads (art 1) "*Sacerdotes Provinciae Americanae subiiciuntur vicario, qui auctoritate dominativa pollet, cui proinde obedientiam praestare tenentur.*" See can. 675, 501.

21 Cfr. Lehmkuhl, *l. c.* I, n 460.

22 Can 88, § 2

23 S. Alph, *l. c.,* n. 229; Lehmkuhl, *l. c.,* n. 458.

24 S Alph, *De Voto,* n 234

this case he may nullify the vow, because his power has not been curtailed by his former consent.[25] This rule is extended by some authors also to the mutual vow of chastity,[26] holding that the husband may irritate the vow, and consequently also his own.

§ 2. Those who have power over the object of the vow, but not over the will of the vowing person, may *suspend* the obligation accruing from the vow if its fulfillment would be prejudicial to them. This, as stated above, is called *indirect irritation.* It is based on the principle that no one can promise anything that would violate the rights of another. Under this heading may be enumerated the following cases:

(1) *Ecclesiastical superiors,* the pope, bishops, religious superiors, also in virtue of jurisdiction, may suspend the obligation of vows that are detrimental to the welfare of the church, either universal or particular, or of their subjects. This holds good also of vows made before the vowing person became dependent on the respective superior.

(2) *Parents* and *guardians* may suspend the obligation of vows made by their dependants until these are of age.

(3) A *wife* may suspend certain vows of her husband, for instance, one which would cause long absence, one of keeping severe abstinence or of not asking the *debitum coniugale.*[27]

(4) Authors add that masters may suspend the vows of their servants. This applies to the ancient relation between master and servant (*herus et servus*), but is hardly applicable to modern conditions.

Direct irritation requires no reason for its validity, but

---

25 *Ibid.;* n. 239.
26 *Ibid.;* cfr. Lehmkuhl, *l. c.,* I,

n. 463, who, however, advises provisional dispensation.
27 St. Alph , *l. c.* n. 235, n. 242.

only for licitness. If the *vovens* demands the irritation of a vow from his or her superior, the reason must be sincerely stated, otherwise the superior would act invalidly, because he is not supposed to make use of this power without a reason.[28] Of his own accord, however, the superior may irritate a vow of his subject without a reason, though he may grievously sin by doing so, if the vow is important.

Indirect irritation requires no reason except the fact that a vow is detrimental to the welfare of the Church, or to authority, or to the salvation of the *vovens*. Of this the superior is the judge.

DISPENSATION FROM VOWS

CAN. 1313

Vota non reservata possunt iusta de causa dispensare, dummodo dispensatio ne laedat ius aliis quaesitum:

1.° Loci Ordinarius quod attinet ad omnes suos subditos atque etiam peregrinos;

2.° Superior religionis clericalis exemptae quod attinet ad personas quae can. 514, § 1, enumerantur;

3.° Ii quibus ab Apostolica Sede delegata fuerit dispensandi potestas.

Vows that are not reserved may be dispensed from, for a just reason, provided the dispensation does not trench on the right acquired by a third person. Such dispensations may be granted:

1.° By the *local Ordinary* to his own subjects as well as to *peregrini*;

2.° By *religious superiors* of *exempt clerical institutes*

---

28 Lehmkuhl, *l c*, n 465.

to all those persons that are mentioned in can. 514, § 1;

3.° By those to whom the power of dispensing has been granted by the *Apostolic See.*

Dispensation here means a relaxation of the rigor of the law in a particular case. More particularly it involves a remission of an obligation *contracted before God* [29]; for a vow is made to God only. A vow may justly be considered a law, because it is based upon the divine law, although made by individual persons, since vows in general have always been sanctioned in Holy Writ. That the divinely instituted Church possesses the power of condoning vows is evident from the universal jurisdiction granted her by Christ. As vows, as well as the power of dispensing from them, are rooted in divine law, it follows that not even the *Sovereign Pontiff can validly dispense from them without a proportionate reason.* Much less, then, may those validly dispense without a cause, who enjoy only a limited and dependent power.

Notice the clause: *dummodo ne laedat ius aliis quaesitum.* A vow may be made in favor of a third person, say a poor girl, for the purpose of endowing her, or of a pious or charitable institution, or it may be a religious vow which affects a community. To dispense from a vow made in favor of a third person, if the latter has freely and fully accepted the same, *per se* exceeds even the power of the Pope. Yet it must be and is admitted by most canonists [30] that the Pope, in virtue of his supreme power and government of the Church, may dispense from vows which affect either physical persons or ecclesiastical communities for the reason that this is necessary for the common welfare. Of course, there must be a solid reason.

---

29 Lehmkuhl, *l. c.,* n. 470.

30 Cfr. S. Alph , n 256, where the negative opinion is said to have been held by some; St Alphonsus himself defends the statement made in the text.

This power cannot, however, be vindicated to inferior prelates, and is therefore excluded in our text.

What are "*vota non reservata*"? Reservation must be interpreted strictly, according to can. 1309. Hence only those private vows are reserved which are enumerated and comply with the conditions laid down in that canon. Thus the vow of entering a religious congregation or embracing a stricter order is *not* reserved.

However, some difficulty arises from the comparison of our canon with can. 1309, because the latter mentions *private* reserved vows, whilst our canon (1313) simply says: "*vota non reservata*," without making a distinction between private and public vows. *Public* vows are those taken in a religious institute approved by the Church,[31] more especially the three that make up the religious state, no matter whether these vows be temporary or perpetual, simple or solemn. Are these religious vows included in the power of dispensation granted by law to those mentioned in can. 1313? It is certain that these vows must be considered as reserved to the Holy See, at least on account of the *ius tertii*.[32] Hence the general rule certainly forbids superiors, even though otherwise empowered, to dispense from them. Yet our bishops formerly could dispense from *temporary vows* of poverty and obedience in favor of non-enclosured members of diocesan institutes; also from the vow of chastity if not taken forever and absolutely[33] The question therefore arises, whether bishops and exempt prelates may

31 Can 488, 1.

32 S. C P F, Aug 24, 1885 (*Coll P F*, n 1642).

33 *Ibid.* and S O, Aug. 2, 1876 (*Coll cit*, n 1461) · "*Quoad vota non reservata paupertatis et obedientiae, posse Episcopum in utroque casu dispensare, dummodo ius ex contractu oneroso acquisitum tertii, ipso rationabiliter invito, non laedatur. Quoad votum non reservatum castitatis, ex potestate ordinaria Episcopi, negative, nisi constet votum non fuisse perpetuum et absolutum.*"

still make use of this power? The answer is yes, because canonists generally hold, and the Code (can. 1309) does not deny, that vows not lasting or perfect in themselves, are not reserved. Hence, *per se loquendo,* the superiors mentioned might still use their power in favor of members with temporary vows, did not the Code, following a decision of the Holy Office, add the provision: *provided no right arising from the onerous contract and acquired by a third person be violated.*[34] Here, then, is the practical rule that should guide superiors: Follow can. 647, which determines the dismissal of religious with temporary vows only. This certainly is the canonically correct way, because it safeguards the rights of the third person, *viz.,* the religious institute.

Here we may supply from St. Alphonsus[35] the information that *no vow is reserved* (a) if it is made with the intention of obliging oneself only *sub levi,* (b) if it is made under the influence of fear, (c) if it is not complete as to the object promised, *e. g.,* the vow of virginity intended only to preserve the integrity of the body; (d) if it is made conditionally, even though the condition was fulfilled.

Concerning the persons mentioned in our text as being endowed with the power of dispensation, we must draw attention to the *peregrini.* For the purpose of this law a *peregrinus* is any one (*hic et nunc*) sojourning in the diocese of the dispensing Ordinary, and no inquiry is necessary as to his future intentions.[36] It goes without saying that by the local Ordinary is understood also the Vicar General and the administrator.

Those who have received *delegated power* to dispense from non-reserved vows from the Apostolic See are,

34 *Ibid*

35 *De Voto,* n. 258; Lehmkuhl, I, n. 477

36 Thus St. Alph., n. 262.

among others, the *regular confessors, i. e.,* confessors belonging to a regular order, for, according to the common doctrine of the school, these can dispense all the faithful from non-reserved vows, either in or outside the confessional. This power, based upon privilege, is granted by papal delegation.[37] How far it may be extended to *papal delegates,* depends on their credentials.

Since none of those named in our canon can dispense without a reason, it may be well to state *some valid reasons* as given by St. Alphonsus:[38]

(1) *Periculum transgressionis ac indispositionis particularis vel communis hominum fragilitas,*

(2) *Magna difficultas in executione, sive praevisa fuit sive non praevisa;*

(3) *Si vovens vexetur magnis scrupulis;*

(4) *Si votum fuit emissum ex perturbata mente vel absque perfecta deliberatione, e. g., ex tristitia, ira, metu, etc.*

COMMUTATION OF VOWS

CAN. 1314

Opus voto non reservato promissum potest in melius vel in aequale bonum ab ipso vovente commutari; in minus vero bonum ab illo cui potestas est dispensandi ad normam can. 1313.

Any good work promised in a non-reserved vow may be changed by the *vovens* into one better or equally good; but only those who may dispense according to canon 1313, can change it into a lesser work.

Commutation is the substitution of a promised good work for another, according to the rules of (at least)

---

37 S. Alph , *l. c.*, n. 257; Lehmkuhl, I, 472.   38 *De Voto,* n. 252 f.

geometrical proportion. The quality of a good work is measured by the spiritual profit of the *vovens* and the degree of divine pleasure and glory involved. This, of course, cannot be determined mathematically. The safest commutation always is a change into greater frequentation of the Sacraments.[39] The confessor, who is supposed to know the condition of his penitent, is the best judge in this matter.

Note that for a private change *no reason is required,* provided the promised good work is commuted into one that is obviously better. To commute the promised work into one less good, the authority that is empowered to dispense, must intervene. Therefore all those mentioned in can. 1313 may commute a non-reserved vow for a *just reason,* though it may be held with probability that the commutation would be valid even if there was no just reason because a commutation is not a complete liberation from a vow. It is also probable that even a vow made under oath may be commuted.[40]

CAN. 1315

Vota ante professionem religiosam emissa suspenduntur, donec vovens in religione permanserit.

Vows made before religious profession are suspended as long the *vovens* remains in the religious institute which he has joined. This includes the vow of entering a stricter, say the Carthusian, order, for this vow is not reserved.[41] But what if this vow has been accepted by the stricter order, or if it was made under oath? Since

39 S. Alph , n 243
40 S. Alph *l c , De Voto,* n. 245, n. 190; Lehmkuhl, I, n 479
41 C 5, 6°, III, 14, but the Pon-

tiff dictates a penance for the vow not fulfilled, although the subject may remain in the more mitigated order.

the text draws no distinction, the vow would be suspended even in that case; in fact the stricter order could not formally accept it until the religious had made his profession there. But this is not intended here because it would be a case of transfer, which is reserved.[42] After dismissal, the vows revive.

[42] Can. 632.

CHAPTER II

OATHS

DEFINITION

Can. 1316

§ 1. Iusiurandum, idest invocatio Nominis divini in testem veritatis, praestari nequit, nisi in veritate, in iudicio et in iustitia.

§ 2. Iusiurandum quod canones exigunt vel admittunt, per procuratorem praestari valide nequit.

§ 1. An oath, that is, the invocation of the Divine Name in witness of the truth, cannot be taken except with truth, judgment, and justice.

§ 2. Oaths demanded or admitted by Canon Law cannot validly be taken by proxy.

There were heretics who rejected oaths as illicit, or minimized their value, or depreciated their gravity, or made little of perjury.[1] The golden mean always held by the Church is that oaths are permitted if made under the conditions[2] laid down in this canon, to wit:

(1) They must be made *in truth,* for what a man solemnly affirms, should be in conformity with the truth,

---

[1] Cfr. *Professio Fidei Waldensibus proposita* (Denzinger, n. 371), *Errores Wicl et Hus* (Denzinger, nn 519, 556–558); *propp. damn.,* 24–28, March 4, 1679 (*ibid ,* nn 1041 ff); *prop. 101, Quesnelli damn ,* Sept. 8, 1713 (*ibid ,* 1316); *prop.* 75 *Syn Pistoriens. damn ,* Aug. 28, 1794 (*ibid ,* n 1438).

[2] Cfr the Commentators on tit. 24, lib II, *de Iureiurando,* S. Thom., II–II, q 89, q. 98; S. Alph, l IV, tr II, c 2, Suarez, *De Relig ,* tr V, *de Iuramento,* t. XIV, 438 ff.

and when he makes a promise, he should have the intention of keeping it.

(2) They must be made *with judgment, i. e.,* with due and reverent consideration of the usefulness or necessity of an oath.

(3) They must be made *in justice,* because no unjust obligation is binding.

Of the various distinctions made by canonists we will consider only the two especially referred to in our Code — the *assertory or affirmative oath,* by which God is called upon to witness an assertion of a past or present fact; and the *promissory oath,* by which God is called upon to witness the execution of a resolution, vow or agreement. In both, the Deity must be invoked as witness and the intention must correspond with the words used in the invocation.

In judging the intention, which is always a difficult matter, the formula or terms of the promise must be taken according to the customary interpretation.

It is strictly forbidden to use a name for the Deity which is commonly considered to mean an evil spirit.[3] It is not necessary to couple the name of God with a verb in the imperative, or subjunctive, or optative form, for the indicative may have the same meaning, as in the formula: " God liveth, God knoweth, before God I speak, I tell the truth." But if these expressions were used as mere enunciations, the intention of swearing would, of course, be wanting.[4]

---

3 Thus *deocce,* with the Gallas, indicates an evil spirit; S. O , June 20, 1866, ad 37 (n. 1293).

4 S. Alph., *l. c.,* n. 134.

THE OBLIGATION ARISING FROM AN OATH

CAN. 1317

§ 1. Qui libere iurat se aliquid facturum, peculiari religionis obligatione tenetur implendi quod iureiurando firmaverit.

§ 2. Iusiurandum per vim aut metum gravem extortum valet, sed a Superiore ecclesiastico relaxari potest.

§ 3. Iusiurandum nec vi nec dolo praestitum quo quis privato bono aut favori renuntiat lege ipsi concesso, servandum est quoties non vergit in dispendium salutis aeternae.

§ 1. One who freely takes an oath, promising to perform something, is under a special obligation, arising from the virtue of religion, to keep what he has promised. The reason is that in a promissory oath God is called upon as solemn witness of our intention to keep what we promise, and as a guarantee and pledge of executing our intention, and hence failure to do so is a slur and an injury to His honor and truthfulness, and involves a sin, either mortal or venial according to the gravity of the matter, against religion.[5]

§ 2. An oath extorted by violence or grave fear is valid, but may be rescinded by one's ecclesiastical superior.

This " great question," as St. Alphonsus [6] calls it, is here solved according to the doctrine laid down in the decretals,[7] viz., that an oath taken under the influence of compulsion or grave fear is valid because man is obliged to keep what he promises under oath, lest God be found a

---

5 Cfr. Suarez, *l c.*, l I, c. 9; 1 III, c. 16, cfr c 1, C 22, q 2; cc 8, 9. 17, 28, X, II, 24; Pius IX, Syllabus, n 64.

6 *L. c.*, II, n. 174, S. Thom , II-II, q 89, art. 7, ad 2
7 Cc. 8, 15, X, II, 24.

false witness. However, the unjust extortioner has no just claim to the thing thus promised, and therefore the ecclesiastical authorities have absolved even sacred ministers who abjured their ministry under compulsion, from the obligation of the oath. Besides, all agree that no obligation of justice arises from an unjustly exacted oath, and that if the object (money, etc.) was already delivered, it could be claimed in court or regained by occult compensation.

§ 3. An oath taken without compulsion or fraud, by which one renounces some private good or favor granted him by law, must be kept, if it does not imply the loss of eternal salvation. The case is taken from the decretals.[8] Women had promised by oath to have their dowries sold. The pope told the judges to observe the canon law, which permitted such alienation, and to instruct the women to keep their oath, as long as no injury was done to others and there was no danger to their salvation.

NATURE OF OBLIGATION

CAN. 1318

§ 1. Iusiurandum promissorium sequitur naturam et conditiones actus cui adiicitur.

§ 2. Si actui directe vergenti in damnum aliorum aut in praeiudicium boni publici vel salutis aeternae iusiurandum adiiciatur, nullam exinde actus consequitur firmitatem.

§ 1. A promissory oath follows the nature and conditions of the act to which it is attached.

8 C. 15, 28, X, II, 24. Thus also an oath made to a *meretrix,* if no sin is involved, would hold, S. Alph., n. 177; even an oath to pay a usurer interest would bind, but the money may be reclaimed; c. 6, X, II, 24.

§ 2. If the oath is attached to an act which implies damage to others, or prejudice to the common welfare or to eternal salvation, the act receives no strength from the oath.

§ 1 explains the meaning of a promissory oath. It is attached to a contract, stipulation, or agreement, and lends higher sanction to the same, but the obligation of the oath cannot be extended farther than the contract or natural promise itself. Hence (a) a sworn promise, in order to be valid, must be *accepted* before it obliges; (b) it cannot be condoned, abated, or forgiven. Besides there may be other mutual or implied conditions, as is the case in every contract; *e. g.,* if I am able, if my superior permits, etc.[9]

§ 2 declares that an oath has no binding force if attached to an act that (a) implies injury to a third person, for this would be evil,[10] or (b) injury to the public welfare, as if a judge would swear not to prosecute criminals, or a clergyman would take a civil oath forbidden by higher authority[11]; or (c) endangers eternal salvation. The underlying principle is that an oath cannot be a chain of iniquity.

CESSATION OF OBLIGATION

CAN. 1319

Obligatio iureiurando promissorio inducta desinit:

1.° Si remittatur ab eo in cuius commodum iusiurandum emissum fuerat;

2.° Si res iurata substantialiter mutetur, aut, mutatis adiunctis, fiat sive mala sive omnino indifferens, aut denique maius bonum impediat;

9 Cfr. c 25, X, II, 24; Lehmkuhl, *l c*, I, n. 419.
10 C 12, X, II, 14, not to speak to parents or relatives.
11 Cfr. c. 21, X, II, 14; c 12, X, II, 2; Engel, l. II, tit. 24, n. 8.

3.° Deficiente causa finali aut conditione sub qua forte iusiurandum datum sit;

4.° Irritatione, dispensatione, commutatione, ad normam can. 1320.

The obligation contracted by a promissory oath ceases:

1.° If condoned by the one in whose favor it was taken;

2.° If the thing promised is substantially changed, or if, by reason of a change in the circumstances, the oath becomes sinful, or entirely indifferent, or an obstacle to attaining a higher good;

3.° If the final cause or condition under which the oath was taken, have ceased to exist or failed;

4.° By irritation, dispensation, or commutation, according to can. 1320.

The first reason has been explained above.

The second reason is a *substantial change* in the thing promised. Thus, one is not obliged to marry a girl to whom he promised marriage under oath, if the girl has undergone a substantial change as to her health, social condition, virginal state, etc., etc.,[12] or if the change affect the *vovens* so that he may incur danger of death, or infamy, or risk the loss of a great good. No one is supposed to have had the intention of obliging himself under oath to something that will gravely [13] embarrass him. If the thing becomes evil or entirely useless, for instance, if one had sworn to punish a child and the child has amended its conduct. Lastly, if one had taken an oath that would deter him from entering the religious or clerical state, it would not be binding, unless the public welfare were at stake.

12 S. Alph., n 180.

13 *Ibid*, n. 187; for instance, the oath of keeping a secret

Can. 1320

Qui irritare, dispensare, commutare possunt votum, eandem potestatem eademque ratione habent circa iusiurandum promissorium; sed si iurisiurandi dispensatio vergat in praeiudicium aliorum qui obligationem remittere recusent, una Apostolica Sedes potest iusiurandum dispensare propter necessitatem aut utilitatem Ecclesiae.

Those who are empowered to annul, dispense from, or commute vows, have the same power with regard to promissory oaths; but in case the dispensation involves a prejudice to a third person, who refuses to condone the obligation, the Holy See alone can dispense on account of the utility or necessity of the Church.

This power is included in the supreme power of the Church and required for the tranquillity and peace of individuals and society. Thus it would certainly be in favor of the public welfare to dispense a child under age from the oath of marrying a certain person, even though the parents should be unwilling to have the oath annulled.[14]

Can. 1321

Iusiurandum stricte est interpretandum secundum ius et secundum intentionem iurantis, aut, si hic dolo agat, secundum intentionem illius cui iuratur.

An oath must be interpreted strictly according to law and the intention of the *vovens,* or if the latter swears de-

---

14 C. 19, C. 22, q. 4; c. 15; C 22, q. 5.

ceitfully, according to the intention of the person to whom the oath is made.

Thus one who swears to keep the statutes of a certain society or congregation is obliged to observe only those which were issued when the oath was taken, not those published later.[15] Nor can the obligation of an oath be extended beyond the intention of the *vovens,* because this intention is the measure of the obligation. But if the person swears deceitfully, he has only himself to blame if his intention is not accepted and that of the person receiving the oath substituted therefor.[16]

---

[15] C. 35, X, II, 24.

[16] Cfr the peculiar case stated in c. 25, X, II, 24.

PART IV

THE TEACHING OFFICE OF THE CHURCH

Although the authority of teaching and preaching the Word of God belongs to the Church by virtue of her divine constitution, and is therefore an inherent attribute of ecclesiastical persons, the manner of exercising this office constitutes part of the administrative rights of the Church. And although the *depositum fidei* can receive no substantial increase, yet its unfolding and explicit declaration are evidenced through the centuries. The material increase of the faithful and the administration of the Word of God have necessitated methods and means which were not so imperative in former times. Hence a certain change is noticeable also in the spread and exposition of the Word of God.

In Part IV the Code sets forth in a preamble the *authority of the Church* with regard to teaching the Word of God, and what is opposed to faith as understood by the Church. Then the text lays down rules for *preaching* (can. 1327-1351); sets up regulations for the *institutions* which hand down the Church's teaching, *viz.*, seminaries and other schools (can. 1352-1383); the warding off of errors as exercised through the *censorship of books* (can. 1384-1405); and, lastly, the obligations connected with the *profession of faith* (can. 1406-1408).

RIGHT OF THE CHURCH TO TEACH

CAN. 1322

§ 1. Christus Dominus fidei depositum Ecclesiae concredidit, ut ipsa, Spiritu Sancto iugiter assistente, doctrinam revelatam sancte custodiret et fideliter exponeret.

§ 2. Ecclesiae, independenter a qualibet civili potestate, ius est et officium gentes omnes evangelicam doctrinam docendi: hanc vero rite ediscere veramque Dei Ecclesiam amplecti omnes divina lege tenentur.

§ 1. Christ, our Lord has entrusted to the Church the deposit of faith, in order that, by the continual assistance of the Holy Ghost, she might preserve the revealed doctrine and expound it faithfully.

The term *"depositum fidei"* (an allusion to I Tim. 6, 20), may be taken in a twofold sense. In the *strict sense* the deposit of the faith comprises all the truths which are either implicitly or explicitly contained in the written word of God or in tradition, and must be believed as revealed with divine faith In a *wider sense* the deposit of faith comprises also those truths which, though not revealed, bear such an intimate relation to revealed truths that, without them, the latter could not be, at least easily and fully, preserved, expounded, and defended.[1] Both kinds of truth are in the lawful possession of the Church, who is entitled to make the deposit of faith in the wider sense an object of her infallible teaching, precisely in order to *preserve the faith holy, i. e.,* unchanged, unsoiled, and unadulterated. The duty of preservation is in itself positive and affirmative and the Church complies with it by *interpretation* or exposition; but it sometimes also re-

1 Cfr Mazzella, *De Religione et Ecclesia,* 1892, p. 615

quires *reprobation* or rejection. Hence the Church has always claimed (a) the right of defining what belongs to the deposit of faith, *i. e.*, faith and morals, or the extent of divine faith; (b) the right of proposing the true meaning of revealed truth in its professions of faith; (c) the right of rejecting or condemning whatever is contrary to the teaching of faith and morals, either by rejecting false interpretations of revealed truth, or reprobating false conclusions of reason, censuring and proscribing erroneous propositions, etc.; (d) the right of infallibly judging dogmatic facts connected with certain doctrines, as in the case of Jansenius.

This office of an infallible teacher belongs to the Catholic Church not merely in virtue of her divine origin, but by reason of the continual assistance of the *Holy Ghost promised to her by Christ,* and which implies no new revelation, but a special providence keeping her free from error in the function of preserving and expounding the deposit of faith.[2]

§ 2. The Church, independently of the civil authority, possesses the *right* of teaching all nations the truth. Correlative to this right is the *duty* of teaching men, and on their part the duty of obtaining a knowledge of the truth and embracing the true Church of God. This obligation, incumbent on all, is derived from the divine law. Our Saviour not merely advised, but commanded, His Apostles to teach all nations and to preach the Gospel to every creature.[3] This command, intended also for their successors, itself forms part and parcel of the deposit of faith. It is attached to the universal mission of the Church, whose real object is nothing else but the union of men

2 Cfr. Matt 28, 19 f; John 14, 26; Mazzella, *l c*, n 789, p. 603. The divine assistance presupposes human coöperation and investigation. 3 Cfr. Matth. 28, 19 f.; Mark 16, 15 f.

with God, or the salvation of all mankind through intimate union with the Creator. This mission is incumbent on the Church to the end of time and is fulfilled first of all by preaching the word of God, because faith is the *conditio sine qua non* of salvation.[4] Faith, of course, must here be taken as including the works of faith, or, in the usual formula, faith and morals. The law of prescription adds weight to the divine law which dictates that everything directly related to the spiritual end or purpose for which the Church was founded, is her proper and exclusive domain, in which she is supreme, having no higher authority than God Himself. The Church, then, is not at liberty to abdicate this right or to shirk this duty, for if she did so, she would cease to exist or give up her divine mission.

On the other hand, as salvation is the individual concern of every rational creature destined to the ultimate end for which he is created, and since salvation begins with faith, it follows that every person endowed with the necessary faculties must coöperate in the attainment of that end by adopting the means without which it cannot be achieved — *necessitate medii.* Each and everyone must hear and believe those who preach the word of God by the authority of the Church. Every preacher must have a divine call, this is communicated to him through the organization founded by Christ. This is the Church in which all those who wish to be saved must be enrolled: " Unless one believeth, he shall be condemned " (Mark 16, 16). Such is, if we mistake not, the meaning of § 1 of our canon. The term *omnes* certainly includes all men who have sufficient use of reason to realize what a grievous sin is, when they are capable of merit and demerit, reward and

4 Rom. 10, 10 ff

punishment. *Omnes,* furthermore, includes every individual without regard to ancestral or paternal prejudice and authority. For the ultimate end of man is not bound up with either national or family traditions, nor is paternal or maternal authority stronger than the divine command. Salvation, as we have said, is a strictly individual concern which involves a serious obligation from the time that reason dawns upon the child. From this viewpoint also is to be understood the phrase: *" independenter a qualibet civili potestate."* For if the duty of acquiring the necessary knowledge of the Gospel and embracing the Church of God is individual, it necessarily follows that the State cannot be allowed to interfere in a matter which transcends its purpose — which lies entirely within the sphere of man's temporal welfare, whereas the object of the Church is spiritual and supernatural, reaching into eternity. Those two ends cannot, *per se,* clash, for although the two societies are supreme each in its own domain, their ends are different and only touch each other at some points. This could not be otherwise, as the author of both societies is one and the same God, who created both the natural and the supernatural world.[5]

THE MATERIAL OBJECT OF FAITH

Can. 1323

§ 1. Fide divina et catholica ea omnia credenda sunt quae verbo Dei scripto vel tradito continentur et ab Ecclesia sive sollemni iudicio sive ordinario et universali magisterio tamquam divinitus revelata credenda proponuntur.

5 Cfr. Leo XIII, *"Immortale Dei,"* Nov. 1, 1885, Cavagnis, *Institutiones Iuris Publici Ecclesiastici,* 1883, p. 6 ff.; Lib IV, c 1; Bachofen, *Summa Iuris Eccl. Pub,* 1910, p 110 ff.

§ 2. Sollemne huiusmodi iudicium pronuntiare proprium est tum Oecumenici Concilii tum Romani Pontificis ex cathedra loquentis.

§ 3. Declarata seu definita dogmatice res nulla intelligitur, nisi id manifeste constiterit.

§ 1. All those truths which are contained in the written word of God, or in tradition, and proposed to our belief as divinely revealed either by a solemn proclamation or by the ordinary and universal magisterium of the Church must be believed by Divine and Catholic faith.

§ 2. To pronounce a solemn judgment of this kind appertains either to a general Council or to the Roman Pontiff speaking *ex cathedra*.

§ 3. Nothing is to be taken as dogmatically declared or defined, unless it is manifestly known to be such.

The material object of faith (*objectum materiale fidei*), or that which is to be believed, is contained either in Holy Writ, as accepted by the Church, or in tradition, as preserved by the Church. However, as Holy Writ itself, without the acceptance of the Church, would be merely a material or indifferent book — though perhaps sacred on account of its venerable age and contents — so tradition would lack sacred character and obligation but for the *infallible judgment* of the Church. This infallible judgment is embodied in the teaching office of the Church, and constitutes a special prerogative granted to the Church by Christ, in virtue of which she cannot deceive nor be deceived in matters of faith and morals.[6]

Our text distinguishes a solemn *ex cathedra* judgment and the ordinary *magisterium* of the Church. But there is no intrinsic difference between the two, as they derive from the same source, *viz.*, the divine promise and provi-

6 Mazzella, *l. c*, n. 782, p 599.

dence, and have the same object and purpose. The object is faith and morals; the purpose, to protect the faithful from error.

The *ordinary and universal teaching body* of the Church consists of the pastors together with their head, the Roman Pontiff, no matter where the former are found, whether scattered over the globe, or sitting united in St. Peter's Dome. This is called the active subject of the infallible magisterium (*subiectum activae infallibilitatis*). To this teaching body corresponds the believing body of the faithful, which latter, however, being the *subiectum passivae infallibilitatis,* cannot be separated from the teaching body or be opposed to it. For the teaching office or authority is the cause of the infallibility of the Church, and both bodies are one in the same faith.

There is, however, a distinction, though not quite adequate, between the *teaching office of the Sovereign Pontiff alone,* and the body of teachers or the teaching Church united to its head, *i. e.,* the Pontiff. Without the latter, or, worse still, in opposition to the latter, there can be no teaching body, whilst the authority of infallible teacher is embodied in the Roman Pontiff alone. Both the Pontiff sole and the body of teachers united with him, enjoy the power of teaching infallibly.

The *"universal [7] and ordinary magisterium"* consists of the entire *episcopate,* according to the constitution and order defined by Christ, *i. e.,* all the bishops of the universal Church,— dependently on the Roman Pontiff [8] Priests and deacons do not, *iure divino,* belong to the hierarchy of jurisdiction, and therefore, are not, prop-

---

[7] The word *"universal"* was added in order to distinguish it from the official attribute of infallibility inherent in the Pontiff. See *Coll. Lac,* t VII, 176.

[8] Cfr Pius IX, *"Tuas libenter,"* Dec. 21, 1863.

erly speaking, judges in matters of faith and morals, nor can they be, *iure ordinario,* bearers of infallible teaching. However, they exercise a certain teaching authority by divine right, inasmuch, namely, as they are helpers and co-workers of the bishops, from whom they receive delegated mission, and preach and testify to the faith preached and expounded by the episcopate. They, too, in a wider sense partake of the assistance of the Holy Ghost.

This teaching authority, then, proposes what must be believed by *divine and Catholic faith.* It is indeed true that what God has revealed may and must be believed with *divine faith,*[9] and that what the Church proposes as part of divine Revelation, may and must be believed with *divine* and *Catholic* faith, or, shortly, with *Catholic* faith. But the material object of divine faith comprises more than the object of Catholic faith, and besides there is something in Catholic faith which is not so clearly expressed or conspicuous in divine faith. For the former is offered by the living word of the Church with a precision and determination that leaves no doubt as to the supernatural origin and medium through which it is conveyed. This Catholic faith then commands our assent and obedience to the full extent of a childlike belief, but from the motive of divine veracity and truth.[10]

The term *proposed* means not merely an official or authentic formulation of a given object or article, but an authoritative promulgation of a law or rule contained in revelation, commanding our full interior and exterior assent.[11]

§ 2 defines, according to Vatican Council,[12] the *solemn*

9 The Blessed Virgin Mary certainly believed the Angel with divine faith, but of Catholic faith there can be no question.

10 Cfr. Scheeben, *Dogmatik,* 1873,

I, p 324; *Coll. Lac ,* t. VII, 72 ff., 159 f.

11 Scheeben, *l. c.,* p. 179 f.

12 *Conc. Vat.,* Sess VII, c II, *De Revelatione,* c. III, *De Fide,* c

judgment of the Church in contradistinction to her ordinary and universal magisterium, not as if the office of
the Supreme Pontiff were extraordinary, in the strict
sense, but because this means of proposing an infallible
truth is uncommon.   Such a solemn pronunciamento or
proclamation may be made either by a *general council*
or by the Pope.   That a council cannot be ecumenical
without the head, is evident, as explained in our Vol. II,
where the other requisites are also discussed.[13]

The *Pope* alone, after having been duly elected and
having accepted the election, is the lawful head of the
Church, and, in virtue of his primacy of jurisdiction,
is the supreme pastor and teacher of the whole Church,
as the Vatican Council has defined.[14]   As such he may
define, or issue decrees on, points of faith and morals,
binding the whole Church.   His decisions do not receive
their obligatory force from the consent of the Church,
as the Gallicans asserted,[15] but embrace the whole extent
of the object of the infallibility inherent in the teaching
Church.   The term *ex cathedra* means: (a) that the Pope
proclaims a dogma as the supreme teacher and pastor of
the Church; (b) that it be a matter of faith and morals,
not of history or politics disconnected with the former;
(c) that he pronounce an authoritative and final sentence
with the manifest intention of obliging (d) the entire
Church, *i. e.*, all individuals as well as the whole body
of the faithful.[16]

However, as § 3 intimates, there may be doubt as to

IV, *De Fide et Ratione, De Revela-*
tione, can. 4, *De Fide,* can. 6; *De*
Fide et Ratione, can. 3; Sess IV,
c. IV, *De Romani Pontificis Infal-*
libili Magisterio

13 See can. 222 ff.; p. 217 f.

14 Sess. IV, *De Eccl.,* c 4 (Denz.,
n. 1682).

15 Art. 2, *Decl. Cleri Gall. dam.*
ab Innoc. XI, April 11, 1682; *ab*
Alex. VIII, "*Inter multiplices,*"
Aug. 4, 1690 (Denz , 1189)

16 Mazzella, *l. c.,* n. 1051, p 821.

what is *declared or defined* either by the universal teaching Church or by means of papal *ex cathedra definitions.* Therefore the theologians have laid down certain *rules,* which we will briefly restate.

a) What has been *solemnly defined,* either by a general council or by the Supreme Pontiff, is certainly *de fide;* but not all the historical or theological assertions which accompany a papal decision (for instance, the Bull "*Ineffabilis*") are *de fide.*

b) What is clearly and undoubtedly contained in *Holy Scripture and Tradition* as a matter of faith or morals, must be believed, although individual errors are not entirely excluded;

c) What the universal and approved practice and discipline proposes as connected with faith and morals must also be believed ("*Lex orandi, lex credendi*").

d) What the *Holy Fathers* and the *theologians* hold unanimously as a matter of faith and morals,[17] is also *de fide.*

There may be some doubt as to the form of infallible decisions. A test for genuine ex cathedra definitions has been found in the following formulas: (1) if those who assert the contrary are declared heretics; (2) if the terms "*si quis*" is used with "*anathema*" following; (3) if it is declared that the doctrine in question must be firmly believed by all the faithful as a dogma.[18]

If after the application of these rules a solid doubt remains, the utterance is not infallibly binding, as is evident from our text.

17 Cfr Simar, *Dogmatik*, 1893, p 41 ff., § 11.
18 For instance, Christ is true man; hence he must have a human body and a soul.

CAN. 1324

Satis non est haereticam pravitatem devitare, sed oportet illos quoque errores diligenter fugere, qui ad illam plus minusve accedunt; quare omnes debent etiam constitutiones et decreta servare quibus pravae huiusmodi opiniones a Sancta Sede proscriptae et prohibitae sunt.

It is not enough to eschew heretical depravity, but those errors also must be carefully avoided which more or less closely approach heresy; and for this reason all must observe also those constitutions and decrees by which the Holy See proscribes and forbids such perverse opinions.

This text is very cautiously worded, no doubt in order to avoid theological controversy. The question here evidently turns about certain *conclusions,* commonly called theological, for there is no doubt that truths either immediately and expressly, or immediately but obscurely contained in Revelation must be believed *fide divinâ,* and, if properly proposed, also fide *catholicâ et divinâ.* But there *is* a controversy as to truths which are not directly and explicitly contained in Revelation, but only virtually (*virtualiter*) deducted therefrom by logical reasoning. Besides there are natural truths, not revealed in the proper sense, which have such an intimate connection with the revealed truths of faith and morals, that the purity and integrity of faith and morals cannot be safely maintained and defended without them. Concerning these some writers have asserted that they must be believed *fide divinâ,* whereas others (*e. g.,* De Lugo) main-

tain that they must be believed *fide ecclesiasticâ* only.[19]
Our Code does not decide this controversy. One thing
is certain, *viz.*, that the *assent* which every Catholic must
give to the judgment of the Church when she pronounces
on certain errors, must be *internal,* and that the condemna-
tions issued by the S. Congregations may not be treated
as if they had no weight.[20] For even the so-called *fides
ecclesiastica* requires not a mere servile silence, but a real
assent, elicited by the will, although the formal reason,
the *auctoritas Dei loquentis,* may not be implied.

PROFESSION OF FAITH

CAN. 1325

§ 1. Fideles Christi fidem aperte profiteri tenentur
quoties eorum silentium, tergiversatio aut ratio agendi
secumferrent implicitam fidei negationem, con-
temptum religionis, iniuriam Dei vel scandalum
proximi.

§ 2. Post receptum baptismum si quis, nomen
retinens christianum, pertinaciter aliquam ex veritati-
bus fide divina et catholica credendis denegat aut de
ea dubitat, haereticus; si a fide christiana totaliter
recedit, apostata; si denique subesse renuit Summo
Pontifici aut cum membris Ecclesiae ei subiectis communicare recusat, schismaticus est.

§ 3. Caveant catholici ne disputationes vel colla-
tiones, publicas praesertim, cum acatholicis habeant,
sine venia Sanctae Sedis aut, si casus urgeat, loci
Ordinarii.

§ 1. The faithful are obliged to openly profess their

---

19 De Lugo, *De Virtute Fidei,*
disp. 20, sect 13, n. 109; Simar,
l. c., p. 49 f., p 640 ff.

20 " *Lamentabili,*" July 4, 1907,
propp. VII and VIII

Christian faith, as often as silence, evasion, or mode of acting would involve an implicit denial of the faith, contempt of religion, dishonor to God, or scandal to their neighbors.

The Apostle says: "With the heart we believe unto justice; but with the mouth confession is made unto salvation." [21] This and the declaration of Christ: "He that shall be ashamed of me and my words, of him the Son of man shall be ashamed," [22] clearly indicate a double duty, namely, (1) to profess the Christian religion, and (2) not to deny it. But as a prohibitive or negative law obliges always, whereas an affirmative or a positive law does not oblige at every moment or on every occasion, so in our case the text states the negative side of the obligation, namely *not to omit the profession* of faith when it is called for. Faith may be concealed by mere *silence,* which, however, is sometimes permissible, for, as stated, we need not profess the faith all the time. Nay, it may even be necessary to hide it, namely, when great damage, such as persecution or vexation,[23] threatens a whole community. On the other hand it is certain that whenever the public and lawful authority demands a profession of one's faith, it is never permitted to refuse it.[24] Besides, in no case is it allowed to conceal the faith entirely and to be a hidden Christian, even though there were danger of life or loss of temporal goods.[25] Such as wish to remain occult Christians always cannot be admitted to baptism.[26]

Faith may also be concealed by *subterfuge,* and various devices have been adopted for this purpose, some of them

21 Rom. 10, 10.
22 Luke 9, 26; Matth. 10, 32
23 Lehmkuhl, I, n 291.
24 S. C P. F., Feb. 7, 1791
(*Coll*, n 604).

25 S. C. P. F., Nov. 24, 1628 (n. 44).
26 S C. P. F., May 28, 1635 (n. 84).

despicable. Thus the custom of Christians assuming pagan or Mohammedan names was branded as deceitful and hypocritical and strictly forbidden by papal constitution.[27] While there is little or nothing in a name as such, if it becomes a shibboleth of heresy or apostasy and is so regarded by the magistrate and populace, it is no longer as sounding brass, even if the bearer interiorly desires to retain the faith. Therefore circumstances must be considered.

A curious kind of subterfuge was devised by certain Christians who wished to graduate or take the doctor's degree in China, a ceremony accompanied by religious rites, such as the offering of flowers, meat, or incense to an idol, etc. This is never permitted. It is also forbidden to bribe the magistrate or to "play sick" on the day of the ceremony, because this would amount to a lie.[28] A somewhat similar artifice was employed in good faith by some missionaries. The mandarins, in order not to lose their office, made an investigation as to the conduct of these missionaries and, in a report to the "Celestial Son," assured him that the missionaries were not priests, had not preached the faith and left no following. This report, together with the sentence of exile (instead of capital punishment), had to be signed by the missionaries themselves, so that they, as it were, condemned themselves in order to be treated more leniently. The S. Congregation decided that the missionaries were not allowed to sign the sentence thus worded. On the other hand, however, they were not bound to protest publicly against the magistrates, if these published the sentence without the signature of the missionaries.[29]

27 Bened XIV, "*Inter omnigenas,*" Feb 2, 1744, § 3–6; "*Quod provinciale,*" Aug. 1, 1754; S O, Nov. 29, 1729 (*Coll. P F*, n. 373).

28 S C P. F., Jan. 4, 1798 (n. 644)

29 S C. P. F., Dec. 9, 1822 (n. 776).

For in that case the malice of the act was imputable entirely to the mandarins.

It may be added that no denial of the faith is involved in the act of hiding one's special or peculiar state (for instance, the priesthood) nor would such an act *per se* amount to a mortal sin.[30]

Lastly, one's conduct, or *ratio agendi,* may imply a denial of the faith. To this class belong certain acts which are indifferent in themselves, but become wrong by the end for which they are performed, or by their object or accompanying circumstances.[31] Thus *eating meat* is in itself an indifferent act, but may become sinful through either or all of three concomitant adjuncts. Thus to eat or prepare meat in *odium fidei,* in contempt of religion, is a grievous sin because the end is sacrilegious, and may amount to a denial of the faith, if the meat is taken as a *signum protestativum of apostasy.* If the act is performed merely for economy's sake, without any religious motive, no denial is involved. Christians in the Orient were permitted to build, or help build, a Mohammedan mosque because compelled to do so by the Turks; at least the S. Congregation decided that they were not to be disquieted.[32] A different answer was given by the Holy Office in reply to the question whether Christians were allowed to build, or coöperate in building, a pagan temple because they feared for their life or were in danger of being exiled. This was declared forbidden.[33] There is an

30 Lehmkuhl, I, n. 292, according to De Lugo, Suarez, etc.

31 S. O., April 19, 1635; May 27, 1671, n 1; June 20, 1866, n 38 (*Coll. P F*, nn. 83, 195, 1293); S C. P. F, June 26, 1820 (n. 747). The end is also perceptible in the following case: Christians may contribute to public funds or public demonstrations, if these may be interpreted as signs of public joy, even though idolatrous customs may be connected with them, but the intention of contributing to idolatry is never permissible S. C. P. F., Sept. 12, 1645, n 114

32 S. C. P F, Sept. 26, 1840, n. 14 (*Coll.,* n. 914).

33 S. O, Jan. 8, 1851, ad 1 (*Coll.,* n. 1055).

essential difference between a mosque and a pagan temple, because the latter involves idol worship, whereas the former does not. Besides, the cases are somewhat different in this that the latter implies voluntary coöperation, whereas the former contains an element of violence.

That *circumstances,* too, may change the nature of an act is evident from the example of certain Christians who were made to trample on the cross. To walk over or to step on an object, is in itself a merely material and indifferent act, but intentionally to trample on the cross, if seen and perceived, is sacrilegious. The case was as follows: The pagans placed crosses across the road and in narrow gates, where Christians had to pass. The decision was: (a) if the Christians were not warned, they should walk as if nothing had happened; but (b) if they were warned, they should take care not to step on the crosses; (c) if they were warned, but could not pass by without stepping on them, they should protest to the bystanders and pass over them as reverently as they could.[34]

Idol worship in whatever form, for instance, in the shape of tablets dedicated to the " seat of such and such a soul," is incompatible with the Christian faith. Therefore such tablets must be destroyed, if they are in the exclusive possession of Christians, or, if pagan families have a share in them, may be restored to these.[35] A convert from the Anglican Church may not hide his faith so as to retain a Protestant minister in his home and assist at the prayer meetings, even though the convert recites the Catholic prayers; nor is he allowed to leave his children in the care of heretical tutors.[36]

Concerning *schismatic* priests the following decisions may be noted: Assistance at schismatic services is not

34 S O , *Inst.,* 1863 (*Coll. P. F.,* n. 1235).

35 S. O , Aug. 20, 1778 (n 530).

36 S. O , July 29, 1699 (n 246)

allowed. An Armenian priest of the Catholic faith is not allowed to pour water secretly into the chalice in the sacristy.[37] Catholic Nestorian priests are not allowed to hear the confessions of their schismatic coreligionists, even though by their refusal they risk losing their support; nor are they permitted to recite the names of Dioscurus or Nestorius at Mass, even though they merely intend to honor the patron saints of these two heresiarchs.[38]

As to *clothes*, the answer is always the same: if they are distinctive and notorious signs or proofs of infidelity, heresy or apostasy, a Catholic is never allowed to wear them.[39]

For the rest, the rules on material and formal co-operation should be consulted.

§ 2 *defines* three classes of Catholics who have suffered "shipwreck of the faith."[40] The first class is that of *heretics* who, having been baptized, retain the name of Christians, but obstinately deny or doubt some of the truths that must be believed by divine or Catholic faith. The second class is that of *apostates*, who have given up the Christian faith entirely and fallen away from it. The third class is that of *schismatics*, who refuse to obey the Sovereign Pontiff or to live in union with those who submit to him.

Heresy, therefore, supposes the valid reception of Baptism, which is the means of Christian initiation. But there is a difference in the attitude of different heretics. Some have been validly baptized and raised in a sect the truthfulness of which they have never doubted.

---

[37] S. O., Aug. 7, 1704 (n. 267). They do it to hide their faith, because the Monophyites abhor a mixture of wine with water.

[38] S. O., Aug. 28, 1669 (*Coll.*, n. 185).

[39] Cfr. Lehmkuhl, *l. c.*, n. 294.

[40] I Tim. 1, 19.

Such are called *material heretics,* who may, nay should remain where they are, as long as no doubt arises in their mind concerning the truth of their sect. Others have doubts, but make no effort to disperse them, and are not ready to accept the truth, even though convinced of it. Such are *formal* heretics. To this we may also reckon those so-called Catholics who interiorly reject or doubt any revealed truth, provided the rejection as well as the doubt be obstinate (*pertinax*), because this characteristic constitutes malice. Obstinacy may be assumed when a revealed truth has been proposed with sufficient clearness and force to convince a reasonable man. Of course, the character of each individual must be taken into consideration.

Apostasy differs from heresy only as to the extent of the material object of faith denied; the specific malice, *viz.,* the denial of God's truthfulness, or of the divine authority, is the same in both.[41] An apostate, therefore, is one who rejects the whole deposit of faith and becomes an unbeliever, whilst a heretic is one who wilfully rejects or doubts only the one or other truth revealed and proposed by the Catholic Church.

Pure schism involves mere stubbornness or disobedience to the Roman Pontiff, or to a bishop, as the case may be; but in reality it hardly ever occurs without heresy. The Puseyites endeavored to convince the Apostolic See of the contrary; but the Holy Office very properly decided that separation from the See of Peter meant a split in the unity and apostolicity of the Church and setting up another Church in place of the one founded by Christ.[42]

§ 3 *warns Catholics against disputations and conferences* with non-Catholics. To hold such a disputation

41 Cf. Lehmkuhl, *l. c.,* I, n. 299.   42 S. O., Sept. 16, 1864 (*Coll. P. F.,* n. 1262).

or conference, especially in public, requires the special permission of the Holy See, or, in urgent cases, of the local Ordinary. This has been the attitude of Apostolic See ever since the beginning of the seventeenth century, though public disputations and conferences — including the so-called congresses or parliaments of religion — are not absolutely forbidden, but may be tolerated, under the condition mentioned, when there is hope of a greater good.[43] The S. Congregation has often expressly forbidden them on the ground that they do more harm than good, since false eloquence may cause error seemingly to triumph over truth.[44] Religious superiors are urged to forbid such public disputations and conferences to their missionaries.[45] This rule in our opinion also affects public disputations with Socialists, because their tenets often contain heresies.[46]

When such disputations are expressly permitted, care should be taken that only capable and prudent speakers be employed to defend the Catholic side.[47]

BISHOPS AS JUDGES IN MATTERS OF FAITH

CAN. 1326

Episcopi quoque, licet singuli vel etiam in Conciliis particularibus congregati infallibilitate docendi non polleant, fidelium tamen suis curis commissorum, sub auctoritate Romani Pontificis, veri doctores seu magistri sunt.

What is said in this canon has been partly explained under can. 1323, where it was said that the bishops,

43 S. C. P. F., Feb. 7, 1645 (n. 112).

44 S. C. P F , Feb. 7, 1625 (n. 8).

45 S. C. P. F , Dec 18, 1862 (n. 148).

46 S. C. pro Neg. Eccl. Extr., Jan 27, 1902, n VIII (*Anal. Eccl.,* X, 74).

47 S. C. P. F., Dec 18, 1662 (n. 148).

dependently upon the Roman Pontiff, are true teachers of the 'flock confided to them. But neither singly nor in councils do they share the infallibility which is their prerogative when acting as the ordinary teaching body of the Church under the leadership of the Sovereign Pontiff, or when united under the same at a general council. One case in particular illustrates the second clause of our text, *viz.*, that the bishops must be regarded as true teachers of their flocks, as long as they obey the ordinances and laws issued by the Roman Pontiff. It is the question of *interest taking* which has repeatedly agitated the minds of confessors and bishops.[48] To take interest on money loaned seemed to be prohibited, especially since Pius VIII (*"Vix pervenit"*) had forbidden the practice to a certain extent. But his words seemed ambiguous and did not cover various cases. Therefore it was left to the bishops to decide in individual cases, whether it was allowed to accept and retain interest, provided they followed the principles laid down in the papal constitution; and the confessors had to abide by their decisions. This may be applied to disciplinary cases in general and also to rubrics. But in case of doubt recourse may be had to the S. Congregations.[49]

[48] Cfr. S. O., Aug. 18, 1830, Aug. 31, 1831; Jan. 17, 1838 (Denz., nn. 1470 ff.).

[49] S. O. May 9, 1821, ad 2 (*Coll. P. F.*, n. 759, Kentucky).

TITLE XX

PREACHING THE WORD OF GOD

CAN. 1327

§ 1. Munus fidei catholicae praedicandae commissum praecipue est Romano Pontifici pro universa Ecclesia, Episcopis pro suis dioecesibus.

§ 2. Episcopi tenentur officio praedicandi per se ipsi Evangelium, nisi legitimo prohibeantur impedimento; et insuper, praeter parochos, debent alios quoque viros idoneos in auxilium assumere ad huiusmodi praedicationis munus salubriter exsequendum.

Preaching the word of God is a necessary means of spreading as well as preserving the deposit of the faith [1] This *office* emanates from the power of jurisdiction, of which the *magisterium ecclesiasticum* is a part The *Sovereign Pontiff* is the supreme teacher of the faithful and consequently has the duty, above all others, of preaching the Catholic faith to the whole Church. This, of course, means that there is no Catholic church on the whole earth in which he is not allowed to preach without interference from any, either ecclesiastical or civil, authority. But it also implies that his *pastoral letters* and other instructions need no approbation or permission from the civil government. St. Peter asked neither Nero (54–68) nor the Jewish synagogue for permission to

---

1 Bened XV, "*Humani generis*,"•June 15, 1917 (*A. Ap. S.*, IX, 305 ff).

address the faithful of Pontus, Galatia, Cappadocia, Asia, and Bithynia, nor do we read of any such permission being asked for by Clement I. Up to the eleventh century there is barely a trace of what later on came to be called *placetum regium*. On the contrary, Pope Paschal II (1099–1118) complained against Henry I of England that letters sent by the Apostolic See were subjected to the *placet* of his royal majesty.[2] The quarrel between Philip IV, the Fair, and Boniface VIII is too well known to need repetition. Other *regalistically tainted governments* followed the perverse example of Henry and Philip up to even the " enlightened " nineteenth and twentieth centuries. Government supervision was, and in some countries [3] is still, applied to the pastoral letters of bishops. That such a course of action is against the divine law needs no proof. Obedience is due to God rather than to men.[4] Nor is there any seditious inference contained in this assertion. For a law is a law in the proper sense only if it conforms to the eternal or natural law, which requires conformity with the Divine Mind, the source of every right and incapable of self-contradiction. Hence no human authority, no matter on what pretext, can lawfully command what runs counter to a divine command. A human law, therefore, forbidding the free and unhampered preaching of the divine law cannot be acknowledged as binding the conscience.[5] This is also evident from the nature and constitution of the Church as a perfect, legal, and necessary society, independent in the choice of the means conducive

2 Cf Friedberg, *Grenzen zwischen Staat und Kirche*, 1872, p 729; Bachofen, *Summa Iuris Eccl Publici*, 1910, p 57.

3 Thus in the Canton of St Gall, Switzerland, the pastoral and even the Lenten letters are still subject to the approval of the cantonal government''

4 Act 5, 29.

5 Cfr Leo XIII, " *Sapientiae*," Jan 10, 1890.

to its spiritual and supernatural end. Finally, if the Vicar of Christ on earth is bound to teach the faithful, it is his inherent right to do so, and in the exercise of this right no human power may hinder him This right is inalienable because inherent in the primacy of jurisdiction that spans the universal Church.

The *bishops,* in virtue of their jurisdiction, are obliged to preach the Catholic faith each within his own district or diocese. This duty, as § 2 states, they must perform personally, unless they are lawfully prevented. For as they are, as a rule, chosen for their personal qualities (*de industria personae*), they are in conscience bound to break the spiritual bread for their flocks.

Some of the *lawful reasons* which may prevent an Ordinary from fulfilling this duty, are mentioned in a papal decretal.[6] They are: manifold pastoral or episcopal occupations, such as the diocesan visitation, attendance at councils or synods, bodily infirmity, hostile invasions, etc. The decretal adds within brackets: "*ne dicamus defectum scientiae, quod in eis reprobandum est omnino, nec de caetero tolerandum.*"

If a bishop is legitimately prevented from preaching, he should entrust this duty to another,[7] as Bishop Valerian did when, on account of defective speech, he commissioned St. Augustine to preach in his place.

Our text continues that bishops should also employ, not only *pastors, but also others who are fit or capable* (men not women) as co-workers in preaching the word of God The pastor's duty is evident, and it is also clear that the bishop is responsible for the pastors under his jurisdiction The S. Congregation once recommended to an archbishop (of Antivari) to explain the catechism

6 C 15, X, I, 31.   7 Reg. Iuris 68, 72 in 6°.

on Sundays and holydays if the pastor failed to do so.[8] The reason is that the bishop is *par excellence* the pastor of the diocese, and the divinely constituted judge in matters of faith and morals, as successor of the Apostles.[9] If the bishop is pre-occupied by other pastoral work, the pastor of the cathedral church is obliged to preach for him.[10]

The text says that the bishop should choose *idoneos viros,* fit or capable men, to assist him in preaching. This means clergymen who possess the qualities necessary for sacred preachers and ministers of God, to wit, a sufficient familiarity with sacred science and the moral virtues that impress the people. Besides, natural gifts are necessary, lest they appear to tempt God.[11] Preachers who possess these qualifications will preach with salutary effect (*salubriter praedicabunt*) because they will not preach for the sake of showing off their eloquence or of gaining applause.[12]

It goes without saying that the bishop may call upon any member of his diocesan clergy (secular or non-exempt religious) to fulfill this duty.

Concerning exempt religious see can. 608, § 1.

MISSIO CANONICA

Can. 1328

Nemini ministerium praedicationis licet exercere, nisi a legitimo Superiore missionem receperit, facultate peculiariter data, vel officio collato, cui ex sacris canonibus praedicandi munus inhaereat.

8 S. C. P F., Nov. 28, 1785 (*Coll*, n 581).

9 Bened XV, "*Humani generis,*" June 15, 1917 (*A Ap S*, IX, 307); *Trid*, Sess 5, c. 2, *de ref.*

10 S. C. C, Sept. 14, 1748 (Richter, *Trid*, p. 22, n. 5).

11 Bened. XV., "*Humani generis*" (*A. Ap S.,* IX, 309).

12 *Ibid.,* (*l c.,* p. 308).

No one is allowed to preach the word of God unless he has received the *missio canonica* from his legitimate superior. This is a requirement of the divine [13] as well as of human law, for the latter clearly supposes that preaching is an attribute of jurisdiction which must be obtained from the lawful authority.

The *missio canonica* may be given either by means of a special faculty, or by virtue of an office to which the right of preaching is attached by ecclesiastical law.

As to the special faculties required, consult Ch. II of this Title. Here we will only state that the *offices* to which the right and duty of preaching are attached by law, are those of the Sovereign Pontiff, bishops, and pastors. Thus a cathedral prior or collegiate provost, to whom the care of souls is entrusted, is obliged to preach. [14]

[13] Rom. 10, 15; "*Humani generis*" (*A. Ap. S.*, IX, 307).

[14] S. C. C., July 30, 1591; May 26, 1639 (Richter, *Trid.*, p. 22, nn 3 f. *et pluries*).

CHAPTER I

CATECHETICAL INSTRUCTION

CAN. 1329

Proprium ac gravissimum officium, pastorum praesertim animarum, est catecheticam populi christiani institutionem curare.

It is the proper and a most weighty duty, especially of pastors of souls, to provide for the catechetical instruction of the people.

The term "catechetical instruction," as is well known,[1] means oral instruction in the elements of religion, especially as a preparation for initiation into the Church. It is now usually, though not exclusively, conducted by means of questions and answers. We need not dwell upon the importance of this instruction, as Pius X has brought its necessity home to all concerned in his encyclical letter "*Acerbo nimis*," of April 15, 1905.

CAN. 1330

Debet parochus:

1.° Statis temporibus, continenti per plures dies institutione, pueros ad sacramenta poenitentiae et confirmationis rite suscipienda singulis annis praeparare;

2.° Peculiari omnino studio, praesertim, si nihil ob-

---

1 *Cath. Encycl.*, Vol. V, 75 ff., *s. v.*, " Doctrine, Christian "

sit, Quadragesimae tempore, pueros sic instituere ut sancte Sancta primum de altari libent.

CAN. 1331

Praeter puerorum institutionem de qua in can. 1330, parochus non omittat pueros, qui primam communionem recenter receperint, uberius ac perfectius catechismo excolere.

CAN. 1332

Diebus dominicis aliisque festis de praecepto, ea hora quae suo iudicio magis apta sit ad populi frequentiam, debet insuper parochus catechismum fidelibus adultis, sermone ad eorum captum accommodato, explicare.

The pastor is obliged:

1.° To prepare the children for receiving the Sacraments of Penance and Confirmation each year by a continuous course of instructions held at stated times;

2.° To instruct the children with special care, if nothing prevents him, especially, during Lent, in order that they may worthily receive First Holy Communion.

Besides the instruction of children mentioned in the preceding canon, the pastor shall not neglect to instruct the boys and girls who have already received their First Communion more fully in Christian doctrine.

On Sundays and other holydays of obligation he shall, at an hour convenient for the people, teach catechism also to his adult parishioners, in a manner adapted to their capacity.

We notice some mitigation in the wording of our text, as compared with the injunctions of Pius X. For instance, no mention is made in can. 1330, n. 2 of instruc-

tions to be given every day in Lent; in can. 1332 the
" full " hour is omitted as well as the addition that no
Sunday shall be excepted, etc. These are wise modera-
tions for a Code binding the universal Church. But
even the rulings of the Code need some modification in
missionary countries, including our U. S., as we know
from experience. Take, for example, a pastor who has
to attend two missions, twelve or more miles apart. He
has perhaps to start a fire in both churches, then to hear
confessions, sing high Mass at least in one church, and
preach in both, perhaps in different languages. Then
he ought to teach catechism for another hour before
making his train — and all this with an empty stomach.
These are not fanciful, but real conditions, which cannot be compared to those existing around Treviso, Man-
tua, or Venice. Hence it must be left to the diocesan
Ordinaries to determine how far the prescriptions of the
code can be carried out. Meanwhile every pastor ought
to impress upon his mind what Pius X says concerning
catechetical instruction: — that it is the milk which St.
Peter wished the faithful to yearn for in all simplicity
like new-born babes; that the labor of the pulpiteer presupposes that of the catechist; that ornate and flowery
sermons often tickle the ears, but utterly fail to touch the
heart,[2] etc.

The best opportunity for effective catechetical instruction is offered by the schools, which, we are happy to say,
flourish in our country as nowhere else. Where such a
school exists, the pastor can easily find convenient hours
for extensive catechetical work.

2 " Acerbo nimis "; see Amer. Eccl. Rev., 1905, Vol. XXXII, p.
606.

CATECHISTS

CAN. 1333

§ 1. Parochus in religiosa puerorum institutione potest, imo, si legitime sit impeditus, debet operam adhibere clericorum, in paroeciae territorio degentium, aut etiam, si necesse sit, piorum laicorum, potissimum illorum qui in pium sodalitium *doctrinae christianae* aliudve simile in paroecia erectum adscripti sint.

§ 2. Presbyteri aliique clerici, nullo legitimo impedimento detenti, proprio parocho in hoc sanctissimo opere adiutores sunto, etiam sub poenis ab Ordinario infligendis.

§ 1. If the pastor is lawfully prevented, he may, nay should employ the help of clerics living in his district, for the religious instruction of the children. He may also, if need be, call upon pious laymen, especially such as belong to the Sodality of Christian Doctrine or a similar organization represented in the parish.

This is an expedient for overburdened pastors and missionaries who can visit their parishes only at intervals. It might be good practice for seminarians of the last year to spend a few hours in the school room, not as hearers, but as teachers, provided the professor of pastoral theology or homiletics has taught some method.

The *Confraternity of Christian Doctrine* was founded in 1560 in Rome and approved by Pius V, in 1571. Of late it has spread all over Italy and other countries.

Laymen, in the text, includes members of the female sex, provided, of course, they enjoy the necessary qualifications of knowledge, virtue, and strength. School-teachers may be supposed to be peculiarly adapted to this task

Male and female *catechists* are frequently employed in

missionary countries. They should be chosen by the missionaries with care and only such should be called to this important office as are at least twenty-five years of age and possess the necessary moral and mental qualities.[3]

§ 2. Priests and other clerics, who are not lawfully prevented, must assist their pastor in this most holy work, and may be punished by the Ordinary if they fail to do so.

It has been the general practice, also of the Roman Court,[4] not to oblige any cleric to work not prescribed in the law or the foundation document. This rule was upheld in principle by Benedict XIV, though the great Pontiff strongly insisted on the necessity of proper instruction in Christian doctrine.[5] He found a means of compelling all priests and clerics, even those not charged with the care of souls, to assist in that holy work. The bishop should not promote clerics who are remiss in this duty to higher orders or better positions if they refuse to obey his commands. This is the punishment adverted to in our canon. It is a powerful weapon in the hands of the bishop, who may lawfully wield it under the law, though no censure can be inflicted for refusal, because neither the old nor the new law mentions such a penalty *sub poenis* or *censuris infligendis*.

OBLIGATION OF RELIGIOUS

CAN. 1334

Si, Ordinarii loci iudicio, religiosorum auxilium ad catecheticam populi institutionem sit necessarium, Superiores, etiam exempti, ab eodem Ordinario requisiti,

3 S. C. P. F., Feb. 29, 1836 (n. 846).

4 S. C. C., July 15, 1882, ad 10 (*A S S*, XV, 324 f.)

5 "*Etsi minime,*" Feb 7, 1742, § 6.

tenentur per se vel per suos subditos religiosos, sine tamen regularis disciplinae detrimento, illam populo tradere, praesertim in propriis ecclesiis.

If the local Ordinary is convinced that the help of religious is required for the catechetical instruction of the people, he may call upon the religious superiors, including those of exempt orders, and they are obliged to comply with his orders, either personally or through their subjects, especially in their own churches, provided the regular discipline does not suffer. Religious, therefore, should give catechetical instructions, especially in their own churches. We may repeat here what Benedict XIV said concerning regulars, to wit, that they should not interfere by their celebrations with instruction in Christian doctrine, nor by their solemnities,[6] draw the people away from their parish churches while instructions are given.

Although no penalty is attached to this law, it imposes a moral obligation, the extent of which must be gauged by the need of the people, as well as the scarcity and physical inability of the secular clergy.

We wish to draw attention to the clause: "*sine tamen regularis disciplinae detrimento*," which also occurs in can. 608, § 1. This means, first and above all, that if the Rule or Constitution approved by the Holy See excludes such work, the religious are not bound by this canon, and therefore the bishop has no right to call on them. It means, secondly, that, if the Constitutions permit such work, the discipline must be safeguarded. Thus at least the ordinary choir service, the school work, either in the seminary, college or school, must not suffer any serious detriment. And, lastly, regular discipline also means community life. Consequently, if by frequent calls

6 "*Etsi minime*," § 15.

the religious should sustain a serious setback in their religious or common life, the religious superior would be entitled to modify the bishop's command. It may also be permitted to state that if the bishop and clergy wish to be aided by the religious of the diocese, they are reasonably expected to aid and support the diocesan institutions conducted by such religious. This is not only a dictate of natural law, but is also insinuated by can. 608, § 2.

DUTIES OF PARENTS

CAN. 1335

Non solum parentes aliique qui parentum locum tenent, sed heri quoque ac patrini obligatione adstringuntur curandi ut omnes sibi subiecti vel commendati catechetica institutione erudiantur.

Not only parents, but also those who take the parents' place, as well as masters and sponsors, are obliged to see to it that their subjects and protegés receive catechetical instruction.

This obligation rests on the natural as well as on a positive law, which latter is here briefly formulated according to Benedict XIV, who urged bishops and pastors to remind all those above mentioned of their grave obligation to instruct their subjects in the catechism.[7] The natural obligation arises from the fact that the ultimate end of all men is God, who must be known in order to be served and loved. It also follows from the superiority of the soul to the body. Hence at least as much care should be bestowed upon acquiring the knowledge of salvation, as upon the acquisition of natural science.[8]

---

7 "*Cum religiosi,*" June 26, 1754, § 4.

8 Cfr Leo XIII, "*Humanum genus,*" April 20, 1884.

DIOCESAN REGULATIONS

CAN. 1336

Ordinarii loci est omnia in sua dioecesi edicere quae ad populum in christiana doctrina instituendum spectent; et etiam religiosi exempti, quoties non exemptos docent, eadem servare tenentur.

This canon corroborates what was said above about the authority of the *local Ordinary* to regulate instruction in Christian doctrine. He is entitled to issue decrees with reference to the instruction of the people in Christian doctrine, and these regulations must be obeyed also by exempt religious, whenever they impart religious instructions to anyone not possessed of the privilege of exemption. It follows that all those persons mentioned in can. 514, § 1, to wit, servants, pupils, guests, and the sick, must, as far as their condition permits, attend the catechetical instructions given by the pastor or his assistants. For these persons are not properly exempt.

CHAPTER II

SERMONS

FACULTY REQUIRED FOR PREACHING

CAN. 1337

Tum clericis e clero saeculari, tum religiosis non exemptis facultatem concionandi pro suo territorio solus concedit loci Ordinarius.

The secular clergy as well as non-exempt religious receive the faculty of preaching only from the local Ordinary for his respective diocese.

According to a medieval decretal, some clerics usurped the office of preaching under the cloak of piety without being authorized either by the Apostolic See or a bishop.[1] There is in this decretal a hint that members of the rising religious orders were at times carried too far by their zeal. It is therefore not surprising that the same papal constitutions [2] which regulated the matter of hearing confessions, also settled the question of preaching. The law was challenged by Wiclif and his followers, who maintained that any deacon or priest may preach the word of God without authority from the Apostolic See or from a Catholic bishop.[3] Therefore the Council of Trent again insisted upon previous examination for all who assume the office of preaching.[4]

1 C. 13, § 6, X, V, 7, *de haereti-cis.*

2 Greg. XV, " *Inscrutabili,*" Feb. 5, 1622, § 3, 6, Clement X, " *Su-perna,*" June 4, 1670, § 1, 3

3 *Prop. 14 dam.* (cf Denzinger, n 490).

4 Sess. 5, c. 2, *De Ref.;* S. C. EE and RR., July 31, 1894 (*Coll. P. F*, n. 1878).

Note the word: *solus loci Ordinarius*. The Ordinary alone is competent to grant the faculty of preaching. Hence no municipality or university may grant it, although they may select the preacher, for instance for Lent, as happened in certain Italian communes.[5] It also means that the faculty given by the bishop is sufficient, and consequently no pastor or rector can lawfully reject one so approved.[6]

RELIGIOUS PREACHERS

CAN. 1338

§ 1. Si concio habenda sit tantum ad religiosos exemptos aliosve de quibus in can. 514, § 1, facultatem concionandi in religione clericali dat eorum Superior secundum constitutiones; qui in casu potest eam concedere etiam iis qui de clero saeculari vel de alia religione sunt, dummodo a proprio Ordinario vel Superiore fuerint idonei iudicati.

§ 2. Si concio habenda sit ad alios, vel etiam ad moniales regularibus subiectas, facultatem religiosis quoque exemptis impertit Ordinarius loci in quo concio fiet; concionator autem, verba facturus monialibus exemptis, licentia Superioris regularis praeterea indiget.

§ 3. Facultatem vero concionandi apud sodales religionis laicalis, quamvis exemptae, dat loci Ordinarius; sed concionator nequit facultate uti sine Superioris religiosi assensu.

Formerly[7] a distinction was drawn between churches

5 S. C. C., April 21, Aug. 11, 1742; Aug 3, 1743 (Richter, *Trid*, p 22, nn. 7 f)

6 S C. C., June 27, 1744 (*ibid*, n. 15).

7 *Trid*., Sess. 5, c 2, *De Ref.*; Greg XV, " *Inscrutabili* ", Clement X, " *Superna.*"

that belonged to regulars and such as did not belong to them, or to another religious order. Our text distinguishes between the persons preached, or the hearers.

§ 1 rules that *religious* of a clerical order obtain the faculty of preaching from their own superiors, according to their constitutions, in case they preach to exempt religious of their own order or to such who are mentioned in can. 514, § 1. For these the respective superior may also grant the faculty to the secular clergy, or to members of another religious institute, provided, however, that the secular cleric has been previously approved or found fit by his Ordinary and the religious by his superior.

This law has been widened, as is apparent from a comparison with former regulations on the same subject. For what was formerly considered a privilege of the regulars in the strict sense, is here applied to *all religious clerical institutes,* whether exempt or not, and the distinctive character is attached to the hearers only, who must be exempt or share exemption *de facto,* as is the case with the persons mentioned in can. 514, § 1, *i. e.,* servants, guests, students, and sick persons, besides the professed members and novices. However, like the Tridentine Council and various papal decrees,[8] our text requires fitness in the preacher, as defined in can. 1340.

The text mentions only *religiosos exemptos aliosve,* in the masculine gender, thereby evidently excluding the female sex, as is patent also from the following section.

§ 2. If the sermon is to be delivered before others, including nuns subject to regular prelates, the faculty of preaching must be granted by the Ordinary in whose diocese the sermon is to be delivered; and the preacher who addresses exempt nuns must also have the permission

8 Sess. 5, c. 2; Sess. 24, c. 4, *De Ref.,* and the constitutions quoted.

of the regular superior to whom they are subject.[9] Preaching to nuns (*moniales* with solemn vows) is done at the grate, so that the preacher is not obliged or permitted to enter the enclosure, which is here understood to be the papal one.

The others (*alios*) are all non-exempt religious, as well as laymen and clerics who do not share the exemption mentioned in can. 514, § 1.

§ 3. To preach for members of a religious lay institute, for instance, the Christian Brothers, even though they may enjoy exemption, a priest must obtain faculties from the local Ordinary, in whose diocese the religious house is located. However, he cannot make use of his faculty unless the *religious superior of the institute gives his consent*. This ruling is partly taken from the Constitution of Leo XIII, "*Conditae*," A. D. 1900, but has an added clause requiring the consent of the religious superior. The superior and his religious are here understood of institutes of men, not of women, § 2 having sufficiently provided for the latter. Moreover, it would not be proper for religious women to refuse to accept a preacher appointed by the bishop. The consent of the religious superior is required for reasons of discipline and to maintain his authority.[10]

RELIGIOUS VS. ORDINARIES

Can. 1339

§ 1. Ordinarii locorum religiosis qui a proprio Superiore exhibeantur, facultatem concionandi, sine gravi causa, ne denegent, concessamque ne revocent, prae-

---

9 Clement X, "*Superna*," § 3.

10 Preachers were sometimes imposed on such institutes, who lacked even a knowledge of the essentials of the religious life, not to mention other defects.

sertim una simul universis domus religiosae sacerdotibus, firmo tamen praescripto can. 1340.

§ 2. Concionatoribus religiosis, ut facultate recepta uti liceat, opus est praeterea sui Superioris licentia.

§ 1 closely resembles can. 880, which concerns the faculty of hearing confessions. It commands the local Ordinaries not to refuse the faculty of preaching to such religious as are presented by their superiors, nor to withdraw it from them without weighty reasons. They should refrain especially from refusing or withdrawing the faculty from all religious of one house at the same time, provided, of course, at least the one or the other was found fit.

Religious formerly had reasons to complain against some Ordinaries, who either had not read the decrees of the Tridentine Council [11] or interpreted them arbitrarily and withdrew the faculty of preaching without any reason. The S. Congregations sustained the complaints and ordered the nuncio (in Spain) to stop such arbitrary proceedings, which prejudiced the Friars. There must be for such action, says the decree in question, a lawful cause proved by documents (*in actis* [12]). Mere caprice or dislike cannot be styled a lawful reason, and a *legitima causa* is one which concerns preaching.[13] However, if a moral defect or want of knowledge render a particular preacher undesirable, and his incapacity can be proved, the bishop may withdraw or refuse the faculty. But it is hardly imaginable that such defects could be imputed to a whole community.

§ 2. *Religious,* in order to make lawful use of the faculty granted by the Ordinary, must in addition obtain

11 Sess 5, c 2; Sess 24, c 4, De Ref., Clement X, " Superna," § 3.

12 S C EE et RR, Jan 13, 1610 (Bizzarri, 243).

13 S. C. EE. et RR, Dec. 14,

permission from their respective superiors. This is required in virtue of the vow of obedience. Those who take the vow of stability, like the Benedictines, have still another reason for asking permission, namely, because the office of preaching may call them away from their habitual residence.

It may not be amiss to draw attention to former regulations which are now out of date. Formerly the religious, before they were allowed to preach in churches not belonging to their own institute, had to obtain a written permission from the bishop, and also to ask his blessing. This was particularly required for the famous Lenten preachers employed by municipalities.[14] These formalities are no longer required, nor need the faculty of the bishop or the permission of the religious superior be given in writing, though the bishop would not exceed his power if he were to demand a written statement of the religious superior as to the ability and moral standing of the religious who wishes to preach in his diocese.

EXAMINATION

CAN. 1340

§ 1. Graviter onerata eorum conscientia, loci Ordinarius vel Superior religiosus facultatem vel licentiam concionandi cuiquam ne concedant, nisi prius constet de eius bonis moribus et de sufficienti doctrina per examen ad normam can. 877, § 1.

§ 2. Si, concessa facultate vel licentia, compererint necessarias dotes in concionatore desiderari, debent eam revocare; in dubio de doctrina, debent certis argu-

---

1674; S. C. C, Feb. 28, 1654 (Bizz.,   S. C. C., *apud* Richter, *Trid.,* p.
l c, p 273).   22, nn. 7 ff.

14 Clement X, *" Superna,"* § 1,

mentis dubitationem executere, novo etiam examine, si opus fuerit.

§ 3. Ob revocatam concionandi facultatem vel licentiam, datur recursus, sed non in suspensivo.

§ 1. Local Ordinaries as well as religious superiors are seriously charged to grant the faculty or permission to preach only to such as have passed an examination with regard to their moral standing and sufficiency of knowledge, according to the rule laid down in can. 877, § 1.

This section of our canon must therefore be compared to can. 877, § 1, which prescribes an examination, but excepts those whose theological knowledge is otherwise known and tried.

The examination is held to establish the moral standing of the preacher and his knowledge. It was prescribed by the Council of Trent[15] and elaborated in an Instruction of the S. Congregation of Bishops and Regulars[16] of 1894.

As to moral standing, it is evident that lack of a good name would hardly recommend a preacher to the people. Hence, neither the bishop nor the religious superior are allowed to give faculties to one who has been rejected or disvowed by another bishop.[17] This rule, of course, applies especially to such clerics or religious as are tainted with Modernism.[18] But mere rumor and defamation should be carefully sifted from true and proved statements.

With regard to *knowledge, sacred eloquence* requires not only piety but also familiarity with the sacred armory

---

15 Sess. 5, c. 2; sess. 24, c. 4, de ref.

16 July 31, 1894 (*Coll. P. F.,* n. 1878).

17 S. C. Consist., Sept. 25, 1910, ad X, XI (*A. Ap. S.,* II, 741).

18 Pius X, "*Sacrorum Antistitum,*" Sept. 1, 1910 (*ib.,* II, 653 ff.).

of Holy Writ, with dogmatic and moral theology and with ecclesiastical history, as well as a delivery worthy of the subjects treated. St. Thomas says: "In order that a preacher may really be the light of the world, he must possess three things; firmness or stability, in order that he may not deviate from the path of truth; clearness, in order that he may not teach with confusion and obscurity; the right intention, in order that he may seek not his own, but God's honor and glory."[19] Therefore he must avoid vainglory and the motive of material gain.[20] As to these points, therefore, the candidate should be examined when passing through the seminary, or when he presents himself for the faculty to preach. If however, as can. 877, § 1 states, his moral standing and knowledge are sufficiently known to either the bishop or the religious superior, the examination may be waived.

§ 2. If a preacher shows that he lacks the necessary requisites after the faculty or permission to preach has been granted to him, the Ordinary and the superior must withdraw it. If a doubt arises as to his knowledge, they should endeavor to disperse it by gathering the necessary information or proofs, and may also subject him to a new examination. The prudent enforcement of this law requires vigilance, so much recommended with regard to the sacred office of preaching by our Holy Father, who warns the bishops against human respect in this regard and requires a strict examination as to the two requisites.[21]

---

19 *Comment. in Matth*, V; S. C. EE. et RR, *l c*, n 5

20 Bened. XV, "*Humani gen-*

eris," June 15, 1917 (*A. Ap. S*, X, 309 ff.).

21 *Ibid*.

EXTRADIOCESAN PREACHERS

CAN. 1341

§ 1. Sacerdotes extradioecesani sive saeculares sive religiosi ad concionandum ne invitentur, nisi prius licentia ab Ordinario loci in quo concio habenda sit, obtenta fuerit; hic autem, nisi eorum idoneitatem aliunde compertam habeat, licentiam ne concedat, nisi prius bonum testimonium super concionatoris doctrina, pietate, moribus a proprio eiusdem Ordinario habuerit; qui, graviter onerata conscientia, secundum veritatem respondere tenetur.

§ 2. Licentiam tempestive petere debet parochus, si agatur de paroeciali ecclesia aliave eidem subiecta; rector ecclesiae, si de ecclesia parochi auctoritati non obnoxia; prima dignitas, de Capituli consensu, si de ecclesia capitulari; moderator seu cappellanus confraternitatis, si de ecclesia eiusdem confraternitatis propria.

§ 3. Si ecclesia paroecialis sit simul capitularis aut confraternitatis propria, ille licentiam petat, qui sacras functiones iure peragit.

The general rule is, as stated in can. 1337, that the Ordinary in whose diocese a priest wishes to preach, grants the faculty. This rule also binds exempt religious who wish to preach to persons not belonging to their own institute.

Now § 1 supposes that *priests from another diocese* are invited to preach. Whether these be seculars or religious, exempt or non-exempt, does not matter, provided only that the hearers are not exempt religious. Such priests need *the faculty of the Ordinary in whose diocese*

they are invited to preach. If, *e. g.*, a Jesuit from St.
Louis University wishes to preach in the cathedral of
St. Joseph, or in the Abbey Church of Conception, to
the parishioners, he requires a faculty from the Bishop
of St. Joseph, which the latter should not grant unless
he has satisfied himself as to the preacher's knowledge,
piety, and moral standing by means of a statement from
the latter's Ordinary. Therefore, in the case mentioned,
the Archbishop of St. Louis has to furnish the Bishop
of St. Joseph with a testimonial as to the qualifications
of said preacher, and he is bound in conscience to state
the truth. This shows how serious the sacred office of
preacher is regarded by the Church.

Yet, in order to avoid red tape, and also, we suppose,
mistrust, the Code adds the wise clause: *"nisi eorum
idoneitatem aliunde compertam habeat."* If the Ordinary who has to give the faculty knows the preacher,
and is convinced that he possesses the necessary qualities, he may dispense with the formality of demanding
testimonials from the other Ordinary. Of course, the
bishop who has to impart the faculty *may*, though he is not
bound to, abide by the statement of the pastor who has
invited the strange priest. The superiors general are
specially cautioned against sending out their subjects to
preach, unless they are certain that these subjects are duly
qualified, and against permitting their religious to preach
without the knowledge of the bishop.[22] This warning
applies also to secular priests, who should not invite an out-
sider to preach without informing the bishop.

§ 2. *Pastors* must, therefore, ask for the permission
in good time, if the preaching is to be done in their own
church, or in one subject to them, as may be the case

22 S. C. EE. et RR., July 31, 1894, n 7 (*l. c.*).

when a pastor governs two parishes, or one with several missions. The same obligation is encumbent on *rectors* with regard to churches not subject to the pastor, and on the first dignitary (provost or dean), who has to ask the consent of the chapter before applying to the bishop for a faculty; also on chaplains or directors of confraternities if the preaching is to be done in their own church.

§ 3. If the parish church is at the same time a chapter or confraternity church the obligation of asking for permission for a strange priest to preach devolves on the one who has the right to perform the sacred functions.

In a parish church which at the same time serves as a cathedral or collegiate chapter church the sacred functions by right belong to the pastor,[23] who must ask the consent of the chapter before he "invites a preacher," as required by § 2. It is the pastor, therefore, and not the first dignitary, who must ask for permission. Does this rule apply also to *monastic chapters?* The text simply says: *ecclesia capitularis,* a chapter church, which term may be applied to an abbey church, which serves at the same time as parish church, as is insinuated in can. 609, § 1.

With regard to confraternities, the general decree of the S. Congregation of Rites may be consulted. It states that confraternities lawfully erected in parish churches *depend on the pastor* for the exercise of all, even non-parochial, functions.[24] From this it follows that the pastor must demand permission for the preacher.

The term *tempestive* (*in good time*) has been officially declared[25] to mean two months before the preaching

---

23 Can. 415, §2.
24 S. Rit. C., Jan. 12, 1704, ad 1 (n. 2123).
25 S. C. C., April 30, 1729 (Richter, *Trid.*, p. 22, n. 9).

commences. However, as communication is swifter now-adays, the time must be left to the prudent judgment of the petitioner, provided the matter is not delayed purposely so that the bishop cannot obtain the necessary information.

WHO MAY PREACH

CAN. 1342

§ 1. Concionandi facultas solis sacerdotibus vel diaconis fiat, non vero ceteris clericis, nisi rationabili de causa, iudicio Ordinarii et in casibus singularibus.

§ 2. Concionari in ecclesia vetantur laici omnes, etsi religiosi.

Only priests and deacons should be given the faculty of preaching, and no other clerics should be allowed to preach, except in particular cases and for a cause which the Ordinary deems reasonable.

Laymen, even though they may be religious, are *forbidden* to preach in church.

It is well known that some Oriental lay monks played a rather conspicuous part in the religious controversies of the fifth century. We need not wonder, therefore, that they were forbidden to preach, because this office demands a canonical mission.[26] There is a remarkable decretal of Innocent III, which shows the ingenuity of some abbesses who, besides hearing confession, also delivered public homilies.[27] This appeared as a novelty to the pope, who stopped the practice. Laymen, too, at times went so far as to hold secret conventicles and to despise the word of God when preached by priests [28] Wiclif and Huss were not the first to demand permission to preach to men and women alike.[29] This prohibitive

26 See c 19, C 16, q 1 (Leo I) 28 C. 12, 14, X, V, 7.
27 C. 10, X, III, 38   29 Art 37 (Denz., 581).

law is based on the requisite of jurisdiction, of which the faculty of preaching is a part.

CAN. 1343

§ 1. Ordinarii locorum ius habent concionandi in qualibet sui territorii ecclesia, quamvis exempta.

§ 2. Nisi agatur de magnis civitatibus, potest quoque Episcopus prohibere ne in aliis eiusdem loci ecclesiis verba fiant ad fideles, quo tempore vel concionem ipse habet vel coram se, ex causa publica atque extraordinaria, convocatis fidelibus, habendam curat.

§ 1 vindicates to the local Ordinaries the right of preaching in every church of their diocese, including the churches of exempt religious.

§ 2 recalls the ancient quarrel between bishops and regulars. The latter maintained that no bishop could forbid them to preach in their own churches and places where the bishop could not himself preach, but engage a preacher to deliver a sermon in his presence. The S. Congregation decided [30] substantially as our text reads, namely, that with the exception of large cities, to which the law does not apply, the bishop may forbid sermons to be delivered to the faithful in other churches of a place in which he or another by his command is preaching at the same time. However, this prohibition binds only when the preaching is done for a special and public cause and the faithful have been properly invited to attend. Such a "special event," as it is called in one decision, would be a Catholic congress or solemn gathering to which the clergy and the faithful have been invited. Large cities are excepted. The size of a city

[30] S. C. C, April 26, 1607; March 10, 1646 (Richter, Trid, p   23, n 17); Bened. XIV, De Synod. Dioec, IX, 17, 7

must here be gauged, not by the total number of its inhabitants, but by the number of Catholics and Catholic congregations it contains. New York, Chicago, and St. Louis are undoubtedly large cities in the sense of this canon.

Can. 1344

§ 1. Diebus dominicis ceterisque per annum festis de praecepto proprium cuiusque parochi officium est, consueta homilia, praesertim intra Missam in qua maior soleat esse populi frequentia, verbum Dei populo nuntiare.

§ 2. Parochus huic obligationi nequit per alium habitualiter satisfacere, nisi ob iustam causam ab Ordinario probatam.

§ 3. Potest Ordinarius permittere ut sollemnioribus quibusdam festis aut etiam, ex iusta causa, aliquibus diebus dominicis concio omittatur.

Pastors are in duty bound to preach the word of God in the customary manner on all Sundays and holy days of obligation, especially during the Mass that is most largely attended.

This obligation is personal and cannot be habitually committed to another, except for reasons recognized as sufficient by the Ordinary.

The Ordinary may allow the sermon to be omitted on solemn feast-days, and, for good reasons, also on the one or other Sunday.

That preaching is a *personal* duty of the pastor is evident from the fact that he is generally appointed for his personal qualities, and as pastor is bound by divine law to break bread to the hungry and to feed his flock with spiritual food.[31] Therefore the custom of not preaching must be styled unreasonable, and has been so styled by the Roman Pontiffs.[32] Nor can the pastor be dispensed from this sacred obligation during Lent or Advent, when other preachers take the pulpit, or other churches in the same city have such preachers.[33]

On the other hand every obligation, no matter how personal, has its equity, which mitigates the rigor of the law. Hence § 2 sets certain bounds to this otherwise strict duty of preaching. The law merely wishes to prevent *habitual* shirking of the obligation, even though the motive be natural shyness, timidity, or lack of confidence. If the *bishop sanctions* the reason for which the pastor shifts the burden to others, the habit or custom may become lawful. Where there is a natural impediment, for instance, throat trouble, failing memory, or other obstacles, the Ordinary may certainly permit a pastor to let others preach for him habitually. Where it is customary for pastors and curates or assistants to take turns at preaching, and the custom has been ratified by the bishop, no breach of the law occurs.

The last section gives the Ordinary the power of dispensing[34] pastors from the duty of preaching on the more solemn feasts of the year, and even on the one or other Sunday. If the bishop pontificates in a parish church, *e. g.*, he may tell the pastor not to preach. A just reason would be the necessity of hearing many confessions, or the reading of a lengthy financial statement of the parish. The text *does not require an express per-*

---

31 *Trid.*, Sess. 5, c. 2; Sess 22, c. 8, *De Sac. Missae;* Sess 23, c. 1; Sess. 24, c. 4, *De Ref*

32 Innoc. XIII, "*Apostolici ministerii,*" May 23, 1723; Bened XIII, "*In supremo,*" Sept 23, 1724, cfr. Bened. XIV, *Instit.,* X, n. 3.

33 S. C. C, Aug. 30, 1817 *et pluries* (*A. S. S.,* IX 465 ff.).

34 This is the term used by S C. C., April 1, 1876 (*A. S. S.,* IX, p. 468).

mission, nor that it be given separately for each occasion, and consequently the bishop may do so in the synod, or through a circular letter, or by a general statement, either written or oral; provided always that no abuses creep in and no contrary custom develops.

INSTRUCTION IN CHRISTIAN DOCTRINE IN OTHER THAN PARISH CHURCHES

CAN. 1345

Optandum ut in Missis quae, fidelibus adstantibus, diebus festis de praecepto in omnibus ecclesiis vel oratoriis publicis celebrantur, brevis Evangelii aut alicuius partis doctrinae christianae explanatio fiat; quod si loci Ordinarius id praeceperit, opportunis datis instructionibus, hac lege tenentur non solum sacerdotes e clero saeculari, sed religiosi, exempti quoque, in suis ipsorum ecclesiis.

What our text prescribes in a mildly optative form was laid own by Benedict XIV, not as a general rule, but as a guiding principle for Ordinaries.[35] The Church desires that in *all churches and public oratories,* even though they are not parish churches, the Gospel or some part of Christian Doctrine should be expounded during the Masses that are attended by the faithful on holy days of obligation. Our text continues: If the Ordinary issues instructions to that effect, all priests, secular as well as religious, including those who are exempt, are bound to obey this law in their respective churches.

The Roman Pontiff will side with Ordinaries even against exempt religious.[36]

[35] *" Etsi minime,"* Feb. 7, 1742, § 15.   [36] *Ibid.*

CAN. 1346

§ 1. Curent locorum Ordinarii ut tempore quadragesimae, itemque, si id expedire visum fuerit, tempore Adventus, in ecclesiis cathedralibus et paroecialibus sacrae conciones frequentius ad fideles habeantur.

§ 2. Canonici aliique de Capitulo huic concioni, si in propria ecclesia continuo post chorum habeatur, interesse tenentur, nisi iusto impedimento detineantur; et illos Ordinarius, poenis quoque adhibitis, ad id adigere potest.

§ 1. The Ordinaries should see to it that during Lent, and if expedient also during Advent, sermons are delivered more frequently in cathedral and parish churches.

Pius X ordained that the young who are preparing for first Communion, should be given daily instructions during Lent.[37] Our text speaks of " sermons to the faithful," but leaves the details (arrangement, frequency, etc.) to the judgment of the Ordinaries.

§ 2. Canons and other members of a Chapter are obliged to attend these sermons, if held immediately after choir service, unless they are lawfully prevented; and the Ordinary may compel them to attend under penalties.

All the canons, except of course the *Canonicus theologus* and the *Pœnitentiarius,* and those employed in other offices with the permission and sanction of the bishop, must be present; also the prebendaries and beneficiaries (*mansionarii*). They must wear the choir dress (*habitus choralis*) and occupy their seats, as usual. This obligation binds even in case the sermon is held in another

[37] "*Acerbo nimis*," April 25, 1905, n. III.

church which (for instance, on account of repairs) temporarily serves as cathedral or collegiate church. The collegiate canons, too, are included.[38]

The penalties depend on the judgment of the Ordinary and may consist of fines.[39]

SUBJECTS OF SERMONS

CAN. 1347

§ 1. In sacris concionibus exponenda in primis sunt quae fideles credere et facere ad salutem oportet.

§ 2. Divini verbi praecones abstineant profanis aut abstrusis argumentis communem audientium captum excedentibus; et evangelicum ministerium non in persuasibilibus humanae sapientiae verbis, non in profano inanis et ambitiosae eloquentiae apparatu et lenocinio, sed in ostensione spiritus et virtutis exerceant, non semetipsos, sed Christum crucifixum praedicantes.

§ 3. Si, quod absit, concionator errores aut scandala disseminet, servetur praescriptum can. 2317; si haereses, in eum praeterea, ad normam iuris, agatur.

§ 1. Sermons should be devoted above all to what is necessary for the faithful to believe and do for salvation.

§ 2. Therefore the preachers shall abstain from profane and abstruse arguments which exceed the capacity of their hearers, and perform their evangelical ministry (as the Apostle warns [40]) not in persuasive words of human wisdom, or for the display of vain and ambitious eloquence, but in showing of the Spirit and power; preaching not themselves, but Christ crucified.

38 S. Rit. C., March 22, 1653; Oct. 1, 1661; March 31, 1703; Dec. 10, 1718, ad 4 (nn. 944, 1217, 2108, 2258).

39 Ibid., nn. 1217, 2258.
40 I Cor. II, 4.

They should not play the rôle of philanthropists, limiting their arguments to this life and disregarding the next. They may speak of the beauty and the blessings arising from religion, but should also mention man's duties to God, the eternal judge.[41]

§ 3. If (what God may avert!) a preacher should disseminate errors and scandals, he should be deprived of the faculty of preaching and removed from the teaching office, and may also be subjected to such penalties as the Ordinary may deem necessary to repair the scandal.[42] Should he preach heresies, the Ordinary must proceed against him according to the law. The first step in the latter case would be to forbid him to preach, followed by a canonical summons, or, where the Holy Office still exercises its jurisdiction, denunciation to the same. But the Council of Trent warns bishops to be careful lest innocent priests be injured by calumny.[43]

DUTY OF THE PEOPLE

CAN. 1348

Monendi et adhortandi diligenter fideles sunt ut sacris concionibus frequenter intersint.

The faithful should be diligently admonished and exhorted to hear sermons frequently. They may also be told that, even when they have no opportunity to hear Mass on Sundays and holy days of obligation, the duty of keeping holy these days by hearing the word of God does not cease. But the exhortation or admonition must not be so worded as if it were an ecclesiastical precept obliging under sin to attend sermons.[44]

41 S. C. EE. et RR., July 31, 1894, n. 6 (*Coll. P. F.*, n. 1878).
42 Can. 2317.
43 Sess. 5, c. 2, *De Ref.*
44 S. C. P. F., Jan. 4, 1798 (*Coll.*, n. 642).

CHAPTER III

CAN. 1349

§ 1. Ordinarii advigilent ut, saltem decimo quoque anno, sacram, quam vocant, missionem, ad gregem sibi commissum habendam parochi curent.

§ 2. Parochus, etiam religiosus, in his missionibus instituendis mandatis Ordinarii loci stare debet.

§ 1. Ordinaries shall see to it that the pastors arrange a holy mission — as it is called — for their flocks at least every ten years.

§ 2. Pastors, including religious, must abide by the regulations of the local Ordinaries in this matter.

Thus, if the local Ordinary orders a mission to be held in a parish church which is in charge of exempt religious and governed by them, they have no right to hinder it or vex the missionary sent by the bishop.[1]

MISSIONS TO NON-CATHOLICS

CAN. 1350

§ 1. Ordinarii locorum et parochi acatholicos, in suis dioecesibus et paroeciis degentes, commendatos sibi in Domino habeant.

§ 2. In aliis territoriis universa missionum cura apud acatholicos Sedi Apostolicae unice reservatur.

1 S. C. EE et R R., July 23, 1694 (Bizzarri, l c., p 281).

§ 1. The non-Catholics living in a diocese or parish are recommended to the benevolent attention of the bishop and the pastors, who should ponder effective means and ways of bringing them back to the one true fold of Christ. This may be accomplished by spreading apologetic tracts,[2] etc. Of course, the social and intellectual conditions of the non-Catholic population must be duly taken into account. Prayers for their conversion should be offered.[3]

§ 2. In all other territories the care of non-Catholics is reserved exclusively to the Holy See. Therefore all foreign missions, the superiors general of missionary societies and their subjects, are under the special supervision of the S. C. de Propaganda Fide, without the consent of which no new mission may be founded or missionary work started. This law binds all religious, exempt and non-exempt, of whatever denomination, under threat of ecclesiastical penalties.[4]

CAN. 1351

Ad amplexandam fidem catholicam nemo invitus cogatur.

No one should be compelled to embrace the Catholic faith against his will.

This golden rule of the great bishop of Hippo[5] was followed in the treatment of the Donatists until they caused troubles which led the civil rulers to interfere. If it has been lost sight of in course of time, this was

2 S. C. P. F, Sept 8, 1869 (*Coll.*, n 1346) *The Faith of Our Fathers*, by Cardinal Gibbons, Fr Conway's Question Box, the pamphlets of the Catholic Truth Societies, "The Antidote," and similar literature may be recommended for this purpose

3 S. C. P. F, *Instructio* of 1879 (*ibid*, n. 1507).

4 S C P. F., Dec. 5, 1640; Jan. 11, 1656 (*Coll*, nn. 101, 125).

5 Cfr cc 3, 5, Dist 45.

due to the mixture of ecclesiastical with political affairs. But it remains as true as it was in St. Augustine's day that faith is a free gift of God, though, of course, men may be instrumental in procuring it. The early Christians were allowed to buy and retain pagan slaves who voluntarily fled to them in order to be more leniently treated; they could use exhortations and persuasive words, but were not allowed to exercise any compulsion.[6]

6 S. O., Sept. 12, 1776 (*Col. P. F.*, n. 515).

TITLE XXI

SEMINARIES

From the second century onward, *i. e.,* as soon as the Church was free to spread, *schools* were instituted which, though called catechetical, offered more than a catechetical training to such as wished to enter the clerical state or to hold some other responsible position. The schools of Alexandria and Antioch resembled theological academies where philosophy was not neglected, though it would be hazardous to identify them with seminaries.[1] More closely resembling our modern seminaries were the cloistral and cathedral schools of the Middle Ages, where clerics and laymen, especially of the nobility, received their education. These nurseries of learning and piety, fashioned after the domestic school of St. Augustine, may be called forerunners of the modern colleges and seminaries established upon the initiative of the Council of Trent.[2] The twenty-third session of that council, held in July, 1563, contains a long chapter on this important subject, in which the colleges for the training of clerics are for the first time called *seminaries.* The council ordained that youths of at least twelve years, especially from among the poorer classes should be received into these schools for the necessary scientific, moral, and practical training qualifying them for the priesthood. A peculiar feature was that the pupils should receive the tonsure when they entered the seminary. The

[1] Cfr *Cath Encycl.,* XIII, 694 ff , *s. v.* " Seminary."   [2] Sess. *23,* c. 18, *De Ref.*

council prescribed two school boards, to be chosen by the bishop, one for the spiritual, the other for the temporal administration.   Such a seminary was to be established in every diocese large enough to maintain one.   The smaller dioceses were allowed to combine.   Thus the terms diocesan, interdiocesan, provincial, and pontifical seminaries were introduced.

A *seminary* may be broadly defined as a school destined either remotely or proximately for the preparation of candidates for the sacred ministry, especially the priesthood.[3]

A *diocesan* seminary is one under the control of the local Ordinary, an *interdiocesan* is one under the control, generally *in solidum,* of all the bishops who send their students there, although interdiocesan may only mean that the control is entrusted to the local Ordinary, whilst other bishops are merely entitled to send their candidates; a *provincial* seminary is one under all the bishops of an ecclesiastical province with the metropolitan as head; a *pontifical* seminary is one under the immediate control and supervision of the Holy See, who generally exercises this right by means of the papal delegate.

RIGHT OF THE CHURCH TO EDUCATE THE CLERGY

CAN. 1352

Ecclesiae est ius proprium et exclusivum eos instituendi qui ecclesiasticis ministeriis sese devovere cupiunt.

3 A promiscuous college with business, scientific, and classical courses, even though erected by the bishop and conducted by the diocesan clergy, *cannot* be styled a seminary, as is apparent from the Council of Trent as well as from our Code

One consequence is that the *seminaristicum* cannot be collected for such colleges, but at most a *subsidium caritatis,* if no other college of the same nature exists in the diocese.

It might seem superfluous to make a law saying that *" the Church enjoys the native and exclusive right to train those who wish to devote themselves to the sacred ministry."* Yet the legislator, taught by experience, has thought it well to emphasize this right. He calls it a *ius proprium,* or inherent right. This is evident from the office of the Church as the divinely constituted teacher of faith and morals. This office demands that those who shall be the bearers of light be imbued with those mental and moral qualities which render the exercise of the teaching office effective and conformable to the principles of faith and virtue. It is a native right of the Church to select those who are in a more particular manner the elect of the Lord, from among the multitude of men and place them in the shadow of the sanctuary, where they are protected against dangerous maxims and practices. In doing this the Church does not violate the rights of the State or of any individual. The *State* has no right to dictate any one's vocation. If God, who is the author of civil authority, calls one to the priesthood or religious state, no human power can hold him back. Individuals are free to choose the clerical state because in doing so they obey their Maker. There is now no longer any danger, as there was in the fifth and sixth centuries, that a wholesale flight from public office and municipal obligations would endanger the existence of an empire. Those were abnormal times suffering from a corrupt system of administration and taxation.

The text says further that the right of training clerics belongs *exclusively* to the Church. The Gallican, Febronian, and Josephinist schools claimed the right of prescribing the programme of studies for the clergy of the State.[4]

4 *Syllabus Pii* IX, n 46 (Denzinger, *l. c*, n. 1594), Pius IX, *" Nunquam forc,"* Dec., 1856.

This claim is based on a false notion of ecclesiastical authority. If the Church, as an autonomous and independent society, is entitled to attain her purpose by the choice of appropriate means, she certainly has the right to train those who are to be the living and successive bearers of her divine mission,— the sacred ministers. From this it naturally follows that the right of choosing the means best adapted for the training of the clergy belongs to the Church exclusively. Her sphere of interests differs essentially from that of the State, though there is no contradiction between the two. The State may monopolize salt and tobacco, but for it to monopolize education, and clerical education in particular, would be usurpation.[5] There is no danger that the clerical training might prove detrimental to the State. For the very fact that loyalty and morality are the principal objects of that training guarantees the foundations of civil society.

THE DUTY OF PASTORS WITH REGARD TO CLERICAL
VOCATIONS

Can. 1353

Dent operam sacerdotes, praesertim parochi, ut pueros, qui indicia praebeant ecclesiasticae vocationis, peculiaribus curis, a saeculi contagiis arceant, ad pietatem informent, primis litterarum studiis imbuant divinaeque in eis vocationis germen foveant.

Priests, and especially pastors, should interest themselves in such boys as show signs of an ecclesiastical vocation, keep them away, as much as possible, from worldly contagion, instruct them in piety and the elements of sci-

[5] Leo XIII, " Iampridem," Jan. 22, 1887 (to Prussia and Bavaria 6, 1886; " Officio sanctissimo," Dec. after the " Kulturkampf ").

ence, and foster in them the germ of their vocation. For it is evident that by such means an ordinary or general vocation may develop into a special or extraordinary one. Suitable surroundings and a favorable atmosphere develop the seeds of a supernatural calling.[6]

DIOCESAN SEMINARIES

CAN. 1354

§ 1. Unaquaeque dioecesis in loco convenienti ab Episcopo electo Seminarium seu collegium habeat in quo, pro modo facultatum et dioecesis amplitudine, certus adolescentium numerus ad statum clericalem instituatur.

§ 2. Curandum ut in maioribus praesertim dioecesibus bina constituantur Seminaria: minus, scilicet, pro pueris litterarum scientia imbuendis, maius pro alumnis philosophiae ac theologiae vacantibus.

§ 3. Si constitui Seminarium dioecesanum nequeat, aut in constituto Seminario conveniens institutio, praesertim in philosophicis ac theologicis disciplinis, desideretur, Episcopus alumnos in alienum Seminarium mittat, nisi Seminarium interdioecesanum vel regionale, auctoritate apostolica, constitutum fuerit.

§ 1. Every diocese should have a seminary or college in a convenient place selected by the bishop. There, according to the revenues and size of the diocese, a certain number of young men should be trained for the clerical state.

§ 2. In the larger dioceses there should be established *two seminaries:* one as a college or *petit seminaire,* the . other for the students of philosophy and theology.

---

6 Cavagnis, *Institutiones Iuris Publ. Eccl*, 1883, 1. IV, n. 76; Vol. III, p 45.

§ 3. If a diocesan seminary cannot be erected, or the philosophical and theological courses cannot be properly given in one already existing, the bishop shall send his students to another seminary, unless there is an interdiocesan or provincial seminary erected by authority of the Apostolic See.

§ 1 prescribes that a preparatory college or *petit seminaire* be established in every diocese. But it wisely sets a limit to this obligation, making it dependent *upon the revenues and size* of the diocese. Where there is a college conducted by religious, the bishop may make use of it for his students.

§ 2 prescribes *two seminaries,* a college and a clerical seminary, for the larger dioceses. The size of a diocese is not determined by its area, but by the number of the faithful, for in extent some apostolic vicariates are large enough to comprise many Italian dioceses or even archdioceses, yet they were told to establish central or provincial seminaries.[7] The revenues, also, are a determining factor, as the same Instruction intimates. Besides it is evident that an efficient staff of teachers and an adequate number of students cannot be expected in a small diocese, not to speak of the expenses necessary for the building and maintenance of the required edifices and the cost of administration.

The two seminaries should, if possible, be separated and conducted as different establishments. This is desired mainly by reason of the different discipline required for younger and for more advanced students.[8]

§ 3 permits bishops to send their students to another seminary, *i e.,* one existing in a different diocese, but only in case there is no interdiocesan or provincial seminary

7 S. C. P F., Oct 18, 1883   8 S. C. Consist., July 16, 1912,
(*Coll*, n 1606)   n. 1 (*A. S. S.*, IV, 492 f).

erected by the Holy See. The latter may intervene either directly or indirectly in the establishment of an interdiocesan or provincial seminary. *Directly* by a formal decree issued by the S. Congregation of Seminaries and Universities,[9] declaring an institution to be an interdiocesan or provincial seminary; *indirectly* by the S. C. Conc. approving the acts of a provincial synod erecting or approving such an institution. The latter mode of approval is intended in certain Instructions of the S. Congregation of the Propaganda.[10] There may be a doubt whether the *"auctoritas apostolica"* is expressly required for both provincial and interdiocesan seminaries,— in other words whether our text intends to draw a real distinction between an interdiocesan and a provincial seminary. Though there is a distinction between the two, this distinction has no practical value in our case, as can. 1357, § 4 simply rules that the government and administration of " an interdiocesan or provincial seminary " are to be conducted according to the rules laid down by the Holy See. This undoubtedly means that interdiocesan and provincial seminaries must have their statutes, and thereby also their existence, approved by the S. Cong. of Seminaries and Universities.

Where such an interdiocesan or provincial seminary exists, therefore, a bishop who has no seminary of his own, in which philosophy and theology are taught, must send his students to that provincial seminary, but only for the strictly clerical, not for the classical, studies.

9 Cfr can. 256.
10 Oct. 18, 1883, IV; Aug. 28, 1893 (*Coll*, nn. 1606, 1848).

Can. 1355

Pro constitutione Seminarii et alumnorum susten-
tatione, si proprii reditus deficiant, Episcopus potest:

1.° Parochos aliosve ecclesiarum etiam exemptarum
rectores iubere ut statis temporibus in ecclesia ad hunc
finem stipem exquirant;

2.° Tributum seu *taxam* in sua dioecesi imperare;

3.° Si haec non sufficiant, attribuere Seminario aliqua beneficia simplicia.

If there are no endowments for the support of a seminary and its students, the bishop may

1.° Command the pastors and other rectors of churches,
even though they be exempt religious, to take up collections for that purpose at stated times;

2.° Impose a seminary tax in the diocese;

3.° If these resources do not prove sufficient, he may
attach some simple benefices to the seminary.

The first means is modern. It imposes the obligation
of taking up a collection, even in churches which are not
parish churches, and in such as belong to exempt religious.

As to the incorporation of benefices, it should be observed that *only simple benefices* are intended, *i. e.,* such
as require no permanent residence in the place of benefice,[11] and the duties of which may be performed by a
substitute or vicar. Thus a *simplex canonicatus* or a
chaplaincy may be united with a seminary; but a parochial benefice may not, without apostolic indult.

Incorporation is either *pleno iure* or *semipleno iure,*
either as to the spiritual and temporal, or as to the tem-

11 Cfr. can. 1411.

poral benefits only; the latter element is especially in-tended here, since incorporation is permited for the pur-pose of support. But the union cannot be made without the advice of the seminary board; that of the chapter or consultors is not sufficient.[12]

An incorporation of benefices made before the sem-inary is in existence, is invalid.[13]

Simple benefices of any kind may be united with a sem-inary, even if the appointment to these falls within so-called papal months, *i. e.*, those in which the right of ap-pointment belongs to the Holy See. But in this case the incorporation must be made before the vacancy occurs.[14]

Can. 1356

§ 1. Tributo pro Seminario obnoxia sunt, quavis appelatione remota, reprobata qualibet contraria con-suetudine et abrogato quolibet contrario privilegio, mensa episcopalis, omnia beneficia etiam regularia aut iurispatronatus, paroeciae aut quasi-paroeciae, quamvis alios reditus, praeter fidelium oblationes, non habeant, domus hospitalis auctoritate ecclesiastica erecta, so-dalitates canonice erectae et fabricae ecclesiarum, si suos reditus habeant, quaelibet religiosa domus, etsi exempta, nisi solis eleemosynis vivat aut in ea col-legium discentium vel docentium ad commune Eccle-siae bonum promovendum actu habeatur.

§ 2. Hoc tributum debet esse generale eiusdemque proportionis pro omnibus, maius vel minus secundum Seminarii necessitatem, sed quinas quotannis centesi-

---

12 S. C. C., Feb 14, 1594; March 3, 1594 (Richter, *Trid*, p. 212, n. 87), Bened XIV, *De Syn. Dioec*, IX, 7

13 S. C. C, June 8, 1595, March 3, 1597 (Richter, *Trid.*, *l. c*, n. 10 f.)

14 S. C. C., Aug. 1586, Aug 31, 1600 (Richter, *l. c*, n 13)

mas partes (5%) reditus vectigalis non excedens, minuendum prout reditus Seminarii augentur.

§ 3. Reditus tributo obnoxius is est qui, deductis oneribus et necessariis expensis, supersit in anno; nec in eo reditu computari debent distributiones quotidianae, vel, si omnes beneficii fructus distributionibus constent, tertia earundem pars; nec fidelium oblationes, nec, si omnes paroeciae reditus coalescant fidelium oblationibus, tertia earundem pars.

Can. 1356 more precisely determines those persons, either physical or corporate, who are obliged to pay the seminary tax (*taxa seminaristica*).

It starts with three clauses, the first of which is "*quavis appellatione remota*. The principal effect of this clause is that no appeal is admitted *in devolutivo,* though a recourse or *restitutio in integrum* is not prohibited. Another effect of this clause is that, even if the seminary tax would be only a side issue in another cause, it would affect the entire cause, at least as long as the secondary one remained unsettled.

The second clause is: "*reprobata qualibet contraria consuetudine.*" This clause abrogates any custom which already exists, or has existed, *i. e.,* whether present or past. As to this there is no controversy, but the question has been raised whether this clause intends to annul future customs.[15] This seems to us to be settled by can. 27, § 1, which says that every custom explicitly reprobated in the Code is unreasonable. Therefore even a future custom is made impossible with regard to the seminary tax, because it would lack the consent of the legislator.

The last clause reads: "*abrogato quolibet contrario*

15 Cfr Barbosa, *Tractus Varii,* Clausulae, nn IX, 87 (ed Lugd., 1660, p. 260 f , 450 f).

privilegio." Each and every privilege, therefore, whether obtained directly or indirectly (by way of communication), must be considered as abolished and void of effect because contraries cannot be comprised under the same subject.[16] Hence if exempt religious have obtained a privilege of not paying the *seminaristicum,* this privilege is now void.

The following are obliged to contribute to the seminary:

1.° The *mensa episcopalis,* which comprises the whole income or salary of the bishop and is administered by him.[17] Hither belong the *cathedraticum* and that part of the pew-rent of the cathedral church that is reserved for salary. In countries where there are endowments these too are included, with due regard, however, to § 3.

2.° *All benefices,* including those of regulars and such as are of lay or ecclesiastical advowson.[18]

3.° *All parishes and quasi-parishes,* even though they have no other income than the offerings of the faithful. Parishes not yet organized as such are probably exempt from paying the *seminaristicum* because rights and duties are correlative terms.

4.° *Hospitals* erected by ecclesiastical authority and provided with funds of their own, for instance, by endowment. Hospitals founded and governed by the civil authority or by private persons (Sisters, etc.), cannot be taxed. The term ecclesiastical authority comprises the Ordinary, the superior major of exempt religious, and the Holy See. Hospitals which subsist on the generosity of voluntary contributors or alms, are not taxable [19]

16 Barbosa, *l c,* p 38, n. 4

17 *Idem, De Officio et Potestate Episc,* P III, alleg 95, n 67.

18 S. C. C, Dec 17, 1836, ad II (Richter, *Trid,* p 213, n 27).

19 S. C. C, July, 1588 (Richter, *Trid,* p 213, n 22); *"loca pia non e bonis ecclesiasticis facta non tenere."*

5.° Canonically erected confraternities and ecclesiastical *fabricae,* provided they have their own income. The term *fabrica* comprises the administrators of a church building, or the counselors. Thus, for instance, the *Reverenda Fabrica S. Petri,* means the whole administration of St. Peter's Basilica. The underlying idea is that such a building is (by *fictio iuris*) an artificial person, or, rather, an ecclesiastical institution. This also applies to confraternities which possess corporate property of their own, either movable or immovable, such as the guilds or confraternities in some parts of Europe. In this country, as far as we are aware, this law does not apply to confraternities or sodalities, because the monthly fees of the members do not constitute *reditus* or income in the proper sense.

6.° *Every religious house, even though exempt.* This includes every religious community, whether *formata* or not, whether belonging to men or to women. *Exceptions* to this rule are: (a) the houses of mendicant orders and others who live from alms,[20] but not the parishes which are entrusted to the care of mendicants; (b) all religious who actually maintain a college of pupils or professors which promotes the common welfare of the church. The latter clause appears ambiguous, but its meaning can be determined from certain official decisions. Thus it has been declared that a monastery which supports a college for monks and professors, or maintains a seminary of its own, is not bound to pay the seminary tax.[21] This was the case in former times at the universities of

---

20 Among these are the orlers of St Dominic, St. Francis (all three branches), the Hermits of St. Augustine, the Carmelites, the Servites, the Minimi, the Society of Jesus; Barbosa, *De Off et Potest. Episc,* P. III, alleg. 77, nn. 14 f. (Vol. II, p. 315).

21 S. C C, Sept. 9, 1594 (Richter, *l. c.,* p 213, n. 18)

Paris and Bologna, where the relgious orders maintained
their own colleges.

A doubt may perhaps arise as to colleges conducted by
religious in their own name, which are not seminaries in
the technical sense. However, our text does not say
" seminary," but *collegium,* and the only condition is that
such a *collegium* promotes the common welfare of the
Church. This, we believe, is verified in any Catholic
college worthy of the name, which is open to all Catholic
youths without discrimination, for such institutions greatly
promote the welfare of the Church at large. A different
answer must be given if the college is intended only for
members of the respective religious family, a so-called
scholasticate, for such institutions are primarily destined
for the benefit of the respective order or congregation, not
of the Church at large. The fact that a scholasticate was
educating boys without means would not free it from the
seminary tax.[22] Nor would the circumstance that the
school or scholasticate was instituted in the monastery
with some grammar school for its members.[23] Lastly, although a monastery may have to contribute to a seminary
of its own order or congregation, it is not exempt from
the diocesan seminary tax.[24]

§ 2 rules that the seminary tax must be general, equal,
and proportionate. It must be *general,* that is to say, no
exception may be made in favor of anyone who is obliged
to contribute. It must be *equal, i. e.,* all are to be taxed
to the same extent, without subjective or personal consideration, according to the objective standard laid down
in § 3. The tax must be *proportionate* to the needs of
the seminary, *i. e.,* it must be diminished if the revenues of

22 S. C. C, Jan 3, 1594 (*ibid.,*   24 S. C. C., Sept. 7, 1714 (*ibid.,*
n. 20).   n 21).
23 S. C. C, April 24, 1723 (Rich-
ter, *l c ,* n. 19).

the seminary increase, and the maximum rate cannot exceed 5% of the net income or capital taxed.

§ 3. The seminary tax can be levied only on the *income which is left after all obligations and expenditures have been deducted*. This is a general principle, which must be applied to the various contributors mentioned in § 1.

(a) As to the *mensa episcopalis* or episcopal income, it must be observed that former decisions cannot be fully adapted to modern exigencies because they apply to real benefices with immovable property. Still these decisions afford at least a clue as to what may be included in deducting obligations and expenditures. An *obligation* may burden the *mensa* in the form of an ecclesiastical pension which the bishop has to pay, for instance, to a disabled priest. Yet a decision says that the bishop would be allowed to charge it to the pensioner.[25] However, this is a rather complicated case. The term *expenditures* covers the total expense of collecting the income, the wages of hired hands and all other employees occupied in harvesting the produce of estates.[26] Applying these rules to modern notions we may say, *salvo meliore iudicio,* that the *mensa episcopalis* is taxable on what is left after the obligations and expenditures accruing from pastoral visits and professional occupations have been duly deducted. Household expenses are not to be deducted.[27] For the rest it is left to the bishop's own conscience to tax himself in a fair amount. The idea of the law is that no one should exempt himself.

(b) The same rules, according to the decision quoted, apply to the holders of *ecclesiastical benefices*. Mass stipends are not taxable.

25 S. C. EE. et RR, *Eugubina,* March 1, 1805 (Bizzarri, *l. c,* p. 405).

26 S. C C, 1673 (Bizzarri, *ibid.*);

Dec. 17, 1836, ad VII, XI (Richter, *l. c.,* p. 214, n. 27).

27 S. C. EE et RR., *l. c.*

(c) *Hospitals, confraternities,* and *fabricae* as well as *religious houses* are subject to the same rule. Hence, for instance, if the obligation of maintaining a number of patients or wards free of charge, or keeping sick or sickly clergymen free of charge, burden a hospital, this expense may be deducted, plus the interest to be paid on capital or mortgage. Thus also *confraternities* would be justified in deducting the expenses of Masses imposed by legacies and of alms imposed by their statutes.[28] *Religious houses* may subtract from the taxable sum the amount which they have to spend on their own seminaries or colleges.[29] In fact a religious house burdened with heavy debts and bound to meet its obligations, could claim either exemption or mitigation, for the terms are general in our text. This of course only in case they have no incorporated benefice or parishes.

(d) *Not taxable* are the *daily distributions* which the beneficiaries of cathedral and collegiate churches receive for actual and active assistance in choir, if they have an income besides these distributions. But if their income consists entirely of daily distributions, the *third part of these distributions* is liable to the tax.[30]

(e) Not taxable are the *offerings of the faithful* if the whole income of a parish consists of such offerings. This is the case in most of our parishes, since by offerings are understood not merely the plate collections, but also pew-rent, subscriptions, and house collections. Of these, then, only two-thirds are to be taxed. However, the general rule stated at the beginning of this section must also be applied to these two-thirds. Therefore the debts and the

28 S. C. C., June 23, 1640 (Richter, *l c.,* p. 213, n. 23).

29 S C. C., Sept. 2, 1714 (*ibid*, n. 21).

30 S. C. C EE et RR, March 1, 1805 (Bizzarri, *l c*); S. C. C., June 23, 1640 (Richter, *l. c.,* n. 23).

necessary current expenses for the priests' salary, the maintenance of buildings and persons (organist, janitor, housekeeper) may be deducted. There will remain very little to be taxed in a good many churches of our country, and no other means is left except what is first stated in can. 1355, *viz.*, the taking up of a collection.

It may be noted that our pastors and curates not being beneficiaries in the canonical sense of the word, are exempt from the seminary tax.

THE BISHOP'S DUTIES IN REGARD TO THE SEMINARY

CAN. 1357

§ 1. Episcopi est omnia et singula quae ad rectam Seminarii dioecesani administrationem, regimen, profectum necessaria et opportuna videantur, decernere, eaque ut fideliter observentur, curare, salvis praescriptionibus a Sancta Sede pro casibus peculiaribus latis.

§ 2. Potissimum studeat Episcopus frequenter Seminarium ipse per se visitare, in institutionem quae alumnis traditur sive litterariam et scientificam sive ecclesiasticam sedulo vigilare, et de alumnorum indole, pietate, vocatione ac profectu pleniorem sibi comparare notitiam, maxime occasione sacrarum ordinationum.

§ 3. Unumquodque Seminarium suas leges habeat ab Episcopo approbatas, in quibus quid agere, quid observare debeant, doceantur tum qui in eodem Seminario in spem Ecclesiae instituuntur, tum qui in horum institutionem operam suam impendunt.

§ 4. Seminarii interdioecesani vel regionalis regimen universum et administratio regitur normis a Sancta Sede statutis.

§ 1. The bishop shall, with due respect to the particular regulations given by the Holy See, decide what is necessary and profitable for the proper administration, government, and progress of the seminary, and enforce his regulations.

§ 2. Above all the bishop shall try to visit the seminary frequently, watch over the mental and moral training of the students, and, especially on the occasion of sacred ordinations, acquaint himself more fully with the character, piety, vocation, and progress of the pupils.

§ 3. Each seminary must have its statutes, approved by the bishop, in which the rules for the conduct of students and teachers are laid down.

§ 4. Interdiocesan or provincial seminaries are entirely governed by the statutes issued by the Holy See.

For Italy special rules have been issued, which may serve as models for other interdiocesan seminaries.[31]

SEMINARY OFFICIALS

CAN. 1358

Curandum ut in quolibet Seminario adsint rector pro disciplina, magistri pro instructione, oeconomus pro curanda re familiari, a rectore distinctus, duo saltem confessarii ordinarii et director spiritus.

In every seminary there shall be a rector to maintain the discipline, professors to teach the students, a procurator to provide for the temporalities, who must be an official distinct from the rector, at least two ordinary confessors, and a spiritual director.

31 Cfr. Micheletti, *Constitutiones Seminariorum Clericalium*, 1919, p. XVIII.

DIOCESAN SEMINARY BOARD

Can. 1359

§ 1. Diocesanis Seminariis bini constituantur coetus deputatorum, alter pro disciplina, alter pro administratione bonorum temporalium.

§ 2. Utrumque deputatorum coetum constituunt bini sacerdotes, ab Episcopo, audito Capitulo, electi; sed excluduntur Vicarius Generalis, familiares Episcopi, rector Seminarii, oeconomus et confessarii ordinarii.

§ 3. Munus deputatorum per sexennium durat, nec electi sine gravi causa amoveantur; sed rursus eligi poterunt.

§4. Episcopus debet consilium deputatorum in negotiis maioris momenti petere.

§ 1. Every diocesan seminary must have two boards, one for discipline, the other for the administration of temporal affairs.

§ 2. Each board consists of two priests, appointed by the bishop with the advice of the chapter or diocesan consultors; excluded are the Vicar-general, members of the bishop's household, the rector of the seminary, the procurator, and the ordinary confessors.

§ 3. The term of each board member lasts for six years, during which he should not be removed from office without a serious reason; he may also be reappointed.

§ 4. The bishop is bound to ask the advice of these boards in important matters.

Such matters of importance are, *e. g.,* the drawing up of statutes, the admission of pupils, the appointment of the rector, confessors and teachers, etc., the selection of textbooks, and the punishment and dismissal of unruly and incorrigible students.[32]

By *familiares episcopi* must here be understood his *commensales, i. e.,* those who partake of the episcopal table or household and live in the episcopal residence as dependants,[33] and since, according to § 2 only priests can be elected *deputati,* they will be the bishop's chaplains, secretaries, or chancellors, provided they live together with the bishop.

The reason for excluding these and the Vicar General, the rector of the seminary, etc., is their dependence; these officials should be as independent as possible.

It may not be superfluous to state that the bishop is in duty bound to have such a seminary board and that he is not allowed to substitute another, made up of other persons, for instance, the rector, or the professors, or other persons prohibited by law [34]

QUALIFICATION OF THE CHIEF SEMINARY OFFICIALS

CAN. 1360

§ 1. Firmo praescripto can. 891, ad munus rectoris, directoris spiritus, confessariorum et magistrorum Seminarii eligantur sacerdotes non doctrina tantum, sed etiam virtutibus ac prudentia praestantes, qui verbo et exemplo alumnis prodesse possint.

§ 2. Rectori Seminarii in propriis muneribus implendis obtemperare omnes debent.

§ 1. For the positions of rector, spiritual director, confessors, and professors in the seminary, only such priests should be chosen as are distinguished not only by learn-

32 S. C C., 1585, July, 1589; Jan. 19, 1595 (Richter, *l. c*, p. 211, n 1 ff.)

33 Barbosa, *De Off. et Potest*

Episc, P II, alleg. 5, n. 2 ff. (Vol. I, 212 f.).

34 S C. C, Aug. 27, 1864 (*A. S. S*, I, 657 ff)

ing, but also by virtues and prudence, so that they may serve as examples to the students in word and deed.

§ 2. All must obey the rector in the discharge of their duties.

As to the qualities of a rector, St. Charles Borromeo demanded that he be of advanced age (*aetate provectus*), of a serious disposition (*auctoritate gravis*), of tried integrity (*speciali probitate*).

With regard to his *external canonical status* the rector is (1) *exempt* from the parish organization, as per can. 1368. If a church is connected with the seminary, he is the canonical rector of the same (see can. 480, § 3). (2) He is obliged and entitled to attend the diocesan synod, as per can. 358, § 1, 3; (3) he is obliged to make the profession of faith according to can. 1406.

Concerning the internal affairs of the seminary; the rector (1) depends in everything and at all times on the Ordinary; (2) he is the supreme authority in the seminary, whom all others, of whatever degree, including the professors and the œconomus and other officials, must obey in matters that pertain to discipline, study, and ordinary administration; (3) he is not allowed habitually to hear the confessions of the students who live under the same roof with him, as per can. 891; (4) he may arrange and change things of minor importance according to his good judgment. (5) In urgent and extraordinary cases, (a) he may expel a student guilty of a grievous public transgression, but must inform the bishop immediately; (b) make changes of a serious nature after due deliberation with the Ordinary; (c) in serious cases which brook no delay he shall consult with the other officials, but not with the spiritual director or the confessors, act upon their advice, and afterwards report to the bishop.[35]

35 Micheletti, *l c.*, p 14 f.

CAN. 1361

§ 1. Praeter confessarios ordinarios, alii confessarii designentur ad quos libere alumni accedere possint.

§ 2. Si ii confessarii extra Seminarium degant, et alumnus aliquem eorum acciri postulet, illum rector arcessat, nullo modo petitionis rationem inquirens neque se aegre id ferre demonstrans; si in Seminario habitent, ipsos alumnus libere adire potest, salva Seminarii disciplina.

§ 3. Quando agitur de alumno ad ordines admittendo vel e Seminario expellendo, nunquam confessariorum votum exquiratur.

§ 1. Besides the ordinary confessors, others should be appointed, whom the students may freely approach

§ 2. If these extraordinary confessors live outside the seminary, and a student desires to approach one of them, the rector shall call him, without in any way asking the reason or showing signs of displeasure. If these extraordinary confessors live in the seminary, the students may freely approach them, with due regard, of course, to the discipline of the house.

§ 3. When a seminarian is to be promoted to sacred orders, or expelled, the opinion of the confessors must never be asked.

The rule for religious communities,[36] that they may have extraordinary confessors at least four times a year, may also be applied to seminaries.

A confessor may be offered *salva disciplina,* means that the granting of such a petition should not constitute a *custom* detrimental to good order, *e. g.,* withdrawing from

36 See can. 566, § 2, 4.

the lecture room, or study hall, or common exercises.   In exceptional cases, of course, a relaxation may be justifiable.

SCHOLARSHIPS

CAN. 1362

Reditus legati pro clericis instituendis tribui possunt alumnis in Seminarium sive maius sive minus rite receptis, licet nondum clericali tonsura initiatis, nisi aliud in tabulis fundationis expresse caveatur.

Legacies or bequests left for the training of clerics may be applied to students of the clerical or little seminary, even though they have received tonsure, provided the foundation does not forbid it.

This ruling is substantially taken from a letter of Pius X to the Cardinal Vicar of Rome.   There are some scholarships in the Roman Seminary (near the Lateran) reserved for aspirants of the diocese of Rome.   Pius X ordered that these be reserved for students of theology, and only in case there be none such may they be given to students of the lyceum (or college).   This also holds for such as are Romans not by birth, but by domicile.[37] Our text is somewhat broader, leaving the choice free between clerical and collegiate students, provided, of course, they have entered the college with the intention of becoming priests, and provided that the terms of the bequest do not ordain differently.   It is, therefore, important that such documents be carefully kept.   If a scholarship is intended only for students of a certain diocese or parish, it cannot be applied to those of another diocese or parish.   If the bequest is for university students, the scholarship cannot be applied to college students.   If it is

37 Pius X, May 5, 1904, n. 2 (Anal. Eccl., XII, 235).

to be given to one student only, it cannot be divided or distributed among several. On the other hand, if the bequest is made in general terms " for a clerical student," without qualification, the president of the college or seminary may give the scholarship to any one attending the college, the petit seminaire, or the clerical seminary proper.

ADMISSION TO SEMINARIES

CAN. 1363

§ 1. In Seminarium ab Ordinario ne admittantur, nisi filii legitimi quorum indoles et voluntas spem afferant eos cum fructu ecclesiasticis ministeriis perpetuo inservituros.

§ 2. Antequam recipiantur, documenta exhibere debent de legitimitate natalium, de susceptis baptismate et confirmatione ac de vita et moribus.

§ 3. Dimissi ex aliis Seminariis vel ex aliqua religione ne admittantur, nisi prius Episcopus etiam secreto a Superioribus aliisve notitias requisierit de causa dimissionis ac de moribus, indole et ingenio dimissorum, et certo compererit nihil in eis esse quod sacerdotali statui minus conveniat; quas notitias, veritati conformes, eorum conscientia graviter onerata, suppeditare Superiores debent.

§ 1. The Ordinary shall admit into the seminary only boys of legitimate birth, whose character and inclination justify the hope that they will devote themselves forever to the ecclesiastical ministry.

§ 2. These, before they are received, must submit proofs of legitimate birth, certificates of Baptism and Confirmation, and testimonials of their life and conduct. These documents, to which a medical certificate might profitably be added, are to be presented to the rector, who shall submit them to the Ordinary. The latter, as stated above, must consult with the seminary board.[38]

§ 3. Such as have been *dismissed* from another seminary or from a religious institute can be admitted only under the following conditions:

(a) The bishop must ascertain, if necessary even by way of secret information from the superiors and other persons, the reasons why they were discharged;

(b) He must satisfy himself about their moral standing, character, and intellectual capacity, and

(c) He must be morally certain that there is nothing in them that would not be compatible with the sacerdotal state.

The superiors who are called upon for such information are bound in conscience to tell the truth as far as they are able. Untruthful recommendations have often done great damage.

PLAN OF STUDIES FOR LITTLE SEMINARIES

Can. 1364

In inferioribus Seminarii scholis:

1.° Praecipuum locum obtineat religionis disciplina, quae, modo singulorum ingenio et aetati accommodato, diligentissime explicetur.

2.° Linguas praesertim latinam et patriam alumni accurate addiscant;

3.° Ea in ceteris disciplinis institutio tradatur quae conveniat communi omnium culturae et statui clericorum in regione ubi alumni sacrum ministerium exercere debent.

---

[38] Micheletti, *l. c.*, p. 90 ff.

1. The first place in the study plan of the *petit seminaire* belongs to *religious instruction,* which should be carefully given and adapted to the intellectual capacity and age of the hearers. Here it may not be amiss to state what is prescribed for the Italian schools. Each week, one period or hour for catechism and one for Bible History in the high school or academic grades; one hour for higher catechism and apologetical instruction in the college, at least in the higher grades.[39]

2. Especially the *Latin language* as well as the vernacular should be learned correctly. Nothing is prescribed as to the number of hours to be devoted to each; but it goes without saying that the language of the Church should be given such a prominent place that the pupils realize its importance as a main branch.

A difficulty may arise in regard to mixed schools, *i. e.,* such as are partly secular and partly ecclesiastical. In these, says Leo XIII as well as the above-quoted Circular of the Consistorial Congregation, the Ordinaries should see to it that the plan of studies be adapted as closely as possible to that prescribed by the civil government.[40] In other words, the colleges conducted by and for ecclesiastics should not fall below the standard prescribed by the State.

Should it be necessary to supplement the instruction in certain branches in keeping with ecclesiastical tradition, certain periods or hours may be added for those who follow the ecclesiastical course. This is a very wise ruling.[41]

3. As to the *other branches,* everything should be taught that is required by the intellectual standard of the country in which the students expect to exercise the sacred

39 S C. Consist , *Litterae Circulares,* July 16, 1912, n 8 (*A. Ap. S.,* IV, 495).

40 Leo XIII, *"Depuis le jour,"* Sept. 8, 1879; *Litt. Circ.,* n. 6 (*l c*).

41 *Litt. Circ , l c.*

ministry. This standard differs in different countries, but everywhere a priest is looked upon as a man of culture and the Catholic clergy in general as the "light of the world" To conform to this ideal students for the ministry must acquire the knowledge and learning expected of them and necessary to enable them to exercise a wholesome influence on their fellowmen. This can only be accomplished by a comprehensive and thorough training in those branches which society at present considers the *sine qua non* of culture. This is more efficaciously and palpably achieved by obtaining the usual academic degrees.[42] This does not mean that all clergymen are called upon or expected to excel in secular learning, but that some at least should be first-class all-around scholars. All, however, are obliged to acquire such a degree of even worldly science as is necessary to their state. in order that there may be no prejudice and unfounded accusations.[43]

PHILOSOPHY AND THEOLOGY

CAN. 1365

§ 1. In philosophiam rationalem cum affinibus disciplinis alumni per integrum saltem biennium incumbant.

§ 2. Cursus theologicus saltem integro quadriennio contineatur, et, praeter theologiam dogmaticam et moralem, complecti praesertim debet studium sacrae Scripturae, historiae ecclesiasticae, iuris canonici, liturgiae, sacrae eloquentiae et cantus ecclesiastici.

§ 3. Habeantur etiam lectiones de theologia pas-

---

42 Leo XIII, "*Officio sanctissimo*,"   43 *Ibid.*
Dec 22, 1887, "*Depuis le jour*,"
Sept. 8, 1899

torali, additis practicis exercitationibus praesertim de ratione tradendi pueris aliisve catechismum, audiendi confessiones, visitandi infirmos, assistendi moribundis.

§ 1. The *philosophical course* must last at least two continuous years and comprise, besides philosophy proper, also the allied branches.

Philosophy is here understood in its proper sense, as the knowledge or science of things in their ultimate principles [44] The *disciplinae affines* are officially described as follows: mathematics, natural or physical science, literature, Latin and Greek, history. The number of lessons to be devoted to each is stated as one hour per day. However, it must be observed that this plan was drawn up for the Italian lyceum, which has a three years' course. Counting five periods a week (they have one full holiday every week) this would be fifteen hours per week for three years. Distributing these lessons over two years, we have about 7 to 8 hours for each per week. To these must be added, according to the same Circular, one hour for review or repetition each week, and one hour for debate or disputation every two weeks.[45] Thus about 8 or 9 periods of philosophy proper are required to do justice to this important branch.

§ 2. The *theological course* should last at least *four full years* and comprise, besides dogmatic and moral theology, the study of Holy Scripture, Church history, Canon Law, liturgy, sacred eloquence, and ecclesiastical chant.

The *number* of hours to be devoted to dogmatic theology, according to the Circular,[46] is one a day, *i. e.*, *five hours per week*, plus one hour for disputation and one

44 Cfr. Turner, *History of Philosophy,* 1903, p. 1.

45 *Litt. Circul. S. C. Consist.,* July 16, 1912, n. 9.

46 *Ibid.,* nn. 11 f. (*A. Ap. S.,* IV, 496 f).

for review, in all, seven hours a week for dogmatic theology.

For *moral* theology no definite number of hours is assigned, but it is added that lectures on sociology and the elements of Canon Law should be given as supplementary to moral theology.

For *Holy Scripture* four periods per week are assigned throughout the four years' course. The first two years are to be devoted to introduction and the last two to exegesis.

Church History has no definite number prescribed, neither have the secondary branches of Biblical Greek, Hebrew, sacred eloquence, patrology, liturgy, sacred archaeology, sacred art, and Gregorian Chant.

It may be noted that this programme, as outlined in the Circular, is to be taken as directive only, not as a law in the strict sense. Details may be left to the seminary board. Note that the same Circular[47] says that there should not be more than four, or at most four and one-half hours school a day, and these should not follow one another consecutively, but should be divided up. Too many lessons are incompatible with the discipline of the seminary, the necessary exercises of piety, and the physical well-being of the students.

§ 3 rules that *pastoral theology* should also be taught. Practical exercises should be added. These should consist in pedagogic instructions, in order that the candidates may learn how to teach catechism, to hear confessions, to visit the sick, and to assist the dying.

[47] *Ibid.,* n. 7.

QUALIFICATION OF SEMINARY PROFESSORS

CAN. 1366

§ 1. Ad magisterii munus in disciplinis philosophicis, theologicis et iuridicis, ii, ceteris paribus, iudicio Episcopi et deputatorum Seminarii, praeferantur, qui laurea doctorali potiti sint in Universitate studiorum vel Facultate a Sancta Sede recognitis, aut, si agatur de religiosis, qui simile testimonium a suis Superioribus maioribus habeant.

§ 2. Philosophiae rationalis ac theologiae studia et alumnorum in his disciplinis institutionem professores omnino pertractent ad Angelici Doctoris rationem, doctrinam et principia, eaque sancte teneant.

§ 3. Curandum ut saltem sacrae Scripturae, theologiae dogmaticae, theologiae moralis, et historiae ecclesiasticae, totidem habeantur distincti magistri.

§ 1. For the teaching of philosophy, theology, and canon law, other qualifications being equal, those should be preferred who have obtained the doctor's degree from a university or faculty recognized by the Holy See. The decision lies with the bishop and the seminary board. The phrase *ceteris paribus* is easily understood in the light of can. 1360, § 1, which demands not only learning, but also virtue and prudence, as necessary qualities of a professor. Teachers taken from the rank of *religious* should have testimonials from their superiors testifying to their doctor's degree or recognized capacity and scholarship.

§ 2. Mental philosophy and theology must be taught according to the method, teaching, and principles of the *Angelic Doctor,* to which the professors should religiously adhere.

The *method* here understood is the *scholastic form* in

which the *Summa Theologica* of St. Thomas and, in fact, all the great *Summae* of the thirteenth century are composed.

The term *doctrina* in this connection is not so easily defined, but, taken as a whole, no doubt means the teaching of St. Thomas, more especially his metaphysics,[48] though not each and every sentence laid down in his works need be accepted.

The *principles* of the Angelic Doctor are the rules or theses around which his system clusters, and upon which it more or less hinges, especially in metaphysics.[49]

It was but natural that the *Summa Theologica* of St. Thomas should be prescribed as the *text-book for theological seminaries.* This does not mean that no other systematic text-book may be used for recitation purposes, but only that the *Summa* must be used and explained for the scholastic part, *i. e.,* in the treatment of purely speculative questions.[50]   Of modern erudition there is but little in the *Summa,* and yet dogmatic theology now-a-days must be treated with the aid of history and Holy Writ.[51]   That it will not be easy for a Scotist or a Molinist to feel at home in the Thomistic system goes without saying; but no other system is condemned by the preference given to St. Thomas.

§ 3. Care should be taken that at least Holy Scripture, dogmatic theology, moral theology, and Church history be taught by different professors.

---

48 Pius X, "*Doctoris Angelici,*" June 29, 1914 (*A Ap S.,* VI, 338).

49 See the 24 theses proposed by S. C Stud, July 27, 1914 (*A. Ap. S*, VI, 383 ff.).

50 Cfr. the documents already quoted and S. C. Sem., March 7, 1916 (*A. Ap. S*, VIII, 157)

51 S. C. Consist, *Lit. Circul.,* n. 11.

THE RELIGIOUS TRAINING OF SEMINARISTS

CAN. 1367

Current Episcopi ut alumni Seminarii:

1.° Singulis diebus communiter matutinas et serotinas preces recitent, per aliquod tempus mentali orationi vacent, sacrificio Missae intersint;

2.° Semel saltem in hebdomada ad sacramentum poenitentiae accedant et frequenter, qua par est pietate, Eucharistico pane se reficiant;

3.° Dominicis et festis diebus, sacris Missarum et Vesperarum sollemnibus adsint, altari inserviant sacrasque caeremonias exerceant, praesertim in ecclesia cathedrali si id, iudicio Episcopi, sine disciplinae et studiorum detrimento fieri possit;

4.° Singulis annis per aliquot dies continuos exercitiis spiritualibus vacent;

5.° Semel saltem in hebdomada adsint instructioni de rebus spiritualibus quae pia exhortatione claudatur.

The bishops shall see to it that the students of the Seminary:

1.° Recite their morning and evening prayers in common, make a short meditation, and assist at Mass;

2.° Go to confession at least once a week and frequently receive holy Communion with proper devotion;

3.° Assist at solemn Mass and Vespers on Sundays and holy-days of obligation, serve at the altar, and perform the sacred ceremonies, especially in the cathedral church, provided the bishop thinks it can be done without disadvantange to discipline and study;

4.° Make a retreat once a year for several successive days;

5.° At least once a week attend a spiritual lecture, which may be followed by a pious exhortation.

We hardly believe that this canon applies to " little seminaries " *in globo.* At most some of its prescriptions may serve as a directive norm for these, as far as circumstances permit. The practice or exercise of sacred ceremonies is certainly only intended for seminarians in the strict sense. Weekly confession for academic and collegiate students cannot be prescribed as a rule. Where there are day scholars, not even 1° can be enforced. Therefore we believe that this canon is primarily intended for clerical seminaries, but may, as stated, serve as a directive norm for high schools and colleges.

To superintend the pious exercises is the special duty of the *rector,*[52] who should see to it that genuine and solid piety be fostered in the candidates to the sacred ministry. Hence he must combat hypocrisy and watch over the freedom of conscience. This presupposes free choice of confessors, according to can. 1361. The rector should be cautious and circumspect in inquiring into the frequentation of the Sacraments, and use no compulsion or moral persuasion in this matter. He shall also inculcate this mode of acting in his officials.

The *spiritual director* conducts the daily, weekly, and monthly devotions of the seminarists, but under the supervision of the rector (can. 1360, § 2). He should be ready to hear confessions whenever asked by the students. But he, too, must leave the freedom of conscience intact, scrupulously abstain from restricting the choice of confessors, and be specially careful about the seal of confession

It may be asked: If perfect liberty of conscience is

52 Micheletti, *l c ,* p. 26 ff.

guaranteed, how can the discipline, and especially the rule laid down in our canon, be observed? We answer as follows: The rector as well as the spiritual director should give warning in their conferences and spiritual lectures as to the obligation in general of observing this rule, a protracted violation of which can not long remain hidden from the eyes of a vigilant rector or spiritual director. The rector, then, when perceiving any case of palpable negligence, must correct the culprit, and, like a religious superior, is bound to correct even apparently slight faults if a serious relaxation of discipline is to be apprehended therefrom.[53] As to individuals, the matter must first be settled with the confessors who are the judges of conscience. It may be that in cases of scrupulosity the confessor would advise less frequent confession. Should a penitent say that he has nothing to confess, the rules of *materia sufficiens* and *necessaria* must be applied. Giving scandal by not going to confession would seem to form a *materia sufficiens*. At least the penitent should present himself to hear the confessor's advice and receive his blessing. Thus freedom can be safeguarded as well as discipline What goes on between the confessor and the penitent is a matter entirely subtracted from public discipline.

Our canon says that the Ordinary must see to the enforcement of this rule. This can be done especially on the occasion of his visits, when the bishop may interpellate the rector as to its observance. The rector is bound to answer his questions truthfully. Of course, neither the spiritual director nor the confessors may reveal anything that they know from confession only. However, the spiritual director, who has every opportunity to watch

53 Cfr. Marc, *Institutiones Morales,* II, n. 2170, q. 3.

the students, may express his judgment in general terms, without mentioning any individual, as to the general observance of our canon. The Ordinary may give weight to the rule by threatening injunctions or penalties, against which no appeal is admitted.[54]

EXEMPTION

Can. 1368

Exemptum a iurisdictione paroeciali Seminarium esto; et pro omnibus qui in Seminario sunt, parochi officium, excepta materia matrimoniali et firmo praescripto can. 891, obeat Seminarii rector eiusve delegatus, nisi in quibusdam Seminariis aliter a Sede Apostolica constitutum.

The seminary is exempt from the jurisdiction of the pastor, whose place is taken by the rector or his delegate for all who live in the seminary in all things except marriage and matters concerning which the Holy See may have differently provided   But the rule laid down in can. 891, that the rector should not habitually hear the confessions of boarding pupils, must not be set aside.

This canon, though quite clear in itself, raises more than one doubt. First of all, there is the very term *seminary*. Does it comprise every seminary, the little as well as the clerical? In view of the definition given above, in the introduction to this title, we believe exemption may be claimed by any seminary which is such in the proper sense of the word. For as the bishop may exempt some religious families and charitable institutions from parish organization,[55] so does the Code exempt the seminaries

---

54 Bened. XIV, "*Ad militantis*," March 30, 1742, § 34

55 Can. 464, § 2   But the defini-

tion of seminary cannot be *eo ipso* applied to colleges of a promiscuous character; the clerical character from the same. Besides, the general rule that, where the law makes no distinction, neither should the interpreter, may here be safely applied, as the law is favorable to the seminaries. But only such seminaries, either little or clerical, as are under the control of the local Ordinary, or interdiocesan and pontifical seminaries, must be understood. Hence seminaries governed by religious cannot claim this privilege, unless the Ordinary should see fit to apply can. 464, § 2, as mentioned above.

The next question is: Who are "*all those who are in the seminary*"? No doubt the officials as well as the professors and pupils who habitually live in the seminary, and as long as they live there, even during vacation, should they spend their vacation there. And we believe that this rule may also be applied to the so-called *villeggiatura,* or summer resort, which is a *desideratum* for all seminaries.[56] This privilege doubtless also applies to laymen working for, and living as boarders in, the seminary, for the text admits this extension. But concerning these laymen it must be understood that, if they want to get married, they must do so in the parish church, according to the law established in can 1094 ff. All other sacraments, including baptism and confirmation, these laymen may receive in the seminary.

But what about the *Sisters* in the seminary? Their presence there is necessary for more than one reason, and is now tolerated by Roman practice. They are subject to the following rules: [57]

1. They may be called or dismissed by the local Ordinary according to his discretion.

must certainly be prevalent, otherwise any school might be called a seminary.

56 *S C. Consist , Litt. Circul.,*

July 16, 1912, n. 3 (*A. Ap S* , IV, 493).

57 Micheletti, *l. c.,* p. 40.

2. The appointment of the superioress and the selection of sisters for service in the seminary is left to the superioress general, who, however, should comply with the wishes of the local Ordinary.

3. The interior government of the Sisters employed in the seminary must be left to the local superioress and neither the rector nor any other official should interfere therewith.

4. A private oratory should be assigned to the Sisters for their spiritual exercises.

5. Their habitation should be entirely separate from the other parts of the seminary, and no one, except the rector, vicerector, and procurator, shall be allowed to communicate with the Superioress or the Sisters.

6. As to confessions the common law, as stated in can. 520, must be applied.

From these observations the question with regard to the rector's rights is easily settled. The Sisters' chaplain must be assigned by the local Ordinary, according to can. 529. Their confessors must have the requisite faculties from the Ordinary; and for the rest, especially for their " peace of conscience," the Sisters may avail themselves of the favors granted in can. 522–523.

SEMINARY DISCIPLINE

Can. 1369

§ 1. Seminarii rector et alii omnes moderatores sub eius auctoritate curent ut alumni statuta ab Episcopo probata studiorumque rationem adamussim servent ac spiritu vere ecclesiastico imbuantur.

§ 2. Saepius eis verae et christianae urbanitatis leges tradant, eosque exemplo suo ad illas colendas excitent; hortentur praeterea ut praecepta hygienica,

vestium et corporis munditiam et quandam in con-
versando comitatem cum modestia et gravitate con-
iunctam, iugiter servent.

§ 3. Sedulo vigilent ut magistri suo munere rite
fungantur.

§ 1. The rector and all other officials subject to his
authority shall take care that the students closely *observe
the statutes* approved by the bishop as well as the *plan of
studies,* and that they be imbued with the true ecclesiastical spirit.

If the students are bound to follow the programme laid
down for the various courses, it naturally follows that the
professors too should follow it (§ 3). Therefore, says
the oft-quoted Circular, the professors should not waste
time in long discussions on some particular subject —
perhaps a " hobby "— but finish their *pensum* within the
period assigned for the same. Ordinaries are exhorted to
see to it, that the lectures on dogmatic and moral theology,
and, as far as possible, also those on philosophy, at least
the general outlines, are given in Latin.[58] This, of course
cannot mean that the vernacular is to be banished   For
the positive parts of dogmatic theology and sociological
questions are certainly more easily and profitably treated
in the vernacular language. But the speculative parts
should be treated in the accurate and precise Latin terminology handed down by tradition.

§ 2. The seminary officials should insist *upon the rules*
of genuine Christian politeness and excite the students to
imitation by their example. They should also exhort
them to observe the rules of hygiene, be cleanly in dress
and appearance, and practice courtesy joined with modesty
and gravity.

[58] *Lit. Circul*, n. 13.

CAN. 1370

Quoties alumni ob quamlibet causam extra Seminarium morentur, servetur praescriptum can. 972, § 2.

When students, for whatsoever reason, live outside the seminary, they should be placed under the care of pious and worthy persons, who shall watch over them and lead them on to piety, as stated under can. 972, § 2.

DISMISSAL OF STUDENTS

CAN. 1371

E Seminario dimittantur dyscoli, incorrigibiles, seditiosi, ii qui ob mores atque indolem ad statum ecclesiasticum idonei non videantur; itemque, qui in studiis adeo parum proficiant ut spes non affulgeat eos sufficientem doctrinam fore assecuturos; praesertim vero statim dimittantur qui forte contra bonos mores aut fidem deliquerint.

Disorderly, incorrigible, and rebellious students, such as appear unfit for the ecclesiastical state on account of their conduct and character, and those who make so little progress in their studies that there is no hope that they will acquire a sufficient knowledge, should be dismissed. Those who offend against faith and good morals — by which latter term the *praeceptum contra sextum* is chiefly meant — should be expelled at once.

TITLE XXII

SCHOOLS

This title sounds more restricted than its contents bear out. Education comprises Christian training of every kind and degree, no matter in what place or form it is given, whereas the term *school* has, at least in common parlance, a narrower meaning, to wit, a place or building where education is imparted; or an institution of learning or training, especially when the latter is carried on in a systematic form. Education in general means mental and moral development of the faculties of man; school means a systematic education offered in a place or building assigned for that purpose. Thus we also speak of compulsory education and compulsory schooling, which terms differ widely, since the former does not necessarily include the latter, as shall be seen under can. 1375. The first of the following canons refers to *Christian education in general.*

THE DUTY OF CHRISTIAN EDUCATION

CAN. 1372

§ 1. Fideles omnes ita sunt a pueritia instituendi ut non solum nihil eis tradatur quod catholicae religioni morumque honestati adversetur, sed praecipuum institutio religiosa ac moralis locum obtineat.

§ 2. Non modo parentibus ad normam can. 1113, sed etiam omnibus qui eorum locum tenent, ius et

411

gravissimum officium est curandi christianam liberorum educationem.

§ 1. All the faithful must from childhood be educated in such way that not only are they taught nothing that is contrary to faith and morals, but that religious and moral training takes the first place.

§ 2. Not only parents, but all those who take their place, have the right and the solemn duty to provide a Christian education for their children.

It seems superfluous to add anything to this pregnant text, which is the concrete embodiment of the many solemn documents which the Holy See issued against the liberalistic tendencies of the last century. One was directed especially to the bishops of the U. S. by the Holy Office.[1] It says that the tender age is most susceptible to the seeds of vice as well as virtue. Experienced teachers and priests could tell a thrilling story of the difference between children brought up in the atmosphere of faith and piety, and those who come from homes where religion has little or no influence.[2]

The right of parents and guardians under God is inalienable and inviolable because the child belongs primarily and before others to the parents. This natural right has its foundation in the very fact of procreation and involves the right of the parent to feed, clothe, and educate his children physically, intellectually, and morally.[3] These rights involve their corresponding duties, which parents may neither evade nor ignore.[4] For by doing so they would violate their natural duties towards their God-

---

1 S. O, Nov 24, 1875 (*Coll P F.*, n 1449).

2 Cfr. Becker, S. J, *Christian Education or The Duty of Parents;* 1899, p. 128 ff.

3 See can 1113.

4 See the excellent paper of Cardinal O'Connell in *Catholic Educational Association Bulletin,* Aug. 1919; Cavagnis, *Instit. Iuris Pub. Eccl.* 1882, Vol. IV, p. 14 f.

given proteges, for whom they are responsible and accountable to the Creator.

From this follows that the parents are entitled and obliged to provide, either themselves or through others, the necessary moral and religious training and to keep their children away from everything and every person that would be dangerous to faith or morals.

RELIGIOUS INSTRUCTION IN SCHOOLS

CAN. 1373

§ 1. In qualibet elementaria schola, pueris pro eorum aetate tradenda est institutio religiosa.

§2. Iuventus, quae medias vel superiores scholas frequentat, pleniore religionis doctrina excolatur, et locorum Ordinarii curent ut id fiat per sacerdotes zelo et doctrina praestantes.

§ 1. In every elementary school religious instruction should be given the children according to their age.

These elementary, popular or grade schools are especially destined for the building up of good character, and since an education which guarantees public peace and tranquillity cannot be solid and lasting without the principles of Christian truth, moral as well as intellectual, it follows that no schooling without religious training is able to produce the desired effects. These words of Pius IX to the Archbishop of Freiburg (Baden)[5] need no further proof than a glance at the present social condition of the world. The programme of the so-called " Liberals," who propose to take the schools away from the influence of the Church, and to limit education to the pursuit of worldly happiness,[6] has never received a more ter-

5 " Quum non sine," July 14, 1864 (Coll. P. F. n 1260).

6 Syllabus of Pius IX, prop. 48 (Denz., n. 1596).

rible shock than in the late war. Unfortunately, the enemies of Christian education have eyes but see not. Ra-
tionalism and materialism clings to their bones and often
has its principal nerve in the pocket.

§ 2. Youths who *frequent the secondary or higher
schools* should be given fuller instruction in Christian
doctrine, and the local Ordinaries should see to it that
this instruction is given by zealous and learned priests.

Such fuller instructions are contained in the larger catechism as well as the so-called evidences of religion, which
should be imparted so that they may be easily grasped
and assimilated by the pupils.[7]

NON-CATHOLIC SCHOOLS

CAN. 1374

Pueri catholici scholas acatholicas, neutras, mixtas,
quae nempe etiam acatholicis patent, ne frequentent.
Solius autem Ordinarii loci est decernere, ad normam
instructionum Sedis Apostolicae, in quibus rerum adiunctis et quibus adhibitis cautelis, ut periculum perversionis vitetur, tolerari possit ut eae scholae cele-
brentur.

Catholic children should not frequent non-Catholic,
neutral, or mixed schools, *i. e*, such as are open also to
non-Catholics. It is for the local Ordinary to decide, according to the instructions of the Apostolic See, in what
circumstances and with what precautions attendance at
such schools may be tolerated, without danger of perversion to the pupils

There is a term used in this canon which recalls the famous controversy waged about the *parochial schools* in

7 Pius IX, " *Acerbo nimis*," April 15, 1905, n. V.

this country a generation ago. It is *"tolerari possit,"* which was given only for particular cases and in view of special circumstances, and may be called an equitable arrangement departing from the letter of the law.[8] The *instructions of the Holy See* for *our country* were contained in a document issued by the Holy Office,[9] Nov. 24, 1875. Others of a similar tenor were given for Canada, Ireland, England and missionary countries.[10] All of them revolve around the question whether the influence of the Church is entirely excluded from the public schools and the Catholic pupils are exposed to danger to the faith; if so, the bishop shall provide for their instruction as far as lies within his power, and at the same time warn the faithful and announce to them that they cannot in conscience permit their children to frequent schools opposed to the Catholic Church.[11]

The *circumstances* in which attendance at non-Catholic schools may be permitted are expressed in the above-named Instruction to the bishops of the U. S. as follows: " Generally speaking, such cause will exist if there is no Catholic school in a place, or if the one that is there cannot be considered suitable to the conditions and circumstances of the pupils." This suitability must not be identified with mere fashionableness, for there is no proportion between the danger to faith and " stylishness." Hence said instruction continues: " Parents who neglect to give this necessary Christian training and instruction to their children, or who permit them to go to schools in

8 See the excellent work of Burns, C. S. C., *The Growth and Development of the Catholic School System in U. S*, 1912, chs XI f

9 *Coll. P. F*, n. 1449

10 S. C P. F, March 14, 1895; Sept. 18, 1819; Jan 16, 1841; April 7, 1860; Aug. 6, 1867 (Oxford and Cambridge); 1659; July 19, 1838, March 20, 1865; April 25, 1868 (*Coll.*, nn 1890, 738, 1190, 1312, 1329)

11 Pius IX, *" Quum non sine,"* July 14, 1864 (*Coll. P. F.*, n. 1260).

which the ruin of their souls is inevitable, or, finally, who send them to the public schools without sufficient cause and without taking the necessary precautions to render the danger of perversion remote, and do so while there is a good and well-equipped Catholic school in the place, and while they have the means to send them elsewhere to be educated; — such parents, if obstinate, cannot be absolved, as is evident from the moral teaching of the Church." [12]

THE RIGHT OF THE CHURCH TO ESTABLISH SCHOOLS

CAN. 1375

Ecclesiae est ius scholas cuiusvis disciplinae non solum elementarias, sed etiam medias et superiores condendi.

The Church has the right to establish schools of every kind, not only elementary, but also secondary and higher schools. Note well, the Church does *not claim* the *exclusive right* to establish schools, as she does with regard to seminaries for the education of the clergy (can. 1352). Our canon claims for her the right of *establishing schools* of *every kind, (cuiusvis disciplinae).* By *disciplina* is generally understood what we call a branch or department of learning. Hence the term includes elementary, secondary, and higher schools, colleges and universities, even the special faculties of theology, philosophy, medicine, and law. Among the secondary schools figure training and professional schools and high schools for boys and girl (academies), whatever name they may go by in different countries, for the terminology varies. [13]

To *establish* a school means to furnish the means

---

12 *Coll. P F*, n 1449
13 See *Cath Encycl*, Vol XIII *s. v* " Schools "

wherewith to commence and continue it. Such an act does not exclude the coöperation of other persons, either public or private, who may participate in the administration or regulation of a school.

A school is a building or other place where education is given in a more or less systematic manner. Now-a-days education is concentrated in schools; hence the "fight for the schools" waged in nearly every civilized country. Yet it cannot be denied that there is not a purely mental or abstract, but a real and well-founded distinction between *education* and *school*. For education comprises the development of the moral and mental faculties in the whole range of science and moral principles. Schools on the other hand are differentiated by the higher and lower degrees of studies, these being divided into various grades, as the appellations elementary, secondary, etc., clearly indicate. Besides, schools are localized and attached to state and municipal machinery, whilst education may and should be the common good of all.

The Code, then, by claiming the right of establishing schools for the Church, leaves aside the question of education in general. Whence this claim to establish schools? Whatever has reference to the purpose or end for which the Church was founded, belongs to her domain. Now schools, as the universal and ordinary means of conveying a Christian education, undoubtedly have a natural connection with the end of the Church. Consequently the Church has the right of establishing and conducting schools.[14] The major premiss follows from the fact that the Church is an autonomous, an independent, and a perfect society endowed with the right of procuring the means necessary to attain its end. It will not do to say

14 Cfr. Cavagnis, *Institut. Iuris Eccl Pub.*, Vol. III, p 69 f, l. IV, n 117 ff

that the State offers to the Church these means, because one sovereign society cannot be at the mercy of another,— the Church subject to the State.   As to the *minor*, viz., that schools are closely connected with the end of the Church, the following observation may suffice.   In itself a school may have a merely temporal purpose, and thus be referred to the State, the end of which is to procure temporal prosperity and order, but a systematic separation between scientific training and moral development results in a one-sided education which can bear no solid and lasting fruits, because the unity of man requires an even evolution of all his faculties, intellectual as well as moral.   And since true morality cannot exist without religious principles, it naturally follows that the whole business of education is closely bound up with religion.   To provide a religious and moral training for her subjects certainly appertains to the Church, whose proper end is spiritual, religious, binding man's temporal to his eternal destiny. Neither is there any danger that religious schools will breed disloyalty or disturb the peace among citizens.   The very fact that religion teaches submission and obedience to lawful authority and love of fellowmen should be sufficient to dispel any misgiving in that direction.   This is acknowledged by honest non-Catholic politicians,[15] and the late war has amply proved that Catholics are as loyal as the members of any other denomination.

Here we may recall the law of *prescription*.   The Church it was who in the turmoil of barbarous invasions held high the torch of civilization and preserved it against the assaults of savage hordes.   To her most of the higher, cloistral and cathedral schools and universities, are indebted for their very existence and endowments.   Many of those very chairs that have been made the catapults

15 Thus Treitschke, *Vorlesungen über Politik*, I, 350.

from which poisonous missiles are hurled against the Catholic Church, owe their foundation to ecclesiastical benefices and persons.

This may suffice to illustrate can. 1375. It is not our task to outline what the State may justly claim. This would require an extensive investigation. Only one statement may be permitted. What is said in the heat of controversy cannot always be accepted as objective truth. Cavagnis [16] vindicates the following functions to the *State:* (1) It should establish schools when private citizens, or other agencies, neglect to do so; (2) It should see to it that the social and civic relations and good order are not disturbed or subverted in private schools; (3) It should repress and punish rebellious disturbances and dangerous machinations. Similar views are expressed by many other Catholic authors,[17] viz., that compulsory education, but not compulsory schooling, may be vindicated to the State, which, as Cavagnis also admits, has the greatest interest in the adequate training of its citizens. It may be quite true that these ideas are imported from the Old World, as Cardinal Manning observed,[18] and that the conditions of the New York are different; but the underlying principles must be as true here as they are there.

UNIVERSITIES, FACULTIES, AND DEGREES

Can. 1376

§ 1. Canonica constitutio catholicae studiorum Universitatis vel Facultatis Sedi Apostolicae reservatur.

§ 2. Universitas vel Facultas catholica, etiam religiosis familiis quibuslibet concredita, sua debet habere statuta a Sede Apostolica probata.

---

16 *Instit. Iuris Publ Eccl,* Vol III, p 64, l. IV, n. 107; for the rest we refer to Burns, *l. c.,* ch IX.

17 Th Meyer, S. J., *Institutiones Iuris Nat,* 1900, Vol. II, 703 ff.

18 Burns, *l. c.,* p 220.

CAN. 1377

Gradus academicos qui effectus canonicos in Ec-clesia habeant, nemo conferre potest, nisi ex facultate ab Apostolica Sede concessa.

The canonical establishment of Catholic universities and faculties is reserved to the Holy See.

These, even when entrusted to religious institutes, must have their statutes approved by the Apostolic See. No academic degree produces any canonical effect unless it has been conferred in virtue of the power granted by the Apostolic See.

The difference between a university and a faculty con-sists in this, that a university includes a so-called *studium generale,* or, in concrete words, the faculties of theology, philosophy, law, and medicine, while the term *faculty,* in its restricted and technical sense, means only one of these. If we say *studium generale* we are aware that this term was first used to signify a school which ad-mitted students from all parts, and then was transferred to the corporate body of teachers and students. To-day a university in the full sense of the word means the total of the four faculties mentioned above.[19] The term " *fac-ulty* " was originally used in the more general sense of sci-ence or knowledge; later it came to indicate some depart-ment of study, as the faculty of arts,[20] or theology, or Canon Law. In this sense it is used in our text. Univer-sities and faculties, then, which enjoy the privilege and power of conferring degrees and are acknowledged as *Catholic* universities or faculties, can be established

---

19 See *Cath. Encyc.,* Vol. XV, 188, *s. v.* " Universities."

20 See *New International Encyc.,*

1904, Vol. XIX, *s. v.* " Universities," p. 738.

only by the Holy See and must have their statutes approved by the S. C. of Seminaries and Universities.[21]

Can. 1377 is to be understood both of degrees conferred after examination and of so-called *honoris causa* degrees. It would seem that the mere acknowledgment and approval of an institution of learning by the Holy See does not convey the right of conferring academic degrees, but this right must be specially mentioned in the petition and the grant. If the Holy See grants the honorary title of doctor, this gives the recipient the same rights and privileges as the degrees conferred by a Catholic university after examination.[22]

RIGHTS ATTACHED TO THE DEGREE OF DOCTOR

CAN. 1378

Ius est doctoribus rite creatis deferendi, extra sacras functiones, annulum etiam cum gemma, et biretum doctorale, firmo praeterea praescripto sacrorum canonum, qui in collatione quorundam officiorum et beneficiorum ecclesiasticorum statuunt eos, ceteris paribus, iudicio Ordinarii, esse praeferendos, qui lauream vel licentiam obtinuerint.

Duly created doctors are entitled to wear, outside of ecclesiastical functions, a ring studded with a gem and the doctor's biretta, and the ruling of the sacred canons remains effective which says that all other things being equal, doctors and licentiates should be preferred in the appointment to ecclesiastical offices and benefices.

The doctor's ring may be worn on the same finger on which prelates wear theirs.[23] The biretta here intended is

21 Pius X, "*Sapienti Consilio,*" June 29, 1908, § 1, n. 11.

22 S. C. Stud., Dec. 19, 1903.

23 S. Rit. C., May 23, 1846, ad 5 (*Dec. Auth.,* n. 2907).

the four-cornered ecclesiastical headgear,[24] not the so-called doctor's hat. These paraphernalia may not be worn at ecclesiastical functions, especially not while saying or singing Mass.[25]

By the way it may be stated that our text grants the right to such distinctions to all duly created doctors, whether of the secular or religious clergy.

CATHOLIC SCHOOLS TO BE ESTABLISHED

CAN. 1379

§ 1. Si scholae catholicae ad normam can. 1373 sive elementariae sive mediae desint, curandum, praesertim a locorum Ordinariis, ut condantur.

§ 2. Itemque si publicae studiorum Universitates doctrina sensuque catholico imbutae non sint, optandum ut in natione vel regione Universitas catholica condatur.

§3. Fideles ne omittant adiutricem operam pro viribus conferre in catholicas scholas condendas et sustentandas.

§ 1. Where there are no *Catholic schools* in the sense of can. 1373, the church authorities, especially the local Ordinary, should take care to establish such.

§ 2. *Catholic universities* should also be founded in provinces or countries where the existing universities are not imbued with Catholic teaching and feeling.

§ 3. The *faithful should not omit to lend their aid, according to their ability,* in the establishment and support of Catholic schools.

This has been a maxim of the Church ever since univer-

24 S. Rit. C., Dec. 7, 1844, ad 1 (16 n. 2877).   25 S. Rit. C., *l. c.*, and June 30, 1883, ad VII (n. 3580).

sities and schools have taken an unchristian turn, as especially the letters of the Holy See to the Irish hierarchy emphasize.[26]

CLERICS TO PURSUE HIGHER STUDIES

CAN. 1380

Optandum ut locorum Ordinarii, pro sua prudentia, clericos, pietate et ingenio praestantes, ad scholas mittant alicuius Universitatis aut Facultatis ab Ecclesia conditae vel approbatae, ut inibi studia praesertim philosophiae, theologiae ac iuris canonici perficiant et academicos gradus consequantur.

It is desirable that the local Ordinaries should, with prudent judgment, send clerical students who excel in piety and talent, to a university or faculty either founded or approved by the Church, that they may there complete their studies, especially in philosophy, theology, and Canon Law, and obtain the academic degrees.

Honorius III already advised prelates and chapters to send talented clerics to universities for at least five years, during which teachers as well as students should be supported from ecclesiastical funds, *i. e*, benefices, by authority of the Apostolic See.

RELIGIOUS INSTRUCTION UNDER CHURCH AUTHORITY

CAN. 1381

§ 1. Religiosa iuventutis institutio in scholis quibuslibet auctoritati et inspectioni Ecclesiae subiicitur.

§ 2. Ordinariis locorum ius et officium est vigilandi ne in quibusvis scholis sui territorii quidquam contra fidem vel bonos mores tradatur aut fiat.

26 Leo XIII, " *Officio sanctissimo,*" Dec 22, 1887 *et pluries.*

§ 3. Eisdem similiter ius est approbandi religionis magistros et libros; itemque, religionis morumque causa, exigendi ut tum magistri tum libri removeantur.

§ 1. The *religious instruction* of the young in all schools is subject to the *authority and inspection of the Church*. This law, it would seem, should need no special stressing, yet it is a sad fact that the Apostolic See had more than once to complain of encroachments on its rights by the civil authorities. Pius IX in his Syllabus proscribed the proposition that the direction of the schools in which the Christian youth are educated, should be entirely withdrawn from the jurisdiction of ecclesiastical authority and given to the civil government. This is a confusion of the sphere of the two societies, Church and State, since religious instruction belongs without a shadow of doubt to the teaching office of the Church by divine right.[27]

§ 2 ascribes to the local Ordinaries the right and duty to watch that in the schools of their territory nothing contrary to faith and morals be taught or done.[28]

There may be a difficulty concerning national or government schools, such as existed in Ireland in the middle of the last century,[29] or as our American public schools, which are under municipal or State authority, entirely withdrawn from the influence of any religious denomination. Here much depends upon the local school board, the directors, and the superintendents, but also upon legislation. Catholic citizens have a powerful weapon in their hands in their vote. The ecclesiastical authorities should prudently draw attention to obnoxious teachers

27 *Syllabus Pii IX*, nn 45, 47 (Denzinger, nn 1593, 1595)

28 *Ibid.*, Pius IX, " *Quum non* sine,*" July 14, 1864; cfr. Math. 28, 19 f

29 S. C. P. F., April 7, 1680 (*Coll*, n. 1190).

and books. The pastors may counteract the bad influence by alertness and the intensified teaching of religion. But all these remedies are insufficient and the necessity of having Catholic schools of our own is imperative.

Of general interest is an instruction of the Holy Office [30] given Aug. 22, 1900, to the bishop of Jassy in Roumenia. There, on account of peculiar circumstances, Catholic schools were permitted to receive schismatic pupils, but only on several conditions, namely: (a) that no danger to faith or morals arise from the practice to the Catholic and schismatic students; (b) that Catholic school boards shall not employ schismatic catechists, though they may permit the schismatics to maintain such at their own expense; (c) that neither Catholic nor schismatic catechists teach the " interdenominational " catechism, *i. e.*, a doctrine which is acceptable to both; (d) that non-Catholics must not be admitted as teachers of metaphysics, ethics, and allied branches; though they may be permitted to teach languages, mathematics, and natural sciences under the supervision of the Catholic schoolboard; (e) that no textbooks, even of profane sciences, written by non-Catholics may be used unless they are known to contain no error, or have been corrected. These rules, as stated, concern only schools governed by Catholic school boards; but they contain some hints which may be applied to our public schools.

§ 3. The local Ordinaries also have the right to *approve the teachers and text-books* of religion and to demand that teachers or books that offend against faith and morals, *be removed.*

The underlying principle is always the same: the teaching of religion belongs to the Church, and the State cannot usurp it without infringing upon a divine right.

30 *Coll P. F.*, n 2093.

SCHOOL INSPECTION BY THE LOCAL ORDINARIES

CAN. 1382

Ordinarii locorum sive ipsi per se sive per alios possunt quoque scholas quaslibet, oratoria, recreatoria, patronatus, etc., in iis quae religiosam et moralem institutionem spectant, visitare; a qua visitatione quorumlibet religiosorum scholae exemptae non sunt, nisi agatur de scholis internis pro professis religionis exemptae.

The local Ordinaries are entitled, either personally or through a delegate, to inspect any school, oratory, asylum,[31] orphanage, etc., in all things concerning religious and moral education. This right of inspection includes the schools of religious with the sole exception of purely internal schools intended for the members of exempt religious institutes.

The Council of Trent vindicated to the bishops the right of visiting all hospitals, colleges, and religious or charitable institutions, except those placed under royal protection.[32] No appeal was or is allowed from this law,[33] but our text, because it concerns schools only, restricts this right of visitation to moral and religious instruction. Our canon covers all schools, elementary, secondary, academic and collegiate, all faculties and universities; none may claim exemption, for the text says: "*quaslibet scholas.*" The reason is because the bishops are the judges in all matters of faith and morals. Theirs is a doctrinal superintendence which they cannot divide with the civil government.

31 *Recreatoria*, from the Italian *ricreatori*, means asylums for the poor or the aged, also conservatories for boys and girls; *patronatus* is generally understood of orphanages, but it may also mean any institution of advowson

32 Sess 22, c 8, *De Ref.*

33 Bened. XIV, "*Ad militantis*," March 30, 1742, § 31.

Universities which are under the immediate protection of the Holy See, cannot be canonically visited by bishops, but only by the Sovereign Pontiff or his legitimate representative.[34]

The domestic or internal schools of exempt religious, established for the sole use of professed members, are not subject to episcopal visitation; but all other schools, as well as orphanages,[35] colleges and faculties conducted by these religious, including the scholasticate, may be inspected by the local Ordinary in the points mentioned, and none other.[36]

CAN. 1383

In religiosa alumnorum alicuius collegii institutione servetur praescriptum can. 891.

In regard to the religious training of college students, can. 1383 recalls the rule laid down in can. 891, namely, that the rector should not habitually hear the confessions of the students.

[34] S C. C., Aug. 1, Sept 1, 1888
A. S. S., XI, 674 ff).
[35] S C. EE et RR , May 14, 1872
(*Coll. P. F.*, n. 1386).

[36] Leo XIII, " *Romanos Pontifices,*" May 8, 1881.

THE CENSORSHIP AND PROHIBITION OF BOOKS

RIGHT OF THE CHURCH

Can. 1384

§ 1. Ecclesiae est ius exigendi ne libros, quos ipsa iudicio suo antea non recognoverit, fideles edant, et a quibusvis editos ex iusta causa prohibendi.

§ 2. Quae sub hoc titulo de libris praescribuntur, publicationibus diariis, periodicis et aliis editis scriptis quibuslibet applicentur, nisi aliud constet.

The Church has the right to demand that the faithful shall not publish books which she has not previously approved by her judgment; she also has the right to forbid for a just reason books published by whomsoever.

The first refers to preventive censorship (*praevia librorum censura*) which touches Catholics only; whereas the second vindicates to the Church the right of prohibiting any and all books which she considers objectionable. The wording of the former clause is rather broad, for it would seem to include all kinds of books, even such on mathematics, agriculture, etc. However this law must be understood in the light of, and by comparison with, the canons of chapter 1, *infra*.

The text says that the Church has the right to censor and forbid books. As to previous censorship there can be no doubt, because the faithful, as well as the matter itself, are subject to the authority of the Church, to whom all Catholics owe obedience in whatever refers to their salvation. Nevertheless the censorship has often been made the target of violent attacks. These attacks are unfounded. Paternal as well as political authorities have the *natural right* to ward off anything that may endanger the moral and physical welfare of their subjects, and to protect them against bad surroundings, company, literature, etc., in fact anything that is apt to cause insubordination, anarchy, or moral decay. The Church, being an autonomous society, with subjects for whom she is responsible within her own sphere cannot be destitute of the authority and power which enables her to keep her children uncontaminated and to safeguard them against the danger of perversion. Of all the dangers that imperil man's salvation bad literature is perhaps the most destructive. Hence the right to control the reading of her children cannot be denied the Church even from the purely natural point of vantage. Historical facts amply confirm the necessity of preventive censorship in Church and State.[1]

The Church, by divine right, is the *guardian and teacher of faith and morals,* the shepherd who must lead his sheep upon wholesome pasture and point out the poisonous weeds that endanger their welfare. This office requires repressive and preventive remedies which the Church is certainly allowed to apply in teaching and preserving the deposit of faith. One of these remedies is the censorship of books.[2] This has been *always exercised by the Church,* not indeed to the same extent and in

---

[1] Cfr. the classical work of J. Hilgers, S J., *Der Index der verbotenen Bucher,* 1904.

[2] Hilgers, *l. c.,* p 15 ff.; see also *The Ave Maria,* Notre Dame, Ind , Jan. 31, 1920, pp. 148 ff.

the same way, but in various ways and by different methods according to the exigencies of the times.[3]   The Apostles frequently warned the faithful against the baneful influence of a too intimate intercourse with the enemies of Christianity either in word or writing.[4]   The first express prohibition of a book is that of Arius' *Thalia*, which was forbidden by the Council of Nicaea (325).   Then followed the lists, which look like incipient indices, of Popes Innocent I and Gelasius I, in which, besides the authentic books of the Old and New Testament, certain "apocryphal" books are enumerated.[5]   Gregory the Great (590–604), Martin I (649–654), and Zachary (741–752) drew up new lists, and the practice was continued in the Middle Ages.

It goes without saying that the *invention of printing* called for more extensive and severer measures.   Innocent VIII, Alexander VI, and Leo X commanded printers to submit all books to be printed to the ecclesiastical authorities for approval.   An index of forbidden books in the modern sense of the word was that of Paul IV, published in 1559.   It was followed by that of 1571, under the pontificate of St. Pius V, and others, which later were made superfluous by the more comprehensive index issued in 1758.   This, together with the Constitution "*Sollicita ac provida*" of Benedict XIV (July 9, 1753) remained in force with scarcely any modification until Leo XIII issued his well-known Constitution " *Officiorum ac munerum,*" Jan. 25, 1897.

3 Hilgers, pp 3 ff.; Hurley, *A Commentary on the Present Index Legislation*, 1908, p 23 ff.

4 I Tim. 6, 20, II Tim. 2, 16, Acts 19, 19.

5 Innocent I, Ep 6, *ad Excep.*, c. 7 (Migne *P. L*, 20, 501 f); Gelasius' decree, see in c. 3, Dist. 16; the authenticity has given rise to doubts (Zahn, *Geschichte des Neutestam. Kanons*, 1890, II, 1, 259 f.), which, however, are not borne out by solid critical research.

This constitution, as such, is now superseded by the Code insofar as it does not agree with the latter. At the same time it is well to remember that the wording, and sometimes even the substance, of the old law will assist us in determining the nature and extension of the new rules.[6]

§ 2 extends the meaning of the term *books* so as to include newspapers and other periodical publications as well as all other published writings, unless the contrary is manifest[7]

Strictly speaking a *book* is a volume[8] consisting of a number of sheets of paper, now-a-days generally printed, and either bound or stitched together, which treats of one subject in a more or less coherent and systematic manner. It is generally held that a book must have some bulk (*aliqua moles*), that is, it should have at least 160 pages. Our text as well as the Constitution of Leo XIII draw a distinction between books and leaflets, etc. The *unitas objecti* is an essential feature of a book Magazines, as a rule, do not treat of only one subject and hence, even if they are bound, do not constitute a book in the technical sense. But if a treatise is published in loose numbers (*fasciculi*), so as to form one whole, the term " book " applies to it. As to the manner of publication it must be observed that now-a-days by *book* we generally mean a *printed* volume, when we use the term without any further attribute. But a book need not necessarily be printed to be a book, else the manuscript treatises published before 1600 could not have been prohibited as books. Our text quite consistently applies the general

6 Hurley, *l. c*, p 51.

7 This is a decidedly new regulation for which Card. Gasparri could give no quotation.

8 Noldin, *Theol. Moralis,* Vol II, 1914, n. 701, p 726 f.

prohibition to all writings, no matter how published, so they be but *published, i. e.,* made accessible to all. As long as a manuscript or book remains the exclusive private property of the author, it cannot be called *editus.* A printer is not *eo ipso* a publisher (*editor*). An *author* may write a book for his own pleasure and have it printed; as long as he keeps it entirely to himself, it is not " published."

CHAPTER I

Previous censorship consists in the submission of a book to the proper authority for inspection, examination, and approval (or rejection). The law binds the author as well as the publisher, placing both under the obligation of submitting an intended publication to the proper authority. If the *imprimatur,* or permission to have the book published, is given, this means not an approval of its contents, but only the judgment of the respective authority that the book may, under present circumstances, be read without detriment to faith or morals.[1]

CAN. 1385

§ 1. Nisi censura ecclesiastica praecesserit, ne edantur etiam a laicis:

1.° Libri sacrarum Scripturarum vel eorundem adnotationes et commentaria;

2.° Libri qui divinas Scripturas, sacram theologiam, historiam ecclesiasticam, ius canonicum, theologiam naturalem, ethicen aliasve huiusmodi religiosas ac morales disciplinas spectant; libri ac libelli precum, devotionis vel doctrinae institutionisque religiosae, moralis, asceticae, mysticae aliique huiusmodi, quamvis ad fovendam pietatem conducere videantur; ac generaliter scripta in quibus aliquid sit quod religionis ac morum honestatis peculiariter intersit;

1 Noldin, *l c* , n 708, p 734.

3.° Imagines sacrae quovis modo imprimendae, sive preces adiunctas habeant, sive sine illis edantur.

§ 2. Licentiam edendi libros et imagines de quibus in § 1, dare potest vel loci Ordinarius proprius auctoris, vel Ordinarius loci in quo libri vel imagines publici iuris fiant, vel Ordinarius loci in quo imprimantur, ita tamen ut, si quis ex iis Ordinariis licentiam denega- verit, eam ab alio Ordinario petere auctor nequeat, nisi eundem certiorem fecerit de denegata ab alio licentia.

§ 3. Religiosi vero licentiam quoque sui Superioris maioris antea consequi debent.

This canon first lays down a general rule as to what books must be submitted to ecclesiastical censorship, and then designates the authority competent to grant the im- primatur.

§ 1. The following books, even though published by laymen, must be submitted to ecclesiastical censure:

1.° The *Books of Holy Writ* and annotations to and commentaries on the same.

Hence the *original text* of each and every one of the forty-five books of the Old Testament and the twenty- eight books of the New Testament must be submitted to ecclesiastical censorship. Also parts of the same (*peri- copes*) and *translations* or versions, whether old or new. *Old versions* are the Latin Vulgate as well as the Itala, the Oriental versions of the Septuagint, the Syriac, Coptic, and Armenian. *New versions* are those made into mod- ern languages. These translations must be submitted, even if only parts or *pericopes* are to be published, for instance, the Epistles and Gospels for Sundays and holy days. For the text simply says "*libri sacrarum Scriptu- rarum*," and can 1384, § 2 finds its application here.

Adnotationes are short explanations or glosses, either

continuous or partial, such as were made on single words between the lines or in the margin, and are now generally placed at the foot of the page (foot-notes). It does not matter whether these notes are printed separately from, or together with, the text, whether they are original or translated, as our canon simply says, *vel*. Nor are foot-notes on the pericopes exempt from this law.

Commentaries are treatises in the form of annotations or explanations of the books of the Old and New Testament, altogether or severally. What was said concerning annotations also holds with regard to commentaries.

2.° The second paragraph of § 1 mentions three classes of books as subject to ecclesiastical censorship, namely, scientific, devotional, and general, especially,

(a) Books treating of Holy Scripture, sacred theology, Church history, Canon Law, theodicy, ethics, and other religious and moral disciplines.

"Books on *Holy Scripture*" here means the treatises called *introductions,* not works of exegesis proper, for the latter, being in the nature of a commentary, falls under no. 1. Introduction includes hermeneutics and "higher criticism," so-called.[2]

"Sacred theology" embraces treatises on dogmatic as well as moral theology, either single tracts, or the whole, written in any language, and published in any form.

"*Church history,*" which is the scientific knowledge of the internal and external development of the Society founded by Jesus Christ, may be written as chronicles or in the form of general accounts, biographies, monographs, etc. It is true that the Church is distinct from the individuals that compose it,[3] but if any individual, for instance, St. Augustine,[4] is treated as the representative of a period

2 Pius X, "*Lamentabili*," July 4, 1904, prop. 1.

3 Hurley, *l. c.,* p. 209

4 See Von Hertling's *Augustinus*

or school of thought, the biography becomes part and parcel of ecclesiastical history. Therefore such a book must be submitted to censorship. The law does not, however, apply to purely secular or political history. The scope, then, or purpose of a book marks the dividing line.

As to *Canon Law*, we all know that this is a distinctly ecclesiastical discipline.

Natural Theology, or Theodicy is that part of philosophy which treats of God and His relations to His creatures from the standpoint of reason unaided by Revelation.

Ethics or moral philosophy, has for its object the moral rectitude of human acts in accordance with the ultimate principles of reason. To this discipline belong books on sociology, unless they are written from the merely economical or political viewpoint.

It would be difficult to explain the phrase, "*other such religious or moral disciplines*," since the sciences expressly mentioned seem to exhaust the subject. Treatises on Spiritism, hypnotism, astrology (formerly also alchemy) must find a place here because they usually touch religion and morals.

(b) Liable to censorship are furthermore: *large and small prayer-books and devotional, catechetical, moral, ascetical, mystical, and the like books and pamplets, even though* they seem to foster piety. To this class belong Bible histories, missals with vernacular translation, catechisms, lives of Saints, the Imitation of Christ, and similar books [5] Of a mystic character are "The City of God"

("*Weltgeschichte in Karakterbild-ern*") Mainz, 1902, without episcopal imprimatur.

[5] S. C. P. F, Jan. 3, 1777 (*Coll.* n. 519); S. Rit C, Aug. 4, 1877

(*Dec. Auth.*, n. 3427), also the translations of the *Officium Parvum B. M V.;* S. Rit. C., April 24, 1896, ad 1 (n. 3827).

by Mary of Agreda, the writings of Anne Catherine Emmerich, St. Catharine of Genoa, and others. Devotion is not always piety and devotional writings require particular vigilance. We may also place in this class all prophesies, private revelations, visions, etc., as well as new devotions of every kind.

(c) The law finally subjects to ecclesiastical censorship *" all writings which contain anything that particularly concerns religion and morals."* No distinction is made between books, but all are comprised that deal in any way with religion or morality. The phrase *" peculiariter intersit "* must be referred to the manner in which the subject is treated *" Peculiariter "* is opposed to *" obiter "* or *" perfunctorie."* The manner of treatment must be measured by the length of the article or treatise A long treatise would not savor peculiarly of religion or morality, if it contained only one or the other sentence bearing on those subjects.

A question has been raised regarding so-called *temperance leaflets.*[6] We will state our opinion fairly and squarely. If these leaflets advocate absolute prohibition, they should be forbidden, for prohibition is opposed to the natural law and clearly touches ethics If they are merely intended to promote temperance, such leaflets come under the category of moral writings, because temperance is one of the four cardinal virtues which in the natural order belong to ethics, and in the supernatural order, to moral theology. From every viewpoint, therefore, these leaflets are subject to the censorship of the Church.

3.° *Sacred images,* no matter how printed, and whether with or without prayers, fall under ecclesiastical censor-

6 Cfr. Hurley, *l. c*, p 214 f

ship. It is evident that only stamped or printed images are intended here, because the text refers only to books or things published in the form of printed matter. But of these all kinds, new and old,[7] are included,— engravings, photographs, chromos, lithographs, etc., etc. Not included are oil or water-colors and statues. If an image belong to the class of printed matter, it is immaterial how customary or unusual it be; for here not the *insolita imago* of can. 1279 is intended, but the image as such, provided, of course, it be *sacred*. Sacred images are all representations of the Blessed Trinity, of our Lord Jesus Christ, of the Blessed Virgin, of the Angels, Saints, and Blessed. Also images which represent a religious mystery, or a sacred scene, or groups of biblical events, or emblems representative of mysteries. The text says it matters not whether such images are printed with or without prayers. If a prayer is added, either at the bottom or on the back, the picture also falls under no. 2 of our canon.

§ 2 and § 3. The permission to publish books and images mentioned in § 1 may be granted by the local Ordinary of the author, or by the local Ordinary of the place of publication, or, finally, by the local Ordinary of the place where the books, etc., are printed. However, if any one of these Ordinaries refuses the *imprimatur,* the author is not allowed to ask it of another, unless the latter has been informed of the refusal.

Religious must obtain the permission of their superiors before applying for the episcopal imprimatur

---

[7] The text does not contain the adjective "*notae*" found in the "*Officiorum ac munerum,*" n 15, hence Vermeersch's view that new designs only must be submitted (*Comm,* n. 20), no longer holds. Not included are *medals,* because these are not printed, but struck; see Vermeersch, *l. c.*

Our text is wider than that of the Leonine constitution [8] in admitting three Ordinaries as competent to give the imprimatur. It is also more liberal in regard to Bible editions, as will be seen under can. 1391. The local *Ordinary* of course is the bishop or the vicar-general, or whoever goes by that name. Since superiors of exempt religious are not local Ordinaries in the meaning of the Code, it would be evident, even if it were not mentioned in § 3, that such religious are not exempt from the obligation of asking the imprimatur of the diocesan bishop; but they may do so through their publisher or printer.

If the local Ordinary himself wishes to publish a book, he needs no imprimatur, even though the book were printed and published outside of his diocese.[9] The reason is that the author's Ordinary may give the *imprimatur*, who, in our case, is the author himself.

Which of the three Ordinaries mentioned should be asked to give the imprimatur is left to the judgment of the author. But in order to prevent deception and to uphold ecclesiastical authority, it is required that in case one of the three Ordinaries has refused the imprimatur, this fact must be stated to the other who is asked for the imprimatur. The latter will probably demand the reasons for the refusal either from the refusing Ordinary or from the author.

Religious, exempt as well as non-exempt, also need the permission of their superiors, who ought to subject every book that is to be published to an examination by competent scholars.[10]

8 " *Officiorum ac munerum,*" nn 7, 35.

9 Formerly, as Noldin states (1 c., n. 710), an Ordinary needed the *imprimatur* of another Ordinary if his book was published outside his own diocese

10 *Trid*, Sess. 4, *De Editione et Usu SS Librorum*, the superiors may abide by the verdict of the censors.

Whether rule 37 of the "Officiorum ac munerum" still holds, may well be doubted. This rule prescribed that if an author residing in Rome wished to have a book printed elsewhere than in the City, he needed only the approval of the Cardinal Vicar and the Master of the Sacred Palace. This rule rather restricts liberty and is not in accord with § 2 of can. 1385. Therefore we hardly believe that one would be obliged to abide by it, unless a local custom or written particular law would be super-added to said § 2.

OBLIGATIONS OF CLERICS AND LAYMEN

CAN. 1386

§ 1. Vetantur clerici saeculares sine consensu suorum Ordinariorum, religiosi vero sine licentia sui Superioris maioris et Ordinarii loci, libros quoque, qui de rebus profanis tractent, edere, et in diariis, foliis vel libellis periodicis scribere vel eadem moderari.

§ 2. In diariis vero, foliis vel libellis periodicis qui religionem catholicam aut bonos mores impetere solent, nec laici catholici quidpiam conscribant, nisi iusta ac rationabili causa suadente, ab Ordinario loci probata.

§ 1. The secular clergy without the consent of their Ordinary, and religious without the permission of their higher superior and of the local Ordinary, are forbidden to publish books on secular subjects and to write for newspapers or other periodicals, publications, or to act as editors of such. The consent of the Ordinary is here clearly distinct from censorship proper, which requires a scientific examination, whereas the consent only means a judgment connected with the manifestation of an act of the will.   However this does not take away from the bishop the right of demanding specimen copies of a publication or the title thereof; nor does it prevent the bishop from refusing his consent if he thinks the author or editor incapable of treating the subject correctly and creditably.

This consent is required even for literary products of a purely worldly or technical character, no science or topic being excepted.[11]   The reason is given in the above-mentioned Constitution of Leo XIII, to wit, "to give an example of ready obedience."   Prompt submission is also required in two other cases; viz.: when clerics wish to contribute to periodic publications or if they desire to act as managers or editors of such publications as *diaria, folia, libelli periodici.   Diaria* are newspapers, daily, weekly, or biweekly.   *Folia* are publications published more or less irregularly, of undetermined size or number of pages, be they leaflets or brochures.   *Libelli periodici* are quarterly, monthly, fortnightly, weekly, etc., magazines or reviews.

To write for such publications, therefore, the secular clergy need the permission of the bishop to whom they are subject, regardless of where the paper or magazine is printed or published.   For the text simply says, "*suorum*," which refers to the clergy, not to the publication. If we say, "to *whom they are subject*," we mean habitually or legally, by virtue of incardination.   Therefore a clergyman on his vacation, who wishes to contribute to a periodical publication, must obtain permission from his own bishop, not from the Ordinary in whose diocese he is sojourning.[12]

11 S C pro Negot Eccl. Extraord., June 27, 1902, n. 3 (*Anal. Eccl*, X, 73).

12 The local Ordinary of religious is the bishop in whose diocese their house is located; but we believe that

The question naturally arises whether clergymen and religious need the simple or double permission for *each and every article* they contribute to any periodic publication. From former legislation it would seem that regular correspondence or contributions are intended. Such at least is the tenor of the "*Sacrorum Antistitum,*" of Sept. 1, 1910, from which our text is evidently taken: "*Ad sacerdotes quod attinet, qui correspondentium vel collaboratorum nomine vulgo veniunt, etc.*" We would not press the term "*scribere*" in our text, though this, too, would seem to involve habitual writing. Hence we hardly believe that a brief occasional article would need episcopal consent. To say that the publication of a notice of a church festival, or parish event, or funeral required the special consent of the Ordinary or religious superior, would render the law ridiculous. On the other hand, a treatise or an elaborate article on any important subject, especially if it touches faith and morals, or ecclesiastical discipline, no doubt falls under the law. Also any important manuscript which religious would like to publish. Nor may religious with either simple or solemn vows publish their writings anonymously or under an assumed name, even with the local Ordinary's permission, if their superior has refused to give his imprimatur.[13]

It may be added that *female religious,* too, must abide by this law.

"*Eadem moderari,*" to direct or manage periodical publications, also requires a double permission for religious, and the permission of the ordinary for secular clerics. This prohibition concerns the management or directorship of all newspapers, pamphlets, and periodicals without ex-

the local Ordinary of any diocese in which a religious lives for some time, may give the required permission, especially in the case of exempt religious

13 Hurley, *l c.,* p. 228.

ception. The canon here is somewhat stricter, at least in its wording, than the old law, but more logical and consistent.

Are *college papers* included? The text does not make a distinction, and hence they, too, need the permission of the local Ordinary in whose diocese the board of managers live, and of the religious superior, if religious are on the board of directors. But if lay students constitute the board, they need no permission from the local Ordinary. Female religious, however, do, no matter how pious the title of their magazine may sound.

What *if the Ordinary refuses* to consent to the publication of a book treating of secular matters only? In that case the author would do well to abide by the bishop's decision, provided there is no reason to assume personal spite. He may, however, demand the reason of the refusal. For although the Holy Office does not need to state its reasons, this prerogative cannot be extended to the bishops, and the S. Congregation of the Index decided that bishops must give their reasons for refusing the imprimatur in case a book is susceptible to correction.[14]

The author has another expedient, namely that offered in can. 1385, § 2; which allows him to seek another publisher or printer. In doing so an author would only be claiming a natural right.

§ 2. Not even *Catholic laymen* — much less clergymen and religious — may write for newspapers, pamphlets or other periodical publications which are accustomed to at-

---

14 S. C. Ind, Sept. 3, 1898, quoted by Hurley, who, in a circuitous way, concludes that the bishop is not bound to state the reasons (*l. c.*, p 200, 224 f); if he is bound to give his reasons in matters of faith and morals, he is surely also obliged to state his reasons for refusing to permit the publication of books of a profane nature; the contrary opinion is frivolous and unworthy of the episcopal office.

tack the Catholic faith or good morals. An exception to this rule may be made only for a just and valid reason, acknowledged to be such by the local Ordinary.

The publications to which even Catholic laymen should not contribute by way of correspondence or collaboration have been named above. Here a special class is singled out which is distinguished by its wicked purpose, *i. e.,* those which habitually attack the Catholic faith or good morals. Is our so-called *yellow press* included in this class of publications? It would be difficult to give a positive answer to this question. For we cannot say that they make it a practice to attack the Catholic faith, though, on the other hand, their scandalous reports on suicides, divorces, etc., are anything but favorable to good morals. Yet as these reports are not strictly attacks on morality, the solution depends on the general tendency of these publications. We think it must be admitted that regular contributions from Catholic pens might promote the sale of an objectionable paper and thereby further religious indifferentism. The law expressly permits extraordinary or occasional contributions for solid reasons. Thus, for instance, if a prelate or prominent priest is interviewed on an important public question, it might be permissible, nay even desirable, that he explain the Catholic position. Again a correction, or the defence of Catholic teaching against an attack might prove useful for the reason that it would reach parties which a Catholic paper could not reach.

VARIOUS EXCEPTIONS

CAN. 1387

Quae ad causas beatificationum et canonizationum Servorum Dei quoquo modo pertinent, sine licentia Sacrorum Rituum Congregationis edi nequeunt.

CAN. 1388

§ 1. Indulgentiarum libri omnes, summaria, libelli, folia, etc., in quibus earum concessiones continentur, ne edantur sine licentia Ordinarii loci.

§ 2. Requiritur vero expressa licentia Sedis Apostolicae ut typis edere liceat, quovis idiomate, tum collectionem authenticam precum piorumque operum quibus Sedes Apostolica indulgentias annexuit, tum elenchum indulgentiarum apostolicarum, tum summarium indulgentiarum vel antea collectum, sed nunquam approbatum, vel nunc primum ex diversis concessionibus colligendum.

CAN. 1389

Collectiones decretorum Romanarum Congregationum rursus edi nequeunt, nisi impetrata prius licentia et servatis conditionibus a Moderatoribus uniuscuiusque Congregationis praescriptis.

CAN. 1390

In edendis libris liturgicis eorumque partibus, itemque litaniis a Sancta Sede approbatis, debet de concordantia cum editionibus approbatis constare ex attestatione Ordinarii loci in quo imprimuntur aut publici iuris fiunt.

Matters pertaining to the *canonization and beatification* of servants of God may not be published without the permission of the S. Congregation of Rites. Urban VIII already ordered that the lives, deeds, and miracles of the venerable servants of God should not be published without the approval of the Ordinary, who had to report each case to the Apostolic See, *i. e.*, the S. Congregation of Rites, in order that frauds, mistakes, and novelties might be avoided.[15]

Can. 1388 refers to books, summaries, booklets, leaflets, etc., containing *grants of indulgences*. These may not be published without the permission of the local Ordinary. The express permission of the *Holy See* is required for publishing, in any language, *authentic collections of prayers and good works* enriched with indulgences by the Apostolic See. The same express permission is required for publishing lists of papal indulgences, and summaries of indulgences, either already collected but not yet approved, or to be made from various grants. Concerning this we refer to can. 919, § 2.

Can. 1389 demands the permission of the respective officials for the republication of *collections of the various Roman Congregations*. If such permission is granted, the conditions laid down by the heads of the respective congregations must be faithfully complied with. What those conditions are is not explicitly stated. One of them is that the original text must be reproduced *ad literam*. Another one undoubtedly will be that a copy of the reprint shall be forwarded to the Cardinal Prefect or Secretary of the respective Congregation, provided permission for *republication* is given.

Notice the phrase, "*rursus edi*"; it supposes that a collection has already been made and published, as those of the S. Rit. C. and the Propaganda.

Can. 1390 concerns the *publication of liturgical books,* or parts thereof, and litanies approved by the Holy See. Reprints of these must agree with the approved text, and the Ordinary of the place where they are printed or pub-

---

15 "*Coelestis Hierusalem,*" July 5, 1634, § 1; S. Rit. C., July 31, 1821 (n. 2617).

lished must testify to such conformity. Of this enough has been said under canons 1257, 1259, and 1264.

CAN. 1391

Versiones sacrarum Scripturarum in linguam vernaculam typis imprimi nequeunt, nisi sint a Sede Apostolica probatae, aut nisi edantur sub vigilantia Episcoporum et cum adnotationibus praecipue excerptis ex sanctis Ecclesiae Patribus atque ex doctis catholicisque scriptoribus.

Translations of Holy Scripture into the vernacular may not be printed, unless they are approved by the Apostolic See or published under the supervision of the bishops, and are provided with notes taken chiefly from the Holy Fathers and learned and orthodox writers.

By Holy Scripture here is understood the text of the Old and New Testament. The plural seems to indicate that parts of Holy Writ are also intended. Hence even a portion of the Old Testament, say the Law, the Prophets and Ketubim, separately taken, fall under this rule; also the Gospels and the Epistles of St. Paul, when translated into the *vernacular*. Old versions, like the Syriac and Latin, which cannot be called vernacular in the proper sense, are excluded. But Arabic, English, French, German, Indian, Italian, Spanish, and the modern Slavic languages, also Chinese and Japanese, are vernacular, and translations of the Bible or any part thereof into any of these languages fall under the present canon, no matter whether the translators are Catholics or non-Catholics.

The *approving authority* is twofold: the Apostolic See and the bishop, the latter under certain conditions only.

(a) The *Holy See* may approve any versions with or without notes; it may even — which is, however, not likely to occur — approve translations made by non-Catholics;

(b) The bishop may approve any translation made under his supervision. *"Vigilantia episcoporum"* here has a special meaning, namely, that the translation must be carefully compared with the original text approved by the Church, or, at least, must substantially agree with a translation already approved.

Of course, a difficulty may arise from the fact that, with the exception of the Latin Vulgate, there is no approved original text,— the Greek text, and much more so the Hebrew-Massoretic text, being subject to many variants. The episcopal censor, therefore, had better keep to the Latin text, but he may make use of the original in doubtful cases. The translator as well as the censor must keep in mind the following canon, 1392.

But supervision is not enough; notes are also required. These notes should be taken from two sources, the writings of the Fathers and learned Catholic authors. The period of the *"Fathers,"* as is generally assumed, ends with the death of Isidore of Seville, A D 636 After that time we speak of Catholic writers The prescribed annotations may be taken from the original works of the " Fathers " or from the current " Catenae," so they be but genuine. The Catholic authors here intended are not only those of the Scholastic period, but also of modern times, provided only they be really Catholic and learned. Purely mystic or devotional writings, where the allegorical sense of the text is unduly emphasized, should be entirely discarded, or at least used sparingly.

Our text employs a term which is not to be found in

Pope Leo's Constitution; it is the word *praecipue,* signifying that the notes should be taken *chiefly* from Catholic authors. This seems to imply that non-Catholic writers need not be entirely neglected. The historical and archaeological explanations and the critical readings of non-Catholic scholars may therefore find a place in the translations approved by the bishops.

WHEN A NEW APPROBATION IS DEMANDED

CAN. 1392

§ 1. Approbatio textus originalis alicuius operis, neque eiusdem in aliam linguam translationibus neque aliis editionibus suffragatur; quare et translationes et novae editiones operis approbati nova approbatione communiri debent.

§ 2. Excerpta e periodicis capita seorsim edita novae editiones non censentur nec proinde nova approbatione indigent.

§ 1. The approbation of the original text of a work does not imply approbation of translations into other languages or of new editions; therefore translations as well as new editions of a work already approved need a new approbation. Thus, for instance, a translation of the Little Office of the B. M V. into the vernacular needs a new approbation every time it is republished. The Ordinary may grant this approbation if the text agrees with that approved by the Church, which agreement is left to the conscientious judgment of the bishop [16] to determine. The same rule applies to translations of the Roman Missal.[17]

16 S Rit. C, Sept. 4, 1875 (n. 3373).   17 S. Rit. C, Aug. 4, 1877 (n. 3427).

One remark must, however, be added.   Our text speaks
of *editions* and translations.   From this it must be con-
cluded that mere *reprints,* either phototyped or lineotyped,
accurately reproduced, require no new approbation.   For
it is evident that the purpose of the law is to prevent
fraud or corruption of the original text.

§ 2. Extracts or *excerpts* from periodicals, published
separately, are not new editions and therefore require no
new approbation [18]   If these so-called reprints (in French
tirages à part) cover a series of articles and develop
into a book and are published in book form, do they require ecclesiastical approbation?   We believe with Noldin [19] that they do, for the reason that the text mentions
only *excerpta capita,* single extracts or chapters.   Besides,
there is always danger that such a reprinted book may
contain substantial changes from the original text as published in the periodical.

Reprints of single articles, or, if the same subject was
treated in two or three issues of a periodical, of several
articles forming one chapter or treatise, need no new
approbation.

DIOCESAN CENSORS

CAN. 1393

§ 1. In universis Curiis episcopalibus censores ex
officio adsint, qui edenda cognoscant.

§ 2. Examinatores in suo obeundo officio, omni personarum acceptione deposita, tantummodo prae oculis
habeant Ecclesiae dogmata et communem catholico-
rum doctrinam quae Conciliorum generalium decretis
aut Sedis Apostolicae constitutionibus seu praescri-

---

18 S C Ind , May 23, 1898, ad 3   19 *De Praeceptis,* 1914, ed 11, n
(*Coll P F.,* n 2000)   706, p. 732 f.

ptionibus atque probatorum doctorum consensu continetur.

§ 3. Censores ex utroque clero eligantur aetate, eruditione, prudentia commendati, qui in doctrinis probandis improbandisque medio tutoque itinere eant.

§ 4. Censor sententiam scripto dare debet. Quae si faverit, Ordinarius potestatem edendi faciat, cui tamen praeponatur censoris iudicium, inscripto eius nomine. Extraordinariis tantum in adiunctis ac perquam raro, prudenti Ordinarii arbitrio, censoris mentio omitti poterit.

§ 5. Auctoribus censoris nomen pateat nunquam, antequam hic faventem sententiam ediderit.

These rules are chiefly taken from the Motu proprio of Pius X, *"Sacrorum Antistitum,"* of Sept. 1, 1910, which was directed against Modernism.[20] They are:

§ 1. *Every diocese must have officially appointed censors,* for the examination of writings that are to be published. *Ex officio* means that there should be a regular censor, not merely one chosen for an emergency. The diocesan censors should be mentioned in the Catholic Directory.

§ 2 The *examiners* in discharging their office, should set aside all human respect and guide themselves solely by the dogmatic teaching of the Church as contained in the decrees of the general councils, in papal constitutions and decisions, and in the consent of approved doctors. This does not mean, however, that any opinion or system tolerated by the Church is to be condemned if it does not fit in with the views of the censor.

---

20 Of course, these rules are not entirely new, having been to a great extent, embodied in former documents like that of Clement VIII on the Index, Benedict XIV, *"Sollicita ac provida,"* July 8, 1753, etc, see Hilgers, *l c*, p 12, p 59 f ; p. 535 ff , *A Ap S* , II, 661.

§ 3. The censors should be taken from *both the secular and the regular clergy,* and be men of mature age, distinguished by learning and prudence, who can safely keep the golden mean in approving or rejecting doctrines.

§ 4. The censor must give his verdict in *writing.* If the verdict is favorable, the Ordinary shall give his permission to publish (*i. e.,* the *imprimatur*), which must be preceded by the censor's verdict (the "*Nihil .obstat*") and his signature. Only in very rare cases and under extraordinary circumstances, if the Ordinary deems it prudent, may the name of the censor be omitted.

§ 5. The censor's name must not be made known to authors before he has given a favorable opinion. This rule clearly presupposes that more than one censor is appointed in each diocese, as § 1 insinuates by using the plural number (*censores*).

We may quote here a remark taken from the "*Sacrorum antistitum,*" namely, that the title of censor has no juridical or canonical value and contributes no weight to the private opinion of the official entrusted with this duty. Therefore if the censor makes a mistake the author has no guaranty in the "*Nihil obstat*" that his book will not be put on the index.

THE IMPRIMATUR MUST BE GIVEN IN WRITING

Can. 1394

§ 1. Licentia, qua Ordinarius potestatem edendi facit, in scriptis concedatur, in principio aut in fine libri, folii vel imaginis imprimenda, expresso nomine concedentis itemque loco et tempore concessionis.

§ 2. Si vero licentia deneganda videatur, roganti auctori, nisi gravis causa aliud exigat, rationes indicentur.

§ 1. The imprimatur should be given in writing and be placed either in the beginning or at the end of the book, leaflet or image, together with the name of the grantor, and the place and date of the grant. It is strongly advisable to print the year of publication on the title page,— a practice which is neglected by some, especially English, publishers.

§ 2. If the imprimatur is denied, the reasons should be given to the author upon demand, unless a weighty motive counsels the contrary. (See can. 1386.)

CHAPTER II

Whilst previous censorship chiefly affects authors, and the faithful at large only indirectly, this second chapter is directly intended to safeguard the faith and morals of all Christians. We purposely say *all Christians*, not merely Catholics, because morality is something universal and common to all who believe in Christ. Of course, the legislator does not concern himself with those outside the Church; but Christians of all denominations ought to be grateful for this directive norm, which, as law, binds all Catholics. The censorship with which we now deal is called *repressiva*, because it aims at suppressing bad literature.[1]

WHO HAS THE POWER TO FORBID BOOKS

CAN. 1395

§ 1. Ius et officium libros ex iusta causa prohibendi competit non solum supremae auctoritati ecclesiasticae pro universa Ecclesia, sed pro suis subditis Conciliis quoque particularibus et locorum Ordinariis.

§ 2. Ab hac prohibitione datur ad Sanctam Sedem recursus, non tamen in suspensivo.

3. Etiam Abbas monasterii sui iuris et supremus religionis clericalis exemptae Moderator, cum suo Capitulo vel Consilio, potest libros ex iusta causa suis

[1] S. C Ind., Aug 24, 1864 (*Coll P. F.*, n. 1264).

subditis prohibere; idemque, si periculum sit in mora, possunt alii Superiores maiores cum proprio Consilio, ea tamen lege ut rem quantocius deferant ad supremum Moderatorem.

§ 1. The right and duty to forbid books for a just cause belongs to the supreme ecclesiastical authority for the whole Church, and to particular councils and local Ordinaries for their respective subjects.

§ 2. Recourse from this prohibition may be had to the Apostolic See, but only *in devolutivo.*

The act of forbidding books is an exercise of jurisdiction, part of which is the teaching office of the Church, which belongs to those who are judges in matters of faith and morals. The supreme authority of the Church exercises its influence over the entire Church, whilst the bishops exercise theirs only over those who are subject to them. Therefore the text properly says: "*pro suis subditis.*" From this we naturally conclude that *exempt religious* are not *juridically* bound to obey the episcopal injunction, that is to say, no penalty can be pronounced against them for not observing the Ordinary's edict. Morally they may be obliged to abide by the bishop's order because of scandal or the danger of weakening the episcopal authority, especially among laymen.[2]

If a *particular council* forbids a book, are the exempt religious living within its jurisdiction obliged to heed that prohibition? If the council is a diocesan synod, the exempt religious are not obliged to obey, since the sole legislator is the local Ordinary, to whom they are not subject. If, however, a provincial or plenary council is understood, its decrees, we believe, are binding on the whole territory,

---

2 Thus Vermeersch, *De Prohibitione et Censura Librorum,* n 12 (ed. 1); Noldin, *De Praeceptis,* ed. 11, n. 704, p. 729.

especially if they are approved by Rome, and therefore also oblige exempt religious.[3]

§ 2 admits *recourse,* not appeal, to the Holy See, but such recourse has no suspensive character. Therefore the prohibition remains in force until the Apostolic See decides otherwise.

§ 3. *Abbots of autonomous monasteries* and the *superiors general* of exempt clerical institutes also may, for just reasons, forbid books to their subjects; but they must proceed together with their chapter or consultors. There is a juridical difficulty in this clause, because, as said above, the act of forbidding books rests on jurisdiction. This text is entirely new, and seems strange, as these superiors are not ordinarily considered to be judges in matters of faith.[4] Yet it is only the logical consequence of § 1, because the local Ordinaries have no jurisdiction over exempt religious. Therefore the reason advanced by the S. C. of the Index for extending the authority to forbid books to local Ordinaries and delegates of the Apostolic See — which extension is now antiquated — may be here applied. The *"pravorum librorum colluvies,"* the flood of perverse literature which is daily increasing in volume, clearly made it imperative to act promptly and efficaciously for the protection of the faithful, and this could be accomplished only by instructing the domestic authorities to stop the danger at the very beginning and, as it were, on the spot.[5]

Whether the chapter or the counsellors have a decisive, or merely an advisory vote, is not explicitly stated in the

3 This seems to follow from can 291, § 2, because such decrees would affect also religious, and we hardly believe that exemption could be claimed in this case, although we readily grant that can. 291, § 2 only mentions territorial, not personal, obligation

4 Can 501, § 2.

5 S C. Ind., Aug 24, 1864 (*Coll P. F*, n 1261).

text. This would seem to be a matter for the Constitutions to decide. To us it appears that a decisive vote is intended, to be given at the regular meeting, for the matter is of great importance. If there is a regular chapter, such as an independent monastery generally has, it is not enough that the abbot call the consultors; he must convene the chapter. *Capitulum* refers to the abbot of an autonomous monastery, *consilium* to the superior general.

The text continues: "If delay should be dangerous, the *other higher superiors* may, with the cooperation of their counsellors, also forbid books, but they are obliged to report the matter immediately to the superior general." The *alii superiores maiores* here intended are the provincials, etc., as explained under can. 488, n. 8. However, note the difference between the first and the second clause. The sentence of the abbots and superiors general is final and no further report is required, whereas that of inferior superiors is only provisional and requires the sanction of the superior general.

The reader may perhaps inquire whether the second clause applies to *female congregations*. No, because they lack a fundamental condition, *viz.*, jurisdiction. But we do not mean to say that a superioress would not be entitled to forbid a book to one of her religious, for this would be an exercise of domestic authority. But she could not forbid it to all as dangerous to faith and morals. Her prohibition would be a merely precautionary measure, and she would have to act according to can. 1397, § 1.

BOOKS FORBIDDEN BY THE APOSTOLIC SEE

CAN. 1396

Libri ab Apostolica Sede damnati ubique locorum et in quodcunque vertantur idioma prohibiti censeantur.

Books condemned by the Apostolic See must be considered as forbidden everywhere and in whatsoever language they may be translated.

The term *"Apostolic See"* comprises the Sovereign Pontiff as well as the S. Congregations, especially those directly concerned with the proscription of books.

(a) The *Pope* himself may forbid a book either by an " Apostolic letter," or without such a letter. There are on record four examples of books forbidden by Apostolic letter and without the coöperation of any congregation.[6]

(b) The *Holy Office* has issued about 900 decrees forbidding books from 1600 to 1900.[7] To this congregation our Code (can. 247, § 4) has affiliated the famous Congregation of the Index, which has the special duty of examining and prohibiting books.

(c) Other Congregations whose decrees figure in the new Index are that of *S. Rites* and that of *Indulgences* (the latter now incorporated with the S. Poenitentiaria). Besides, all other S. Congregations may take cognizance of and condemn books having special reference to their respective departments.[8]

As to the authority of the decisions rendered in regard to books the following may safely be stated:

The decisions given either by the Pope himself, or by

6 Cfr. Hilgers, *l c*, p. 89; Genovesi, Langeois des Chatellier, De Potter, Siegwart Muller.

7 *Ibid*, p. 88
8 *Ibid.*, p 89.

a congregation of the Roman Court *do not, per se, contain a dogmatic or an ex cathedra definition, i. e.,* an infallible verdict as to the doctrine defended or proposed in the forbidden book. It goes without saying that the Pope *may* issue a decree condemning a book with infallible authority, but in that case his intention must be apparent from the wording of the decree. The Thursday sessions of the Holy Office, on account of the personal presence of the Sovereign Pontiff, are regarded as more weighty than the others; but even the decrees issued at these sessions cannot be called infallible or irreformable.[9]

It need not be added that these decisions must be received with the greatest respect and obedience and with internal as well as external submission.

Our canon says that the books condemned by the Apostolic See must be considered forbidden *everywhere.* The reason is because the Holy See is the supreme tribunal in matters of faith and morals. Books of purely local interest usually are left to the local Ordinaries. This also explains why *translations* of forbidden books are also forbidden, for the difference of language is merely accidental. The poison is the same, although the channel may differ.

THE OBLIGATION OF DENOUNCING BOOKS

CAN. 1397

§ 1. Omnium fidelium est, maxime clericorum et in dignitate ecclesiastica constitutorum eorumque qui doctrina praecellant, libros quos perniciosos iudicaverint, ad locorum Ordinarios aut ad Apostolicam Sedem deferre; id autem peculiari titulo pertinet ad Legatos

9 *Ibid.,* p 74 f , p 88

Sanctae Sedis, locorum Ordinarios, atque Rectores Universitatum catholicarum.

§ 2. Expedit ut in pravorum librorum denuntiatione non solum libri inscriptio indicetur, sed etiam, quantum fieri potest, causae exponantur cur liber prohibendus existimetur.

§ 3. Iis ad quos denuntiatio defertur, sanctum esto denuntiantium nomina secreta servare.

§ 4. Locorum Ordinarii per se aut, ubi opus fuerit, per sacerdotes idoneos vigilent in libros, qui in proprio territorio edantur aut venales prostent.

§ 5. Libros qui subtilius examen exigant vel de quibus ad salutarem effectum consequendum supremae auctoritatis sententia requiri videatur, ad Apostolicae Sedis iudicium Ordinarii deferant.

Denunciation savors of sycophancy, yet it may become an official duty. A prosecuting attorney, for instance, has to denounce crimes and criminals. Every society which cares for the observance of its laws must have custodians and guardians of the public welfare Protestant sects promoted sycophancy by giving part of the fine imposed upon the guilty to their denouncers [10] The Catholic Church does not hold out any material gain, but imposes a strict obligation on all concerned. However, there is a gradation of duty in regard to denouncing. Those who are bound *ex officio, i. e.,* the official guardians and judges in matters of faith and morals, are obliged *in justice* to denounce transgressors. The obligation is grave, as a rule, when the matter is serious, and the damage resulting from negligence would be great. Ordinary *Christians* on the other hand are as a rule bound to make

10 Cfr. Hilgers, *l c* pp 70, 270 (in " free " Switzerland denunciation flourished), p 304 (Hungary) and elsewhere, for inst., the Netherlands.

denunciation only when the matter is very important, as when a book causes great injury to faith and morals, or if a positive law imposes denunciation. Besides, it is evident that less educated persons are as a rule exempt from the obligation of denouncing books, unless their conscience raises an irresistible scruple, in which case they may refer the matter to the confessor. But cultured Catholics who move in the higher circles of society most certainly are bound to perform this duty. It is a natural duty enforced by positive law.[11] Hence our canon rules:

1. That it is the duty of all the faithful, especially of *clergymen, ecclesiastical dignitaries* and persons distinguished by learning to denounce books which they deem pernicious, to the local Ordinaries or to the Apostolic See. More especially is this duty incumbent on *papal legates, local Ordinaries,* and the *rectors of Catholic universities.* The last named organizations in the Middle Ages always were conspicuous for their zeal in maintaining orthodoxy, as is proved by their statutes, which forbade the professors as well as librarians to publish or sell manuscripts that had not been corrected and examined by the faculty.[12] Now-a-days, too, on account of the number of students as well as by reason of extensive literary acquisitions and communications, the Catholic universities are favorably situated for watching scientific productions.

2. When denouncing a book it is expedient that *not only the title of the book* be indicated, but also the *objectionable passages be singled out* which call for a prohibition. Such coöperation facilitates the work of the consultors and censors, who are usually overburdened, and, besides, guarantees the acumen and sincerity of the denouncing person.

11 Cfr. " *Officiorum ac munerum,*" n. 27 ff.
12 Hilgers, *l. c.,* p. 404.

3. Those who receive the denunciation, *i. e.,* usually the officials of either the Roman or the diocesan court, are strictly bound to keep the *name of the denouncer secret.* This is a grievous obligation, enhanced for the officials of the Sant' Uffizio by their sacred oath. The Secretary of the S. Congregation, however, is authorized to communicate to the author the objections made to his book, but he may not divulge the name of the denouncer or censor.[13]

4. The local Ordinaries, either personally, or, if necessary, through capable priests, should watch the books that are published and sold in their territory. This was the duty of the so-called *vigilance commissions* prescribed by Pius X against the Modernists.[14] Although the Code does not enforce this law, the Holy Office has decided that it remains in force until the Apostolic See orders differently.[15]

The members of the diocesan vigilance commission may perform their duty at regular sessions, to be held every other month, or by written communication.[16] It is clear that an effective control can be exercised only over *Catholic* firms, who may be deprived of their title of Catholic book-sellers if they refuse to obey episcopal orders. Even if a book has the *imprimatur,* but is proved to be infected with modernism, it must be withdrawn from sale or exhibition.[17] Priests, especially pastors and confessors, should watch over the reading of the faithful, particularly over circulating libraries and also public libraries. Much can be accomplished by prudent vigi-

---

13 Benedict XIV, "*Sollicita ac provida,*" July 9, 1753, § 12

14 "*Sacrorum Antistitum,*" Sept. 1, 1910 (*A. Ap. S.,* II, 664).

15 S. O., March 22, 1918 (*A. Ap. S.,* X, 136).

16 S. C. Consist., Sept. 25, 1910, ad II, III (*A. Ap. S.,* II, 740 f).

17 "*Sacrorum Antistitum,*" n. III (*A. Ap. S.,* II, 660)

lance in keeping these institutions free from objectionable books.

5. Books which require a more thorough examination or call for the judgment of the supreme tribunal, should be referred to the Holy See by the Ordinaries — by all Ordinaries, not only the diocesan bishops. Sometimes the matter at issue may not be delicate or difficult, but the author's name and reputation require an emphatic and more solemn sentence, to produce the desired effect.

THE EFFECTS OF PROHIBITION

CAN. 1398

§ 1. Prohibitio librorum id efficit ut liber sine debita licentia nec edi, nec legi, nec vendi, nec retineri, nec in aliam linguam verti, nec ullo modo cum aliis communicari possit.

§ 2. Liber quoquo modo prohibitus rursus in lucem edi nequit, nisi, factis correctionibus, licentiam is dederit qui librum prohibuerat eiusve Superior vel successor.

§ 1. The prohibition of books has this effect that a forbidden book may not be published, nor read, nor kept, nor sold, nor translated into another language, nor communicated to others in any way.

The term *edere* (to publish) concerns the author, the editor, and the printer: the *author* of the book is forbidden to have it printed and published; the *editor* may not sell it, and the *printer* may not print and bind it, either personally or through others. Accessory helpers and remote cooperators are hardly affected, as otherwise there would be an indefinite number of persons included.

Reading a book means the operation by which the

contents of a book are conveyed to the mind through the senses of vision or hearing. If one would employ another to read a forbidden book to him, he would certainly read it himself and would incur the penalty of the law.[18]

To *keep a book* (*retinere*) means to possess it permanently as one's personal property or to have it in one's possession temporarily or transiently so as to be able to make free use of it. Librarians are not said to keep, but rather to guard the books entrusted to their care. The length of time is immaterial, but must amount to a somewhat protracted action, as the reduplicative particle *re* indicates.

Books may be *sold* in stores or at auction, at wholesale or retail, of which more under can. 1404.

What *translations* are is generally known. Here we will only observe that it does not matter whether the objectionable passages or parts of a forbidden book are omitted or explained in the translation; as long as the original text is forbidden, the translation is also forbidden, unless expressly approved.

Communicare aliis means to loan a book to others or to exchange it for another. It may also imply making the contents known to others. In this latter sense the reading of a forbidden book to others, for instance, by a teacher to his pupils, is forbidden.[19]

18 To read a book means to assimilate a considerable part thereof (Vermeersch, *l. c ,* n. 32, n. 11); the opinion of St Alphonsus, referred to by Noldin (*l. c.,* n 702, p. 728), and opposed to what we say in the text, is contrary to Reg Iuris 72 in 6°. Of course, if one would hear some parts of a forbidden book read by mere chance, he would not fall under the law. Readers are also those who read the proofsheets of a book.

19 Under this heading as well as under that of "retaining" fall restaurants, hotels, boarding houses, etc., which keep objectionable papers and magazines and place them at the disposal of their guests. The owners of these places are certainly not allowed to keep literature which is manifestly contrary to faith and morals

Here may be added some explanations given by the
Holy Office. A book may not be read, even if the contents are not understood or the errors are not accepted.
This applies also to Protestant Bible translations: they
may not be read even if the missionaries, for instance,
have corrected the erroneous passages.[20] Neither may a
forbidden book be read or retained for a good and holy
purpose.[21]

Books which are forbidden with the clause, *"donec
expurgentur,"* may not be retained until they have been
corrected.[22]

§ 2. A book forbidden no matter how, *may not be republished* until after it has been corrected and the one
who forbade it, or his superior or successor, has granted
permission to republish it. Therefore, if the bishop has
forbidden a book, and recourse was had to the Roman
Congregation, who granted the imprimatur, the book may
be published. Note also the term *quoquo modo,* in whatever manner forbidden. The Constitution of Leo XIII
(n. 31) applied that rule to books prohibited by the Apostolic See. But our text says in a general way, no matter how and by whom forbidden, whether by general
rules or special prohibition, whether by the Ordinaries or
by the Apostolic See. The latter is always ready to accept corrections made by the author, provided he has
duly submitted himself and his corrections are accepted
by the examiners.

20 S. O., July 26, 1848 (*Coll.
P. F*, n. 1030)

21 S O., June 29, 1817 (*ibid.*,
n. 718)

22 *Prop. 45 damn.*, March 18, 1666
(Denzinger, n. 1016).

Can. 1399

Ipso iure prohibentur:

1.° Editiones textus originalis et antiquarum versionum catholicarum sacrae Scripturae, etiam Ecclesiae Orientalis, ab acatholicis quibuslibet publicatae; itemque eiusdem versiones in quamvis linguam, ab eisdem confectae vel editae;

2.° Libri quorumvis scriptorum, haeresim vel schisma propugnantes, aut ipsa religionis fundamenta quoquo modo evertere nitentes;

3.° Libri qui religionem aut bonos mores, data opera, impetunt;

4.° Libri quorumvis acatholicorum, qui ex professo de religione tractant, nisi constet nihil in eis contra fidem catholicam contineri;

5.° Libri de quibus in can. 1385, § 1, n. 1 et can. 1391; itemque ex illis de quibus in cit. can. 1385, § 1, n. 2, libri ac libelli qui novas apparitiones, revelationes, visiones, prophetias, miracula enarrant, vel qui novas inducunt devotiones, etiam sub praetextu quod sint privatae, si editi fuerint non servatis canonum praescriptionibus;

6.° Libri qui quodlibet ex catholicis dogmatibus impugnant vel derident, qui errores ab Apostolica Sede proscriptos tuentur, qui cultui divino detrahunt, qui disciplinam ecclesiasticam evertere contendunt, et qui data opera ecclesiasticam hierarchiam, aut statum clericalem vel religiosum probris afficiunt;

7.° Libri qui cuiusvis generis superstitionem, sortilegia, divinationem, magiam, evocationem spirituum, aliaque id genus docent vel commendant;

8.° Libri qui duellum vel suicidium, vel divortium licita statuunt, qui de sectis massonicis vel aliis eiusdem generis societatibus agentes, eas utiles et non perniciosas Ecclesiae et civili societati esse contendunt;

9.° Libri qui res lascivas seu obscenas ex profcsso tractant, narrant, aut docent;

10.° Editiones librorum liturgicorum a Sede Apostolica approbatorum, in quibus quidpiam immutatum fuerit, ita ut cum authenticis editionibus a Sancta Sede approbatis non congruant;

11.° Libri quibus divulgantur indulgentiae apocryphae vel a Sancta Sede proscriptae aut revocatae;

12.° Imagines quoquo modo impressae Domini Nostri Iesu Christi, Beatae Mariae Virginis, Angelorum atque Sanctorum vel aliorum Servorum Dei ab Ecclesiae sensu et decretis alienae.

By law (*i. e.,* common law) are forbidden:

1.° *Editions* of the original text and of ancient Catholic versions of *Holy Scripture,* also of the Oriental Church, which have been published by non-Catholics; also *translations* of the same into any language made or published by non-Catholics.

The *original text* of the O. T. is in Hebrew, except portions of the Book of Esdras and about half of Daniel, which are written in Chaldean. The Books of Judith, Tobias, Baruch, Ecclesiasticus, I Machabees and parts of Daniel were written either in Hebrew or in Chaldean, but are preserved only in translations, of which the Greek Septuagint is the oldest. The book of Wisdom, II Machabees and the whole of the N. T. were composed in *Greek,* and have come down to us in that language.

Ancient translations are several Greek and Chaldean translations of the O. T.; a Samaritan version of the

Pentateuch, some Syriac versions (especially the Peshitto of the Ist century), several Arabic (mainly made in the Xth century by a Jewish rabbi), one Armenian (IVth century) one Coptic (IIIrd century) one Ethiopian (IVth century), one Slavonic, one Gothic (by Wulfilas, IVth century) ; and especially the Latin versions called Itala and Vulgate.[23] All these texts and versions, if published by non-Catholics, are forbidden, for the reason that there is danger of perversion and hypercriticism, which may lead to the elimination of genuine texts or wrong punctuation, etc. By issuing this prohibition, of course, the Church does not wish to slur well-deserving non-Catholic editors or their work. She merely desires to safeguard the text of S. Scripture and the faith of her children.

More liable to carelessness and perversion than the ancient versions are the *translations into modern languages,* of which the King James Bible furnishes an example. Most of them entirely omit the so-called deutero-canonical books and thus offer a mutilated Bible.

2.° The *books of writers defending or championing heresy and schism, or attempting in any way to undermine the very foundations of religion.*

The text omits the term *"apostates,"* found in the Leonine legislation, for the reason, apparently, that they are included either in this paragraph or the following two. *Propugnare* means an argumentative defence. Heresy and schism have been defined in can. 1325, § 2.

The foundations of religion are the fundamental truths of both the natural and the supernatural, i. e., revealed, order,— the existence of God, the immortality of the soul, the possibility and reality of miracles, etc., as generally set forth in handbooks of fundamental theology or

---

23 Seisenberger, *Practical Handbook for the Study of the Bible,* (Engl. Transl) 1911, p 213; p 235.

apologetics.[24] The undermining, *evertere,* may be done by casting ridicule upon these fundamental truths; hence satirical, also sceptical writings would suffice.

3.° *Books which purposely attack religion or good morals.* *Data opera* appears to mean the same as *ex professo,* and is opposed to such expressions as *perfunctorie* and *obiter.* It may be, however, that *data opera* is intended to signify the intention. This would have to manifest itself in some way, whereas *ex professo* rather refers to the way and style of handling the arguments or subject. Practically the two phrases are hardly to be distinguished from each other.

What is understood by *religion* is not expressly determined, but there can be no doubt that the term here denotes first and above all the true religion of Christ, and secondarily natural religion, which governs the relations between God and His creatures.

" *Good morals* " comprise the principles laid down by ethics as well as moral theology, not only the system as a whole, but any part of it. Thus, for instance, a book defending " race suicide " or profiteering would no doubt be opposed to good morals.

Impetere means not only to make incoherent statements, as is done in newspapers, but to launch an elaborate or a systematic attack.

4.° *Books by non-Catholics which professedly treat of religion,* unless it is certain that they contain nothing contrary to the Catholic faith.[25]

The *author* must be a non-Catholic,—*i. e.,* a pagan, Jew,

24 Thus Wernz, *Ius Decret.,* Vol. III, ed 1, p 119, n. 111. Vermeersch (*l. c,* n. 13) excludes " *praecipua dogmata ipsius fidei* " and seems to insist too much on the distinction between scientific and religious foundations; it is not true that all these are included in heresy and schism, for not all heretics and schismatics attack them.

25 Wernz, *l c.;* Hurley, *l. c.,* p. 62.

Moslem, heretic, schismatic, or an apostatized Catholic, for our Code always uses the term non-Catholic in this wide sense.

The phrase *"ab acatholicis quibuslibet"* in no. 1 of the present canon shows that, as in the Constitution of Leo XIII, so here also the term "non-Catholic" must be interpreted in the widest sense.[26]

The *subject* is religion, without any further determination, therefore natural as well as supernatural religion, for in the final analysis all religion affects the attributes of God.

The *mode* of treating religion must be *ex professo*, which, as stated before, signifies not a mere transient or cursory statement, but a formal and developed argument dealing with at least a notable and considerable part of the subject in question. Such, for instance, are sermons or discourses written by non-Catholics, histories of religion, etc.

The *restrictive clause "nisi constet . . ."* permits the reading of such books if it is morally certain that they contain nothing against the Catholic faith, either by way of assertion, innuendo, or induction. The word *nihil* is a wide term, as it marks a universal negation and generally admits of no restriction. Still stronger would be the expressions, *"nihil penitus,"* or *"nihil omnino,"* which absolutely exclude everything and anything.[27] But since the simple term "nothing" is used here, we may admit the adage *"parum pro nihilo putatur,"* and say that one or the other sentence of little importance against the Catholic faith might be overlooked, especially if there is a palpable absence of malicious intent.

It is said that one must be *morally certain* that the book

26 Wernz, *l. c.*, p. 119 f.
27 Barbosa, *Tractatus Vari*, Dictio 214 (ed. Lugdun., 1660, p. 725).

contains nothing objectionable. This certainly may be obtained by reading the book, either privately or officially, on the part of persons who are capable of judging it and possess a conscientious disposition.

5.° *Bibles and Biblical annotations and commentaries,* modern translations of the Bible, *i. e.,* into the vernacular, and all books mentioned in can. 1385, § 1, n. 2, books and booklets which narrate new apparitions, revelations, visions, prophecies, miracles or aim to introduce new devotions, even though they pretend to be purely private, if published without regard to the rules prescribed, *i. e.,* without complying with the law of previous censorship (can. 1393).

Note the word *narrare,* which is historical rather than theological or scientific. However, a mere report in a newspaper or magazine could hardly be intended, because the term appears to require a longer treatise.[28] This rule also applies to " war prophesies," of which we heard so much of late. It does not matter whether the facts narrated are objectively true or not.

New devotions are such as have not yet been approved by ecclesiastical authority. In regard to new devotions, as well as to *apparitions,* for instance, of the Blessed Virgin Mary, observe that, if they were believed and tolerated for a long time, and never disapproved by the Holy See, they may continue to be tolerated by the local Ordinary, who may also approve them and thus render them permissible. In case of episcopal approbation, the Ordinary should add a declaration to the effect that the respective devotion is tolerated on account of immemorial custom.[29]

28 Thus also Vermeersch, *l c.,* n. 14. This seems also evident from the opposition: books and booklets. Their chief purpose must be the narration of such things, no matter whether the narrator himself believes the story or not.

29 S. Rit. C., Feb. 6, 1875, May 12, 1877 (*Dec. Auth,* nn. 3336, 3419).

The previous *censorship,* therefore, is required for all these books, and without the Ordinary's imprimatur no one may read them, even for private devotion.

6.° This number contains several classes of books which are best kept separate, namely:

(a) *Books which attack or ridicule any dogma of the Catholic Church.* Dogma here means an article of divine or Catholic faith. The attack may be made by argument or in the form of a simple statement. Ridicule may be contained in one sentence.

(b) *Books which defend errors that have been pro-scribed by the Apostolic See, i. c.,* by the Pope himself, or by one of the S. Congregations.[30] This law refers principally to formally condemned errors of heretics, *e. g.,* Jansenius, Bajus, Molinos, etc., also to the propositions censured in the Syllabus of Pius IX and the so-called New Syllabus of Pius X.

(c) *Books which disparage divine worship. Cultus divinus* is here evidently to be taken in the same sense in which the Code uses the term in can. 1255 ff., *i. e.,* the worship paid to God and His Saints as well as the liturgical functions of the Church, which are nothing else but visible manifestations of internal worship.

Detrahere signifies a kind of slander of a person or disparagement of some object connected with that person. Thus the worship of relics and sacred images is disparaged by iconoclastic propositions.

(d) *Books which seek to undermine ecclesiastical discipline.* To this class belong writings directed against the Canon Law and the divine liturgy. Ecclesiastical discipline comprises all the measures taken by the Church to preserve and develop the society founded by Christ. The

---

30 It is not necessary that any specific qualification (*erronea, temera-ria, scandalosa, piarum aurium offensiva,* etc) be added

term includes the holy seasons, the sacred liturgy, the duties and privileges of clergy and laymen,[31] etc.

(e) *Books which of set purpose insult the ecclesiastical hierarchy or the clerical or religious state.* The term insult is liable to a more or less subjective interpretation. Essentially it means an undeserved affront or indignity offered to one's self-respect. The insult, to bring a book within the prohibited class, must strike at the hierarchy *as such,* not at single persons. The same is true of the clerical or *religious state.* Therefore an insult hurled against a clergyman, or several clergymen, or against a religious, or one house or congregation of religious, or even a whole order could not be called an affront against the religious state.[32]

7.° *Books which teach or approve any kind of superstition, fortune-telling, divination, magic, the evocation of spirits, and other similar practices.*[33]

Superstition seems to be here taken as a distinct and co-ordinate, not as a comprehensive term, and hence means a specific form of belief, which manifests ignorant or abnormal credulity, such as the belief in omens, charms, etc. The other terms include the whole broad field of occultism or Spiritism, witchcraft, sorcery, clairvoyancy, and so forth. Hypnotism and somnambulism, if superstitious, are also included. Books *teaching or approving* such practices are forbidden, not, of course, books written for the purpose of combatting them.

8.° *Books which defend the lawfulness of duelling or suicide or divorce; or which try to prove that Freemasonry*

---

31 However, this must be understood, not of single canons or rubrics, but of the law and liturgy as a whole, or at least some compact part thereof.

32 Thus the commentators generally; see Wernz, *l. c.,* p. 123.

33 Somewhat different appears to be the meaning in " *Officiorum ac munerum,*" art. 12.

and other similar sects are useful and not detrimental to Church and State.

Statuere, in the first clause, means literally to establish, determine, pass judgment or demonstrate. To do this requires no *ex professo* treatise, but the tendency to make duelling, etc., appear lawful, must be manifest. Law books which admit divorce are excepted from this prohibition, because they are merely repositories of laws. But a pamphlet written to recommend a divorce bill would certainly be prohibited.

The second class treats of *Masonic and similar sects.* Masonic societies are those which have special rites, secret oaths, and advocate subversive principles. The last mentioned feature is now regarded as a characteristic feature,[34] and hence all anarchistic, Bolshevist, and extremely Socialistic societies are included.[35] However, such books or pamphlets, to fall under the prohibition of our canon, must *make a serious attempt* to prove the usefulness or harmlessness of these sects. This requires argumentation which is apt to convince the reader.

9.° *Books which of set purpose treat of, relate, or inculcate lascivious and obscene things.* Hither belongs the whole class of strictly so-called pornographic literature, as well as innumerable romances, novels, and poems. To treat of (*tractare*) implies a frivolous or alluring style. *Narrare* refers to a minute or detailed account of obscene facts, whilst *docere* may be taken as indicating that the reader deduces false conclusions from the description or narrative. From this it is evident that scientific treatises on medicine, surgery, pastoral medicine, and moral theology do not belong to the category of for-

---

34 Cfr. S C. P F., Sept 24, 1867 (*Coll.,* n. 1320).

35 Vermeersch (*l. c.,* n. 13)

doubts whether Socialists are included because they are, he maintains, neither a *factio* (*une partie,* a

bidden books [36] unless they are written in a style which clearly betrays the purpose of the author to be other than scientific.

The term "books" here excludes images, pictures, drawings, engravings, photogravures, etc.

10 ° Editions of *liturgical books* approved by the Apostolic See, which have been altered so as *no* longer to agree with the *authentic texts*.

11.° Books which spread apocryphal indulgences or indulgences that have been proscribed or recalled by the Holy See.

12.° Images, however printed, of our Lord Jesus Christ, the Blessed Virgin Mary, the Angels, the Saints, and other Servants of God, if not in keeping with the spirit or decrees of the Church.

These last three classes of publications have been sufficiently explained under canons 1257, 1279, 919.

EXCEPTION IN FAVOR OF THEOLOGICAL STUDENTS

CAN. 1400

Usus librorum de quibus in can. 1399, n. 1, ac librorum editorum contra praescriptum can. 1391, iis dumtaxat permittitur qui studiis theologicis vel biblicis quovis modo operam dant, dummodo iidem libri fideliter et integre editi sint neque impugnentur in eorum prolegomenis aut adnotationibus catholicae fidei dogmata.

Editions of the original text of Holy Scripture, of the ancient versions by non-Catholics, and translations into

party), nor a secret (*occulta*) sect. But the latter characteristic is not absolutely needed, according to the preceding note; and the attribute of faction or party can certainly not be denied to such Socialist bodies as the Spartacists in Germany.

36 Wernz, *l. c.*, p. 122

the vernacular made and published either by non-Catholics or by Catholics without previous censorship, are allowed to such as are in any way engaged in theological or biblical studies, provided, however,

(1) that these editions are faithful and entire, and

(2) that neither the introduction nor the annotations contain attacks on Catholic dogmas.

There is, then, a privileged class of persons, who may make use of the aforesaid forbidden books, but not of others mentioned in the preceding canon, namely those engaged in *theological* or *biblical studies*. Theology comprises first and above all dogmatic theology, but may be taken as coextensive with the theological course of can. 1365, § 2, and therefore includes all branches usually taught with theology. This interpretation is not contradicted by the declaration of the S. C. of the Index, of June 21, 1898, which (*ad 2am partem*) excludes from this privilege those who simply read the Hebrew or Greek text of S. Scripture without reference to *theological studies*.[37] Hence one purpose of using these otherwise forbidden books is theological study. Another is the pursuit of *biblical studies, viz.,* introduction, hermeneutics, and exegesis. Now both these studies may be pursued not only by professional theologians and biblical scholars or professors, but also by students in seminaries, universities, etc. All these share in the privilege extended by can. 1400.[38]

Is the use of these editions allowed if one has to prepare a sermon or lecture? Our answer would be that for a usual Sunday or holyday sermon no special theological or biblical study is required, and therefore we could not

---

37 Cfr. Wernz, *l c.,* p. 120, mistaken is Hurley's interpretation, *l. c.,* p. 69.

38 Cfr. S. C. Indic., May 23, 1898, ad 1 (*Coll. P. F ,* n. 2000).

say that these preachers are engaged in (*operam dant*) such studies.[39]   But if one would have to deliver an elaborate *lecture* on a theological subject, say for instance, on creation, on the Real Presence, or on Holy Orders, he would certainly have to study his subject, and therefore would be allowed to make use of these editions.[40]

PERSONS EXEMPT FROM THE PROHIBITION

CAN. 1401

S. R. E. Cardinales, Episcopi, etiam titulares, aliique Ordinarii, necessariis adhibitis cautelis, ecclesiastica librorum prohibitione non adstringuntur.

Cardinals, residential as well as titular bishops, and other Ordinaries, provided they employ the necessary precautions, are not bound by the law of forbidden books, (but must obey the law of previous censorship).

What precautions are to be taken is not determined by the Code.   They may be described as follows:

(a) The natural as well as positive law requires that one should not expose his faith and morals unnecessarily to danger (cfr can. 1405, § 1), for no one is immune from temptations.

(b) No one is allowed to read lascivious or obscene books unless bound to do so *ex officio,* to examine them;

(c) If the persons mentioned retain forbidden books, they must see to it that they do not fall into the hands of those not permitted to read them.   This does not mean, however, that Ordinaries, etc., may not communicate

---

39 If one, by way of exception, should need a critical edition, or should have no other text at hand, he would be excused

40 The best known editions by non-Catholic authors are those of Tischendorf, Tregelles, and Westcott and Hort.

among themselves or converse with their censors about such books.

Here it may be useful to add a word about *librarians.* These, being custodians, not proprietors or retainers, of the books in their care, should see to it that forbidden books are kept separate, or if this is impossible or impracticable, that a warning sign be placed on the shelves containing forbidden or dangerous books.

The *prelates or superiors of exempt clerical institutes,* who, according to our canon and canon 198, are free from the restrictions of the law regarding forbidden books, should take care that their libraries are so managed as to preclude danger to their subjects.

This rule may also be applied to *parish libraries,* though these, as a rule, will hardly keep forbidden books, with the exception perhaps of non-Catholic editions of the Bible.

What we have said is nothing but a logical deduction from *can. 1403, § 2,* which strictly obliges those who have obtained faculties for reading or retaining forbidden books, to guard them carefully, so that they do not fall into the hands of others.

FACULTIES

CAN. 1402

§ 1. Ordinarii licentiam, ad libros quod attinet ipso iure vel decreto Sedis Apostolicae prohibitos, concedere suis subditis valent pro singulis tantum libris atque in casibus dumtaxat urgentibus.

§ 2. Quod si generalem a Sede Apostolica facultatem impetraverint suis subditis permittendi ut libros proscriptos retineant ac legant, eam nonnisi cum delectu et iusta ac rationabili causa concedant.

CAN. 1403

§ 1. Qui facultatem apostolicam consecuti sunt legendi et retinendi libros prohibitos, nequeunt ideo legere et retinere libros quoslibet a suis Ordinariis proscriptos, nisi in apostolico indulto expressa iisdem facta fuerit potestas legendi et retinendi libros a quibuslibet damnatos.

§ 2. Insuper gravi praecepto tenentur libros prohibitos ita custodiendi, ut hi ad aliorum manus non perveniant.

Can. 1402 mentions two kinds of faculties, one granted by the law itself, the other by the Apostolic See.

1. *Ordinaries, i. e.,* all who go by that name [41] in virtue of can. 198, § 1, may grant permission to their subjects to read books forbidden either by law (*i. e ,* by the Code) or by a special decree of the Apostolic See, but they can impart this faculty only for individual books and in urgent cases. The term "*pro singulis tantum libris*" means that each book must be distinctly mentioned by title and no wholesale permission may be issued. The plural form, *singulis libris,* permits the faculty to be given for more than one book at a time, provided they are duly specified.

Urgent cases are such as arise suddenly and unexpectedly. Thus if a writer needs a certain book for immediate use, he may apply to his Ordinary, (either the local Ordinary, if he is subject to him, or the exempt religious superior, if he is an exempt religious) and obtain the permission needed

It may have surprised the reader to find *libri lascivi vel*

---

41 Wernz, *l c.,* p. 129 correctly held against Pennacchi that all ordinaries, hence also religious superiors who, according to can 488, n. 8 and can. 501, § 1, have jurisdiction *in foro externo,* must here be understood

obscoeni mentioned under n. 9 without the restriction or mitigation found in rule 10 of the Constitution of Leo XIII, in favor of *classical writers.* Does the New Code abolish this mitigation? It does, though § 1 of can. 1402 permits teachers and others whose office necessitates such reading, to apply to their superiors for the faculty, if the case is urgent, as it generally is

§ 2 mentions a general faculty granted by the Apostolic See (Holy Office).[42] If such a general faculty has been given to Ordinaries for the benefit of their subjects, it should be communicated to the latter with discretion and only for a just and reasonable cause.

The term *" cum delectu "* doubtless refers to the *persons* subject to the Ordinaries. These persons are described in the Clementine Instruction as men of learning and piety who labor for the public welfare and that of the Catholic Church. Being engaged in such work constitutes a reasonable and just cause for granting the permission.

Ordinaries who have this general (either triennial or quinquennial) faculty, before granting either perpetual or revocable permission to their subjects,[43] should carefully read the text of the grant, for it may be that some classes of books (*e. g., libri obscoeni* or books *ex professo* defending heresy and schism or undermining the foundations of religion) are excepted.

Can 1403 rules that those who have obtained a papal faculty for reading and keeping forbidden books, are not thereby entitled to read and keep books proscribed by their Ordinaries unless the indult which they have ob-

42 Secular prelates have to petition the Holy Office if they are under the ordinary hierarchical jurisdiction, otherwise the S. C de Propaganda Fide Religious prelates must apply to the S. C Relig

43 Wernz, *l. c.*, p. 129.

tained contains the express clause that they may read and keep books *no matter by whom condemned.*[44]

What was said under can. 1395, also applies here and should be compared with rule 26 of the Constitution of Leo XIII, which employs the term " local Ordinaries " (*Ordinariis locorum*), whereas our canon mentions Ordinaries in general. The consequence is that if the local Ordinary or bishop forbids a book, or magazine, or paper, exempt religious are not, juridically speaking, bound to heed the proscription, until their superior has approved it. On the other hand, the religious superior of an exempt clerical institute may forbid a book or pamphlet or magazine not forbidden by the local Ordinary. Therefore a religious who has obtained a papal indult to read and keep forbidden books is not allowed to read or retain a book forbidden by his (exempt) religious superior, unless the above-mentioned clause is found in the papal indult. This rule holds good even if the local Ordinary or religious superior should prohibit a book already proscribed either by common law or by a special decree of the Apostolic See; for there may be a special local or personal reason why this book should be doubly forbidden.

We may finally admit a certain *epikeia* when an adequate reason of utility or necessity exists for not observing the law, as far as its positive side is concerned, provided, of course, there be no danger to faith or morals.[45]

BOOKSELLERS

CAN. 1404

Librorum venditores libros de obscenis ex professo tractantes ne vendant, commodent, retineant; ceteros

---

[44] Hurley, *l. c*, p 172 f   [45] Vermeersch, *l. c.,* n. 34.

prohibitos venales ne habeant, nisi debitam licentiam
a Sede Apostolica impetraverint, neve cuiquam vendant, nisi prudenter existimare possint ab emptore legitime peti.

Catholic booksellers [46] are bound in conscience:

1.° Not to sell, loan, or keep books which treat *ex professo* of *obscene subjects*. Here again no distinction is
made between classical and ordinary authors, and therefore all obscene books are included. However, it stands
to reason that purged or corrected editions of classical
authors may be sold.

2.° Not to *offer for sale any other forbidden books*, except with the permission of the Apostolic See (*i. e.,* the
Holy Office), nor to sell any such books to anyone of
whom it cannot be reasonably supposed that he asks for
them lawfully.

Venales habere means to exhibit or offer for sale.
Since the term "*retinere*" does not occur in this clause,
we may reasonably suppose that booksellers are allowed
to keep such books in stock, but only in a hidden or secret
place, not publicly. But they may not list them in their
catalogues or advertise them unless they have obtained a
papal indult to this effect. Even if they have such an
indult, they should be careful not to sell forbidden books
indiscriminately. If a customer asks for a forbidden
book, they are not indeed obliged to ask whether he has
permission to read and keep it, but they should be morally
certain that he does not ask unreasonably.

[46] A distinction between Catholic and non-Catholic booksellers was drawn in "*Officiorum ac munerum*," n. 46, but it is not repeated in our Code, because the Code legislates for Catholics only.

CAN. 1405

§ 1. Licentia a quovis obtenta nullo modo quis eximitur a prohibitione iuris naturalis legendi libros qui ipsi proximum spirituale periculum praestant.

§ 2. Ordinarii locorum aliique curam animarum habentes opportune moneant fideles de periculo et damno lectionis librorum pravorum, praesertim prohibitorum.

§ 1. A license to read forbidden books does not in any way exempt one from the prohibition of the natural law against reading books which are to him a proximate occasion of sin. Therefore

§ 2. The local Ordinaries and all those in charge of souls should warn the faithful of the danger and injury caused by reading bad, especially forbidden, books.

It is obvious that one who disobeys the law of the Church and neglects the precautions dictated by reason, cannot expect supernatural help against temptations.

For completeness' sake we here add can. 2318.

PENAL SANCTION

CAN. 2318

§ 1. In excommunicationem Sedi Apostolicae speciali modo reservatam ipso facto incurrunt, opere publici iuris facto, editores librorum apostatarum, haereticorum et schismaticorum, qui apostasiam, haeresim, schisma propugnant, itemque eosdem libros aliosve per apostolicas litteras nominatim prohibitos defendentes aut scienter sine debita licentia legentes vel retinentes.

§ 2. Auctores et editores qui sine debita licentia sacrarum Scripturarum libros vel earum adnotationes aut commentarios imprimi curant, incidunt ipso facto in excommunicationem nemini reservatam.

§ 1. Those who publish books written by apostates, heretics, and schismatics defending apostasy, heresy, or schism, incur the excommunication reserved *speciali modo* to the Holy See. The same penalty is incurred by those who defend such books or others nominally forbidden by Apostolic letter, or who knowingly read or retain them without due permission.

§ 2. Authors and publishers who, without due permission, print books of Sacred Scripture or annotations and commentaries thereon, incur excommunication reserved to no one.

TITLE XXIV

THE PROFESSION OF FAITH

CAN. 1406

§ 1. Obligatione emittendi professionem fidei, secundum formulam a Sede Apostolica probatam, tenentur:

1.° Coram praeside eiusve delegato, qui Oecumenico vel particulari Concilio aut Synodo dioecesanae intersunt cum voto seu consultivo seu deliberativo; praeses autem coram eodem Concilio vel Synodo;

2.° Coram Sacri Collegii Decano, Cardinalibus primis in ordine presbyterorum et diaconorum et S. R. E. Camerario, promoti ad cardinalitiam dignitatem;

3.° Coram delegato ab Apostolica Sede, promoti ad sedem episcopalem etiam non residentialem, vel ad regimen Abbatiae vel Praelaturae *nullius,* Vicariatus Apostolici, Praefecturae Apostolicae;

4.° Coram Capitulo cathedrali, Vicarius Capitularis;

5.° Coram loci Ordinario eiusve delegato et coram Capitulo, qui ad dignitatem vel canonicatum promoti sunt;

6.° Coram loci Ordinario eiusve delegato et coram aliis consultoribus, assumpti ad officium consultorum dioecesanorum;

7.° Coram loci Ordinario eiusve delegato, Vicarius Generalis, parochi et ii quibus provisum fuit de beneficiis quibusvis, etiam manualibus, curam animarum habentibus; rector, professores sacrae theologiae, iuris canonici et philosophiae in Seminariis, initio cuiuslibet anni scholastici vel saltem initio suscepti muneris; omnes promovendi ad ordinem subdiaconatus; librorum censores, de quibus in can. 1393; sacerdotes confessionibus excipiendis destinati et sacri concionatores, antequam facultate donentur ea munia exercendi;

8.° Coram Ordinario eiusve delegato Rector Universitatis vel Facultatis; coram Rectore vero Universitatis vel Facultatis eiusve delegato, professores omnes in Universitate seu Facultate canonice erecta, initio cuiusque anni scholastici vel saltem initio suscepti muneris; itemque qui, periculo facto, academicis gradibus donantur;

9.° Coram Capitulo vel Superiore qui eos nominavit eorumve delegato, Superiores in religionibus clericalibus.

§ 2. Qui, priore dimisso, aliud officium vel beneficium aut dignitatem etiam eiusdem speciei consequuntur, rursus debent fidei professionem emittere ad normam huius canonis.

The profession of faith was generally connected with the oath of obedience imposed on prelates since the XIIth century, especially on those immediately subject to the Holy See.[1] The Pope himself used to send a kind of public profession to the patriarchs of the East soon after his accession to the papal throne[2]; and documents of the VIIth century testify that a public profession of faith was made by the Pontiff on the occasion of his election or cor-

1 Cfr. c. 4, X, I, 6; c 13, X, I, 33; c 4, X, II, 24 The formula for the Italian bishops in Sickel, *Liber Diurnus*, form 73, 75.

2 Cfr. Reg. Greg I, ed Ewald-Hartmann, I, 5, 28, 39, 438, 448.

onation.[3]   The Council of Trent established substantially the present discipline, and later decrees specified more closely the persons who had to make profession of faith.[4] The present prescribed *form* is contained in our Code and must be followed always.   Besides this profession, there is no special oath prescribed in the Code, and therefore the oath demanded by Pius X in the "*Sacrorum Antistitum*" (Sept 1, 1910) would be abolished (according to can. 6, n. 6) had not the Holy Office since declared that the *Antimodernist Oath* continues in force until the Holy See expressly abrogates it.[5]   Our canon deals only with the *profession of faith,* which, according to § 1, must be made by the following ecclesiastics:

1.° By all those who attend a general or particular *council* or *diocesan synod* with the right to cast either an advisory or a decisive vote.   These must make their profession of faith before the presiding officer or his delegate; the presiding officer himself before the synod or council.

2.° Newly created *cardinals* must make profession of faith before the Dean of the Sacred College, the first in rank among the cardinal priests and deacons, and the Camerlengo of the Holy Roman Church.

3.° *Bishops,* residential as well as titular, Abbots or Prelates *nullius,* Vicars Apostolic and Prefects Apostolic, before the papal delegate.

4.° The Vicar Capitular before the cathedral chapter. Since in this country the consultors supply the cathedral chapter (can. 427), our diocesan administrators must make their profession of faith before the consultors as a body.

---

[3] Wernz, *Ius. Decret*, III, n. 14, p 15 f.

[4] *Trid*, Sess 24, c. 1, 12, *De Ref*, Pius IV, "*Iniunctum Nobis*,"

Nov. 13, 1504, S C C, Jan. 20, 1877 (*Coll. P F.*, n. 1464).

[5] S. O, March 22, 1918 (*A. Ap. S.*, X, 136)

5.° Those who have been promoted to a *dignity or canonicate* must make their profession of faith before the local Ordinary or his delegate, and at the same time before the chapter. We say: " at the same time," for if the bishop or his delegate (who *propter decentiam* should be an ecclesiastical dignitary) is not present when the profession is made before the chapter, it would have to be made again.[6] There cannot be any doubt that *canons of collegiate chapters,* too, are now obliged to make the profession of faith before they take possession of their office or benefice.[7]

6.° *Diocesan consultors* must make their profession of faith before the local Ordinary or his delegate and, at the same time, before the other consultors, who should therefore meet together with the bishop in a convenient place, — the cathedral or another church, the episcopal residence, or a priest's house.

7.° The following must make profession before the *local Ordinary or his delegate:* (a) the vicar general; (b) *pastors* [8] and those provided with a benefice (even though manual only) to which the care of souls is attached; (c) *rectors of seminaries* and *professors* of sacred theology, canon law, and philosophy, at the beginning of each scholastic year,[9] or at least when they assume office; (d) those about to be ordained subdeacons; (e) the censors of books, as mentioned in can. 1393; (f) all priests who are to act as *confessors* or *preachers,* before they are given their appointment or faculties. Under this

---

[6] S. C. C., Jan. 25, Feb 9, 1726, ad III (Richter, *Trid.*, p. 353, n. 19).

[7] Although the decision just quoted (ad I) would exempt them, yet can. 405, § 2, requires it.

[8] See can. 461; pastors are not obliged to make this profession of faith on the day of installation before the people; S. Rit C., July 21, 1855 (*Dec. Auth*, n. 3035).

[9] This rule might also be observed concerning the Antimodernist oath, for it appears very awkward—to say the least—to repeat it every year.

heading, no doubt, also come our assistants or curates, and the confessors and chaplains of nuns [10] and religious institutions.

8.° The *rector* of a *university or faculty* must make his profession of faith before the local Ordinary or his delegate; all the *professors* of a canonically established university or faculty, before the rector at the beginning of each scholastic year, or at least when they assume the office of teaching; the same rule applies to all those who receive *academic degrees,* after they have passed their examinations. Academic degrees, in the proper sense, are the licentiate and the doctorate; the baccalaurate is regarded only as a stepping-stone to the former. The time for making the profession of faith for such graduates is between the examinations and the ceremony of conferring the degree. The profession may most properly be made in the chapel or church, before the staff, board, or faculty of the university, and in presence of the students, or in the *aula academica* before the rector and some professors.

9.° *Superiors of clerical institutes* must make their profession of faith before the chapter or the superior who has appointed them. Thus an abbot should make it before the president or vice-president of his congregation and the monastic chapter.[11] If the superior is appointed by a higher one, this latter, or his delegate, should receive the profession.

§ 2 requires *that the profession of faith* be repeated, according to the rules prescribed in § 1 of this canon, whenever one assumes a new office, benefice or dignity, after giving up the former, even if the new office is of the same species. If a canon or dignitary of a cathedral

10 See can. 529.

11 The profession of faith is not to be identified with the *sacramen-* *tum* at the *benedictio abbatis,* cfr. *Pontif. Rom., s. h. t.*

church obtains a new benefice, office, or dignity in the same cathedral (or collegiate) church, he must renew his profession of faith; and if the change should occur during the vacancy of the episcopal see, the renewal must take place before the vicar-capitular and the chapter.[12]

This rule also applies to pastors who obtain another parish in the same diocese.

Can. 1407

Obligationi fidei professionem emittendi non satisfacit qui eam per procuratorem vel coram laico emittit.

Can. 1407 declares a profession of faith made *by proxy* or before a layman invalid. The validity of such an act had been sustained by canonists of note, such as Navarrus, Sanchez, Barbosa, Reiffenstuel, and Boekhn; but the S. C. C. was of contrary opinion, and its view is here espoused.[13] This is so true that if, for instance, a prelate or canon had made his profession before the Cardinal Vicar of Rome, he would nevertheless have to renew it upon his return to the benefice.

A *layman* cannot validly receive a profession of faith because he lacks spiritual power.

Can. 1408

Reprobatur quaelibet consuetudo contra canones huius tituli.

Every custom contrary to the canons of this title (XXIV) is hereby reprobated.

What we said under can. 1356, § 1, also applies here.

12 S C C , 1595, 1622 (n 19); Nov. 23, 1630 (Richter, *l c.* n. 22)

13 S C. C , Jan. 25, Feb 9, 1726, ad II (Richter, *l c* , 19).

PART V

BENEFICES AND OTHER NON-CORPORATE ECCLESIAS-TICAL INSTITUTIONS

Part V treats of a subject which was once of great importance for the Church at large and, therefore, lavishly discussed by canonists. We can limit ourselves to a few observations.

The term *benefice,* taken from the Germanic law, signifies a grant, especially of real estate or landed property, to subjects or vassals in recognition of services rendered. The practice dates back to the Vth century, and benefices were sanctioned as a permanent source of ecclesiastical revenue by civil and ecclesiastical law. The ecclesiastical benefice arose from the distribution of clerical support, which was formerly held in common, under the supervision of the bishop. The bishop was supposed, through his deacons, to distribute all the voluntary offerings into four, or three, parts, one portion of which was especially assigned for the maintenance of the clergy. With the increase of country parishes and the growth of ecclesiastical holdings, especially in land, it was but natural that the bishops should grant to the country clergy a certain portion of the land destined for their support.[1] This appor-

---

[1] Concerning England, see Lingard, *History and Antiquities of the Anglo-Saxon Church,* ed 2, 1858, pp. 162 ff on benefices in general; see Thomassin, *Vetus et Nova Eccles. Disciplina circa Bene-*

tionment was made upon a *precaria* or petition presented by the clergyman concerned, which had to be renewed every time the place became vacant. When, in the VIth century, the revenue or grant became legally attached to the church itself, the *precaria* was turned into a permanent title or claim, or was attached to the property and church served by the respective cleric.

A similar development is noticeable in the property and revenues of cathedral churches. When the canons ceased to live in common, about the Xth century, each received from the common stock (*massa communis*) a share, which was called *praebenda*. When the so-called secularization set in the ecclesiastical benefice did not lose its character of a benefice, but was distributed in the form of a yearly salary from the government. Thus it is still in Italy, where the pastors, and canons, and all other priests acknowledged by the State receive their income from the public treasury.

In the *U. S.* benefices are almost unknown. A solitary example in New Orleans figured as a notable exception in the decrees of the Second Plenary Council. A few parochial benefices are found in the province of San Francisco. In England, also, benefices are the exception, but in Canada they are more common.[2]

ficia, 1688; N. Garcias, *Tractatus de Beneficiis*, 1636, P. Lewienius, *Forum Beneficiale* 1742; U. Stutz, *Geschichte des Kirchl. Benefizial-wesens*, 1895; Idem, *Die Eigen-* kirche, 1895; and the commentators on X, III, 5

[2] See *Cath. Encycl*, II, 474; as to Canada, see Pouliot, *Le Droit Paroissiale*, 1918.

TITLE XXV

ECCLESIASTICAL BENEFICES

DEFINITION

CAN. 1409

Beneficium ecclesiasticum est ens iuridicum a competente ecclesiastica auctoritate in perpetuum constitutum seu erectum, constans officio sacro et iure percipiendi reditus ex dote officio adnexos.

A benefice is a *juridical entity* permanently established or erected by competent authority, and consisting of a sacred office and the right of receiving the revenues from the endowment attached thereto.

Ens iuridicum is the genus of all institutions, with or without corporate character, having a legal foundation. We may say that the material element, the *beneficium* proper, is personified, inasmuch as it is presented as the subject of rights and duties. It may also be called a fictitious person, but without personal rights. It is the end (*finis*) alone that specifies these rights, and therefore becomes, as it were, the subject of them. The end or purpose of a benefice is spiritual, *viz.*, the sacred office, and the revenues are granted for the sake of the service one renders (*beneficium propter officium*).[1]

A benefice is a *juridical* entity, because the ecclesiastical law[2] has, if not introduced, at least sanctioned the com-

---

1 C. 10, X, III, 1; c. 15, 6°, I, 3.   2 *Ibid.*

bination of two widely different elements, the material and the spiritual. This connection could be effected only by *ecclesiastical authority,* for the end being entirely spiritual, it cannot be attached to any material object except by the authority which controls the spiritual element, and this is the Church.

The revenues of a benefice are granted on account of the sacred office, but in order that they may be given, there is need of a source or treasury from whence they may be taken. This is the endowment (*dos*), which term has a wide significance.

CAN. 1410

Dotem beneficii constituunt sive bona quorum proprietas est penes ipsum ens iuridicum, sive certae et debitae praestationes alicuius familiae vel personae moralis, sive certae et voluntariae fidelium oblationes, quae ad beneficii rectorem spectent, sive iura, ut dicitur, stolae intra fines taxationis dioecesanae vel legitimae consuetudinis, sive chorales distributiones, exclusa tertia earundem parte, si omnes reditus beneficii choralibus distributionibus constent.

The *various sources of ecclesiastical endowment* are:

1.° Property of any kind, movable or immovable, *owned by the benefice itself* as a juridical entity or fictitious person; for instance, a piece of land owned by a church, in which case the owner is the church, not the pastor, or the trustees, or the congregation;

2.° Contributions imposed on families or corporations, such as tithes to be paid by the persons themselves (*decimae personales*), or on goods, produce, stock (*decimae praediales, reales, animalium*);

3.° *Voluntary offerings of the faithful,* which belong

to the rector of the benefice, such as pew-rent, at least in part, plate collections, and subscriptions;

4.° *Stole fees,* to be paid according to diocesan taxation or lawful custom; but never manual mass stipends, as is clear from the text;

5.° *Choir distributions,* except the third part of the same, if the entire revenue of the benefice consists of such distributions. This provision is manifestly intended for canons Note that these revenues must be connected with the office permanently (*in perpetuum*).

This quality was styled by canonists the *obiectiva perpetuitas* of a benefice and constitutes an essential element of the same, but no longer of a parish.[3]

What about *our parishes?* The conclusion is forced upon us that the elements of a benefice may also be found in them. For there can no longer be any doubt that when the three conditions pointed out by the Code and by the decree of the S. C. Consist. of Aug. 1, 1919, are verified (*viz.,* residence, endowment, and boundaries), the rectors of such parishes are pastors. This would mean at least objective perpetuity.

A doubt may reasonably be maintained concerning " national " parishes, because they are actually and almost necessarily more or less subsidiary and fluctuating. On the other hand, the *ens iuridicum,* as well as the purpose of this quasi-corporate entity, are contained in every parish. Besides, since our Code has considerably enlarged the notion of endowment, it is almost impossible to deny the character of benefices to our parishes. Yet a solid doubt remains as to the permanent and stable character of a separate or distinct juridical entity.

3 The law of Justinian (Cod I, 2) supposed that the Saint to whom the church was dedicated was the quasi-proprietor.

DIVISION OF BENEFICES

CAN. 1411

There are different kinds of ecclesiastical benefices, to wit:

1.° *Consistorial benefices, i. e.,* such as are bestowed in consistory (now-a-days chiefly prelatures with dignity); all others are called non-consistorial;

2.° *Secular benefices* are those which may be claimed by the secular clergy, who are, by reason of legal presumption, entitled to all benefices established outside a church or house of religious, even to those which are doubtful. But if a lawful custom or the will of the founder reads differently, there can be no doubt. *Religious benefices* are those existing in the churches or houses of religious, as well as those existing outside these churches or houses that have been given to religious by lawful custom or the will of the founder.

3.° *Double or residential* are those benefices which require residence in addition to service. Those which demand no permanent residence are called *simple* or *non-residential.*

Here it may be noted that a somewhat different characteristic is assigned to double benefices, because they are said to have the care of souls or jurisdiction attached. However, since these latter functions certainly require residence, it was logical to draw the distinction from this obligation.

4.° *Manual, temporary, or removable* are those benefices which are bestowed subject to the will of the appointer; *perpetual* or *irremovable* those which are not only themselves perpetual, but have an incumbent who cannot be removed at will.

5.° *Curata* are benefices that involve the care of souls. They are sometimes united with simple benefices which oblige the holder, for instance, to recite the office or to say Mass in some chapel or on a certain altar.

CAN. 1412 AND 1413

The following *do not go by the name of benefices* in law, although they may resemble benefices:

1.° The office of parish vicar when not erected forever;

2.° Lay chaplaincies not established by competent ecclesiastical authority, that is to say, founded by lay persons from their own money with the obligation of saying Mass;

3.° The office of coadjutor, with or without the right of succession;

4.° Personal pensions;

5.° *Temporary* grants of income made from the property of a church or monastery to an ecclesiastic on condition that if he looses his claim, the revenues shall revert to the church or monastery.

Canons 147–195, unless the contrary is manifest, apply only to non-consistorial benefices that are benefices in the proper sense of the term, for these canons treat of appointment to, and loss of, offices.

CHAPTER I

COMPETENT AUTHORITY

CAN. 1414

1.° Consistorial benefices are erected by the *Apostolic See* alone.

2.° Besides the Roman Pontiff, the *local Ordinaries* can establish in their respective dioceses, non-consistorial benefices, with the exception of dignitaries of cathedral and collegiate chapters (can. 394, § 2).

3.° The Vicar-General needs a special commission from his Ordinary for establishing a benefice.

4.° A Cardinal may erect non-curate benefices in his own title or *diaconia,* unless the church belongs to exempt clerical religious.

REQUISITES OF ERECTION

CAN. 1415-1418

These four canons sum up the conditions required for the lawful erection of a benefice, *viz.,* the endowment, the coöperation of the persons concerned, and the necessary document; can. 1417 refers to conditions in the strict sense.

The *endowment (dos)* must be *stable, viz.,* prospectively durable and *sufficient* for the maintenance of the building, the divine worship, and the ministers.[1]

If the endowment is made in specie or cash, the Ordinary should, in union with the board of administration, see to it that the money is safely invested in *interest-bearing property or titles, i. e.,* stocks or bonds.

It is not forbidden to establish a parish or quasi-parish, even if a sufficient endowment is not immediately available, provided it can be reasonably foreseen that the necessary support will be forthcoming.

Can. 1416 rules that, before a benefice is erected, those *who are interested* in its erection should be *invited and heard,* to wit, the parishioners, and others who may have to contribute or who will probably suffer a detriment. But the omission of this formality does not invalidate the establishment of a benefice or parish.[2]

Can. 1417 permits the founder to lay down *certain conditions* in the charter with the *consent of the Ordinary, i. c ,* the diocesan bishop or the superior of exempt clerical religious if the benefice is to be a religious one. These conditions may be contrary to common law, but they must be *reasonable* and *compatible with the nature of the benefice.* Thus, for instance, the founder may stipulate that the holder of the benefice must be of a certain nation or family,[3] or the youngest among a certain group. This may contravene the common law requiring a certain age; yet the law in our case upholds the will of the founder.[4] However, if a stipulated condition would be subversive of ecclesiastical discipline, or derogatory to divine worship, or contrary to sound morality, it would not bind.[5] Im-

1 Cfr c 9, Dist 1, *de cons ,* c. 26, X, III, 5; c 1, X, III, 29.

2 Cfr c 3, X, III, 48

3 This was not infrequently done in monastic foundations in Ireland, see Bury, *Life of St Patrick,* 1905, p. 174 ff

4 Reiffenstuel, III, tit. V, n 110.

5 A *coniugatus* is unfit, and hence this condition would be invalid; S,

possible conditions would be looked upon as not existing. Concerning irregular persons mentioned in the conditions, a distinction should be made: if the irregularity is not plainly against the honor of the sacred ministry and is, as a rule, dispensed from by the Holy See, we believe that a dispensation should be asked for, provided the candidate is otherwise fit. For to install unfit candidates would be against the nature of an ecclesiastical benefice. If the irregularity is great and one not easily dispensed from, the condition should be treated as impossible.

Conditions once accepted *cannot be validly suppressed or changed* by the local Ordinary, unless the change be favorable to the Church, and even then only with the consent of the founder or patron if the benefice is one of advowson.[6] This rule also holds good if the condition is added that the benefice or beneficiary is not bound to assume other obligations, for instance, preaching, hearing confessions, etc. In this case the Ordinary has no right to compel the beneficiary to accept such obligations.

Can. 1418 requires for the establishment of a benefice a *legal document,* in which the place of the benefice is designated, and the endowment, rights, and obligations are described. Such a paper must be drawn up by the ecclesiastical authority, in our country with the coöperation of a notary public.

C. C., Sept. 20, 1727; Aug. 19, 1730 (Richter, *Trid.,* p. 443); Santi-Leitner, 1898, III, tit. 5, n. 40.

6 Reiffenstuel, III, 5, n. 112 ff.

CHAPTER II

UNION

CAN. 1419–1420

1°. A union of benefices is called *extinctiva,* or *per con-*
'fusionem, when out of two or more suppressed benefices
an entirely new one is created, or when two or more benefices are combined with a third so that they cease entirely
to exist, *i. e.,* as a juridical entity. In both cases the new
benefice assumes all the rights and obligations of the suppressed or united benefices. However, if these rights and
obligations should conflict, only the more substantial and
favorable ones are to be retained.

2°. A union is called *aeque principalis* if two or more
benefices, though united, remain as before, neither one becoming subordinate to the other. In this case each benefice retains its nature, rights and obligations, but one and
the same cleric may hold titles to all. Two independent
dioceses held by one and the same bishop would afford an
example of such a union (*e.g.,* Viterbo-Aoscanella).
Two dioceses thus united may hold their synods either
separately or together, have two vicars-general, distinct
revenues, feasts, etc.[1] The same rule applies to two par-

[1] S. C. C., Jan 11, 1783 (Richter, *Trid.,* p. 35 f.).

ishes united *aeque principaliter:* — their boundaries remain distinct, so that marriages must be performed in the respective parish churches, etc. There is no overlapping in this case, but one and the same pastor attends to both parishes and holds the titles to them.

3.° *Minus principalis* is a union *per subiectionem* or *per accessionem,* in which the several benefices remain distinct, but one is made subordinate or accessory to the other. In this case the accessory benefice follows the principal one, upon which it depends, so that the clergyman who obtains the principal, *eo ipso* receives the accessory benefice, and is bound to comply with the obligations incumbent on both. No doubt this is the meaning of the term *subsidiary parishes* or *chaplaincies,* which the S. Congregation had in view when it directed our American bishops to create such within the boundaries of existing parishes whenever lack of endowment or shifting of the population do not permit the erection of new parishes.[2]

TRANSFER, DIVISION, DISMEMBERMENT, ETC.

CAN. 1421

A benefice is *transferred* when its seat,— for instance, a chapel or church,— is changed from one place to another, whilst the benefice remains the same as to its nature, rights, and obligations.

A *division* of benefices is made if two or more benefices are created out of one; this is also applicable to our parishes.

Dismemberment takes place when a part of the territory or the revenues belonging to one benefice is taken away and united to another benefice, or to a charitable or ecclesiastical institution, as, for instance, a seminary.

2 S C Consist, Aug. 1, 1919 (*Eccl. Rev,* Vol 61, p 551 f.).

Transformation is a specific change of benefices, for instance, if *non curata* would be turned into *curata,* or a collegiate into a cathedral benefice.[3]

Suppression is the extinction of a benefice; this cannot be lawfully done by the civil government.

CAN. 1422

The extinction, suppression, and dismemberment of benefices, when the revenues are withdrawn and no new benefice is erected; the union, whether *aeque* or *minus principalis,* of a religious with a secular benefice, or *vice versa;* and the transfer, division, and dismemberment of benefices belonging to religious, are reserved to the Apostolic See.

RIGHTS OF THE LOCAL ORDINARIES

CAN. 1423

§ 1 and § 2. Local Ordinaries may, for reasons of necessity or great and evident utility of the Church, either *aeque* or *minus principaliter unite parish churches* with one another or with *non-curate* benefices. However, a *unio minus principalis* of a parish with a *non-curate* benefice must be made in such a manner that the latter becomes an accessory to the parish.

This union cannot be performed by the *Vicar-Capitular,* on account of can. 436, nor by the *Vicar-General,* unless he has obtained a special commission for that purpose.

§ 3 rules that such a union must be made for good (*in perpetuum*), in order to avoid a cumulation or plurality of benefices.[4] Reasons of *necessity or utility* would be

---

3 S C C, July 24, 1875 (*A. S. S.,* IX, 8 ff.).
4 *Trid.,* Sess. 21, c 5, *De Ref*

poverty, decrease of the population, the settling of quarrels, increase of divine worship, etc.[5]

Ordinaries *may not unite* a parish with the *mensa* of the chapter or of the bishop, nor with a monastery or church in charge of religious (this being reserved to the Holy See), nor with any corporation, nor with cathedral or collegiate dignities or benefices. However, they *may* unite a *parish with the cathedral or collegiate church* if the latter is located within the boundaries of the same, but in doing so must provide that the parish revenues are invested in the cathedral or collegiate benefice and the actual pastor or his substitute is paid a decent income (the *congrua*).

Can. 1424

Can. 1424 forbids Ordinaries to unite either curate or non-curate benefices *against the will of the actual incumbents,* if the latter suffer damage by that union. It also forbids them to unite benefices of advowson (*iurispatronatus*), either lay or ecclesiastical, with benefices of free collation, without the advowee's consent, and to unite *benefices of one diocese with such of another diocese,* even though both are united *aeque principaliter* and governed by the same bishop. Finally it forbids Ordinaries to unite *exempt* benefices, or such as are *reserved* to the Apostolic See, with others. The reason for this prohibition lies partly in the danger of alienation, partly in the confusion of rights and subsequent litigation.

5 Wernz, *Ius. Decret.*, II, n. 271, p. 372.

CAN. 1425

This canon distinguishes between unions *semipleno iure* and *pleno iure,* made by the Apostolic See. The latter term, according to can. 1422, must be understood of perpetual union, not merely *ad tempus,* for a temporary union may be made by the Ordinary, if it is only partial. The law is:

§ 1. If a parish has, by papal rescript,[6] been united to a religious house as to *temporalities* only, the religious house is entitled to the revenues, and the superior must present to the local Ordinary a member of the *secular clergy,* who is then appointed pastor and receives his salary from the religious house. This arrangement was sometimes made to support religious houses or colleges.[7] Note that the clergyman to be presented for appointment must belong to the diocesan clergy and that he obtains his spiritual jurisdiction from the local Ordinary, upon whom he is entirely dependent as to pastoral rights. The clergyman presented by the religious superior, if he has the necessary qualifications, must be appointed by the bishop, who would otherwise infringe upon the rights of the religious.[8]

§ 2. If a parish is incorporated *pleno iure* with a religious community by the Holy See,[9] the religious superior may designate one of his subjects to take charge of the same; but the local Ordinary has the right to subject the appointee to an examination and to give him his canon-

6 See can 452
7 S C C, Sept. 20, 1727, Jan. 30, 1740; Sept. 20, 1692 (Richter, *Trid.,* p 367, nn 2 ff.)

8 S. C C, July 18, 1761, *et plures* (Richter, *l. c.,* p. 53, n. 11 ff).
9 See can. 456.

ical appointment.[10] Besides, the *pastor religiosus* is subject to the jurisdiction, coercive power, and visitation of the local Ordinary in whatever belongs to the care of souls, as explained under can. 631.

TRANSFER OF SECULAR PAROCHIAL BENEFICES

CAN. 1426

For reasons of necessity, or great and evident utility, Ordinaries may *transfer* the seat of a secular parochial benefice to another place within the boundaries of the same parish; but other benefices they may transfer to the mother church, or to another church of the same or a nearby place, only if the church in which said benefices were founded, has collapsed and cannot be restored. If such a transfer has to take place, the altars or chapels should, if possible, be erected in the church to which the benefice was transferred under the same titles which they had in the original benefice, and all the revenues and burdens of the former church are transferred to the latter.

DIVISION OF PARISHES

CAN. 1427

§ 1. Possunt etiam Ordinarii ex iusta et canonica causa paroecias quaslibet, invitis quoque earum rectoribus et sine populi consensu, dividere, vicariam perpetuam vel novam paroeciam erigentes, aut earum territorium dismembrare.

§ 2. Causa canonica ut divisio aut dismembratio paroeciae fieri possit, ea tantum est, si aut magna sit diffi-

---

10 If the religious has not obtained this appointment, the bishop may recall him at any time, S C   C, Nov. 10, 1734 (Richter, *l. c*, p 54, n 21).

cultas accedendi ad ecclesiam paroecialem, aut nimia sit paroecianorum multitudo, quorum bono spirituali subveniri nequeat ad normam can. 476, § 1.

§ 3. Paroeciam dividens, Ordinarius debet vicariae perpetuae aut paroeciae noviter erectae congruam portionem assignare, servato praescripto can. 1500; quae, nisi aliunde haberi queat, desumi debet ex reditibus ad ecclesiam matricem quoquo modo pertinentibus, dummodo sufficientes reditus eidem matrici ecclesiae remaneant.

§ 4. Si vicaria perpetua aut nova paroecia dotetur ex reditibus ecclesiae a qua dividitur, debet matrici honorem deferre modo et finibus ab Ordinario praestituendis; qui tamen vetatur baptismalem fontem matrici ipsi reservare.

§ 5. Divisa paroecia quae ad aliquam religionem iure spectat, vicaria perpetua aut paroecia noviter erecta non est religiosa; pariter divisa paroecia iuris patronatus, nova paroecia est liberae collationis.

It is evident that this canon refers not only to benefices in the strictly canonical sense of the word, but also to parishes and quasi-parishes. We say, this is evident, because not only this canon, but also can. 476, § 8, expressly mentions parishes. Hence this *canon is law also in the United States.*

§ 1. Ordinaries may, for a just and canonical reason, *divide parishes of any kind* by establishing a perpetual chaplaincy or a new parish, or dismembering the territory of such parishes; and they may do so even against the will of the rectors of the parishes, and without the consent of the people.

This part of our canon should create no difficulty, since the right of the Ordinary to divide or dismember parishes was established by the Decretals as well as by the Council of Trent.[11]   However, there is a canonical hitch concerning parishes which belong (*pleno iure*) to religious.   According to can. 1425, § 2, such a parish is a " religious parish," and can. 1422 strictly reserves the division and dismembration of religious benefices to the Apostolic See. Can. 1427 speaks of *quaslibet paroecias,* whilst can. 1422 uses *quaelibet* in speaking of division or dismembration. Here, then, two canons seem to clash. · However, we may apply here the juridical axiom: " *generi per speciem derogatur,*" which finds its application whenever general and specific terms occur [12] in the same law.   Taken in this light, the *genus* would be benefice, and the *species,* parish.   Consequently, the general rule of can. 1422 would suffer an exception as to parishes.   This is probably the mind of the lawgiver, because Ordinaries with regard to parishes have *intentionem fundatam in iure.* This was also the guiding principle of that passage of " *Romanos Pontifices* " which refers to parishes in England, subsequently applied to the U. S.,[13] and does not question the right of Ordinaries to divide parishes belonging to regulars.   The necessity of abiding by all the formalities was the real point under discussion, and the Constitution decided that these are not strictly required because the missions in England (and the U. S.) are not parishes erected according to the rules of canon law. From this it may be seen that the practice of the Roman Court [14] gives free sway to our Ordinaries and those of England (and other countries, too) in the matter of dividing or dismembering parishes of religious.   However,

11 C. 3, X, III, 48; *Trid ,* Sess. 21, c. 4; Sess. 24, c 13, *De Ref.*

12 Barbosa, *Tractatus Varii,* Axioma 107 (ed. Lugd , 1660, p. 72 f).

13 May 8, 1881; extended to the U. S. in 1885 (*Coll. P. F.,* n. 1552).

14 See S. C. C , June 22, 1743 (Richter, *Trid.,* p. 117, n. 5).

since an incorporated parish of religious can only be obtained by the Holy See (can. 452; can. 1425), it would seem rather presumptuous for an Ordinary to proceed to a division or dismembration without informing the Apostolic See. This seems at least a reasonable assumption, especially since the boundaries of every religious parish are accepted and sanctioned by the Holy See.[15]

§ 2. The sole *canonical reasons* for dividing or dismembering a parish are: great difficulty on the part of the people to come to the parish church or impossibility of properly attending to their spiritual needs because of too great a number.

Note the expression " *ea tantum* "; only the two reasons mentioned are acknowledged as canonical. Hence a desire to create more parishes within a city or diocese cannot be considered a canonical reason for dividing the existing parishes. The *distance* has been sometimes described in Roman decisions [16] as of one or two hours (to be walked, of course), sometimes as 1500 *passus* (about a mile and a quarter), sometimes three Italian miles, sometimes simply a long and arduous way, especially if impeded by a torrent or river.

The phrase " *too great a number* " is relative; it means, if the spiritual welfare of the faithful suffers because there are too many souls to be taken care of. In 1905 and 1907 the S Congregation [17] decided the case of a parish in charge of the Capuchins, which numbered about 6,500 souls and was well taken care of, but divided by the Ordinary. The S. Congregation first refused to sanction the

15 This information, of course, is not required *ad validitatem*

16 S. C C, June 22, 1743; Sept. 27, 1732, Jan 29, 1735, etc. (Richter, *Trid*, 117, nn. 5 ff); a distance of 30 miles would certainly

be sufficient; S. C. C, March 28, 1903 (*Anal. Eccl.*, XI, 116 ff.).

17 S. C C, Jan 21, 1905, July 27, 1907 (*Anal. Eccl.*, XIII, 23 ff.; XV, 338 ff); a legacy of 30,000 lire was promised to the newly erected church.

decree, but new reasons advanced by the episcopal court finally led to a ratification of the same. However, neither the distance [18] from church nor the number [19] of parishioners has ever been definitely settled by the Roman authorities, and it would be futile, therefore, to try to determine either. Local circumstances must be considered and the welfare of souls looked to as the supreme law. The latter does not, however, demand that a flourishing congregation, say of four or five hundred or more families be broken up for the sake of a few " kickers " or to make a vain display of parishes. The fact that old parishes are sometimes loaded down with debts and new parishes often require heavy sacrifices should be duly taken into account.[20] The faithful should not be needlessly burdened, especially in critical times such as ours. A parish with 300 or 400 families who live within a radius of about one mile and a half with good roads or streets, and sometimes street railways and automobiles, can easily be taken care of by the pastor with the aid of one or two assistants and certainly does not call for dismembration, unless perhaps dangerous tracks, or factories, or undesirable quarters would have to be passed by a considerable number of the parishioners.

§ 3. The Ordinary, when he divides a parish, must assign sufficient revenues or provide in some other way (see can. 1500), for the new parish or chaplaincy. If no other source of revenue is available to provide the new parish with sufficient funds, these must be taken from the

18 A distance of one Italian mile has never been considered sufficient for dismembration; see *Anal. Eccl*, XIII, 27

19 One parish had 26,000 souls (= about 5,000 families), which number appeared too great for one

pastor with his assistants to attend to properly, S C. C., Jan. 25, 1879 (*A. S. S.,* XIII, 287 ff)

20 This reason was also advanced in the petition mentioned above of 1905 and 1907.

mother church, provided, however, that a sufficient income is left to the latter. Of course, this holds also if the new parish was detached from a religious parish. Here it is not superfluous to remark that the accounts of a parish in charge of religious should be kept strictly separate from those of the monastery. If there are any accrued funds, the salary to the pastor, as well as the expenses for the upkeep of the church and divine worship must first be deducted, and if anything is then left, the old parish is bound to share it with the newly erected one.

But what if there are *debts on the old parish?* Here the injustice of some divisions becomes apparent. As it is entitled to a share of the revenues, the new parish has to share also the debts,[21] for it would be unjust to saddle a debt which was calculated for 400 or more families, on 150 or even less.

§ 4. If the chaplaincy or new parish is endowed from the revenues of the old, the latter, as the *mother church, is entitled to certain marks of honor,* which should be determined by the Ordinary, who, however, is not allowed to reserve the right of the baptismal font to the mother church. Sometimes a candle had to be offered, sometimes the baptismal water had to be gotten from the mother church,[22] but the latter practice is now forbidden, and justly so, for a parish without a baptismal font is badly handicapped. The bishop may decide what signs of honor should be paid, for instance, a procession, an invitation to preach, etc.

§ 5. A parish detached from one which belongs to religious, does not become a religious parish, and the relig-

21 See can 1500, which confirms what is said in the text

22 S C C, Sept 20, 1879; April 24, 1880 (*A S S.,* XIII, 298, 514 ff).

ious may not claim it, but to obtain it need the recommendation of the bishop and a papal indult.[23]

CAN. 1428

§ 1. Locorum Ordinarii uniones, translationes, divisiones, dismembrationes beneficiorum ne faciant nisi per authenticam scripturam, auditis Capitulo cathedrali et iis, si qui sint, quorum intersit, praesertim rectoribus ecclesiarum.

§ 2. Unio, translatio, divisio, dismembratio facta sine canonica causa irrita est.

§ 3. Adversus decretum Ordinarii unientis, transferentis, dividentis aut dismembrantis beneficia, datur in devolutivo tantum recursus ad Sanctam Sedem.

Can. 1428 mentions certain *formalities* which the local Ordinaries must observe when they unite, transfer, divide, or dismember benefices. One of these is that an *authentic document* be drawn up, signed, and sealed with the diocesan seal. The other formality consists in hearing the *advice* of the chapter; or, with us, of the *diocesan consultors,* which is to be given *collegialiter, i. e.,* at a meeting.[24] Besides, the bishop must also *summon all those who are interested* in the transaction, *viz.,* the parishioners or their representatives, and especially the *rectors of the churches.* However, if these formalities (viz., writing, obtaining the advice of the consultors, hearing the parishioners and pastors) were omitted, it would *not affect the validity of the act.*[25]

---

23 Cfr Leo XIII, *Romanos Pontifices,* May 8, 1881; S. C C., Jan. 25, 1879, (*A. S. S.,* XII, 287 ff.).

24 Formerly the *consent* of the chapter was required for validity (Wernz, *l c*, II, n 267, p. 367), though in this country only the advice of the consultors and the rector of the mission needed to be obtained; *Conc Balt III,* n. 20.

25 Cfr. *A. S. S*, III, 396 ff.

§ 2. A union, transfer, division, or dismembration made *without a canonical reason is invalid,* because every such act involves a change in the status of a church or benefice, and is therefore a species of alienation which no one inferior to the Supreme Pontiff can validly perform without a reason.[26] Therefore if neither the distance nor the number of parishioners demands a division, it is invalid.

§ 3. If the Ordinary deems the reason just and canonical, whilst the greater part of the congregation and the old pastor think it unjustified, the union, transfer, division, or dismembration takes effect, but *recourse is open to the Holy See.* This recourse, however, is not properly an appeal, and, therefore, does not suspend the effect of the episcopal decree, but devolves the matter on the S. C. Concilii.[27]

PENSIONS

CAN. 1429

§ 1. Beneficiis quibuslibet nequeunt Ordinarii locorum pensiones perpetuas aut temporarias imponere quae ad vitam pensionarii durent, sed possunt, dum beneficium conferunt, ex iusta causa in ipso collationis actu exprimenda, eisdem imponere pensiones temporarias, quae durent ad vitam beneficiarii, salva huic congrua portione.

§ 2. Beneficiis autem paroecialibus non possunt, nisi in commodum parochi vel vicarii eiusdem paroeciae a munere abeuntis, imponere pensiones, quae tamen ne excedant tertiam partem reditus paroeciae, quibusvis deductis expensis et incertis reditibus.

§ 3. Pensiones beneficiis sive a Romano Pontifice

26 C 8, X, III, 5.

27 C 3, X, III, 48, Benedict XIV, "*Ad Militantis,*" March 30, 1742, §§ 11, 16, 32; Leo XIII, "*Romanos Pontifices,*" May 8, 1881

sive ab aliis collatoribus impositae, cessant morte pensionarii, qui tamen nequit eas alienare, nisi id expresse
concessum sit.

An ecclesiastical pension may be called an annual allow-
ance from an ecclesiastical benefice, granted by the competent authority either to its former holder, or to a stranger,
generally for some service rendered to the benefice itself,
or to the beneficiary, or at least to the church.

A pension is *personal* if paid by the ecclesiastical beneficiary; *real* if incumbent on the benefice itself. If a
real pension is attached to a benefice in such a way that
not only the present pensionary, but after his death others
are entitled to the pension, it is a *strictly perpetual* pension, whereas one paid during the lifetime of the pensionary only is called *relatively perpetual,* and one paid during
the lifetime of the beneficiary, although paid from the
benefice itself, is called *temporary.*[28]

§ 1 rules that the local Ordinaries may not impose on
any kind of benefice either *perpetual* or *temporary* pensions, which last during the lifetime of the pensionary,
but may, when conferring a benefice, for a just reason to
be mentioned in the act of bestowal, impose a temporary
pension to be paid during the lifetime of the beneficiary,
provided, however, the latter's income is safeguarded.

§ 2. On *parochial* benefices the Ordinaries can impose
pensions only in favor of a pastor or substitute (*coadiu-
tor*) when he leaves his office (as *rector* or *pastor emeri-
tus*). But the amount of this pension shall never exceed
the third part of the entire parish revenues, after all expenses and uncertain revenues have been deducted.

Note the expression *"parish revenues,"* which is not

---

28 Traces of pensions are found
in the acts of the Council of Chalce-
ton, A. D. 451; they were increased
after separate parish and canon's
benefices had been introduced;
Wernz, *l. c,* II, n 321, p. 433.

synonymous with the "pastor's revenues." Hence in our country only the pew-rent, plate and house collections, sure subscriptions, and perhaps interest from money loaned out would have to be considered. From these revenues the current expenses for the pastor's salary and the upkeep of the church, etc., may be deducted.

§ 3. Pensions imposed on benefices either by the Roman Pontiff, or by other collators, cease with the death of the pensioner, who, unless expressly empowered to do so, may not alienate his pension.

TRANSFORMATION

CAN. 1430

Benefices that have the cure of souls attached to them cannot be transformed by the Ordinaries into such as have no such charge, nor can religious benefices be changed into secular ones, or *vice versa*. On the other hand, simple benefices may be changed into *curate* ones, provided there be no express stipulation to the contrary on the part of the founder.

CHAPTER III

CAN. 1431

The Roman Pontiff, being the supreme authority and endowed with universal jurisdiction, may confer benefices in the whole Church and reserve their collation to himself. This proposition is directed against the libelous book of Eybel, which is full of invectives against the Holy See from the point of view of the Febronian and Josephinist schools.[1]

CARDINALS AND ORDINARIES

CAN. 1432

§ 1. Cardinals may confer benefices in their titular churches or deaneries, and Ordinaries in their own dioceses, because they have the priority or right in their favor (*habent intentionem fundatam in iure*).[2]

§ 2. The vicar general, however, cannot confer benefices unless he has received a special commission for this purpose by his bishop. The *Vicar-Capitular* or Administrator, however, can confer parochial benefices, but only

[1] The book: *Was ist der Papst?* was put on the index, and Pius VI, Nov. 28, 1876, issued a special Brief, "*Super Soliditate*", see Denzinger, n 1303.

[2] This is truly called a presumption in law, which has the effect that the bishop in our case is released from proving his right, and the burden of proving it against the bishop devolves on the plaintiff or the one who disputes the bishop's right, see Reiffenstuel, II, tit. 23, n 45.

according to can. 455, § 2, n. 3; other perpetual benefices he may not confer at all, on account of can. 436.

§ 3. If the Ordinary does not make an appointment to a vacant benefice within six months from the time when the vacancy became known to him, the right of making the appointment passes to the Apostolic See, unless (can. 458) special reasons permit a delay, and an administrator is left in the place.

CAN. 1433

Can. 1433 reserves the appointment of *coadjutors* to beneficiaries, with or without the right of succession, to the Apostolic See. But this reservation does not apply to the temporary coadjutors and assistants mentioned in canons 475 and 476.

BENEFICES RESERVED TO THE HOLY SEE

CAN. 1434-1435

Benefices *reserved to the Apostolic See* cannot be validly conferred by inferior prelates, for instance, bishops.

Besides all consistorial benefices and dignitaries in cathedral and collegiate chapters (can. 396, § 1) the following are reserved to the Apostolic See, even though the latter be vacant:

1.° All benefices, including *curata,* which become vacant by the promotion, resignation, or transfer of cardinals, papal legates, the higher officials (assessor, prefect, secretary, subsecretary, regent) of the Roman Congregations, tribunals and offices of the Roman Court and the papal household, even though they be purely honorary.

2.° All benefices which, though founded outside the

Roman Court, become vacant by the death of the beneficiary in the city of Rome.[3]

3.° All benefices invalidly conferred by reason of
simony.

4.° Finally all benefices in which the Roman Pontiff,
either himself or through a delegate, is interested for one
of the following reasons:

(a) Because he had declared the election to the benefice
null and void;

(b) Because he had forbidden the electors to proceed
to an election;

(c) Because he had accepted the resignation of the incumbent;

(d) Because he had promoted, transferred, or deprived
the beneficiary of his benefice:

(e) Because he had given the benefice *in commendam.*

No manual benefices, or such of lay or mixed advowson
(*iurispatronatus*) are reserved, unless expressly stated.

As to the bestowal of benefices founded in Rome, the
particular laws in force there must be observed.[4]

ACCEPTANCE

Can. 1436–1437

No benefice can be validly conferred on a cleric who is
unwilling to accept it, or who does not expressly declare
his acceptance of the same

No one can bestow a benefice upon himself, because
the one who bestows and the one who accepts must be
different persons.[5] This is true also of a clergyman
whose father holds a benefice.[6] Hence, for instance, a

3 This is part of *Regula XIX* of
the Cancellaria Apostolica
4 S. Pius V, "*Intolerabilis,*" June
1, 1569, § 8

5 C. 7, X, III, 7
6 C. 15, X, III, 38; there is not
much danger of this, except in
case of advowson

bishop cannot validly bestow a benefice of his own diocese upon himself; an abbot cannot be a canon of a cathedral or collegiate chapter, even though it be a simple canonicate.[7] Consequently, too, an abbot cannot confer upon himself a parish benefice, nor could the bishop validly give it to him, even though he has all the necessary qualities.

PROVISION TO BE MADE FOR LIFE

Can. 1438

All secular benefices must be conferred for *life*, unless the will of the founder, or an immemorable custom, or a special indult rules otherwise.

QUALITIES OF BENEFICIARIES

Can. 1439

§ 1. No clergyman is capable of accepting or holding *several benefices,* either in his own name, or *in commendam* (see. can. 156).

§ 2. Benefices, the obligations of which the beneficiary cannot fulfil personally, as well as benefices of which one suffices for the decent support of the incumbent, are *incompatible.*

NO DEDUCTIONS PERMISSIBLE

Can. 1440–1441

" Ecclesiastical benefices must be conferred without diminution," was the complete and authentic title of one of the Decretals (III, 12), and the commentators comprised under this heading the imposing of new burdens,

---

7 S. C. C, March 3, 1880 (*A. S. S*, XIII, 461).

division, dismemberment and suppression of benefices.[8] Our canon exclusively intends the first only, *viz.*, the *imposition of new burdens*. These may be of two kinds: *spiritual* and *temporal*. By law, then, the bishops may not impose new *obligations* which would burden either the office holder or the benefice, if these obligations are not mentioned in the original grant.

Such new burdens would be the duty of performing pastoral work, saying more Masses than required, etc., etc. No such burdens may be imposed, although the beneficiaries may be asked to assume them, if necessary.[9]

Temporal obligations would be the giving up of part of the revenues, of charges for certain purposes, etc. All such are forbidden and savor of simony.

Can. 1441 forbids and *reprobates* as simoniacal all deductions made from the revenues, all compensations and payments in the act of preferment, no matter whether they accrue to the appointer, or to the advowee, or to others.[10]

ON WHOM BENEFICES MAY BE CONFERRED

CAN. 1442

Secular benefices may be conferred on secular clerics only, religious benefices only on religious of the institute to which the benefice belongs.

Hence a benefice belonging, *e. g.*, to the Franciscans should not be conferred on a Benedictine, and *vice versa*. This rule also holds with regard to prelacies,[11] and must

8 Cfr. Engel, III, 12, n. 1 f.
9 Wernz, *l c.*, II, n. 321, p 430 f.
10 C. un. X, III, 12; ec. 8, 9,
41, 44, V, 3, *Trid.*, Sess. 24, c. 14, *de Ref.*
11 C. 1, Clem. I, 3.

be observed when a higher superior confers a benefice [12] by devolutive right.

Can. 1443-1445

No one shall take possession of a benefice conferred upon him, on his own authority, or before he has made profession of faith, if the benefice requires such profession. In regard to non-consistorial benefices, the right of installation belongs to the local Ordinary, who may, however, delegate another ecclesiastic,— generally the rural dean.

The *manner* in which installation should take place is prescribed by particular — for instance, diocesan — statutes, or by custom, and the prescribed rite must be observed unless the Ordinary has granted a written dispensation, in which case the dispensation takes the place of the formal installation.

The installation may be performed *by proxy* if a special mandate to that effect has been issued by the appointee.

PRESCRIPTION AND TITULUS COLORATUS

Can. 1446

If a cleric who possesses a benefice is able to prove that he has had peaceful possession of the same for three full years and in good faith, the benefice is his by prescription, even though his title was invalid, provided, however, that no simony was committed.

Concerning the application of prescription to benefices, there was a controversy among canonists [13]; our Code has

---

12 C. un. Clem I, 5   13 Cfr Reiffenstuel II, 26, n. 35.

adopted the affirmative view, under certain conditions, *viz.*:

(a) The possession must have been *peaceful*, with no suit pending;

(b) This peaceful possession must have lasted *three full years*, without interruption;

(c) The possessor must have been honestly ignorant of the fact that he held the benefice unlawfully; and

(d) No simony must have been committed either by him or his proxy.

All this the incumbent has to prove by witnesses or documents. If he succeeds, the benefice is his, even though his original title was doubtful for some reason, for instance, that he was appointed by the administrator or vicar-general against the common law. This benefit is granted to avoid unnecessary litigation.[14]

A LITIGANT BENEFICE

CAN. 1447

To understand this canon it is necessary to know what a petitory and a possessory trial is. A petitory trial turns about the question whether a title or claim is just and valid, whilst in a possessory trial the plaintiff claims the object or right, or asks that he be not disturbed in its possession. A " peacefully possessed benefice " is one that is not disputed, either as to title or as to actual possession (*de iure et facto possessum*).

The text rules that the one who claims a benefice that is peacefully possessed by another, on the supposition or pretence that it is vacant, must clearly state in his petition the name of the possessor, how long he has been in possession, and the particular reason why he has no right

---

14 C un Clem II, 6, but only *ad argumenti instar*.

to the benefice. But the benefice cannot be conferred upon the plaintiff or claimant before a petitory trial has cleared up the title. For the general rule is that only benefices which are vacant by right and in fact (*de iure et facto*) can be validly conferred.

CHAPTER IV

The *iuspatronatus* arose from a transfer of landlord-ism, plus feudalism, to ecclesiastical soil. The Church accepted the protection of the civil power as well as that of laymen who should have been her patrons (*advocati*, hence advowson), but frequently played the part of oppressors and robbers. In course of time certain spiritual rights were granted to lay benefactors,[1] chief among them the right of presenting candidates for ecclesiastical benefices and some honorary and material privileges. If the balance betwen advantages and disadvantages accruing to the Church from advowson were fairly drawn, we believe the latter would exceed the former. Hence we need not be surprised that the Code is not very enthusiastic in this matter, as is apparent from can. 1449, which defines, divides, and limits the *iuspatronatus*.

CAN. 1448

The *iuspatronatus* is the sum total of the privileges and obligations that belong, by ecclesiastical authority, to Catholic founders of churches, chapels, or benefices, and

---

[1] A Latin verse comprises the reasons for admitting advowson thus: *Patronum faciunt dos, aedi-ficatio, fundus*, see the commentators on the Decretats III, 38; also Wernz, *Ius Decret.*, III, n. 401 pp. There is no mention of the iuspatronatus in the *Acta Conc. Balt. III; Conc. Balt II* (n. 184) according to *Prov Balt. I* (1829) rejects the iuspatronatus in this country (*Coll. Lac* III, p. 27).

also to such as have obtained a canonical title from the founders.

The *ecclesiastical authority* alone can connect a material right or favor with a spiritual right, such as presentation radically is. Whether this is done explicitly or implicity is irrelevant.

The *founder* must be a *Catholic,* as shall be seen from can. 1543, although it must be confessed that in Hungary, even Jews tried to obtain the *iuspatronatus.* The term *founder* must not be too strictly interpreted. It includes not only the original or first founder, endower, maintainer, but also those who have restored a church, chapel, or benefice.

" *Qui ab illis causam habent,*" means that the *iuspatronatus* may be obtained not only by a direct privilege or prescription, but also by succession, donation, exchange, and sale; not directly, but indirectly, by reason of another right. That *obligations* correspond to the privileges is evident, because these two terms are always correlative.

Can. 1449

The *iuspatronatus* is *real* if attached to an object or thing, as, for instance, real estate, or a building, or an office. It is *personal* if it inheres in a person. It is *ecclesiastical* if the title itself is ecclesiastical, for instance, a church, a prebend, an office. It is *laical* (lay patronage) if the title is secular, for instance, a civil office or right like that of inheritance. It is *mixed* if it springs from both an ecclesiastical and a civil title, for instance, if a pastor has the right of presentation as pastor and as a member of a certain family. It is *hereditary* if it is obtained through succession or by last will. It is a *family* patronage if it remains among, and is limited to, the next descendants.

It is a clan patronage if it extends to all the descendants comprised by the name *gens,* tribe, or clan, for instance, all the *O'Rourkes.* It is *mixed* if one or more of the above-mentioned titles concur.[2]

CAN. 1450–1451

No patronage can be established validly on any title in future. *Local Ordinaries* may, however,

(a) Grant to those of the faithful who build churches or found benefices, either entirely or in part, a claim to *spiritual suffrages* in proportion to their generosity, either for a certain time, or forever; for instance, a founded Mass or office;

(b) Admit the foundation of a benefice on condition that for the first time the founder himself, if he is a clergyman, be appointed to the benefice or another clergyman presented by him.

Local Ordinaries should endeavor to induce patrons to abdicate their *iuspatronatus,* or at least the right of presentation, in exchange for *spiritual suffrages* for themselves and their families. If a patron is unwilling to cede the *iuspatronatus,* this can be exercised only in accordance with the following canons.

POPULAR PATRONAGE

CAN. 1452

Elections and presentations to *parochial benefices by the people* (*i. e.,* congregations, as for instance, in Switzerland) can be *tolerated* only if the people elect one of three candidates designated by the local Ordinary. Hence

---

2 The distinction between *familiare* and *gentilitium* is not explained in the same way by all writers.

neither the government, nor the municipality, nor the congregation as such, are allowed to reject all three candidates proposed by the Ordinary.

TRANSMISSION OF PATRONAGE

Can. 1453

A personal *iuspatronatus cannot be validly transmitted,* either by inheritance, donation, change or sale, to infidels, public apostates, heretics, schismatics, members of secret societies condemned by the Church, or to any one who is under a declaratory or condemnatory sentence of excommunication.

That a personal *iuspatronatus* may be validly transmitted to others, the written consent of the Ordinary is required, with due regard to the last will of the founder, which, once accepted, must be kept sacred.

If a *real* patronage passes to any of the above-named persons it remains suspended, *viz.,* until said person becomes reconciled to the Church.

AUTHENTIC PROOF REQUIRED

Can. 1454

No *iuspatronatus* can be admitted unless it is established by an authentic document or other lawful proofs, as seen in Book IV.

PRIVILEGES OF PATRONS

Can. 1455

The privileges of patrons are the following:

1.° To *present* a clergyman (not a layman) for a vacant church or benefice;

2.° To obtain *support* from the revenues of the church or benefice, if there are any left, should he (the patron) become reduced to poverty without his fault. This claim remains even if the patron has renounced the advowson in favor of the church, or if a pension was by mutual agreement reserved to the patron but proves insufficient for his support. However, this equitable right can be claimed only if the patron has complied with his obligations as advowee, and the beneficiary has a decent support.

3.° To enjoy certain *honorary* prerogatives, where these are customary. These prerogatives are:

(a) To have his family coat-of-arms placed in the church;

(b) To precede all other laymen at processions and other similar functions;

(c) To occupy a more prominent seat in the church, but outside the sanctuary and without a canopy.

Sometimes two swings of the censer at the incensation are permitted.

WIFE AND MINORS

CAN. 1456

A wife exercises the *iuspatronatus* herself, children who are not yet of age, through their parents or guardians; if the parents or guardians are non-Catholics, the patronage remains suspended until the minors come of age, or the parents or guardians become Catholics.

TIME OF PRESENTATION

CAN. 1457–1458

The presentation for a vacant benefice, whether lay, ecclesiastical, or mixed, must, if there be no obstacle, be made within at least *four months* from the day on which the collator, *i. e.*, generally the local Ordinary, has notified the patron of the vacancy, and from among the priests who have successfully passed the concursus, if the benefice requires a concursus.

Exceptions to this rule are:

(a) Any legitimate obstacle which prevents the patron from making the presentation, *e. g.*, illness, or suspension, or a journey to Rome [3];

(b) The fact that a *shorter time* is prescribed either by the will of the founder or by lawful prescription.

If no presentation has been made within the prescribed time, the church or benefice becomes, for this time only, one of *free collation, i. e.*, the Ordinary can appoint whom he pleases, without consulting the patron. But if a quarrel or *dispute* arises during the four months, concerning the right of presentation, either between the Ordinary and the patron, or between different advowees, or about the candidates, who of them should be accepted, the *appointment must be suspended* until the controversy is settled, and, if necessary, an administrator (*oeconomus*) shall be appointed by the Ordinary for the church or benefice.

COLLEGIATE PRESENTATION

CAN. 1459–1460

§ 1. If several individuals are patrons, they may agree among themselves, both for themselves and for their successors, to exercise the right of presentation alternately.

§ 2. But in order to be valid this agreement must have the written consent of the Ordinary, which consent, when once given, cannot be validly revoked against the will of

---

[3] C 5, X, III, 8; formerly ecclesiastical patrons had six, lay patrons only four months for making the presentation; c 22, X, III, 38.

the patrons either by the Ordinary himself or by his successor.

Whilst canon 1459 treats of patrons severally, can. 1460 mentions a body or college of patrons, which may be a corporation, for instance, a monastery or university which possesses the *iuspatronatus*. For such collegiate presentation the following rules are laid down:

§ 1. If the advowson is exercised by a *college* or *body of patrons,* the candidate who obtains the *majority of votes,* according to can. 101, § 1, must be considered as chosen or presented. After two ballots have been cast without result, all those are to be considered as presented who obtain a majority in the third ballot, even though they receive the same number of votes.

§ 2. The same principle is applied to a *non-collegiate body, i. e.,* when several patrons have an individual right of presentation. If they cannot agree as to alternate presentation, the candidate who obtains at least a relative majority of the votes cast by the litigant patrons is regarded as presented, and if several candidates are selected with the same number of votes, they must all be considered as presented.

§ 3. He who is entitled to exercise a patronage on *various* grounds, (for instance as founder, endower, builder, or by reason of inheritance) enjoys as many votes as he has titles.

§ 4. Every patron may, before the presentation is accepted, present more than one candidate, either at once or successively, because the *ius ad rem* is not yet acquired; but he must present these candidates within the prescribed time and not exclude those whom he presented first.

CANDIDATES

CAN. 1461-1464

No one, even though he be a clergyman and the most worthy candidate available, *can present himself,* nor vote with others in order to obtain the number of votes necessary for presentation. To do this would savor of ambition, and is forbidden, even by proxy.[4]

The patron, even if he be a layman, can not present for a church or benefice a cleric who has not successfully passed the *concursus,* whenever this is required.

The *candidate to be presented must be fit, i. e.,* he must have all the qualities required by common law, or particular statutes, or the charter of foundation on the day when the presentation is made, or at least on the day when he accepts the presentation. The qualities required by common law are laid down in Book II of our Code.

The *presentation must be made to the local Ordinary,* to whom it appertains to judge whether the candidate is fit.

To form his judgment the Ordinary shall make inquiry about the candidate,[5] and obtain information, if necessary in secret.

The Ordinary is not obliged to manifest to the patron the reasons for rejecting a candidate.

He may do so, but cannot be compelled, because compulsion might involve unnecessary odium.

---

4 Cc. 15, 26, X, III, 38; Reiffen-   5 See can. 149.
stuel, *h t.,* n. 72.

REJECTION OF THE CANDIDATE PRESENTED

CAN. 1465

§ 1. If the candidate is found unfit, *i. e.*, if he lacks the qualities required (can. 1463) and is therefore rejected by the Ordinary, the patron (no matter whether he be an ecclesiastical or a lay advowee), provided the four months have not elapsed through his own negligence or carelessness, *may present another candidate* within another four months. If this one, too, is found *unfit*, the Ordinary may, for this occasion, freely appoint one of his own *choice*, and we believe he not only may but should make use of this right, unless the patron has recourse to the Holy See within ten days from the day when he was notified of the rejection. If recourse is taken, this fact must naturally be communicated to the Ordinary. Pending a decision, the benefice remains vacant. In the mean time, the Ordinary shall, if necessary, appoint an *oeconomus* to the vacant church or benefice.

§ 2. A presentation tarnished with the stain of simony is *null and void* by law, and the same rule holds of the subsequent installation of the candidate by the Ordinary.

EFFECT OF ACCEPTED PRESENTATION

CAN. 1466–1468

Every candidate who has been lawfully presented and found fit, by accepting presentation, obtains the right (*ius ad rem*) to be canonically installed.

The right to grant canonical institution belongs to the local Ordinary, but not to the Vicar-General, unless he has obtained a special mandate to that effect.

If several candidates have been lawfully presented, and all are proved fit, the Ordinary may choose from among them the one whom he deems most suitable or worthy.

The canonical installation for any and every benefice, even if it has no cure of souls attached to it, should take place *two months* from the date of presentation, unless a legitimate obstacle prevents.

If the candidate presented resigns his right or dies before the canonical installation has taken place, the patron again has the right of presentation, to be exercised, as before, within four months.

OBLIGATIONS OF PATRONS

CAN. 1469

§ 1. The burdens or *obligations* of patrons are the following:

1.° To notify the local Ordinary if the property of the church or benefice is suffering material damage, without, however, meddling in the administration of the same;

2.° To *rebuild* a church if it has collapsed, or to make the repairs that are judged necessary by the Ordinary, if the advowson was obtained by reason of having built the church and this burden of repairing or rebuilding is not incumbent on others, according to can. 1186.

3.° If the patronage is based upon the title of *endowment,* the patron must supply new revenues in case the old revenues of the church or benefice become so insufficient, that either divine worship cannot be properly kept up, or the benefice cannot be conferred.

§ 2. In case the church has collapsed, or is in need of urgent repair, or if the endowment has become insufficient, the *iuspatronatus* remains suspended until the patron is able or willing to comply with his obligation.

§ 3. If the patron rebuilds or repairs the church, or supplies the needed revenues, the *iuspatronatus* within the time set by the Ordinary, revives; otherwise it ceases *ipso iure* and without any declaration after the expiration of the term.

LOSS OF THE IUSPATRONATUS

CAN. 1470

§ 1. The *iuspatronatus* is lost, as we have seen in the preceding canon, if the patron fails to rebuild, repair, or re-endow the benefice. It may also cease for one of the following reasons:

1.° If the patron renounces his right; this renunciation may be either total or partial; but if one of several individual patrons gives up his right, no prejudice is thereby created to the others.

2.° If the Holy See revokes the right or permanently suppresses the church or benefice.

3.° If there is a legitimate *prescription* against the patron. This is but another form of tacit resignation.

4.° If the property or office in which the *iuspatronatus* inheres perishes; or the family, clan (*gens*) or line to whom the advowson was reserved, dies out. In this latter case the patronage does not become hereditary, nor can the Ordinary validly permit it to pass over to persons not connected by blood relationship with the patron, family, or clan.

5.° If, with the consent of the patron, the church or benefice is united with another, which is of free collation, or if it becomes elective or regular. This, too, is a kind of tacit resignation.[6]

---

6 Cfr Santi-Leitner, III, 38, n. 43 f.

6.° By *crime*, as follows:

(a) If the patron attempts, even though unsuccessfully, to transfer his *iuspatronatus* to another by *simony;*

(b) If he becomes an apostate, a heretic, or a schismatic;

(c) If he unjustly usurps or retains rights and property belonging to the church or benefice;

(d) If he, either personally or through another, kills the rector or any other cleric attached to the advowson church, or the beneficiary.

§ 2. This last-named crime affects also the heirs, whilst the three first mentioned concern only the patron himself.

§ 3. To incur privation of advowson on account of any of the four crimes mentioned, a declaratory sentence is required and suffices.

§ 4. No one is allowed to exercise the *iuspatronatus*, or to enjoy its privileges, who has incurred a censure or infamy by law, inflicted by a condemnatory or declaratory sentence, as long as this censure is not removed.

INDULT OF PRESENTATION

CAN. 1471

If the Apostolic See has, either by a concordat or otherwise, granted the privilege of presentation to a vacant church or benefice, this grant must *not* be construed as *iuspatronatus,* but the indult must be interpreted strictly according to its tenor. This is clearly intended for countries where the separation of Church and State is not yet in effect, either totally or partially. The interpretation must be applied in a similar manner to concordats.

CHAPTER V

RIGHTS AND DUTIES OF BENEFICIARIES

RIGHTS IN GENERAL

CAN. 1472–1473

Every beneficiary, after having taken canonical possession of his benefice, is entitled to all the rights, temporal
and spiritual, attached to the same.

These rights are, of course, the rights specially connected with the benefice. Besides these there are the general rights arising from the clerical state, as set forth in
can. 118–123, which are by no means curtailed through
the fact of one's being installed in a benefice.

Of the *temporal rights* the foremost is that of enjoying
the revenues derived from the benefice, as far as they are
needed for the beneficiary's decent support. He is entitled to these revenues even though he may possess other
property, but is *obliged* to devote the superfluous *revenues* to the poor or to charitable institutions.

Since this canon is undoubtedly intended also for pastors and curates who hold no strictly so called benefices,
it may be well to recall the *different kinds of clerical
property*. They are:

(1) *Patrimonial,* if derived from the cleric's patrimony, *e. g.,* by inheritance;

(2) *Quasi-patrimonial,* or industrial, if acquired by
the clergyman's own industry or diligence, from work

which has no connection with his benefice, for instance, as a lecturer, a musician, an author;

(3) *Parsimonial,* if acquired from ecclesiastical or beneficiary revenues by living very frugally, so that something is left over and above the expenditures for decent support;

(4) *Beneficiary,* if acquired from the benefice after a decent support has been deducted, in other words from the surplus revenues.

What is a *decent support* must be decided according to the circumstances of time and place. It includes moderate and customary hospitality, which has always been inculcated by the Church, and suitable recreation and provision for old age and inability, for instance, by life insurance or interest-bearing investments.[1]

Our text speaks of *superfluous* revenues. What are they? Discarding the patrimonial and quasi-patrimonial, there can be question only of parsimonial and strictly beneficiary income. However, since the Code mentions *congrua,* it is not likely that parsimonial incomes are understood, and canonists generally do not apply the law to them. Hence only the *strictly beneficiary* revenues, which are left after one has provided for his decent support, can be understood. These are *superfluous,* and must therefore be applied, as the law says,[2] *to the poor or to charitable institutions.* Note that this is a strict *obligation,* not *ex mera caritate,* but *ex iustitia.* Our text is quite explicit on this point, since it calls the beneficiary only the *usufructary,* not the possessor or lord, of his benefice. Usufruct is the right of enjoying a thing

---

[1] Cfr Santi-Leitner, III, tit 25, n 2 f.

[2] Cfr. c. 16, X, III, 5; c. 44, X, V, 3; *Trid.,* Sess. 25, cc. 1, 9, *de Ref ;* Santi-Leitner, III, tit. 25, n. 7, opposes this interpretation, but without a good reason.

which is not one's property. This law is very logical, because the right of property in case of a benefice, by a fiction of law, is invested in the juridical entity, which is the benefice itself.

CAN. 1474–1475

If a benefice requires the reception of an *order*, be it minor or major, the beneficiary must receive that order before he can be installed.

§ 1. A beneficiary is obliged faithfully to fulfill the special obligations connected with his benefice, and, besides, to recite the *canonical hours* daily.

§ 2. If he neglects the obligation of reciting the divine office without a lawful reason, he is bound to make *restitution* of the revenues received, in proportion to the extent of his culpable omission, and should give the amount due to the church building, or to the diocesan seminary, or to the poor.

The obligation of reciting the divine office (*Breviary*) has been dealt with in Vol. II of this Commentary. From the decisions of the Holy Office we here supply the following points: One who holds either a chaplaincy or other ecclesiastical benefice cannot comply with the obligation of reciting the divine office through another, on the ground that his time is occupied with literary studies.[3] Nor is the recitation of the entire office on one day sufficient for the next.[4] Those who cannot recite Matin and Lauds, but are able to recite the little hours, are obliged to say the latter.[5]

[3] *Prop.* 21 *damn. a* S. O., Sept. 24, 1665 (Denzinger, n 992).

[4] *Prop.* 35 *damn a* S. O., March 18, 1666 (*ibid.*, n 1006).

[5] *Prop.* 54 *damn. a* S. O., March 4, 1679 (*ibid.*, n. 1071).

The *proportion* in which restitution is to be made has been declared by Pius V as follows: Those who omit the entire office, lose all their revenues corresponding to the day or days on which this duty was entirely neglected; those who neglect Matins only lose one-half of the revenues; those who omit the rest of the hours, also one-half, and for each single hour the sixth part of the revenues of the respective day.[6] These rules, however, apply only to such beneficiaries as have no other duty than to recite the divine office.[7]

OBLIGATIONS OF ADMINISTRATION

CAN. 1476–1478

§ 1. As guardian of his benefice, the beneficiary must administer the goods belonging to the same according to law.

§ 2. If he has been culpably *negligent,* he is bound to *repair the damage,* and the local Ordinary shall compel him to make up for the loss. If the beneficiary is a pastor, he can be removed (can. 2147 ff.).

§ 1. The *ordinary expenses* of administration and of collecting the revenues must be borne by the beneficiary.

§ 2. *Extraordinary* expenses incurred for repairing the beneficiary's residence must be borne by those who are obliged to make these repairs, unless the charter of the foundation or mutual stipulation and custom provide otherwise.

§ 3. *Minor repairs* which the beneficiary has to make at his own expense should be made as soon as possible, to avoid greater ones.

6 S Pius V, " *Ex proximo,*" Sept. 20, 1571

7 A pastor, for instance, even supposing he were a beneficiary, receives his salary chiefly for pastoral work; and therefore the duty of

The local Ordinary is obliged to see to it, through the rural deans, that the property belonging to benefices is preserved and properly administered.

LEASFS

CAN. 1479

In leasing property belonging to benefices it is not permitted, without the consent of the Ordinary, to demand that the money be paid over six months in advance. In extraordinary cases the Ordinary should provide by appropriate precepts, that such a lease does not result in damage to a pious institution or to the beneficiary's successors.

HOW THE REVENUES ARE TO BE DIVIDED IN CASE OF THE BENEFICIARY'S DEATH

CAN. 1480

In case of death, the yearly revenues must be divided between the beneficiary's successor and predecessor, or their heirs, in proportion to the time either has served the benefice, taking into account all the revenues and expenses. If the predecessor was in office four months, for example, he or his heirs are entitled to one-third of the revenues, minus any obligations that remain unpaid.

However, legitimate custom or particular statutes may provide another mode of distribution.

restitution is reduced to a minimum. Cfr. Noldin, *De Praeceptis,* 1914, n. 758, f., p. 794, who justly maintains that barely the tenth part of the revenues would have to be restored.

WHAT IS TO BE DONE IN CASE OF VACANCY

CAN. 1481–1482

All revenues accruing during the vacancy of a benefice go in equal parts to the endowment or common fund, and to the building or vestry (sacristy) of the Church. The expenses, especially the salary of the administrator, may, of course, be deducted.

Lawful custom may permit these funds to be applied to the common good of the diocese.

As to the so-called *media annata, i. e.,* the taxes to be paid for certain benefices from the income of the first year (*fructus primi anni*), this should be retained wherever it is in vogue, and the peculiar statutes and praiseworthy customs of each diocese or region with regard to the *media annata* should be upheld.

The *media annata,* which originated under Boniface VIII, was never introduced into this country.

EPISCOPAL REVENUES

CAN. 1483

The property of the *mensa episcopalis* shall be carefully administered by the bishop. His residence must be kept in good condition, and if repairs are required, the expenses are to be paid from said *mensa,* unless others are obliged to defray them.

The bishop shall also take care that an accurate inventory is made of all the movable property belonging to the episcopal residence, and that everything is safely transmitted to his successor.

CHAPTER VI

RESIGNATION

CAN. 1484–1486

The general principles governing the resignation of beneficiaries are the same as those laid down in can. 184–191, to which we may therefore refer the reader (see Vol. II of this Commentary). The substance of the above three canons is as follows:

1. Since sordid occupations or begging are unbecoming to the clerical state in general,[1] and more particularly to *clerics in higher orders,* the Ordinary is not allowed to accept the resignation of any cleric in *major orders* unless he is certain that the beneficiary has other means of procuring a decent support. Proof to this effect must be given before the Ordinary can lawfully accept such a resignation. The oath of the beneficiary alone would not suffice, but at least one trustworthy witness is required and he must testify under oath.[2]

2. This rule holds more especially if the benefice which a cleric wishes to resign, constitutes the title upon which he was ordained (*titulus beneficii*). Such a resignation would be *null and void,* unless the beneficiary expressly

---

1 *Trid*, Sess 21, c 2, *de Ref.*
2 S. C P. F, April 18, 1757, ad
1 (*Coll.*, n. 405), S. C. C., Feb 9,

1726, ad III and IV (Richter, *Trid*, 113, n 7).

stated that he had been ordained to that title *and* had substituted another legitimate title with the consent of the Ordinary. Two, or rather say, three conditions are therefore required:

(a) An express statement of the title of ordination;

(b) Proof that another title has been substituted, and

(c) The consent of the Ordinary into whose hands the benefice is resigned.

An express statement is one to which no qualification (for instance, " perhaps," " I believe," etc.) is attached.

The consent of the Ordinary must be given by means of a declaration that the substitution has been lawfully made.[3]

A legitimate title is any one of those mentioned in can. 979, and, no doubt, now also one of those enumerated in can. 981, because *service* and *mission* have been legitimated by our Code.

A *conditional resignation* (canon 1486) may be made in favor of another (*in commodum aliorum*) or under some condition proper which either affects the appointment to the benefice itself, or its revenues, or burdens imposed upon the benefice. Such a resignation in favor of another is strictly forbidden by reason of the danger of introducing hereditary succession.[4] The other kind, too, is here forbidden, and Ordinaries may not accept it.

The *provisio beneficii* may be affected by a threefold kind of resignation, which the canonists designate by *accessus, ingressus,* and *regressus.*

A resignation by *accessus* is that made by a cleric who has obtained only the *ius ad rem, i. e ,* a claim to the benefice by accepted presentation or nomination.

---

3 S C C , Feb 9, 1726 (*l c.*).   April 1, 1568; "*Intolerabilis,*" June
4 *Trid.,* Sess 25, c 7 *de Ref ,*   1, 1569; this was called a resigna-
S. Pius V, "*Quanta Ecclesiae,*"   tion with the clause "*non aliter,*"

A resignation by *ingressus* is that made by a cleric who has the *ius in re,* that is to say, the right to hold the benefice, but has not yet taken possession thereof.

A resignation by *regressus* is that made by a cleric of a benefice which he actually possesses.[5] This, too, is forbidden, for the reason alleged above, and also because of the restriction imposed on the bestower as well as on the patron.

But the Code admits one conditional resignation, viz., that of a *benefice disputed* either by a petitory or a possessory claim, provided the resignation is made in favor of one of the contestants, in order to end the quarrel.

EXCHANGE OF BENEFICES

CAN. 1487–1488

An exchange is a mutual transfer of equal interests, the one in consideration of the other [6]; and if the objects are ecclesiastical benefices, the exchange is a *permutatio beneficiorum.*

Such an exchange, says can. 1487, can be made only for a reason involving the necessity or utility of the Church, or for some other just cause, provided, moreover, that both beneficiaries really possess their benefice.[7] Valid exchange further requires:

(a) That no other interested persons suffer a detriment;

(b) That, if the benefice be one of advowson, the consent of the patron be obtained;

(c) That the exchange be made with the permission of the local Ordinary, *i. e.,* the bishop; the Vicar-general

---

5 Santi-Leitner, I, tit. 9, n 24.   7 C. 13, X, II, 25.
6 Blackstone-Cooley, *Comment,*
II, 323.

needs a special mandate to ratify such an exchange and the Vicar-Capitular cannot ratify it at all;

(d) That, finally, the exchange be made either in writing or before two witnesses.

The local Ordinary must either refuse his consent or give it within *a month,* and the exchange is valid from the date of the consent given. But the local Ordinary cannot ratify an exchange if one or both of the benefices involved are reserved to the Holy See; because the latter's right of free collation might thereby be injured.[8]

An exchange supposes benefices of equal or nearly equal value and importance. When *two benefices are unequal* as to income or other value, an exchange, according to can. 1488, is not permissible if it is made by reserving part of the revenues or the payment or grant of any valuable object, because of the danger of simony. This rule, it appears, comprises all kinds of unequal exchange, between conventual as well as parish benefices, between individuals as well as corporations.[9]

An exchange of benefices cannot be made between more than *two* beneficiaries. Hence no triangular or quadrangular exchanges are permitted, except by special permission from the Supreme Pontiff.[10]

8 Santi-Leitner, III, 19, n. 8.   10 Reiffenstuel, I, 9, n. 123 ff.
9 C. 5, X, III, 19, c. 6, X, III,
19 is antiquated.

TITLE XXVI

OTHER NON-CORPORATE ECCLESIASTICAL INSTITUTIONS

Can. 1489–1494

§ 1. Local Ordinaries may erect hospitals, orphanages and similar institutions destined for religious or charitable (spiritual or temporal) works; they may also endow such institutions with the character of ecclesiastical corporations.

The right of the Church to found such institutions cannot be disputed. This right is set forth in Part VI, which immediately follows. The canonical nomenclature for a hospital, orphanage, or similar institution under ecclesiastical control is *domus religiosa,* a religious or rather *ecclesiastical* foundation or house. To deserve this name, an institution must be destined for works of piety or charity by the *ecclesiastical authority, i. e.,* the local Ordinary or an exempt religious superior. An institution founded by private persons without ecclesiastical authority, even though its purpose be sacred, is called merely *domus pia.*

The text says: *et per eius decretum persona iuridica in ecclesia constitui.* The *corporate character* attached to such an institution by the decree of the Ordinary may be taken in a twofold sense: as a corporation proper and as an institute or juridical entity. The corporate character can only be given if the house belongs to a community or religious corporation which owns and administers it,

546

either by itself or in the name of the Church.   For neither patients nor orphans constitute a corporation; they are merely beneficiaries or *destinatarii*.   In the wider sense, the object (*finis*) of an institute is, by a legal fiction, the carrier or subject of its rights and duties, *i. e.*, generally the officials or representatives acknowledged by law.

§ 2.   Before the local Ordinary gives his approval, or issues a decree, he must *assure himself that the foundation is really useful and sufficiently endowed,* or that it has prospects of obtaining sufficient funds.   If he neglects this duty, the blame falls on the Ordinary, together with such undesirable consequences as debts, etc.

§ 3.   In all such institutions the rector or syndic shall *administer the temporalities* according to the by-laws laid down in the charter.   His rights and obligations are the same as those of the administrators of other ecclesiastical property.

The *charter must contain an accurate description of the constitution,* purpose, endowment, administration, and government of the institution, also of the use to be made of the revenues and who is to succeed to the property in case the institution goes out of existence.

Of the charter and by-laws *two copies* must be made, one of which is to be kept in the archives of the institution itself, the other in the diocesan court.

The local Ordinary has the *right and the duty of visiting* all such institutions, even though they are corporations or otherwise exempt.   •

If non-corporate institutions are in charge of a *religious diocesan* community, they are entirely (*i. e.,* both in spiritual and temporal matters) subject to the jurisdiction of the local Ordinary; if they are in charge of a *pontifical* or papal religious community, they are under the supervision of the local Ordinary in whatever concerns faith and morals, pious devotions, and the administration of the Sacraments.

Although a pious or ecclesiastical institution may, in virtue of its charter, or by prescription, or by a papal privilege, have obtained exemption from the jurisdiction and visitation of the local Ordinary, the latter is *entitled to demand an account* of its affairs, and every contrary custom is hereby reprobated.

If a founder insists that the administrators should not be obliged to render an account to the local Ordinary, the foundation cannot be accepted as an ecclesiastical one.

The local Ordinary shall see to it that the *pious desires* of the faithful, as set forth in the charter of such institutions, be *fully carried out*.

Without the *permission of the Apostolic See* such institutions cannot be suppressed or incorporated with others, or converted to purposes other than those prescribed by the founders, unless the charter provides differently.

PART VI

THE TEMPORAL POSSESSIONS OF THE CHURCH

This last part of the administrative law of the Church treats first of the property-right of the Church and then of the mode of acquiring temporal goods and their administration. To this are added two specific kinds of obligation which involve some peculiarities as to form and object, *viz.*, contracts and pious foundations.

That this part of the Code brings the Church into closer relation with the State and the world at large goes without saying, for it forms the sensible or commercial link between the two societies, but also the necessary bridge between the spiritual and the temporal domain.

RIGHT OF THE CHURCH TO POSSESS PROPERTY

CAN. 1495

§ 1. Ecclesia catholica et Apostolica Sedes nativum ius habent libere et independenter a civili potestate acquirendi, retinendi et administrandi bona temporalia ad fines sibi proprios prosequendos.

§ 2. Etiam ecclesiis singularibus aliisque personis, moralibus quae ab ecclesiastica auctoritate in iuridicam personam erectae sint, ius est, ad normam sacrorum canonum, bona temporalia acquirendi, retinendi et administrandi.

The first of the four introductory canons of this Part vindicates the natural and historic right of the Church to possess material property in these words:

§ 1. The *Catholic Church and the Apostolic See have the inherent right, freely and independently of any civil power, to acquire, retain, and administer temporal goods for the pursuit of their own ends.*

§ 2. Individual churches and other *corporations* established as such by ecclesiastical authority, are also endowed with the right of acquiring, retaining, and administering their own property, according to Canon Law.

To a practical American these propositions appear as evident as that two and two are four.[1]

1. The Catholic Church, being a perfect, *i. e.*, autonomous, legal, and visible society, with its own proper end, cannot lack the means which are necessary to attain that end. Now, one of these means is the right to possess property. For the Church is founded for men who are endowed not only with a soul, but also with a body that needs support and is subject to the senses. The Church needs temples, sacrifices, and sacraments, and it needs ministers, who also are men. All these things are *essential* to the society founded by the Son of One, who is at the same time, God. His ministers cannot live on the word alone; they need at least some bread. Divine worship also requires material aid and support. Now, divine worship certainly belongs to the Church, in virtue of her very existence and end. Nor can we imagine that God in

[1] It is not necessary to recall all the obnoxious laws of *morte main* which were made from the twelfth to our century, see Coulondre, *Des acquisitions des biens par les Etablissements de la Religion Chrétienne en Droit Romain et dans l'Ancien Droit Français,* 1886, Mamacchi, *Del Diritto Libero della Chiesa di acquistare e di possidere Beni Temporali si mobile che stabili,* 1769, C. Scheys, *De Iure Ecclesiae acquirendi et possidendi Bona Temporalia,* Louvain, 1892, *Archiv. fur Kath. K.-R*, 1904, 22 ff.

his providence should have left her destitute of the power necessary to procure these necessary means, or that He should have thrown her upon the mercy of the State, for this would involve a handicap and a dependence which would make her the mercenary and slave of a society which, as to its end, is inferior to the Church.

Neither can there be, *per se,* any conflict between the spiritual and the temporal society, as if the latter would be curtailed by the acknowledgment of the property right vested in the Church. For although the State has a material right to temporal goods, yet this right is neither absolute nor unlimited. It is not *absolute* because the State is not independent of the Supreme Governor of the universe. It is not *unlimited* because the State is entitled to material goods only as far as its end requires it, and as far as the rights of individuals are not trespassed upon. For the individual citizen has a right to exist, and consequently also to own what is necessary for his existence, prior to any right of the State. And if the State interferes without necessity and in violation of that natural freedom which belongs to every human being, then the individual has a natural right to resist.[2] If this is true of the individual, it is also, and *a fortiori,* true of the society founded by God, which is also made up of individuals If we say that *per se* no conflict is possible between Church and State, we suppose, of course, that each society keeps within its own proper sphere, claiming only what is necessary for the pursuit of its specific and well defined end.

2. There is another, more specific reason for the Church's claim. The Church has the innate right and duty to establish, foster, and protect *charitable* works of

2 See Fr. Cuthbert, O S. F. C , *Catholic Ideals in Social Life,* 1905, p 27.

all kinds, which are commanded by her divine Founder.[3] The most luminous pages in her history are those recording her deeds of charity. To sever these from the Church would be the same as tearing a child away from his mother. The exercise of charity, however, requires substantial means and unhampered liberty, which again is possible only if the Church is endowed with the inherent right to possess property.

3. Not only the first Church historian, St. Luke,[4] but also many later writers [5] bear witness to the fact that the Church always possessed temporal goods. Even pagan emporers acknowledged that right. Thus Aurelian (270–275) adjusted a question of property in favor of the Church against Paul of Samosata. To mention the edict of Milan 313 is sufficient to prove that Constantine did not grant, but merely *restored,* the property right of the Church.[6] It is superfluous to add further proofs. It was but natural and logical that the Holy See condemned the contrary tenet, namely, that " the Church has no inherent and lawful right to acquire and possess property." [7]

The present canon vindicates this right of holding property to the Church at large and to the Apostolic See; then, with some limitation, also to single corporations.

The term *Apostolic See* must be understood according to can. 7 of the Code. However, here it evidently has the special meaning of the primatial See of St. Peter, and there seems to be a covert allusion to the *temporal power of the Pope.* To set forth the whole *Roman Question,* so-

---

3 See Matth. 25, 35 ff., Acts II, 29 ff., Gal. 2, 9 f , I Cor. 16, 1; II Cor 8 ff., Rom 15, 26

4 Acts 2, 44 f , 4, 34 ff.

5 Justin, *Apol.,* I, nn. 14, 67; Tertull , *Apologet ,* n. 39, Cyprian, *Ep* 66, c. 16.

6 Cfr Lactantius, *De Mortibus Persecutorum,* c 12; Eusebius, *Hist Eccl.,* VII, 13; S Brandi, S. J., *Di Chi Sono le Chiese?* 1898, p. 16 ff.

7 Syllabus of Pius IX, n. 26; Heiner, *Der Syllabus,* 1905, p. 142 f.

called, would require a treatise for itself.   Let us emphasize but two points, namely, (1) that the temporal dominion of the Pope, in its limited sense, *i. e.,* as it actually
existed before 1870, cannot be said to be *iuris divini,*
though it may justly be called providential.   Providence
and divine right are not identical terms, else the Church
would have lacked an essential feature for about 700
years; (2) that temporal dominion is compatible with
spiritual power[8]; the latter, as the superior power, may
subject to itself a temporal rule or government, but not
conversely, because the power of assimilation is wanting
in a merely temporal factor.

The Apostolic See, then, being the Church personified
or visibly vested in the Supreme Pontiff, enjoys the right
to possess property to the same extent and in the same
sense as the Church at large.

" Individual churches " are dioceses or organizations
which have their own superiors, endowed with jurisdiction *in foro externo,* who act as representatives of the
universal Church.   *Parishes* are not such corporations in
the ecclesiastical sense because their purpose is entirely
dependent on the superior end of the diocese, of which
they form a subordinate part, and, besides, the pastor is
not a representative *in foro externo.*   However, by participation, parishes may share in the nature of a corporation proper, and thus be acknowledged by the Church
for the sake of convenience in administration.   The State
may recognize them as corporations, provided the local
Ordinary is not excluded.   Note that single churches or
corporations (for instance, religious communities) are
capable of exercising ecclesiastical property rights only
so long and in so far as they belong to the body of the

8 Syllabus Pii IX, n. 75, Heiner, *l c.,* p. 331 ff.

Catholic Church. The reason is that the partial end, such as pursued by single churches and corporations, necessarily follows the universal end of the Church at large, and borrows from it its juridical entity. Hence if a particular church or organization departs from unity of faith or government, or adopts a worship different from that of the universal Church, it can lay no claim to any property which it enjoyed whilst united to the entire, supremely sovereign organism. This has also been ruled by courts in the United States.[9]

These individual churches and corporations, then, are dependent upon the Church for their existence, for they cannot grow except on ecclesiastical soil, and become dead outside the pale. They depend on the universal Church also in as far as the *common law of the same* is binding on them concerning the acquisition, possession, and administration of property. It does not follow from this proposition that there are two subjects of such ecclesiastical property rights, one the Church universal, and the other an individual corporation. The Code is against such a splitting up of the one and indivisible property right. "*Ius est,*" it is a right, dependent only in as far as the welfare of the whole Church requires. In a similar manner our civil corporations depend on the State, but enjoy the complete and autonomous right to possess and administer their property.[10]

CAN. 1496

Ecclesiae ius quoque est, independens a civili potestate, exigendi a fidelibus quae ad cultum divinum, ad honestam clericorum aliorumque ministrorum susten-

9 Zollmann, *American Civil Eccl Publ*, 1910, p 42, Tanquery, *Church Law*, 1917, p 194. *Summa Theol. Moral*, ed. 2, III, 10 Cfr Bachofen, *Summa Iuris* p 85.

tationem et ad reliquos fines sibi proprios sint necessaria.

Can. 1496 is a corollary of the preceding canon, and vindicates to the Church, independently of any civil power, the right to *demand of the faithful* whatever is necessary for divine worship, for the support of her clergy and other servants, and for the pursuit of her proper ends. This is a corollary, or logical deduction, from what was stated above, because it follows from the inherent right of the Church to possess property sufficient for her support. The legal standing of the Church requires such an independent right, since the faithful belong to her by divine right, having been consecrated to her by baptism.

To this right, of course, corresponds a *duty on the part of the faithful.* What was said under can. 463, must here, proportionately, be applied to all the purposes mentioned.[11]

CAN. 1497

§ 1. Bona temporalia, sive corporalia, tum immobilia tum mobilia, sive incorporalia, quae vel ad Ecclesiam universam et ad Apostolicam Sedem vel ad aliam in Ecclesia personam moralem pertineant, sunt *bona ecclesiastica.*

§ 2. Dicuntur *sacra,* quae consecratione vel benedictione ad divinum cultum destinata sunt; *pretiosa,* quibus notabilis valor sit, artis vel historiae vel materiae causa.

§ 1. All kinds of church property are, according to can. 1497, called *ecclesiastical,* no matter whether it belongs to the universal church, or to the Apostolic See, or to an

---

11 See Vol II, 539 f.

ecclesiastical corporation, and no matter whether it is corporeal (movable or immovable) or incorporeal.

" Right of property " is taken in the subjective sense as the moral faculty of doing something, or of holding or exacting property. Hence it is something intellectual and moral, not perceived by the senses. If a distinction is drawn between corporeal and incorporeal property it is because of the objects which these categories comprise; they are *corporeal,* if they fall under the senses; such are landed property, buildings, chattel, objects, etc.; *incorporeal* if they cannot be seen or perceived by the senses, except as far as they are asserted; such are advowsons, titles, franchises, pensions, rents, leases, etc.[12]

§ 2. If goods or objects belonging to the Church have received a consecration or blessing by which they were destined for divine worship, they are called *sacred.* This character, of course, adheres to corporeal things only. *Precious* objects are such ecclesiastical things as have a considerable value on account of the artistic skill with which they are wrought, or because of their antiquity or historical associations, or on account of the material contained in them.

CAN. 1498

In canonibus qui sequuntur, nomine Ecclesiae significatur non solum Ecclesia universa aut Sedes Apostolica, sed etiam quaelibet persona moralis in Ecclesia, nisi ex contextu sermonis vel ex natura rei aliud appareat.

By the term *Church* in the following canons are understood not only the universal Church, or the Apostolic See, but any ecclesiastical corporation, unless the contrary appears from the context.

12 Blackstone-Cooley, *l. c.,* II, 15 ff.

TITLE XXVII

THE ACQUISITION OF ECCLESIASTICAL PROPERTY

CAN. 1499

§ 1. Ecclesia acquirere bona temporalia potest omnibus iustis modis iuris sive naturalis sive positivi, quibus id aliis licet.

§ 2. Dominium bonorum, sub suprema auctoritate Sedis Apostolicae, ad eam pertinet moralem personam, quae eadem bona legitime acquisiverit.

Can. 1499 vindicates to the Church the right of acquiring property by all *just means* which are permitted by either natural or positive law to *other citizens or individuals, i. e.,* by contract, donation, inheritance, etc.

The title or ownership is vested in the corporation itself, though, of course dependently on the Holy See, *i. e.,* on common law.

Here it may not be amiss to point out the different forms of holding church property. They are: (a) by *corporation sole,* which consists of one person, who transfers it to his successor in office; thus a bishop or pastor holds property in the name and as officer of the diocese or pastor; (b) by *corporation aggregate,* when the church members are the incorporators and whatever property they possess or acquire is vested in the body corporate;[1]

---

1 Cfr Zollmann, *American Civil Church Law,* 1917, p. 38 ff.

557

(c) in *fee simple,* which conveys absolute and direct ownership of the property, and was looked upon in former days as vested in the bishop for all diocesan property.[2]

DIVISION AND TRANSFER OF CHURCH PROPERTY

CAN. 1500

Diviso territorio personae moralis ecclesiasticae ita ut vel illius pars alii personae morali uniatur, vel distincta persona moralis pro parte dismembrata erigatur, etiam bona communia quae in commodum totius territorii erant destinata, et aes alienum quod pro territorio contractum fuerat, ab auctoritate ecclesiastica, cui divisio competat, cum debita proportione ex bono et aequo dividi debent, salvis piorum fundatorum seu oblatorum voluntatibus, iuribus legitime quaesitis, ac legibus peculiaribus, quibus persona moralis regatur.

CAN. 1501

Exstincta persona morali ecclesiastica, eius bona fiunt personae moralis ecclesiasticae immediate superioris, salvis semper fundatorum seu oblatorum voluntatibus, iuribus legitime quaesitis atque legibus peculiaribus quibus exstincta persona moralis regebatur.

If a territory, say a diocese or corporation, is *divided* so that part of its territory is united to another corporation, or a distinct juridical person is established out of the dismembered part, the *property* that belonged to the territory as a whole must be divided and the *debts* distributed by the competent ecclesiastical authority. This division must be made according to the *principles of justice and*

2 Blackstone-Cooley, *Comment*, II, 104 f. The S C. prefers ownership by corporation sole

equity, with due regard to the will of the founders or do-
nors and to the acquired rights and the particular statutes
governing the moral person who sustained the division.
This is a corroboration of what was stated under can. 1427
concerning the division of parishes, to which also the note
of Cardinal Gasparri refers, thus hinting that this canon
must also be applied to parishes, even though they may
not come up to the notion of a corporation proper.   But
persona moralis may also signify a juridical entity of the
species of benefices, and as these may be divided or dismembered, so also parishes.

The *proportion* to be observed is twofold: general and
particular.   The *general proportion* is indicated by the
phrase, "*bonum et aequum.*"   But since it is a maxim
that equity follows the law, it is evident that justice must
be the first measure, to be taken not in the arithmetical,
but in the geometrical sense, for it would be next to impossible to make such an equal division that cent for cent and
inch for inch would be shared.   The *particular proportion*
is to be gauged by the acquired rights (because *melior est
conditio possidentis*), the charter and by-laws.   This same
proportion in can. 1501 is applied to the case where a
moral or juridical person *ceases to exist.*   For this particular proportion means that all the property left by such an
extinct person passes to the immediate superior.   Thus,
for instance, the property of an extinct parish goes to the
diocese; if a diocese were suppressed, we suppose the S. C.
Consistorialis would provide.   If a monastery or convent
of a centralized order becomes extinct, its property passes
to the province, unless the constitutions rule otherwise.

Can. 1502

Ad decimarum et primitiarum solutionem quod attinet, peculiaria statuta ac laudabiles consuetudines in
unaquaque regione serventur.

As to tithes (*dimes*) and first-fruits, the special statutes
and praiseworthy local customs should be observed.

BEGGING

Can. 1503

Salvis praescriptis can. 621–624, vetantur privati tam
clerici quam laici sine Sedis Apostolicae aut proprii
Ordinarii et Ordinarii loci licentia, in scriptis data, stipem cogere pro quolibet pio aut ecclesiastico instituto
vel fine.

Private persons, whether clerics or laymen, are *forbidden to collect alms* for any charitable or ecclesiastical
institution or purpose, unless they have the *written permission* of the Apostolic See or that of their own and of
the local Ordinary.

Concerning religious enough has been said under can.
621–624, which must be strictly followed. It is hardly to
be presumed that collectors will go about collecting alms,
as they formerly did,[3] under false pretences, even promising people eternal joy. But churches are still being built,
and hospitals and schools erected, which require an appeal
to Christian charity. Hence this regulation, which is intended to keep order.

Who are the private persons here intended? All those
who beg without official or public capacity, authority or
warrant, no matter whether they belong to the ranks of

---

3 C. 2, Clem. V, 9.

the clergy or the laity. A *pastor* is no private person, and may therefore collect within the boundaries of his parish, but not beyond without the required permission, because outside his own district he has no official capacity. It is a wise ruling, and in keeping with our canon, if diocesan statutes forbid priests in charge of souls to collect either directly or indirectly, for instance, by selling tickets or chances.[4] The so-called chain-letters belong in the waste-basket.

Are *bishops* allowed to collect in another diocese than their own? If they have obtained the written consent of the respective Ordinary, they certainly are allowed to do so.

The text says, "for any charitable or ecclesiastical *purpose.*" This means that a pastor, or any other priest, is not allowed to collect for others, say a hospital or sisterhood, unless he has the permission of the Apostolic See (S. Congregatio Concilii; can. 250), or of the two Ordinaries concerned. Of course, if the collector does not cross the boundary line of another diocese, he needs only the written permission of his own Ordinary. If he has obtained this, he requires no permission from the pastor in whose parish he wishes to collect, although courtesy may move him to apply for it. Besides, the diocesan statutes must be observed.

THE CATHEDRATICUM

CAN. 1504

Omnes ecclesiae vel beneficia iurisdictioni Episcopi subiecta, itemque laicorum confraternitates, debent quotannis in signum subiectionis solvere Episcopo ca-

---

[4] Thus the diocesan statutes of Leavenworth and St. Joseph, n. 58; but the first clause must now be changed according to our canon.

thedraticum seu moderatam taxam determinandam ad normam can. 1507, § 1, nisi iam antiqua consuetudine fuerit determinata.

In Spain and in Italy it was customary, in the sixth century, to pay two solidi to the diocesan bishop, either on his visit or otherwise, "*propter honorem cathedrae.*" [5] This tribute was, as the Latin term shows, paid as a token or earnest of the dependence and submission of the church and clergy. After exemptions became more numerous, the monasteries paid a certain tribute to the Holy See as a sign of papal patronage and exemption from episcopal jurisdiction. Hence exempt regulars did not pay the cathedraticum to their diocesan bishop unless they held incorporated benefices or parishes.[6] Those who were wont to pay this tribute, usually offered it at the diocesan synod, whence it came to be called *synodaticum.*

Our canon rules that *all churches and benefices subject to the jurisdiction of the bishop,* as well as lay confraternities, are obliged to pay annually, as a sign of subjection, the so-called cathedraticum, a moderate tax to be levied according to can. 1507, § 1, unless some other method exists by ancient custom.

Hence, (1) *all churches and public oratories* subject to episcopal jurisdiction must pay the cathedraticum, even though they may not have been subject to it formerly. This certainly holds concerning all churches ruled by the secular clergy. Churches or public oratories in which *exempt religious* hold services for themselves only, and not for outsiders, or for these only *per accidens,* need not pay the cathedraticum. But if exempt religious have a

5 Cc. 1, 4, 6, C. 10, q. 3—the underlying idea being that all churches sprang from the cathedral church.

6 C. 16, X, I, 31; c. 1, X, III, 35.

parish church, even though it be an abbey or a convent church, or an incorporated public oratory, and even though one of their own number acts as pastor or chaplain, they are obliged to pay this tax.[7]

(2) All *benefices* not exempt from episcopal jurisdiction must also pay the cathedraticum. Thus canons beneficiaries, who possess a distinct benefice, also the *theologus* and *poenitentiarius,* are bound by this obligation.[8]

(3) *Lay confraternities* must pay the cathedraticum if they own not merely a chapel erected in honor of a saint in some church, but a church or public oratory of their own, even though no benefice is connected with that church or oratory.[9]

(4) The *amount* of this tribute was formerly established at *two solidi* (about $6.00) a year.[10] But the Code leaves it to be settled by provincial councils.

SUBSIDIUM CHARITATIVUM

CAN. 1505

Loci Ordinarius, praeter tributum pro Seminario, de quo in can. 1355, 1356, aut beneficialem pensionem de qua in can. 1429, potest, speciali dioecesis necessitate impellente, omnibus beneficiariis, sive saecularibus sive religiosis, extraordinariam et moderatam exactionem imponere.

When there is particular need on the part of the diocese, the *local Ordinary* may demand, besides the *seminaristicum* and the pension mentioned in can. 1429, a con-

---

7 *Ibid ,* and the commentators, Reiffenstuel, III, tit 39, n. 12 f ; Santi-Leitner, III, 39, n 6; S C C, Feb 26, 1707 (Richter, *Trid ,* p. 336, n 19); also churches *iuris-patronatus laicalis,* S C C, July 24, 1760 (Richter, *l c ,* n 22)

8 S C. C , March 18, 1775, April 7, 1742 (Richter, *l. c.,* n 20 f).

9 S C C , May 22, 1734, July 24, 1734 (Richter, *l c ,* n 24 f).

10 See cc. 4-6, C 10, q. 3.

tribution from all beneficiaries, secular as well religious, but this contribution must be moderate and can be demanded only extraordinarily, not regularly. It is called a charitable subsidy, and, as such, differs from the regular diocesan taxes, though it may be demanded in justice, and therefore under threat of penalty.

The term *Ordinaries* here, according to the common opinion of canonists, based on the Decretals,[11] means only the bishops or Ordinaries themselves, not the Vicars-General.

Metropolitans cannot impose this tax on their entire province, but only on their own archdiocese.[12] Apostolic administrators and coadjutors appointed by the Apostolic See, also Vicars Capitular (our administrators) are entitled to demand this subsidy.[13]

Those upon whom the *subsidium charitativum* may be imposed are the *beneficiaries,* as explained under can. 1504, and to the same extent, also exempt religious if they hold a parish church or other benefice.

The *reason* is stated as being a *special need of the diocese.* Such special needs are: a large indebtedness contracted by the bishop or his predecessor for the welfare of the diocese; extraordinary support of the Apostolic See; expenses required for the *visitatio ad limina* or a journey to a general or provincial council.[14]

It must, however, be observed that the S. Congregation has forbidden bishops to collect this subsidy if they possess a rich income or revenues (*pingues reditus habentes*) or if no real and urgent reason exists, or if the beneficiaries from whom the tax is demanded have but a bare living.[15]

11 C. 6, § *Prohibemus,* X, III, 39.
12 Reiffenstuel, III, tit. 37, n. 20
13 *Ibid.,* n. 23.

14 *Ibid.,* n. 31.
15 S. C. C., Feb. 27, 1603 (Richter, *Trid,* p. 336, n. 27).

CAN. 1506

Aliud tributum in bonum dioecesis vel pro patrono imponere ecclesiis, beneficiis aliisque institutis ecclesiasticis, quanquam sibi subiectis, Ordinarius potest tantummodo in actu fundationis vel consecrationis; sed nullum imponi tributum potest super eleemosynis Missarum sive manualium sive fundatarum.

Can. 1506 forbids Ordinaries to impose any other tax besides those mentioned, for the benefit of the diocese or a patron (advowee), upon churches, benefices, and other ecclesiastical institutions, subject to their jurisdiction, except on the occasion of their foundation or consecration. All other taxes are against the common law (can. 1429) and looked upon as either simoniacal or as an unjust diminution of benefices. *Never* can a tax or contribution be imposed upon either manual or foundation *masses*.

CAN. 1507

§ 1. Salvo praescripto can. 1056 et can. 1234, praefinire taxas pro variis actibus iurisdictionis voluntariae vel pro exsecutione rescriptorum Sedis Apostolicae vel occasione ministrationis Sacramentorum vel Sacramentalium, in tota ecclesiastica provincia solvendas, est Concilii provincialis aut conventus Episcoporum provinciae; sed nulla vi praefinitio eiusmodi pollet, nisi prius a Sede Apostolica approbata fuerit.

§ 2. Ad taxas pro actibus iudicialibus quod spectat, servetur praescriptum can. 1909.

Can. 1507 governs the manner of *fixing ecclesiastical taxes*. It should be done at a *provincial council* or meeting of the bishops, but needs the approval of the Holy See to have legal force. The taxes here comprised are (a) those levied for the exercise of voluntary jurisdiction, *i. e.,* dispensations, commutations (except matrimonial dispensations; can. 1056), and funeral taxes (can. 1234); (b) the *executoriae* or fees for the execution of papal rescripts; (c) charges for the administration of the Sacraments and sacramentals. Not included are taxes imposed for ecclesiastical trials, which are subject to the rules laid down in can. 1909.

PRESCRIPTION

CAN. 1508

Praescriptionem, tanquam acquirendi et se liberandi modum, prout est in legislatione civili respectivae nationis, Ecclesia pro bonis ecclesiasticis recipit, salvo praescripto canonum qui sequuntur.

This canon admits for ecclesiastical property *prescription,* as it is current or in vogue under the civil law in each country; the following canons limit prescription.

Prescription (called in Roman law *usucapio*) is the mode of acquiring a title to property by long-continued and uninterrupted possession. It also means freeing oneself from an obligation due to another, for instance, tithes or pensions, in which case the term signifies the loss of a property right brought about by omission to assert the same within a given time. Finally, prescription also has the meaning of the period or time required for legal acquisition or loss of this right.

The new Code accepts prescription in the same sense and with the same conditions under which it operates according to the laws of different countries, provided the following canons are observed.

CAN. 1509

Praescriptioni obnoxia non sunt:

1.° Quae sunt iuris divini sive naturalis sive positivi;

2.° Quae obtineri possunt ex solo privilegio apostolico;

3.° Iura spiritualia, quorum laici non sunt capaces, si agatur de praescriptione in commodum laicorum;

4.° Fines certi et indubii provinciarum ecclesiasticarum, dioecesium, paroeciarum, vicariatuum apostolicorum, praefecturarum apostolicarum, abbatiarum vel praelaturarum *nullius*.

5.° Eleemosynae et onera Missarum;

6.° Beneficium ecclesiasticum sine titulo;

7.° Ius visitationis et obedientiae, ita ut subditi a nullo Praelato visitari possint et nulli Praelato iam subsint;

8.° Solutio cathedratici.

Can. 1509 excepts from prescription the following objects and rights:[16]

1.° *Things enjoined either by the natural or by divine law,* for instance, the right of parents to their children, the primacy of the Roman Pontiff, the Sacraments, the constitution of the Church.

2.° *Things that can be obtained only by an Apostolic privilege,* for instance, exemption of persons not comprised by law.

3.° *Spiritual rights of which laymen are incapable,* if prescription concerns things or rights in favor of laymen, for instance, lay investiture, or election of laymen to an ecclesiastical benefice.

16 Cfr the commentators on lib. II, tit. 26; Wernz, *l. c.,* III, n. 298; p. 333 f ; see under can 1701 ff.

4.° *Certain and undisputed boundary lines* of ecclesiastical provinces, dioceses, parishes, vicariates apostolic and prefectures apostolic, abbacies and prelacies *nullius.*

5.° *Alms or mass stipends and obligations;* however, although these as such cannot be prescribed against by any contrary custom, yet they may be transferred from one to another; thus if the canons or prebendaries of a church were in turn obliged to say and apply Mass for the benefactors, this obligation could be imposed upon the dean or provost of the chapter by prescription.[17]

6.° *Ecclesiastical benefices obtained without title, i. e.,* without at least a *titulus coloratus* (see can. 1446).

7.° *The right of canonical visitation and obedience,* so that the subjects could not be visited by any prelate or would not be under obedience to any prelate. But a mere transfer of obedience or visitation from one prelate to another (*translativa praescriptio*) may take place by prescription.[18] The fact is that exemption rested, centuries ago, on prescription.

8.° *The payment of the cathedraticum,* which cannot itself be subject to prescription, although the amount is liable to prescription.[19]

CAN. 1510

§ 1. Res sacrae quae in dominio privatorum sunt, praescriptione acquiri a privatis personis possunt, quae tamen eas adhibere nequeunt ad profanos usus; si vero consecrationem vel benedictionem amiserint, libere acquiri possunt etiam ad usus profanos, non tamen sordidos.

§ 2. Res sacrae, quae in dominio privatorum non

---

17 S. C. C., June 17, 1879, April 27, 1901 (*Anal. Eccl.* IX, 201 ff.)

18 Reiffenstuel, II, 26, n 52 ff.

19 Santi-Leitner, III, 39, n. 6.

sunt, non a persona privata, sed a persona morali ecclesiastica contra aliam personam moralem ecclesiasticam praescribi possunt.

Can. 1510 concerns sacred things (*res sacrae*) owned
by *private persons*. These may be acquired by prescription, but not used for profane purposes, unless they have
lost their consecration or blessing, and even then the purpose must not be unbecoming (*sordidus*). Sacred objects
which are not owned by private persons cannot be acquired by prescription by a private, but only by a *juridical
person*, against whom only an artificial person can prescribe.

Can. 1511

§ 1. Res immobiles, mobiles pretiosae, iura et ac-
tiones sive personales sive reales, quae pertinent ad
Sedem Apostolicam, spatio centum annorum praescribuntur.

§ 2. Quae ad aliam personam moralem ecclesiasticam, spatio triginta annorum.

Can. 1511 reasserts the ancient privilege of the *Roman
Church,* against which only a prescription of 100 years
is admitted, no matter whether it concerns landed property, precious movable property, rights, or personal as well
as real actions. Against other ecclesiastical corporations
or juridical entities a term of thirty years suffices for
prescription.

Can. 1512

Nulla valet praescriptio, nisi bona fide nitatur, non
solum initio possessionis, sed toto possessionis tempore ad praescriptionem requisito.

No prescription, however, is valid which is not based upon good faith at the beginning as well as throughout the whole period permitted for prescription. This rule has always been upheld by the Church against the Roman law, which required good faith only at the beginning.[20] Hence modern civil law, which follows the Roman law, cannot be accepted in this case. Good faith, which is the prudent and sincere judgment that one holds or possesses a thing by right or without infringement of another's rights, is required by natural law, because bad faith would render the possession sinful and therefore illicit, and no human or divine positive law could declare it just or lawful.

DONATIONS AND LEGACIES

CAN. 1513

§ 1. Qui ex iure naturae et ecclesiastico libere valet de suis bonis statuere, potest ad causas pias, sive per actum inter vivos sive per actum mortis causa, bona relinquere.

§ 2. In ultimis voluntatibus in bonum Ecclesiae serventur, si fieri possit, sollemnitates iuris civilis; hae si omissae fuerint, heredes moneantur ut testatoris voluntatem adimpleant.

He who, by natural and ecclesiastical law, is free to dispose of his property, may bequeath the same, either by donation or last will and testament, in favor of pious institutions or causes.

Testamentary bequests of the faithful in favor of the Church should, if possible, be made in legal form, *i. e.,*

---

20 Cfr. cc. 5, 8, 17, 20, X, II, 26;   1 un. *Inst.,* II, 6; l. un., *Cod.,* VII, 31.

according to the rules prescribed by civil law. If this precaution has been omitted the heirs must be admonished to carry out the testator's will.

Wiclif's propositions: that it would be sinful to found convents, that to bequeath money to the clergy would be against the teaching of Christ, and that the emperors were mistaken in endowing the Church, were deservedly condemned.[21] Nevertheless, the nineteenth century revamped these impious theories.[22]

The question whether a last will or donation not drawn up in legal form is binding in conscience was decided by the S. Poenitentiaria, which said that it is the Roman practice to hold such legacies valid and binding in conscience, but the heirs are easily admitted to an agreement with the church or pious institution.[23]

CAN. 1514

Voluntates fidelium facultates suas in pias causas donantium vel relinquentium, sive per actum inter vivos, sive per actum mortis causa, diligentissime impleantur etiam circa modum administrationis et erogationis bonorum, salvo praescripto, can. 1515, § 3.

CAN. 1515

§ 1. Ordinarii omnium piarum voluntatum tam mortis causa quam inter vivos exsecutores sunt.

21 Propp 31-33 (Denzinger, nn. 507-509)

22 Pius IX, "*Quanta Cura*," Dec. 8, 1864.

23 S Poenit, Jan 10, 1901 (*Coll. P. F.*, n. 2099). As to the *legal form* to be observed in making wills, see *Am Eccl Rev.*, Vol 33, 306 ff ; also "*After My Death,*" 1918,

Jones, *Legal Forms*, 7th ed Notice also that "contracts to procure a third person to make a will in favor of a particular person or object, or to use his influence to procure such testamentary disposition, are illegal;" see Harriman, *The Law of Contracts*, 1901, § 214

§ 2. Hoc ex iure Ordinarii vigilare possunt, ac debent, etiam per visitationem, ut piae voluntates impleantur, et alii exsecutores delegati debent, perfuncti munere, illis reddere rationem.

§ 3. Clausulae huic Ordinariorum iuri contrariae, ultimis voluntatibus adiectae, tanquam non appositae habeantur.

Can. 1514 and 1515 emphasize the great care which the Church has ever bestowed on the faithful *administration* and *distribution* of property left by donation or bequest. They are specially intended for executors, who are obliged to attend to speedy execution, according to the term permitted by civil law. In the business of execution they must chiefly attend to the wording of the will. They are not allowed to substitute one pious institution for another, unless the document permits them to do so, nor are they permitted to apply a legacy " for the poor " to one poor person only. Among the poor those of the deceased person's home town should be favored and the most needy selected.[24]

These general rules should also guide the *Ordinaries,* who, according to can. 1515, are the executors of all pious gifts, by donation as well as by last will (*mortis causa*). They may and must, at the canonical visitation, take cognizance of pious bequests, and other executors are obliged to render an account to the Ordinaries after they have discharged their office. Every *clause* which runs counter to this right of the Ordinary must be looked upon as non-existing.

" Ordinaries " here includes the superiors of exempt religious. Religious, too, (except Friars Minor) may

---

24 Reiffenstuel III, tit. 26, n 772 ff.

be executors of last wills, but must in each case obtain previous permission from their superiors.[25]

CAN. 1516

§ 1. Clericus vel religiosus qui bona ad pias causas sive per actum inter vivos, sive ex testamento fiduciarie accepit, debet de sua fiducia Ordinarium certiorem reddere, eique omnia istiusmodi bona seu mobilia seu immobilia cum oneribus adiunctis indicare; quod si donator id expresse et omnino prohibuerit, fiduciam ne acceptet.

§ 2. Ordinarius debet exigere ut bona fiduciaria in tuto collocentur et vigilare pro exsecutione piae voluntatis ad normam can. 1515.

§ 3. Bonis fiduciariis alicui religioso commissis, si quidem bona sint attributa loci seu dioecesis ecclesiis, incolis aut piis causis iuvandis, Ordinarius de quo in §§ 1, 2, est loci Ordinarius; secus, est Ordinarius eiusdem religiosi proprius.

Can. 1516 plainly shows that not only the *secular clergy* but religious, too, may be executors and trustees. If a cleric or religious receives a donation or a bequest *in trust*, he must notify his Ordinary of that fact and indicate to him all the property held in trust, movable as well as immovable, together with the obligations attached thereto. Should a donor have expressly forbidden the intervention of the Ordinary, no religious or cleric can accept the bequest or donation.[26]

The Ordinary must insist that the property held in trust is *safely invested* and watch over the fulfillment of the testator's will, according to can 1515. A safe investment, according to Roman practice, is that in land.

25 *Ib.*, n 777 ff.
26 S. C C, Aug 7, 1909, (*A. Ap. S.*, I, 766).

When a *religious* has received property in trust, the Ordinary referred to in § 1 and § 2 of this canon is the local *Ordinary* if the property is destined for a church of the town or diocese, or for the inmates of charitable institutions existing in that town or diocese; in all other cases the Ordinary is the superior of the exempt religious; for only exempt clerical superiors go by the name of Ordinaries, according to can. 198.

It seems doubtless that by "*loci seu dioecesis ecclesiis*" must be understood such churches as are either incorporated or parish churches. For if a donation or bequest were made to a church belonging exclusively to exempt religious, who use it for their own purposes only, even though it were a public oratory, it is incredible that the local Ordinary should have to intervene. This interpretation is borne out by the obvious meaning of the term, "*dioecesis ecclesiae*," churches of the diocese, in the *genitivus subjectivus;* for in that sense churches owned by religious, but not as parish or beneficiary churches, are not *of* the diocese, although *in* the diocese.

CHANGE OF LAST WILL

CAN. 1517

§ 1. Ultimarum voluntatum reductio, moderatio, commutatio, quae fieri ex iusta tantum et necessaria causa debent, Sedi Apostolicae reservantur, nisi fundator hanc potestatem etiam Ordinario loci expresse concesserit.

§ 2. Si tamen exsecutio onerum impositorum, ob imminutos reditus aliamve causam, nulla administratorum culpa, impossibilis evaserit, tunc Ordinarius quoque, auditis iis quorum interest, et servata, meliore quo fieri potest modo, fundatoris voluntate, poterit

eadem onera aeque imminuere, excepta Missarum re-
ductione quae semper Sedi Apostolicae unice competit.

§ 1. To reduce, mitigate, or change testamentary bequests is reserved to the *Apostolic See,* which can proceed only for a just and necessary cause. The *local Ordinary* may act only if the founder has expressly granted
this power to him, and he too is bound by reasons of
justice and necessity, for both the natural and the divine
law, as well as positive law, demand that the last will of the
faithful be conscientiously executed and the money be-
queathed by them expended for those purposes for which
it was intended. It may not be applied to a seemingly
better cause, or in a more suitable manner, because such a
change would frustrate the last will of the testator and in-
jure the Church, since the faithful would hesitate to make
donations if they were not certain that the money would
be properly applied. Hence, even the Sovereign Pontiff
is bound by the law of justice and necessity and cannot
validly make a change or reduction [27] in a will without a
proportionate cause. It is therefore quite natural to find
that very rare use has been made of this power, and the
negative answers of the S. Congregatio Concilii are more
numerous than the permissive ones. Thus a change of a
mansionariatus (simple benefice of a chapter) into a canonicate was rejected; a proposed change of manual masses
into chaplaincies was rejected, etc., etc.[28]

§ 2. However, if, on account of decreased revenues or
for other reasons not due to faulty administration, the
obligations cannot possibly be complied with, the Ordinary,
after having heard those concerned, may equitably dimin-

[27] S. C. P. F., 1807, (*Coll*, n. 689).
[28] S. C C, Nov 4, 1705; Feb

27, 1734; June 26, 1772 (Richter, *Trid.*, p. 164).

ish the burdens, but must, as well as he is able, abide by the will of the founder. From this power is *excluded the reduction of Mass obligations,* which is reserved to the Holy See.

This canon makes quite a concession to the Ordinaries, because formerly such faculties were granted only for very particular reasons of distance or slow travelling.[29] But the local Ordinaries are obliged in conscience to make use of this privilege only for *just and solid reasons.* Besides, since it has always been the practice of the Roman Court to ascertain the probable or *likely mind of the testator* before permitting a change,[30] this should also be the guiding principle for Ordinaries. Here is a case in point: A pious Catholic had left a sum of money for the purpose of founding a home for poor girls exposed to danger. The legacy proved insufficient (here the reason) and the foundation appeared rather useless for the town in question. Hence the money was assigned to a convent for nuns on condition that they would receive a poor girl without the dowry otherwise required (here the interpretation of the probable desire of the founder).[31]

From this now *ordinary episcopal power,* in which exempt religious superiors do not participate, is excluded the reduction of *mass obligations,* which is strictly reserved to the Apostolic See (S. C. Consilii), as will be further explained in can. 1551.

29 S C P F, 1807 (*l. c*)
30 S. C C, Feb 12, 1735 and *pluries* (Richter, *l. c.,* p. 135, n. 8).
31 S. C. C., Aug. 19, 1724 (*l. c.,* n. 2)

TITLE XXVIII

THE ADMINISTRATION OF CHURCH PROPERTY

CAN. 1518

Romanus Pontifex est omnium bonorum ecclesiasti-corum supremus administrator et dispensator.

The Roman Pontiff is the supreme administrator and steward of all church property.

This right flows, of course, from the plenitude of his power, which embraces the final end of the Church as well as its means. Waiving the question as to the rights which were formerly vindicated to him by reason of the relation of vassalage that existed between some nations and the Apostolic See,[1] it is evident that the Code considers only actual or present-day conditions. The name *dispensator* was given to the Pope by St. Bernard[2] as well as by St. Thomas. The Angelic Doctor says: The possessions of the Church belongs to the Pope, not as their lord and owner, but as their principal dispenser. This means that the Pope may dispense or dispose of all church property, even that owned by single corporations, in favor of the universal Church if an urgent reason exists and the welfare or tranquillity of the Church requires it. This power is given for the edification of the society founded

---

[1] See Hergenrother, *Kath. Kirche und Christl. Staat,* 1872–1878.

[2] *De Consideratione,* l. IV; see Fagnani in c. 7, *Relatum,* III, 50.

by Jesus Christ, not for its destruction, or for the enrich-
ment of the Pontiff or of his family or nation.[3] There is
nothing absurd in the exercise of this power, for the State,
too, claims the right of *eminent domain,* in virtue of which
it confiscates or expropriates private property. The law
is based upon the well-known maxim: "*Bonum privatum cedere debet bono publico.*"

THE LOCAL ORDINARIES

CAN. 1519

§ 1. Loci Ordinarii est sedulo advigilare adminis-
trationi omnium bonorum ecclesiasticorum quae in suo
territorio sint nec ex eius iurisdictione fuerint sub-
ducta, salvis legitimis praescriptionibus, quae eidem
potiora iura tribuant.

§ 2. Habita ratione iurium, legitimarum consuetudinum et circumstantiarum, Ordinarii, opportune
editis peculiaribus instructionibus intra fines iuris
communis, universum administrationis bonorum ecclesiasticorum negotium ordinandum curent.

§ 1. The local Ordinaries should watch carefully over
the administration of all church property located in
their dioceses, except that which has been withdrawn
from their jurisdiction. If lawful prescription gives the
bishop the right to administer property otherwise not subject to his power, he may make use of this right. The
reason is that the bishop has the "*intentio fundata in
iure,*" i. e., the original right of administering all diocesan
property because he is the pastor of the whole territory.

Exemption, as the term implies, spells an exception
from the rule. Therefore, if exempt religious or other

---

3 Benedict XIV, "*Cum Encyclicas,*" May 24, 1754, § 4.

exempt communities or individuals permit prescription against themselves, the original right revives. But exemption creates a right of independent administration as far as the canons admit. For it signifies freedom from episcopal jurisdiction as well as from the law of the diocese; from the right in *dando* as well as from the right in *recipiendo,* with due regard, of course, to the common law.[4] But note well, the Ordinaries are only the administrators,[5] not the dispensers of diocesan property.

Therefore § 2 of can. 1519 provides that the Ordinaries should regulate the whole business of the administration of diocesan property according to the *common law of the Church* and with due regard to special, lawful customs, which are the best interpreters of the law, and to circumstances. To this effect, and with these objects in view, they may issue, either in synod or outside, particular statutes which bind the whole diocese, provided they keep within the common law.

DIOCESAN BOARD OF ADMINISTRATION

Can. 1520

§ 1. Ad hoc munus rite obeundum quilibet Ordinarius in sua civitate episcopali Consilium instituat, quod constet praeside, qui est ipsemet Ordinarius, et duobus vel pluribus viris idoneis, iuris etiam civilis, quantum fieri potest, peritis, ab ipso Ordinario, audito Capitulo, eligendis, nisi iure vel consuetudine peculiari iam alio aequivalenti modo legitime fuerit provisum.

§ 2. Citra apostolicum indultum, ii a munere administratoris excluduntur, qui cum Ordinario loci primo

---

4 Cfr c 24, C 12, q 1, c 18, X, I, 31, and the gloss to the same.   5 S C. P. F, April 1, 1816 (*Coll. P F*, n 712).

vel secundo consanguinitatis vel affinitatis gradu coniuncti sint.

§ 3. Loci Ordinarius in administrativis actibus maioris momenti Consilium administrationis audire ne praetermittat; huius tamen sodales votum habent tantum consultivum, nisi iure communi in casibus specialiter expressis vel ex tabulis fundationis eorum consensus exigatur.

§ 4. Sodales huius Consilii iusiurandum de munere bene ac fideliter adimplendo coram Ordinario emittant.

§ 1. In order that this business be properly attended to, every Ordinary shall establish in his episcopal city a *board of administrators,* consisting of the president, who is the bishop himself, and two or three capable men, experienced also in civil law, if possible, to be appointed by the Ordinary after having heard the advice of his chapter (or consultors). Should there be in the diocese a particular law or custom which provides an equally effective mode of administration, this may be retained. But some kind of a council (*consilium*) there must be, according to the admonition of the wise man: "Do nothing without counsel, and thou shalt not repent, when thou hast done."[6]

§ 2. Excluded from this council of administrators are all relatives in the first and second degree (*affines et consanguinei*) of the local Ordinary, unless the Apostolic See should grant a dispensation to the contrary.

§ 3. Local Ordinaries shall not fail to call the council of administrators as often as any business of importance is to be transacted. Such business would be alienation of property, for which a papal indult is required, the effective exercise of supervision over the administration of tem-

6 Ecclus. 32, 24.

poralities, and the rendering of accounts to be given annually by those who are obliged to do so.[7]   But the vote of these administrators is *advisory* only, unless a decisive vote is required in certain cases expressed in law or in the charter of a foundation.

§ 4. The members of this board must take oath to the effect that they will perform their duty well and faithfully.

It may be observed that these administrators may also be laymen, provided, of course, they are Catholics.

ADMINISTRATORS OF INDIVIDUAL INSTITUTIONS

CAN. 1521

§ 1. Praeter hoc dioecesanum Consilium administrationis, Ordinarius loci in administrationem bonorum quae ad aliquam ecclesiam vel locum pium pertinent et ex iure vel tabulis fundationis suum non habent administratorem, assumat viros providos, idoneos et boni testimonii, quibus, elapso triennio, alios sufficiat, nisi locorum circumstantiae aliud suadeant.

§ 2. Quod si laicis partes quaedam in administratione bonorum ecclesiasticorum vel ex legitimo fundationis seu erectionis titulo vel ex Ordinarii loci voluntate competant, nihilominus universa administratio nomine Ecclesiae fiat, ac salvo iure Ordinarii visitandi, exigendi rationes et praescribendi modum administrationis.

§ 1. According to Roman as well as ecclesiastical law each institution should have an administrator, or, as he was formerly called, *syndicus*.[8]   Our Code prescribes the appointment of such syndics, in addition to the diocesan

---

7 S. C. P. F., Oct. 18, 1883, n. XIV, (*Coll*, n. 1606)

8 Cfr   Cod   Iust., I, 2; c 2,

Clem, III, 11; *Trid*, Sess. 7, c. 5; Sess 25, c. 8, *de Ref*.

board of administrators. For all churches or pious institutions which have no syndics either by law or charter, the Ordinary should choose prudent and capable men of good repute to administer the property. The term of these administrators lasts three years, unless local circumstances counsel a more or less frequent change. It is evident that our American parishes need no special administrators, because the parish priests themselves, aided by the trustees, administer the property.

§2. If the charter or the will of the local Ordinary calls upon *laymen* to take part in the administration of ecclesiastical property, the whole administration must nevertheless be conducted in the name of the Church, and the Ordinary's right of visitation and of demanding a regular account and prescribing the mode of administration must be safeguarded.

THE GENERAL DUTIES OF ADMINISTRATORS

The following canons set forth the duties of administrators appointed by law or charter or by order of the Ordinary; first, before assuming office:

CAN. 1522

Antequam administratores bonorum ecclesiasticorum, de quibus in can. 1521, suum munus ineant:

1.° Debent se bene et fideliter administraturos coram Ordinario loci vel vicario foraneo iureiurando cavere;

2.° Fiat accuratum ac distinctum inventarium, ab omnibus subscribendum, rerum immobilium, rerum mobilium pretiosarum aliarumve cum descriptione atque aestimatione earundem; vel factum antea inventarium acceptetur, adnotatis rebus quae interim amissae vel acquisitae fuerint;

3.° Huius inventarii alterum exemplar conservetur in tabulario administrationis, alterum in archivo Curiae; et in utroque quaelibet immutatio adnotetur quam patrimonium subire contingat.

Before they assume office, the administrators of church property, (a) must *take an oath* before the local Ordinary or the rural dean, by which they promise that they will perform their obligations properly and faithfully. (b) They must *sign the inventory,* which must be made accurately and distinctly, of all the immovable property, as also of precious movable goods, clearly described and appraised; or accept an inventory already made, which should account for things either lost or acquired in the meantime. (c) Of this inventory *two copies* must be drawn up, one of which must be kept in the archives of the administrative council and the other in the archives of the diocesan court, in each of which all changes in the property must be duly noted.

Can. 1523

Administratores bonorum ecclesiasticorum diligentia boni patrisfamilias suum munus implere tenentur; ac proinde debent:

1.° Vigilare ne bona ecclesiastica suae curae concredita quoquo modo pereant aut detrimentum capiant;

2.° Praescripta servare iuris tam canonici quam civilis, aut quae a fundatore vel donatore vel legitima auctoritate imposita sint;

3.° Reditus bonorum ac proventus accurate et iusto tempore exigere exactosque loco tuto servare et secundum fundatoris mentem aut statutas leges vel normas impendere;

4.° Pecuniam ecclesiae, quae de expensis supersit et

utiliter collocari potest, de consensu Ordinarii, in emolumentum ipsius ecclesiae occupare;

5.° Accepti et expensi libros bene ordinatos habere;

6.° Documenta et instrumenta, quibus iura ecclesiae in bona nituntur, rite ordinare et in ecclesiae archivo vel armario convenienti et apto custodire; authentica vero eorum exemplaria, ubi commode fieri potest, in archivo vel armario Curiae deponere.

Administrators of ecclesiastical property should administer their office like a good father of a family; in particular,

1.° They should see to it that nothing entrusted to their care is lost or damaged;

2.° They shall observe the rules laid down by both ecclesiastical and civil law, and the regulations imposed by the founder or donor, or by lawful authority;

3.° They shall collect the revenues and fees (produce, rent, etc.), at the proper time, keep them safely, and use them in accordance with the will of the founder and the rules of the charter;

4.° They shall invest the surplus profitably, with the consent of the Ordinary, and to the advantage of the Church;

5.° They shall keep the books of income and expenditures in good order;

6.° They shall keep the holographs and title deeds of the church in good order and place them in the archives or safe of the church, and copies or abstracts in the diocesan archives or safe.

CAN. 1524

Omnes, et praesertim clerici, religiosi ac rerum ecclesiasticarum administratores, in operum locatione de-

bent assignare operariis honestam iustamque merce-
dem; curare ut iidem pietati, idoneo temporis spatio,
vacent; nullo pacto eos abducere a domestica cura
parsimoniaeque studio, neque plus eisdem imponere
operis quam vires ferant neque id genus quod cum
aetate sexuque dissideat.

This canon refers to a duty incumbent on administrators of church property, which is of a preëminently social
character because it enjoins on them the obligation of
paying *fair wages* to workingmen. All administrators, it
says, especially clerics and religious, must pay their employees a just and adequate wage; they should also see to
it that the workingmen be allowed a convenient time for
fulfilling their religious duties; they should never keep
them from their domestic duties or from habits of thrift
nor impose upon them more work than their strength, age
or sex enables them to perform. The whole famous encyclical letter of Leo XIII " On the Condition of the
Working Classes " is here contained in a nutshell.[9] We
will not, although the temptation is strong, dwell on this
point. On the one hand, an example is to be set of
really religious interpenetration of work and prayer, and
on the other, the world is to be shown that the Church is
opposed to slavish drudgery, but not to wholesome social
and domestic pursuits. If priests and religious fail to do
justice to workingmen, how can the world expect enlight-
enment and guidance from the Church in the solution of
the labor question?

[9] " *Rerum Novarum,*" May 15,
1891; J. A. Ryan, *A Living Wage.* This canon also applies to house-
keepers and janitors.

SPECIAL DUTIES OF ADMINISTRATORS

CAN. 1525

§ 1. Reprobata contraria consuetudine, administratores, tam ecclesiastici quam laici, cuiusvis ecclesiae etiam cathedralis aut loci pii canonice erecti aut confraternitatis, singulis annis officio tenentur reddendi rationem administrationis Ordinario loci.

§ 2. Si ex peculiari iure aliis ad id designatis ratio reddenda sit, tunc etiam Ordinarius loci vel eius delegatus cum his admittatur, ea lege ut aliter factae liberationes ipsis administratoribus minime suffragentur.

§ 1 of canon 1525 *reprobates any custom contrary* to the duty, established by long standing law,[10] of *rendering annual accounts to the local Ordinary*. This law is binding on clerical as well as lay administrators

(a) *Of every church,* including the cathedral church, and every public oratory, with the exception of churches belonging to *exempt religious* exclusively and solely by reason of their own service and for their own purpose, without being a parish or incorporated church by way of a benefice. Parish churches governed by religious must also render an account of their administration.[11]

(b) Accounts must also be rendered of any and all *charitable or pious institutions canonically erected,* no matter whether governed by secular or religious, even exempt, clergymen. Thus, if religious conduct a hospital or an asylum of any kind, an account must be given, the reason being that such charitable institutions concern the faithful, or the Church at large, and are often of the na-

---

10 C. 11, C. 10, q. 1, (*Synod. Tolet. IV*)

11 C 31, X, III, 5; see can. 532 f.; can. 1504.

ture of foundations connected with a last will.[12]   This rule holds also concerning institutions under royal protection.[13]

(c) The syndics of *each and every confraternity,* without exception, even though affiliated with an archconfraternity in the City of Rome, for instance, that of the "Good Death," and even though it be erected in a church of exempt religious,[14] must likewise render an account to the bishop.   Of course, this is to be understood only of such confraternities as have revenues of their own, and form at least a juridical entitiy (*un' ente morale*).

§ 2. If there is a special statute requiring that accounts be rendered to others designated for that purpose, the local Ordinary or his delegate must also be allowed to inspect the accounts, and all stipulations made for the purpose of excluding the Ordinary are void.   Thus, for instance, if a municipality is entitled to receive the account of a pious foundation, which contains a clause to the effect that the local Ordinary be excluded, this clause would be invalid in the ecclesiastical court.[15]   The same is true of any custom that may have crept in against the present canon.[16]

CAN. 1526

Administratores litem nomine ecclesiae ne inchoent vel contestentur nisi licentiam obtinuerint scripto datam Ordinarii loci, aut saltem, si res urgeat, vicarii

12 Cfr c 2, Clem III, 11, where *xenodochia, leprosariae, eleemosynariae, hospitalia,* though exempt, are mentioned, see Leo XIII, "*Romanos Pontifices,*" May 8, 1881.

13 S. C C , Dec 10, 1621, and *saepius* (Richter, *Trid ,* p 168, n 4 f).

14 S C. C , Sept 20, 1710; March 24, 1725 (Richter, *l c ,* nn. 6 f.).

15 S C. C , June 6, July 11, 1750 (Richter, *l. c ,* n 2)

16 S. C. C , Jan 18, 1757 (*ibid.,* n. 3).

foranei, qui statim Ordinarium de concessa licentia certiorem reddere debet.

Administrators of church property must not *institute or contest a lawsuit* in the name of the church without having obtained written permission from the local Ordinary or, in urgent cases, from the rural dean, who shall immediately inform the Ordinary when he has granted such a permission.

"*Nomine ecclesiae*" means in the name of the church or pious foundation. For going to law the administrators need the formal and written consent of the local Ordinary, because he is *the* administrator of all church property in his diocese.

CAN. 1527

§ 1. Nisi prius ab Ordinario loci facultatem impetraverint, scriptis dandam, administratores invalide actus ponunt qui ordinariae administrationis fines et modum excedant.

§ 2. Ecclesia non tenetur respondere de contractibus ab administratoribus sine licentia competentis Superioris initis, nisi quando et quatenus in rem suam versum sit.

If they disregard his advice and are defeated in a lawsuit, they are bound in conscience and by ecclesiastical law to make up for the loss sustained.[17] The *church is not responsible* for contracts made by the administrator without the permission of the competent superior, unless the contract is favorable. This *favor ecclesiae* is to be extended to lawsuits as well.

According to § 1 of can. 1527, administrators per-

17 S. C. EE. et RR., Nov. 29, 1850, ad 1 (Bizzarri, *l c.*, p. 125 ff.).

form even otherwise legal acts *invalidly* if they exceed the limits and mode of ordinary administration without having obtained the necessary written permission of the local Ordinary.

Ordinary administration as a rule excludes the acceptance or refusal of legacies, bequests, donations, the purchase of immovable property, mortgages and rents for more than three years, alienation of precious objects, borrowing a considerable sum, building new edifices and cemeteries, making repairs of importance, suppressing parishes and institutions, imposing taxes or taking up collections.[18] For all these acts, therefore, the bishop's permission is required.

CAN. 1528

Etsi ad administrationem non teneantur titulo beneficii vel officii ecclesiastici, administratores qui munus expresse vel tacite susceptum arbitratu suo dimittunt ita ut damnum ecclesiae obveniat, ad restitutionem tenentur.

Administrators are obliged to *restitution* if they relinquish an office which they have either explicitly or tacitly assumed and thereby cause loss to the church. This rule holds even though they were not bound to act as administrators by reason of an ecclesiastical benefice or office.

Hence also laymen may be bound to make restitution according to the rules laid down in moral theology.

18 S C P. F, July 21, 1856, n. 20 (*Coll.*, n. 1127).

TITLE XXIX

CONTRACTS

ECCLESIASTICAL AND CIVIL CONTRACTS

CAN. 1529.

Quae ius civile in territorio statuit de contractibus tam in genere, quam in specie, sive nominatis sive innominatis, et de solutionibus, eadem iure canonico in materia ecclesiastica iisdem cum effectibus serventur, nisi iuri divino contraria sint aut aliud iure canonico caveatur.

Whatever the civil law of a country determines with regard to contracts, general and specific, named and nameless, as well as payments, shall be observed also in ecclesiastical law and with the same legal effects, unless the civil laws run counter to divine law, and, unless the canons provide otherwise.

A contract is a formal agreement made between two or more parties (*"duorum vel plurium in idem placitum consensus"*).[1] Contracts are sometimes divided into *nominati and innominati,* the former being such as have obtained special names in law, as, for instance, contracts of sale, rent, lease, whilst nameless contracts are comprised under the fourfold class of: *do ut des, facio ut facias, do ut facias, facio ut des.* The third is especially applied to pious foundations (can. 1544).

The essential elements of a contract are: the consent of

---

1 Cfr Engel, I, tit. 25, n. 7 ff.

the contracting parties, their ability to contract, and the consideration itself. The civil law prescribes formalities or rules which must be observed in order that a contract be valid. These formalities may concern all contracts in general or only a *certain class* of contracts. These civil formalities, says our canon, must be observed even if the subject matter, or the consideration, or the contracting parties belong to the Church. But there are two exceptions: (1) provided the contract does not contravene the divine positive law, and (2) provided the canon law is not against its observance. Whether the term " divine law " includes natural law is not quite evident. Neither is the doubt completely solved by can. 1513, where natural and ecclesiastical law only are mentioned, and where a will lacking the formalities required by civil law is held to be valid in the court of conscience. We leave it to the theologians to decide this problem. Clearly opposed to divine law would be a civil law excluding ecclesiastical persons, either physical or moral, from the right of making contracts. The ecclesiastical law differs in some respects from the civil law with regard to religious, as may be seen in can. 536. Against ecclesiastical law is also the obligatory form of civil marriage, which, besides, violates the divine law. These exceptions admitted, it is safe to follow the civil law, because after all, a law worthy of the name should be nothing else than a more detailed application of the natural law, and jurists should be grateful that the new Code offers an illustrious example of the conciliatory spirit of the Church and her readiness to adapt herself to the reasonable demands of the State. Modern jurists define a contract as " a promise or agreement enforceable by law," but complain that the definition is not satisfactory.[2] All

2 Harriman, *The Law of Contracts,* 1901, § 3 ff ; § 610 ff.

more or less agree that a formal contract at least needs the support of law. Which is true, as far as material coercion is concerned; but a contract may be binding in conscience. However, our Code accepts the *formal contract* with the reservation pointed out. Formal contracts in our law are those the existence of which can be established by a record or a deed. *Unilateral* contracts impose an obligation on one party only, whereas *bilateral* contracts impose obligations on both parties. Requisites for valid contracts are set forth by the jurists as affecting the promise itself, the one who makes it, and the one to whom it is made. Yet, though all the elements of a contract be present, there may be a law which prevents their effecting a contractual obligation, and therefore, renders a contract illegal. Of these there are quite a number in canon law.[3]

ALIENATION

Can. 1530

§ 1. Salvo praescripto can. 1281, § 1, ad alienandas res ecclesiasticas immobiles aut mobiles, quae servando servari possunt, requiritur:

1.° Aestimatio rei a probis peritis scripto facta;

2.° Iusta causa, idest urgens necessitas, vel evidens utilitas Ecclesiae, vel pietas;

3.° Licentia legitimi Superioris, sine qua alienatio invalida est.

§ 2. Aliae quoque opportunae cautelae, ab ipsomet Superiore pro diversis adiunctis praescribendae, ne omittantur, ut Ecclesiae damnum vitetur.

Alienation implies the turning away of a thing from its proper purpose or destiny.[4] From this it was but logical

---

3 *Ibid*, § 171 ff.

4 Cfr. c. 2, C. 12, q. 2: "*quae a religioso aliena sunt proposito.*"

to apply the term to any act by which the ownership or
usufruct or any right belonging to the Church was transferred to another.   However, it also implies a transfer
that is detrimental,[5] which indeed is verified in any loss
of a right, but may nevertheless be more useful than its retention.   Besides, it must be remembered that the purpose of Church property is wide, and that the poor and
captives always had a special claim on the property of
the Church.   Hence the alienation even of sacred vessels
was not considered forbidden if captives had to be re-
deemed or the poor succored.[6]   Forbidden, however, was
any unwarranted and purposeless alienation, (under the
feudal system any alienation without the consent of the
Lord.)[7]   This is still traceable in the present legislation,
the reason for which is stated in can. 1518.

Alienation, then, is the transfer of an object or right
from one to another and partakes of the nature of an
onerous contract, which involves a deterioration in the
condition of the holder.   The *acts* by which this transfer
is made are · sale, exchange, payment, donation, mortgage,
leases for more than three years, bailment and security,
and *cessio iuris,* or cession of a right acquired, such as admitting a servitude.[8]   The *objects or rights* which are or
may be transferred by way of alienation are things of
material value or price (*res pretio aestimabiles*) ; hence
movable as well as immovable goods

Movable goods are either such as can be preserved or
kept without loss, (*quae servando servari possunt*), for
instance, title deeds, books, treasures, etc.; or things that

---

5 Thus c 52, C, 12, q 2· "*ut me-
liora prospiciat*"

6 Cfr. cc 14, 15, 70, C 12, q 2.

7 Blackstone-Cooley,   *Comment,*
II, 288 f

8 All these acts occur in the
sources of law; see Santi-Leitner,
III, 13, n 1, Wernz, III, n 154,
who justly observes that a *repudiatio
lucri,* though illicit, is no alienation,
because it is not yet property acquired

are easily consumed or corrupted, for instance, produce.[9] Movable goods may be *precious,* or have little value, at least for the time being. Precious things, can. 1497, § 2 says, are such as have a considerable artistic value (paintings, sculptures by great artists) or a *historical* value (manuscripts or archaeological objects) or are made of precious material (jewelry, rare stones, pearls). The term *precious* might also be applied to an entire library, or to the sacred treasure of a church.

Immovable property consists of land, buildings, lakes, rivers, mines, etc. These too are estimated in proportion to their value, according to the canon " *Terrulas* " (c 53, c. 12, q. 2).[10] Immovable, though incorporeal, property are rights of way, the privilege of fishing or hunting, etc. To give up such rights or privileges or to surrender them when in dispute (*cessio litis*), would be alienation.

Alienation is not forbidden absolutely, for, as stated above, this act signifies a deterioration of the material condition of a church or corporation, which the common law endeavors to prevent by administrative restrictions or regulations. An absolute prohibition might involve a *summa iniuria,* which the legislator certainly does not intend. Therefore can. 1530 sets forth certain conditions which render alienation lawful and valid.

For the alienation of sacred relics the express permission of the Holy See is required, according to can. 1281, § 1. All other ecclesiastical goods, whether immovable or movable, may be alienated, under the following conditions:

9 To this class also belong· young stock, calves, pigs, lambs, chickens, the right of selling which canonists admit, but not the entire herd at once.

10 The value of this less valuable property, according to an antiquated opinion, would be about $50, or 268 francs; Santi-Leitner, *l c.,* n. 6.

1.° An appraisement of the goods must be made by conscientious experts;

2.° There must be a just cause, *i. e.*, urgent necessity, or evident utility on the part of the church, or piety;

3.° The competent superior must give his permission, without which alienation would be invalid.

The superior may also prescribe other precautions and formalities, as the circumstances of the case may demand, in order to prevent damage to the church.

Here it may be noted that *perishable* or easily consumable goods require no formalities; hence live stock or produce may be bought, sold, or exchanged without any scruples of conscience, unless the competent superior has prescribed special rules, as, for instance, that no exports shall be made in time of public calamity beyond certain boundaries, or nothing be bought from a place or country infected by a contagious disease or an epidemic.

Valuation or appraisement is not required under pain of nullity. Nor is the *cause* required under such a penalty. However, if alienation were made without any reason, the one who made it to the detriment of the church would certainly be obliged to restitution, because administrators of church property are not possessors, but trustees.

Just reasons for lawful alienation are these three: necessity, utility, piety. *Necessity* must be *urgent* here and now, for instance, the paying of a debt, redeeming a mortgage, the indispensable support of the ministers, repair of the church, etc. The *utility* must be *evident, i. e.*, considering all the circumstances of the case, alienation must be more profitable than the retention of the property, for instance, buying a piece of property to round out one already held, a rare occasion of buying a library, etc. *Piety* may mean gratitude towards those from whom we have received favors, aid and succour of the poor and captives, as stated above, in fact the whole field of practical corporeal works of Christian mercy and charity.

CAN. 1531

§ 1. Res alienari minore pretio non debet quam quod in aestimatione indicatur.

§ 2. Alienatio fiat per publicam licitationem aut saltem nota reddatur, nisi aliud circumstantiae suadeant; et res ei concedatur qui, omnibus perpensis, plus obtulerit.

§ 3. Pecunia ex alienatione percepta caute, tuto et utiliter in commodum Ecclesiae collocetur.

This canon rules, not, however, under pain of nullity,

1.° That no thing should be alienated for less than what it was appraised at, because this would involve injustice and grafting;

2.° That alienation should take place by *auction,* or at least by advertisement of a public sale, unless circumstances advise the contrary; and the property to be disposed of should, everything being considered, be given to the highest bidder;

3.° That the sum realized from alienation should be invested safely and profitably.

Concerning the public auctioning of church property, the rules usually given by canonists are somewhat out of date and inapplicable to modern conditions.[11] But public auction is still commendable, in as much as it is apt to prevent favoritism and nepotism. For the rest, the civil law governing public auctions may safely be followed. *Circumstances* may demand less publicity, as when church property has to be sold on account of bankruptcy, or to

---

11 Bened. XIV, "*Essendo,*" Nov. 23, 1742; S. C. EE. et RR., March 18, 1835 (Bizzarri, *l. c.,* p. 62 f).

protect the church against an iniquitous civil law, or to spare the good name of an institution.[12]

Can. 1532

§ 1. Legitimus Superior de quo in can. 1530, § 1, n. 3, est Sedes Apostolica, si agatur:

1.° De rebus pretiosis;

2.° De rebus quae valorem excedunt triginta millium libellarum seu francorum.

§ 2. Si vero agatur de rebus quae valorem non excedunt mille libellarum seu francorum, est loci Ordinarius, audito administrationis Consilio, nisi res minimi momenti sit, et cum eorum consensu quorum interest.

§ 3. Si denique de rebus quarum pretium continetur intra mille libellas et triginta millia libellarum seu francorum, est loci Ordinarius, dummodo accesserit consensus tum Capituli cathedralis, tum Consilii administrationis, tum eorum quorum interest.

§ 4. Si agatur de alienanda re divisibili, in petenda licentia aut consensu pro alienatione exprimi debent partes antea alienatae; secus licentia irrita est.

Can. 1532 determines the *lawful superior* whose permission is required for valid alienation. This superior is:

1.° The *Apostolic See, i. e.,* the S. C. Concilii (can. 250, § 2), if (a) *precious things* of any kind or amount are to be alienated, for they are not precisely appraised in our

---

12 That the investment should be made in safe securities, is a wise ruling, but has nothing to do with the validity of the act, if the sum does not exceed the value stated in can. 1532 Hence, despite the decision of the S. C. C., quoted in the *Irish Eccl Record*, Jan , 1920, p. 67, the answer there given shoots beyond the mark and is against can. 1530, § 1, n 3

canon; or (b) if property is to be disposed of, the value of which exceeds the sum of 30,000 lire (or francs),[13] *i. e.,* about $6,000 to $10,000.

2.° If the value of the property to be alienated *does not exceed the sum of 1,000 lire (or francs)*, i. e., about $200, the local Ordinary may proceed after having heard the advice of the board of administrators — unless the property is of very little value — and with the consent of those concerned.

" Those *concerned* " are the contracting parties, who, however, must be in a condition to give their consent. While a benefice is vacant, or while an episcopal see is vacant, no alienation of property belonging to the benefice or to the *mensa episcopalis* is permitted, even though the amount would be small. Hence the canon " Terrulas " cannot be applied here, because it would be contrary to can. 436: " *Sede vacante nihil innovetur.*"[14]

3.° If the value of the property to be alienated is *between 1,000 and 30,000 lire (or francs)*, the local Ordinary may proceed, provided a threefold consent has been obtained, viz., (1) that of the cathedral chapter (or diocesan consultors), which must be given *collegialiter, i. e.,* by vote at a meeting; (2) the consent of the board of administrators, and (3) that of the persons concerned. The penalties are stated in can. 2347.

4.° If the property to be alienated is *divisible,* the parts which have been previously alienated must be mentioned in the petition for permission or consent, under pain of nullity. Hence no concealment is admissible, because it may endanger the validity of the transaction.

---

13 What was said under can. 534 (see this Commentary, Vol. III, p. 186) must be reaffirmed, provided, of course, the valuta is normal.

14 See C. 1, X, III, 9; S C EE. et RR , June 14, 1788 (Bizzarri, *l. c.,* p. 40 f.).

This holds concerning the papal indult as well as with regard to anyone's consent.

We call attention to can. 81, which certainly may be applied in cases that brook no delay or where delay would entail serious loss.

FORMALITIES OF ALIENATION

CAN. 1533

Sollemnitates ad normam can. 1530-1532 requiruntur non solum in alienatione proprie dicta, sed etiam in quolibet contractu quo conditio Ecclesiae peior fieri possit.

Can. 1533 applies the formalities set forth in can. 1530–1532 not only to alienation in the technical sense of the word, but to any contract by which the status of the Church might be impaired. Prelates may improve the condition of their churches, but are not allowed to render it worse.[15] A deterioration may be brought about by mortgages or securities as well as by donations (see can. 1535) and onerous contracts.[16] Alms or offerings collected by missionaries also constitute ecclesiastical property and may not be acquired or disposed of at will by the missionary, even though it were for the benefit of the mission.[17] This rule, of course, includes the *making of debts,* which is always dangerous, especially if done by such as do not know the value of money or lack business capacity.

CAN. 1534

§ 1. Ecclesiae competit actio personalis contra eum qui sine debitis sollemnitatibus bona ecclesiastica alienaverit et contra eius heredes; realis vero, si alien-

[15] C. 2, X, III, 24.
[16] C. 2, X, III, 23.

[17] S C. P. F., May 27, 1881 (*Coll*, n. 1553); see can. 534.

atio nulla fuerit, contra quemlibet possessorem, salvo iure emptoris contra male alienantem.

§ 2. Contra invalidam rerum ecclesiasticarum alienationem agere possunt qui rem alienavit, eius Superior, utriusque successor in officio, tandem quilibet clericus illi ecclesiae adscriptus, quae damnum passa sit.

The Church, *i. e.*, each single church corporation, or juridical entity (through its syndic) has the right to bring a *double action*. A *personal* action may be brought against anyone who has alienated church property without observing the formalities required by law. This action, brought to recover the damage or property itself, is also extended to the *heirs* of the one who is guilty of illegal alienation, because the heir is supposed to be identical in law with the deceased who acted unlawfully. *Real action* may be brought, in case of invalid alienation, against any one who acquired church property that was alienated illegally, even if he bought it in good faith. However, the possessor thus brought to law may, on his side, bring suit against the one who performed an illegal alienation.[18] But it also must be added that if the illegally alienated property was obtained by personal action, no real action is to be brought against the possessor, because the same thing cannot be demanded twice, and *vice versa*.

§ 2 says that *invalid alienation* can be revoked either by the alienator himself, or by his superior, or by the successor of either, and, finally, by any clergyman assigned to the church which has sustained a loss by the invalid alienation. The text from which our canon is taken threatens with penalties the clergyman who neglects to denounce the illegal alienator or donator.[19]

---

18 Cfr. c. 6, X, III, 13; I. 3, X, III, 21; Reiffenstuel, III, 13, n. 62.
19 C. 6, x, III, 13; c. 2, x, III, 14; c. 2, x, III, 24 (against donation).

DONATIONS

Can. 1535

Praelati et rectores de bonis mobilibus suarum ecclesiarum donationes, praeterquam parvas et modicas secundum legitimam loci consuetudinem, facere ne praesumant, nisi iusta interveniente causa remunerationis aut pietatis aut christianae caritatis; secus donatio a successoribus revocari poterit.

Prelates and rectors are allowed to make *only small and moderate donations* from the *movable property* of the Church, according to legitimate local custom; large donations may be made only for a just reason, as reward, piety, or Christian charity. Donations made against this rule may be revoked by the successors.

Donations are free gifts and are here understood of movable property only, to the exclusion of immovable property.[20] Since prelates are not the owners of church property, but only the administrators, they are not allowed to deteriorate the condition of their church. Therefore only *small* and infrequent donations are permitted. The judgment concerning quantity and quality is left to the donor, who must be guided by *local custom* and by the circumstances of time and persons. But local custom must not be stretched so as to cover large donations because such a custom would be a corruption and therefore unreasonable. However *three reasons* may justify larger and more important donations: reward or remuneration, piety, and charity. *Reward* is here understood as a remuneration for services done to the church or to the

20 It is evident that the text intends only donations *inter vivos*, gifts to living persons, not donations *mortis causa*, made to go into effect after the donor's death, see commentators on lib. III, tit 24

prelate or rector, provided a certain equality or proportion be observed between the merits and the reward. *Piety*, as stated, may signify gratitude and duty either to one's relatives and friends, or to outsiders. Household, town, and diocese should determine the gradation. *Christian charity* is wider, embracing, as it does, all *causae piae* of every description. But the donor must always keep in view the condition of the church; for to go beyond the means at hand would be unreasonable and involve an unjustice.[21]

CAN. 1536

§ 1. Nisi contrarium probetur, praesumendum ea quae donantur rectoribus ecclesiarum, etiam religiosorum, esse ecclesiae donata.

§ 2. Donatio facta ecclesiae, ab eius rectore seu Superiore repudiari nequit sine licentia Ordinarii.

§ 3. Repudiata illegitime donatione, ob damna quae inde obvenerint actio datur restitutionis in integrum vel indemnitatis.

§ 4. Donatio ecclesiae facta et ab eadem legitime acceptata, propter ingratum Praelati vel rectoris animum revocari nequit.

§ 1 says that *donations* made to rectors of churches, secular or religious, are supposed to be made *to the church*, unless there is reason to presume the contrary (see can. 533).[22]

§§ 2 and 3 lay down certain rules concerning the refusal of donations. In order lawfully to refuse a donation made to a church, the rector or superior of the same needs the permission of the Ordinary. An illegal refusal, if a

21 Reiffenstuel, III, 24, n. 37 ff
22 See this Commentary, Vol. III, p. 182

loss is caused thereby, justifies an action for *restitutio in integrum* or indemnity.

§ 4 departs from the Decretals,[23] inasmuch as the Code does not permit a donation made to a church and lawfully accepted by the latter, to be revoked on account of ingratitude or enmity on the part of the prelate or rector.

CAN. 1537

Res sacrae ne commodentur ad usum qui earundem naturae repugnet.

Sacred things, i. e., such as have received ecclesiastical consecration or blessing,[24] *may not be loaned for a purpose repugnant to their nature.* Thus a church should never be turned into a concert hall, a chalice is not to be used for banquets,[25] even though it were only by a transitory loan and the money were sorely needed. The rule is absolute and admits of no exception.[26]

MORTGAGES AND DEBTS

CAN. 1538

§ 1. Si ecclesiae bona, legitima interveniente causa, oppignoranda vel hypothecae nomine obliganda sint, vel agatur de aere alieno contrahendo, legitimus Superior, qui ad normam can. 1532 licentiam dare debet, exigat ut antea omnes, quorum interest, audiantur, et curet ut, cum primum fieri poterit, aes alienum solvatur.

§ 2. Hac de causa annuae ratae ab eodem Ordi-

---

23 C. 10, x, III, 24 admitted revocation on account of qualified ingratitude, such as violence, atrocities, serious injury.

24 Can 1497, § 2
25 See Dan 5, 2 f
26 Reg Iuris 51 in 6°.

nario praefiniantur quae exstinguendo debito sint destinatae.

§ 1. If, for a lawful reason, church property has to be pawned or mortgaged, or debts have to be made, the lawful superior who is entitled to grant permission, according to can. 1532, shall first hear all concerned, *i. e.*, the administrators and rectors, or syndics, and endeavor to pay off the debt as soon as possible.

§ 2. For this purpose the Ordinary should determine the amount of annual payments. If the church has fixed revenues, this may be done by subtracting the necessary amount therefrom.[27] But if no fixed endowment or revenues are available, as is the case with most of our churches, a " sinking fund " should be established to wipe out the debt.

SALE AND EXCHANGE

CAN. 1539

§ 1. In venditione aut permutatione rerum sacrarum nulla ratio consecrationis vel benedictionis in pretii aestimatione habeatur.

§ 2. Administratores possunt *titulos ad latorem,* quos vocant, commutare in alios titulos magis aut saltem aeque tutos ac frugiferos, exclusa qualibet commercii vel negotiationis specie, ac de consensu Ordinarii, dioecesani Consilii administrationis aliorumque quorum intersit.

§ 1. When *sacred things* are sold or exchanged, the fact that they are consecrated or blessed shall not influence their valuation, *i. e., no higher price* can be lawfully

---

[27] S. C. P. F., July 30, 1867, n.4 (*Coll.*, n. 1310).

charged for a consecrated or blessed object merely be-- cause it is consecrated or blessed. To do so would be simony.[28]

§ 2. The administrators may convert *notes payable to bearer* into other titles or investments which are safer than, or at least equally safe and profitable as, the former.

In doing so, however, they must avoid every species of trading or speculation, and, besides, obtain the previous consent of their Ordinary, of the diocesan board of administrators, and other interested persons.

ADMINISTRATORS AND RELATIVES EXCLUDED

CAN. 1540

Bona ecclesiae immobilia propriis administratoribus eorumque coniunctis in primo aut secundo consanguinitatis vel affinitatis gradu non sunt vendenda aut locanda sine speciali Ordinarii loci licentia.

Immovable church property cannot lawfully be sold or leased to the administrators themselves, or to persons related to them in the first or second degree either by blood or marriage, without special permission of the local Ordinary.

LEASE OR RENT

CAN. 1541

§ 1. Contractus locationis alicuius fundi ecclesiastici ne fiant, nisi ad norman can. 1531, § 2; et in iis addantur semper conditiones de limitibus custodiendis, de bona cultione, de rite solvendo canone, de opportuna cautela pro conditionibus implendis.

---

[28] See can. 730.

§ 2. **Pro locatione bonorum ecclesiasticorum, servato praescripto can. 1479:**

1.° Si valor locationis excedat triginta millia libellarum seu francorum et locatio sit ultra novennium, requiritur beneplacitum apostolicum; si locatio non sit ultra novennium, servari debet praescriptum can. 1532, § 3;

2.° Si valor contineatur intra mille libellas et triginta millia libellarum seu francorum et locatio sit ultra novennium, servari debet praescriptum eiusdem can. 1532, § 3; si locatio non sit ultra novennium, praescriptum eiusdem can. 1532, § 2;

3.° Si valor non excedat mille libellas seu francos et locatio sit ultra novennium, servari debet praescriptum can. 1532, § 2; si locatio non sit ultra novennium, fieri potest a legitimis administratoribus, monito Ordinario.

§ 1. Land belonging to a church should not be rented except by public auction or announcement, as stated under can. 1531, § 2, and exact conditions must be laid down in the lease or rent contract as to the boundaries, appropriate methods of cultivation, payment of rent, and the necessary safeguards for the fulfillment of the conditions.

§ 2. Anticipated payments being excluded according to can. 1479, the *following rules* must be observed in leasing or renting church property:

1.° If the rental exceeds 30,000 lire (or francs) and the lease is made for more than *nine years,* a *papal indult* is required; if the contract is made for less than nine years, the *local Ordinary* may give the permission, with the consent of his cathedral chapter (or diocesan consultors), the board of administrators, and those interested.

2.° If the rental is between 1,000 and 30,000 lire (or

francs) and the lease runs *more than nine years,* the local Ordinary may grant permission, with the consent of those just mentioned; but if the contract is made for *less than nine years,* the local Ordinary has only to consult with the board of administrators and obtain the consent of those concerned.

3.° If the rental is *less than* 1,000 lire (or francs) and the contract reads for more than nine years, the local Ordinary has to consult with the board of administrators and obtain the consent of those concerned; if the contract is for nine years or less, the administrators themselves may sign the contract and notify the Ordinary.

The Code has extended the time limit from three to nine years.

CAN. 1542

§ 1. In emphyteusi bonorum ecclesiasticorum emphyteuta nequit canonem redimere sine licentia legitimi Superioris ecclesiastici de quo in can. 1532; quod si redemerit, eam saltem pecuniae vim ecclesiae dare debet, quae canoni respondeat.

§ 2. Ab emphyteuta congrua exigatur cautio pro solutione canonis et conditionibus implendis; in ipso instrumento pacti emphyteutici forum ecclesiasticum arbiter statuatur ad dirimendas controversias inter partes forte exorituras et expresse declaretur meliorationes solo cedere.

Emphyteusis has little practical value, at least in our law. Ancient jurists distinguished it from *locatio,* defining the latter as an informal contract by which the usufruct, or use, of an object, or the labor of a person is let or hired,[29] whereas *emphyteusis* was a species of indefinite

---

29 Santi-Leitner, III, 18, n. 1; n. 11.

lease of immovable property, under which the tenant paid rent, but had all but the nominal ownership of the land.[30] *Enfeoffment* would most nearly correspond to emphyteusis; but the general term *lease* conveys the idea just as well. Now our canon says that the lessee of church property cannot redeem the rent without the permission of the competent ecclesiastical superior, and if he does redeem the fee — which is generally paid annually —he must give at least as much as the whole rent for the entire time would amount to. Besides the lessee must give security for the payment of the rent and for complying with the other conditions. The lease itself must contain the clause that the ecclesiastical court is the competent court to settle disputes between the parties and that all improvements accrue to the soil.

INTEREST

CAN. 1543

Si res fungibilis ita alicui detur ut eius fiat et postea tantundem in eodem genere restituatur, nihil lucri, ratione ipsius contractus, percipi potest; sed in praestatione rei fungibilis non est per se illicitum de lucro legali pacisci, nisi constet ipsum esse immoderatum, aut etiam de lucro maiore, si iustus ac proportionatus titulus suffragetur.

" Fungible " goods are such as can be replaced in kind If such goods are given to a person in such a way that he becomes the owner thereof, and are restored in kind to the same amount, no interest can be demanded by reason of the contract itself, for it would be usury to demand back

---

30 Blackstone-Cooley, *Comment*, II, 309 ff.; Stimson's Law Dictionary, 1911, *s. v.* " Emphyteusis."

more than was given (*" nihil in mutuo vi mutui accipiendum ultra sortem principalem"*). However, it is not *per se* forbidden to make loans under the usual legal conditions, provided no excessive interest is charged; nor is it forbidden to stipulate a higher rate of interest if a just and proportionate reason can be advanced.

The quintessence of this canon is that interest on loans is permitted according to the usual and legal rate, not precisely by reason of the contract, but by reason of the risk incurred and other circumstances.[31]

31 Cfr. Bened. XIV, *" Vix pervenit,"* Nov. 1, 1745; S. C. P. F., Instr. 1873 (*Coll.,* n. 1393, where the documents referring to these subjects are given and the question is treated *ex professo*).

TITLE XXX

PIOUS FOUNDATIONS

DEFINITION

CAN. 1544

§ 1. Nomine piarum fundationum significantur bona temporalia alicui personae morali in Ecclesia quoquo modo data, cum onere in perpetuum vel in diuturnum tempus ex reditibus annuis aliquas Missas celebrandi, vel alias praefinitas functiones ecclesiasticas explendi, aut nonnulla pietatis et caritatis opera peragendi.

§ 2. Fundatio, legitime acceptata, naturam induit contractus synallagmatici: *do ut facias.*

CAN. 1545

Loci Ordinarii est normas praescribere de dotis quantitate infra quam pia fundatio admitti nequeat et de eius fructibus rite distribuendis.

The term "pious foundation" signifies temporal goods conveyed to some ecclesiastical juridical person with the perpetual or long-continued obligation to say Masses, or to perform certain ecclesiastical functions, or works of piety or charity, in consideration of the revenues received from said endowment. Hence every foundation, after it has been duly accepted, has the nature of a bilateral contract: "*do ut facias.*"

If Title XXVI is compared with the present, the difference between them may appear very slight; however, there is a distinction between the institutions mentioned there and the foundations named in our canon. First, temporal goods enter into can. 1544, *in directo,* whereas in can. 1489 they are omitted as a member of the definition. Besides, our canon presupposes an artificial person already in existence, whereas can. 1489 mentions a decree that creates such persons. In other words, there is a juridical person existing either really or at least by a legal fiction and represented by legal authority. Lastly, the purpose of a pious foundation does not constitute the legal person, but obliges the respective person to perform certain things or acts in consideration of the goods donated. There is the temporal element on one side and the spiritual on the other, and between both stands the mediator, *viz.,* the moral person. Hence such foundations can be called neither corporations nor institutions, but there is a juridical person who accepts the object of the contract, and the contract itself is called: "*do ut facias.*" For in every contract, whether express or implied, there must be something given in exchange for something else, a mutual or reciprocal consideration. This is the case between master and servant, or employer and employee, when the former agrees to give the employee a certain sum for performing certain work. Hence the *do* are the temporal goods, while the *ut facias* is the performance of certain works. But since the works to be performed are mostly spiritual, it is necessary that the competent authority should intervene. Hence can. 1545 demands that the local Ordinaries should fix the *minimum* of endowment below which no pious foundation may be accepted, as well as the manner in which the interest is to be distributed. This is somewhat similar to fixing the amount of mass stipends.

CAN. 1546

§ 1. Ut huiusmodi fundationes a persona morali acceptari possint, requiritur consensus Ordinarii loci, in scriptis datus, qui eum ne praebeat, antequam legitime compererit personam moralem tum novo oneri suscipiendo, tum antiquis iam susceptis satisfacere posse; maximeque caveat ut reditus omnino respondeant oneribus adiunctis secundum cuiusque dioecesis morem.

§ 2. In acceptatione, constitutione et administratione fundationis patronus ecclesiae nullum ius habet.

This canon (§ 1) commands that *no more obligations* be accepted than can be complied with, and that none be accepted *for less* than the customary tax. The *written consent* of the local Ordinary is required for the acceptance of foundations by ecclesiastical persons. This consent should never be given unless the Ordinary is assured that the institution is capable of fulfilling the new as well as any old obligations it has assumed or is to assume. The Ordinary shall also see to it that the consideration is in proportion to the obligations, according to local custom.

§ 2 provides that the *patron* has nothing to say about the acceptance, constitution, or administration of such pious foundations.

It may not be amiss to state that the *local* Ordinary is here intended for foundations under his jurisdiction.

CAN. 1547

Pecunia et bona mobilia, dotationis nomine assignata, statim in loco tuto, ab eodem Ordinario designando, deponantur ad eum finem ut eadem pecunia vel bonorum mobilium pretium custodiantur et quamprimum caute et utiliter secundum prudens eiusdem Ordinarii arbitrium, auditis et iis quorum interest et dioecesano administrationis Consilio, collocentur in commodum eiusdem fundationis cum expressa et individua mentione oneris.

This canon provides for the *safekeeping and safe investment* of pious foundations. All money and movable property assigned as an endowment, must be deposited in a safe place, to be designated by the local Ordinary. This, with us, generally is a bank. Titles and other valuable papers may be put in a safety vault. If stock or produce were offered, the easiest way would be to sell them.

The Ordinary shall then consult with those interested, *i. e.*, the founder or his heirs, those who have accepted the foundation, and the diocesan board of administrators, as to the safest and most profitable way of *investing* the property for the benefit of the foundation. Each investment of this kind must be accompanied by express and specific mention of the *obligation* resting on the investment.

FORMALITIES

CAN. 1548

§ 1. Fundationes, etiam viva voce factae, scripto consignentur.

§ 2. Alterum tabularum exemplar in Curiae archivo, alterum in archivo personae moralis, ad quam fundatio spectat, tuto asservetur.

Pious foundations, even when made orally, must be *set down* in *writing;* one of the records must be kept in the diocesan archives, the other in the archives of the institution which is obliged to fulfill the obligation.

Can. 1549

§ 1. Servatis praescriptis can. 1514-1517 et can. 1525, in qualibet ecclesia onerum ex piis fundationibus incumbentium tabella conficiatur, quae apud rectorem in loco tuto conservetur.

§ 2. Pariter praeter librum de quo in can. 843, § 1, alter liber retineatur et apud rectorem servetur, in quo singula onera perpetua et temporaria eorumque implementum et eleemosynae adnotentur, ut de iis omnibus exacta ratio Ordinario loci reddatur.

In every church there must be kept a list of the obligations arising from pious foundations; this list must be preserved in a safe place in the rectory.

Besides the book for manual stipends,[1] mentioned in can. 843, § 1, there must be another, kept by the rector, in which each and every obligation, whether perpetual or temporary, is duly entered, as also the record of fulfillment (when a mass was said) and the amount of the alms, — so that an accurate account may be rendered to the local Ordinary.

EXEMPT RELIGIOUS

Can. 1550

Si agatur de piis fundationibus in ecclesiis, etiam paroecialibus, religiosorum exemptorum, iura et offiicia

---

[1] We cannot accept the theory advanced in a magazine that a priest who receives, say, $100 for " masses," can satisfy his obligation by saying 20 " high or sung masses," intead of 100 low masses. For this is a substantial, not merely an accidental, change, the ceremony of singing being a mere *accidens*, and the priest would therefore defraud the donor of eighty masses Who can admit such a pious fraud?

Ordinarii loci, de quibus in can. 1545–1549, exclusive competunt Superiori maiori.

As to pious foundations made and accepted by churches belonging to exempt religious, even if they be parish churches, all the rights and duties of the local Ordinary mentioned in canons 1545–1549, devolve on the *major superior exclusively,* according to the constitutions of the respective institute.

It may be added that the Constitution *" Nuper,"* of Innocent XII,[2] from which these laws are chiefly taken, revokes and annuls all contrary privileges granted to any order.

REDUCTION OF OBLIGATIONS

Can. 1551

§ 1. Reductio onerum quae pias fundationes gravant, uni Sedi Apostolicae reservatur, nisi in tabulis fundationis aliud expresse caveatur, et salvo praescripto can. 1517, § 2.

§ 2. Indultum reducendi Missas fundatas non protenditur nec ad alias Missas ex contractu debitas nec ad alia onera piae fundationis.

§ 3. Indultum vero generale reducendi onera piarum fundationum ita intelligendum est, nisi aliud constet, ut indultarius potius alia onera quam Missas reducat.

The reduction of obligations arising from pious foundations is reserved to the Apostolic See, unless the charter contains an express provision to the contrary and with due regard to can. 1517, § 2, which admits the reduction of certain foundations under certain conditions, but excepts masses.

2 § 30.

The S. C. Concilii sometimes grants an *indult* reducing foundation-masses, but this indult does not extend to masses to be said by some other species of contract different from that by which a foundation is accepted, nor to other works imposed by a pious foundation. Hence this particular kind of indult must be strictly interpreted. If a *general indult* is granted for reducing the obligation arising from a pious foundation, this must be understood and interpreted to mean that the grantee should reduce other works rather than the masses, unless the text of the indult reads differently. Thus if, besides Masses, the recitation of the divine office or certain prayers are prescribed in the foundation, the latter should be reduced rather than the masses.[3] Sometimes the wording of a general indult, or a particular indult, expressly permits the reduction of masses. Such indults need close inspection. For instance, it may be that the indult mentions *legata taxative* or *demonstrative concepta*. A legacy which is drawn up *taxative* is one which first fixes the sum of the endowment, say $1,000, and then the obligations to be fulfilled, say a requiem high mass every year on such and such a day. If the obligation is mentioned first, and the endowment afterwards, we have a legacy worded *demonstrative*. This kind of legacy is also called approximate and has this peculiarity that the heirs of the founder could, by ecclesiastical law, be compelled to supply the deficient funds so as to continue the fulfillment of the obligation, although the value of the endowment may have decreased.[4] However, this is often impossible. Hence, if the indult draws no distinction between the different kinds of bequests, the heirs are not to be bothered.

3 S. C C, May 6, 1803 (Richter, *Trid*, p 139, n 80), if the will of the founder does not appear, this rule must be followed; S. C. C., Sept. 11, 1717 (*ibid*, n. 81).

4 S. C. C, Sept. 9, 1702; Bened. XIV, *De Syn Dioec*, XIII, 25, 32.

The *practice* of the Roman Court, mentioned in rescripts, is to change *missae cantatae* into low Masses, provided the funds suffice for the same number.[5] If a reduction has already been granted, and another is asked for, there must be new reasons to justify the request.[6]

Reasons for granting a reduction of mass obligations are *insufficiency of funds* brought about by a considerable decrease in the endowment; and the *poverty of the priests* who would be obliged to say them.[7] In some cases the needy condition of the patron and the necessity of repairing the church were considered sufficient reasons at least for a temporary reduction.[8]

5 S. C. C., Feb. 3; Aug. 4, 1725 (Richter, *l. c.*, p. 140, n. 83 f,).

6 S. C. C., Sept. 7, 1793 (*ibid.*, n. 82).

7 S. C. C., Aug. 17, 1793, and *pluries* (*l. c.*, n. 82).

8 S. C. C., Dec. 2, 1775; Nov. 29, 1777 (*ibid.*).

END OF VOL. VI

www.ingramcontent.com/pod-product-compliance
Lightning Source LLC
LaVergne TN
LVHW012208040326
832903LV00003B/198